The Metamorphosis of Love

Pablo Irizar

The Metamorphosis of Love

Body, Word and Free Will in On the Song of Songs *by Bernard of Clairvaux*

BRILL
FINK

Bibliographic information published by the Deutsche Nationalbibliothek

The Deutsche Nationalbibliothek lists this publication in the Deutsche Nationalbibliografie; detailed bibliographic data available online: http://dnb.d-nb.de

www.fink.de

Cover design: Evelyn Ziegler, Munich
Production: Brill Deutschland GmbH, Paderborn

ISBN 978-3-7705-6750-8 (hardback)
ISBN 978-3-8467-6750-4 (e-book)

To Ephraïm and Rachelle

Ἡ ἀγάπη οὐδέποτε ἐκπίπτει
1 Cor 13.8

Préface de *La métamorphose de l'amour*

Emmanuel Falque
Institut catholique de Paris

La métamorphose de l'amour, de Pablo Irizar, fait œuvre nouvelle. Non pas d'une nouveauté abstraite faisant fi du passé, mais d'une nouveauté enracinée dans la tradition et qui nous enseigne aujourd'hui comment penser. On ne fait du neuf qu'à partir de l'ancien. Mais l'ancien demeurerait à jamais enfoui dans le passé s'il n'était autrement interrogé. Et tel est probablement le caractère magistral de l'ouvrage ici publié. On a longtemps, et longuement, cantonné l'œuvre de Bernard de Clairvaux soit à une mystique déracinée de tout support anthropologique, soit à un simple commentaire biblique sans portée proprement philosophique. Tel est ce que ne fait pas, et ne veut pas, l'ouvrage de Pablo Irizar. Soutenant une thèse qui lui est propre, fût-elle aussi inspirée par d'autres, la « métamorphose de l'amour » a de beaux-jours devant elle, et on ne peut que souhaiter à l'auteur ici de poursuivre en ce chemin si bien commencé. Car il est une "voie propre de l'amour" que Bernard de Clairvaux avait autrefois défrichée, et que l'on a sinon trop peu aperçue, au moins oubliée. C'est ainsi *à l'aune de la philosophie contemporaine* qu'il faut interroger le cistercien, et l'actualiser pour nos contemporains. Une « actualité » du *Commentaire sur le Cantique* du cistercien qui n'est pas simplement une "mise au gout du jour" d'un auteur ancien, mais le "déploiement de toutes ses possibilités insoupçonnées" (mise en acte ou actualisation).

Les traditions grecques et chrétiennes n'ont en effet cessé de se croiser – et la démonstration ici en fait plus, et mieux, que jamais. « Métamorphose de l'amour » certes, mais aussi « métamorphose de la tradition » telle que saint Bernard lui-même a su l'opérer, telle est la double démonstration qui ici est faite. L'*éros* est grec, on le sait, et l'*agapê* chrétien. Mais on aurait tort soit de fusionner, soit de séparer, les termes comme aussi les héritages culturels. Les uns ont soutenu l'« équivocité » de l'éros et de l' « agapê » (Nygren), les autres ont revendiqué leur « univocité » (Marion), alors que par le passé on préférait l'« analogie » (Thomas d'Aquin). Au regard de ces trois modèles, l'ouvrage de Pablo Irizar ne tient pas à les rejeter, mais à montrer au contraire qu'ils ne trouvent sens, et ne s'achèvent, que dans la « transformation » ou le « métamorphose » de l'éros par l'agapê. Il y a la « métamorphose de la finitude » certes par la résurrection, mais elle produit en même temps une « métamorphose de l'amour » dans l'union de l'âme à Dieu. « L'amour change tout » en théologie, comme l'« incarnation change tout » disait Merleau-Ponty en philosophie cette fois. Tel est le « changement » qui fait de la rencontre de Dieu non pas une simple *metanoïa* ou conversion, mais une véritable incorporation de l'homme en Dieu, par quoi la résurrection ne sera plus pensée comme un événement ontique *dans* le monde, mais une transformation ontologique *du* monde. Dieu n'est pas venu au monde pour nous aimer, mais c'est en nous aimant, et parce que déjà il nous aimait, qu'il est venu s'incarner. L'amour n'est jamais un résultat mais un principe. L'amour comme « force », ainsi que l'indique si bien la deuxième partie de l'ouvrage, produit le monde plutôt qu'il ne se découvre comme une dimension du monde. Tel est ce que sait, et que voit, Bernard de Clairvaux, ou plutôt que l'ouvrage de Pablo Irizar nous fait voir, si tant est que nous l'ayons oublié.

Y aurait-il alors et déjà du Nietzsche chez le cistercien, ou plutôt les concepts de « métamorphose » et de « force », chrétiennement pensés s'entend, ne doivent-ils pas s'insérer dans le *corps*, ou plutôt produire du « corps », pour véritablement se donner et s'incorporer ? Telle est la seconde nouveauté de l'ouvrage de Pablo Irizar, après la transformation de l'éros par l'agapê. Car l'amour n'est pas une dimension de Dieu seulement, mais aussi de l'homme. Mieux, et Bernard de Clairvaux l'a parfaitement montré, ce n'est qu'en passant par l'expérience de l'homme (éros) que l'on atteint et que l'on comprend l'expérience de Dieu (agapê), sachant qu'il revient à l'amour divin de transformer l'amour humain et de l'incorporer en lui. *Hodie legimus in libro experientiae* – « aujourd'hui nous lisons au livre de l'expérience ». Cette formule au sermon 3 du *Commentaire sur le Cantique* du cistercien, justifie pleinement que *La métamorphose de l'amour* commence, et débute, par l'expérience. Car il ne suffit pas d'abstraire, en matière d'amour plus que partout ailleurs. C'est dans la concrétude de l'acte d'aimer que se dit, pour l'homme comme pour Dieu, la meilleure manière de s'incarner. L'« amour fait le corps » plutôt que le « corps ne fait l'amour ». Cela Bernard de Clairvaux l'a absolument compris, et Pablo Irizar parfaitement démontré. Pas d'éros sans agapê désiré, et pas d'agapê sans éros transformé.

D'où la dimension du *désir* – troisième grande originalité de *La métamorphose de l'amour*. Le « désir du corps » doit être pensé comme la "clé herméneutique" de l'ensemble de la lecture du *Commentaire du cantique*, ainsi que le montre, et le souligne, si bien l'ouvrage. Le corps amoureux certes, mais aussi le corps malade ou le corps affamé, appartiennent au désir, l'attendent ou le provoquent. « J'ai désiré d'un grand désir manger cette Pâques avec vous » (Lc 22, 15). Le redoublement du désir ici (le désir du désir) l'extrait du simple besoin (simple désir). Il en va du désir proprement humain lorsque celui-ci désire non pas l'autre uniquement, mais le désir de désir de l'autre (désir anthropogène). Et ainsi en va-t-il aussi de Dieu – qui ne désire par l'homme au sens d'un manque, mais d'un partenaire pour s'accomplir lui-même (désir théogène). « Qu'il me baise de baiser de sa bouche » (Ct 1, 2). La magnifique formule qui ouvre le *Cantique des cantiques* sert pour Bernard de Clairvaux d'ouverture à son *Commentaire*, et devient pour Pablo Irizar la clé de voute de son interprétation de saint Bernard.

Il y a en effet et non seulement du philosophique, mais aussi du mystique, dans *La métamorphose de l'amour*. Et quiconque le lira pas-à-pas verra enfin les champs croisés, plutôt qu'opposés. Les frontières ne sont jamais des barrières, et les franchir n'est pas outrepasser des bornes à jamais fixées, mais plutôt faire preuve d'audace et nouvellement créer. Une "lecture contemporaine" des *Sermons sur les Cantiques* de Bernard de Clairvaux attendait d'être réalisée. Pablo Irizar en a parfaitement accompli la tâche. Il ne suffit pas d'historiciser, encore faut-il *pour aujourd'hui* penser. Les anciens interrogent les modernes, parce qu'ils ne sont eux-mêmes jamais autant "modernes" que lorsqu'ils nous renvoient aux problèmes les plus anciens. L'amour est de ceux-là. « Philosophie » – "amour de le sagesse", ou plutôt "sagesse de l'amour", tel ce que saint Bernard vient nous enseigner. Ni éros d'un côté, ni agapê de l'autre, on attendra de la « *métamorphose de l'éros par l'agapê* » qu'elle prennent en charge l'humain comme tel, et convertisse « en Dieu » ce qu'il y a de plus profond en lui – des passions moins dominées par la raison qu'habitées du divin pour autrement les envisager : *o emos eros estaurotai* – « c'est mon amour (*éros*) qu'ils ont crucifié », convient-il ici de s'exclamer à suite d'Ignace d'Antioche (cité et commenté par Denys l'Aréopagite [*Noms divins*, ch. II, 12, 709 a-b]).

La métamorphose de l'amour nous aurait manqué s'il n'avait pas été si bien produit et écrit. Le voilà aujourd'hui publié. Il est heureux, pour celui aussi qui a l'honneur de préfacer l'ouvrage, d'avoir pu accueillir l'auteur à Paris et le diriger dans ses recherches. Le dialogue n'est jamais aussi fécond que lorsqu'il se vit et s'éprouve « en chair et en os ». Renouveler la tradition certes, mais aussi s'interroger sur notre présent – telle est la tâche de la philosophie, en particulier lorsqu'elle accepte de « passer le Rubicon », et de mesurer le "choc en retour de la théologie sur la phénoménologie". Pablo Irizar a su l'accomplir, sûr que présent ouvrage ouvrira sur d'autres essais, car jamais on ne s'arrête en si bon chemin lorsque l'on a si bien commencé : « Ainsi celui qui monte ne s'arrête jamais d'aller de commencements en commencements, par des commencements qui n'ont jamais de fin » (Grégoire de Nysse).

Preface to *The Metamorphosis of Love*

Emmanuel Falque
Catholic University of Paris

The Metamorphosis of Love, by Pablo Irizar, is a new work; not an abstract novelty that ignores the past, but a novelty rooted in tradition that teaches us how to think today. One can only make something new from the old. However, the old would remain forever buried in the past unless it were questioned otherwise. Such is probably the masterful character of the work published here. For a long time, Bernard of Clairvaux's work has been confined either to a mysticism deracinated from any anthropological support, or to a simple biblical commentary without any philosophical consequence. This is what Pablo Irizar's work does not do, and does not want to do. Supporting a thesis of his own, even if inspired by others, "the metamorphosis of love" has a bright future ahead, and we can only hope that the author will continue on this path, that has been so well begun. For there is a "proper way of love" that Bernard of Clairvaux had once pioneered, and that we have, if not seen too little, at least forgotten. It is thus *in the light of contemporary philosophy* that we must question the Cistercian, and apprise him for our contemporaries: an "actualizing" of the Cistercian *On the Song of Songs* which is not simply an "updating" of an ancient author, but the "deployment of all its unsuspected possibilities" (putting into action or actualizing).

The Greek and Christian traditions have indeed never ceased to intersect – and the demonstration here shows it better than ever. "Metamorphosis of love" certainly, but also "metamorphosis of the tradition," which Saint Bernard himself executes. Such double metamorphosis is shown in this œuvre. *Eros* is Greek, as we know, and *agape* is Christian. However, it would be a mistake either to merge or to separate the terms as well as the cultural heritages. Some have maintained the "equivocity" of *eros* and *agape* (Nygren), others have claimed their "univocity" (Marion), while in the past "analogy" was preferred (Thomas Aquinas). With regard to these three models, the work of Pablo Irizar does not want to reject them, but to show, on the contrary, that they only find meaning, and are completed, in the "transformation" or "metamorphosis" of *eros* by *agape*. There is the "metamorphosis of finitude" certainly by the resurrection, but it produces at the same time a "metamorphosis of love" in the union of the soul with God. "Love changes everything" in theology, just as the "incarnation changes everything", said Merleau-Ponty, in philosophy this time. This is the "change" that makes the encounter with God not a simple *metanoia* or conversion, but a true incorporation of man into God, by which the resurrection will no longer be thought of as an ontic event in (*dans*) the world, but as an ontological transformation of (*du*) the world. God did not come into the world to love us, but it is by loving us, and because he already loved us, that he came to be incarnated. Love is never a result but a principle. Love as a "force", as the second part of the book so well indicates, produces the world rather than discover itself as a dimension of the world. This is what Bernard of Clairvaux knows and sees, or rather, what Pablo Irizar's work makes us see, in case we have forgotten.

Does the Cistersian anticipate Nietzsche or, rather, does Bernard address, from a Christian perspective, the concepts of "metamorphosis" and "force"? Must these concepts not be inserted in the *body*, or rather, must they not produce "body", to truly give themselves and incorporate? This is, after the transformation of *eros* by *agape*, the second novelty of the work by Pablo Irizar. For love is not only a dimension of God, but also of man. Better still, and Bernard of Clairvaux showed this perfectly, it is only by passing through the experience of man (*eros*) that one reaches and understands the experience of God (*agape*), knowing that it is up to divine love to transform human love and incorporate it into itself. *Hodie legimus in libro experientiae* – "today we read from the book of experience." This formula in sermon 3 of the Cistercian's commentary on *Song of Songs* fully justifies that the metamorphosis of love begins (*commencer*), and originates (*débuter*), with experience. For it is not enough to abstract, in matters of love more than anywhere else is. The concreteness of the act of loving is the best way to be incarnated, for man as for God. "Love makes the body" rather than "the body makes love". Bernard of Clairvaux understood this absolutely, and Pablo Irizar demonstrates it perfectly; no *eros* without desired *agape*, and no *agape* without transformed *eros*.

Hence the dimension of desire – the third great originality of *The Metamorphosis of Love*. The "desire of the body" must be thought of as the "hermeneutical key" of the whole reading of *On the Song of Songs*, as this work so well shows and underlines. The body in love, of course, but also the sick body or the hungry body, belong to desire by awaiting it or by generating it. "I have *longed* to eat this Easter with you" (Lk 22.15). The doubling of desire here (the desire of desire) extracts it from simple need (simple desire). This is true of human desire, which not only desires the other, but also desires the desire of the other (anthropogenic desire). It is thus with God also – who does not desire man in the sense of a lack, but of a partner to fulfill himself (theogenic desire). "Let him kiss me with the kiss of his mouth" (Sg 1.2). The magnificent formula that opens the *Song of Songs* serves for Bernard of Clairvaux as the opening of his commentary, and for Pablo Irizar it becomes the foundation of his interpretation of Saint Bernard.

There is indeed not only the philosophical, but also the mystical, in *The Metamorphosis of Love*. Whoever reads it gradually will finally see the fields crossed, rather than opposed. Boundaries are never barriers, and crossing them is not overstepping boundaries that are forever fixed, but rather being bold and newly creative. A "contemporary reading" of Bernard of Clairvaux's *On the Song of Songs* was waiting to be done. Pablo Irizar has done it perfectly. It is not enough to historicize, it is also necessary to think for today. The ancients question the moderns because the latter are themselves never so "modern" than when they send us back to the most ancient problems. Love is one of them. "Philo-sophy" – "love of wisdom", or rather "wisdom of love", such as Saint Bernard comes to teach us. With neither *eros* on the one hand, nor *agape* on the other, we await for the "metamorphosis of *eros* by *agape*" to take charge of the human being as such, and to convert "into God" what is deepest in him – passions less dominated by reason than inhabited by the divine in order to consider them differently: *o emos eros estaurotai* – "it is my love (*eros*) that they have crucified," it is appropriate here to exclaim following Ignatius of Antioch (quoted and commented by Dionysius the Areopagite [*Divine Names*, ch. II, 12, 709 a-b]).

We would have missed *The Metamorphosis of Love* if it had not been so well produced and written. Here it is today published. For the one who has the honor of prefacing the work it is also a joy to have been able to welcome the author in Paris to direct him in his research. Dialogue is never as fruitful as when it is lived and experienced "in the flesh". To renew the tradition, of course, but also to question our present – such is the task of philosophy, especially when it accepts to "cross the Rubicon", and to assess the "backlash of theology on phenomenology". Pablo Irizar has been able to do this, and it is sure that this work will lead to other essays, because one never stops on such good path when one has begun so well: "He who climbs never stops going from beginning to beginning through beginnings that have no end" (Gregory of Nyssa [*Homilies on the Song of Songs*, ch. VIII, 941 c]).

Contents

Acknowledgements

Years ago, I first encountered a philosophical treatment of love and its academic problematization, in a beautifully-written work by Josef Pieper entitled *Faith, Hope, Love*. Nearly a decade later I returned to the question when, having completed philosophical studies in Leuven and in Rome, and as I was exploring the prospects of pursuing doctoral research, Professor Emmanuel Falque of the Catholic University of Paris [Institut catholique de Paris (ICP)] insisted – and rightly! – that I explore the theme of love in the monastic (philosophical) theology of Bernard of Clairvaux. Thereafter I avidly read through a delightful French-Latin version of Bernard's *On the Song of Songs*, which Professor Falque lent me – a gesture of generosity accurately measurable by the weight of the *heavy* collection which Falque painstakingly carried on the train for hours to then bring to me on a hot summer day in Paris –, and which soon turned into a thesis proposal for a canonical doctorate at the Faculty of Philosophy. The present study is the outcome of my (speculative) reflection on the question of love based on a phenomenological reading of Bernard's *On the Song of Songs*. Reflection and the discipline of the mind, as I have learned from Bernard, is but an echoing chamber when it is not rooted in experience and vice versa. As the project, which has been maturing for some years, now joyfully comes to term, I gratefully acknowledge those around me on whose shoulders the project steadily advanced. I count meeting Professor Emmanuel Falque, first through his work on Augustine in *Dieu, la chair, et l'ature*, and then in person or, to use a favorite biblical expression of his, "in flesh and bones," among the many spontaneous and surely providential encounters in my life. Falque's insight awoke in me anew the philosophical wonder, which I had once thought lost. Having introduced me to Bernard of Clairvaux, Falque unwaveringly accepted to help me formulate a doctoral research question, and patiently supervised and supported my academic growth along the way. Thanks to Professor Falque, and of course to my colleagues at the Faculty of Philosophy of the ICP, my formative and memorable stay in France proved to be a time of rewarding and fruitful philosophical reflection. I fondly recall the International Network for Philosophy of Religion (INPR) seminars on Friday afternoons followed by convivial drinks at the nearby *Café Le Doucet* on rue Vaugirard (which is now sadly closed, following the pandemic, and which has been rebranded, thereafter), not to mention the philosophical retreats in Tivoli and Val d'Aulnay. My philosophical questions and ideas were forged, and continue to be forged, in the midst of philosophical and intellectual fellowship. Professor Falque continually reminds an emerging generation of young scholars that philosophy is an essential activity of life. Philosophy, and theology, come to life in disputation (*disputatio*), in loving struggles (*les combats amoreux*), in blows and counterblows (*le choc-en-retour*), in liminality and passage (*passer le rubicon*), in transformation and manifestation (*la métamorphose de la finitude*) and in courageously attempting to contend with mystery and with the incomprehensible (*l'hors phénomène*). For his insight, guidance, encouragement, understanding, and for the growing body of his philosophical *corpus*, I am deeply grateful to Professor Falque. If I persevered in the study of Bernard it is because, among other things, Bernard is a close reader of Augustine, in the study of whose work I began my academic journey. Therefore, I must too express gratitude for the wonderful collaborative community of Augustinian scholars throughout the world, and especially to Professors Anthony Dupont, Matthew Drever and Robert Dodaro (in no specific order), through whose work the world of Augustine was opened to me, and through whose support I have learned to read Augustine in my own terms; my work on Bernard is a but a natural extension thereof. The doctoral defense in Paris was, for me, an occasion to better understand my work through the eyes of others, albeit virtually. For this formative experience I am grateful to the members of the doctoral defense jury (*le jury de soutenance*) for taking the time to consider my work and for offering critical and constructive feedback: Dr. Laure Solignac (ICP), Dr. Marielle Lamy (Sorbonne) and Dr. Yves Meessen (Lorraine Metz). The examination report, to which I have carefully returned for consultation numerous times over the past two years, has enriched my analysis of Bernard, my understanding of my own work, and the shape of this book, specially its conclusion. After my time in Leuven and Paris, I found an institutional home at McGill University. For this, I am joyfully indebted to Professor Garth W. Green at the School of Religious Studies (SRS) who graciously welcomed me to contribute to the vibrant life of SRS since my arrival at the Newman Centre of McGill University in 2019. Through my involvement at SRS, I have been delighted to contribute to Catholic Studies, where my research, teaching and discussions with colleagues have continued to feed my reflection and academic development. At SRS, I have found a hospitable intellectual home to continue exploring philosophy of religion and the Catholic intellectual tradition. Over the years, generous financial support from various institutions has made my research (pleasantly) possible, including the FWO Research Foundation – Flanders, the *Fondations Catholiques Anglaise et Écossaise* in Paris, and now the research funds of the Kennedy Smith Chair in Catholic Studies at McGill University. I am grateful to Dr. Henning Siekmann, Catharina Krallmann, and all the editorial team at Brill | Fink for accepting to consider my manuscript and for inviting me to publish it as part of its program; the timely, helpful and professional support throughout the publication process has been encouraging. I am grateful also to my colleagues at the Newman Centre of McGill University. Gratitude is equally due to all my colleagues and friends who have support my academic journey along the way, knowingly or unknowingly in Canada, Belgium, Italy, Poland, France, and beyond. As always, to my wife, her family, and mine, I remain ever grateful, for the unfailing gift of love (*donum amoris*), which is, I recognize, all the more precious because it has been granted in spite of me, undeservedly, and unreservedly, even when recognized thus belatedly; you are *all* a living testament to unfailing love, about which Paul the Apostle beautifully writes: “Ἡ ἀγάπη οὐδέποτε ἐκπίπτει” (1 Cor 13.8).

29 June 2022
Montréal, Québec
Solemnity of the Feast of Ss. Peter and Paul

Note on Texts and Translations

Various versions and translations of *On the Song of Songs* (*Sermones in Cantica canticorum*) by Bernard of Clairvaux were consulted, including the French-Latin edition published by Cerf in Paris, with the accompanying French translations of J. Leclercq, P. Verdeyen and M. Zink. The French translation in the *Oeuvres competès* by Louis Vivès (Paris, 1877) was initially, and joyfully, consulted also. The Latin text primarily consulted was *Sources Chrétiennes* (*SC*) by Leclercq, Rochais, Talbot, Verdeyen and Fassetta (n. 414 for ss. 1-15, n. 431 for ss. 16-32, n. 452 for ss. 33-50, n. 472 for ss. 51-68, n. 511 for ss. 69-86). The Latin in the collection of *Patrologia Latina* (*PL*) of J. P. Migne was also consulted (v. 182-185). The English edition and in-text translations and citations are all from the translation by K. Walsh and I. Edmonds, published by Cistersian Publications, Kalamazoo, Michigan. The prologue, *La métamorphose de l'amour* (*The Metamorphosis of Love*), previously published in Vol. 1 (2020): 96-100, has been reporduced with the gratious permission of the editors of *Crossings: The INPR Journal.*

Introduction

There are many kinds of loves. What these loves are is simple enough to say – the love of things, the love of places and the love of people. In daily parlance some even say, 'I love God' which, intuitively and unambiguously – at least in the mind of the speaker – seems to mean differently from statements like 'I love my mom', 'I love chocolate' or 'I love myself'. Explicitly stating how these somehow similar yet essentially diverse predications of love relate is no easy task, however. Furthermore, the experience of love, while easily recognizable, at least in appearance, escapes definition, nevertheless. What, then, is love?[1] Is there one love, the Love – upper-case 'L' – from whence all loves – not *the* Love, but *a* love, lower-case 'l' – *are* loves and through which all things, places, and people, are *loved*? Alternatively, are there only scattered instantiations of an experience nominally though truly non-existent referential called love? The question is even more pressing considering that love is the kernel of Christianity and of God's revelation therein *as* love. To ask *what* or *who* love is, is to pry into the divine mystery and to ascertain the relationship between God and human beings and to discover, within this relationship, what it means to be human *tout court*. The aim of this book is to explore the locus of encounter between divine love, which Christians from early times called *agape*, and passionate or erotic human love, which the ancient Greeks called *eros* – a love among others, like *storge* (affection), *epithymia* (desire) and *philia* (friendship).[2] The novel idea of *agapeic* love dawned upon the horizon of history with the advent of Christianity. Against the backdrop of Greek philosophy and culture – condemningly characterized by a commentator as "a world without [*agapaic*] love"[3] – the challenge to uphold human passionate erotic love with the new form of altruistic *agapeic* love emerged in Christian life, reflection and religious practice. Since the revelation of God as *agape* is the kerygma of the Christian message, the task of defining *agape* in relation to *eros* captivated the Christian imagination from early times, soon after the crucifixion of Jesus and as Christian communities began to form and to define themselves throughout the ancient world around the experience of persecution

1 Helpful introductory books to the problem of love in (Western) Christianity include Bernard V. Brady, *Christian Love* (Washington: Georgetown University Press, 2003); Carter Lindberg, *Love: A Brief History Through Western Christianity* (Oxford: Blackwell Publishing, 2008).

2 Lindberg, *Love: A Brief History*, 1.

3 These words are attributed to Gerhard Uhlhorn, in his monumental study on Christian charity, as cited by Lindberg, *Love: A Brief History*, 36.

 | DOI:10.30965/9783846767504_002

and martyrdom. Then and thereafter, conceptualizing and describing how *agape* and *eros* relate unfolded in varied directions, yet always as a demand of Christian commitment, mainly through indirect and mostly according to experiential, not ideological, accounts. A notable consensus within the sophisticated early Christian tradition on this question is the paradigmatic view of the Christian as a pilgrim. The pilgrim is always on the way (*in via*), ever exiled, ever estranged and torn between heaven and earth, desiring the city of God, while navigating the city of man (to borrow Augustine's expression), embroiled in the bubbling and zizzing cauldron of erotic loves, while in the search for the transformative gift of divine charity in Christic *agape* on the cross.[4] What is, then, the role of love in the Christian pilgrim's journey, in Christian praxis and, ultimately, in resolutely pursuing the *imitatio Christi* even unto ordinary, or extraordinary, martyrdom? Wrestling with the problem of love paves the way to appreciate the existential problem of the Christian life and determines its experiential demands.

The rich repository of Christian sources, and its reception and transformation of the Greek philosophical tradition, about which important histories have been written, sheds light on this question. Attempting a review of the primary and secondary literature by way of introduction is, admittedly, a daunting and frankly impossible task. Suffice it, therefore, for our purposes, to present a *heuristic* classification according to paradigms, patterns or models (*παράδειγμα*) operative in Christian discourse, on the problem of love. Four observable models usefully chart implicit views on love and explicit understandings of the interrelation between *eros* and *agape* in terms of (1) *univocity*, (2) *equivocity*, (3) *analogy* and (4) *metamorphosis*. These models need not be mutually exclusive and their proponents often interlace them. The first of these models, hereby presented in no particular order, is the model of *univocity*. *Univocity*, from the Latin *univocus*, meaning 'in one voice', suggests that varied senses of a word are unequivocal and have only one meaning. When speaking about love according to the model of univocity, *eros* and *agape* indicate the single, univocal reality of love with different names and perhaps through different expressions, but without thereby entailing a real difference. In this view, *eros* and *agape* are two of the manifold and perhaps even endless possible manifestations of the single reality, which has the name of love, though inaccurately but inevitably, for it escapes all categories of understanding. This is why, according to the model of univocity, the varied expression of love, like *eros* and *agape*, may be easily confused, as they often are, with realities other than love, or,

4 Augustine, *Confessions*, 3.1. Augustinus, *Opera Omnia, editio Latina, Patrologia Latina* 32. URL: http://www.augustinus.it/latino/confessioni/index2.htm, accessed throughout August 2022.

conversely, the expressions of love may be considered distinct realities altogether, without underlying unifying relationships. In reality, however, in the model of univocity, *eros* and *agape* mean the same underlying and unifying reality that is love. Now, the *equivocity* model advances a different view in contrast to the *univocity* model. As the Latin word *aequivocus* implies, following the literal meaning of the Greek *ὁμώνυμος* (meaning 'of the same name'[5]), an equivocal term is ambiguous and is therefore expressed according to a dual sense (*à double sense*).[6] Equivocity refers to terms "of like significations, ambiguous, equivocal."[7] According to the *equivocity* model, *eros* and *agape* are ambiguous significations of the same reality, which is love. In *equivocity*, although *eros* and *agape* somehow express similar aspects of love, these aspects remain distinct and irreducible to each other. Thus, the experience of *eros* does not imply an experience of *agape*, and vise-versa. The question of the relationship between *eros* and *agape* as ambivalent manifestations of love therefore begins to emerge poignantly. The third model, which is *analogy*, neither equivocates or univocates the relationship between *eros* and *agape* but seeks, rather, to find a proportionality according to *ratio*. The word *analogy*, from the Latin *analogus*, means proportionate.[8] In Greek, the word analogy (*ἀνάλογος*) is a composite of the prefix '*-ana*' and the word '*logos*', which together literally mean 'according to proportion'.[9] To speak according to proportion, or by analogy, consists in recognizing that certain aspects of *agape* are transferable to *eros*, and vise-versa, in a restricted sense, and according to resemblance and dissemblance of proportionality.[10] That is, "ressemblence ou comformité de plusieurs choses entre elles."[11] This means that while *eros* and *agape* remain distinct (*equivocity* model), some of their aspects relate nevertheless (*univocity* model), though always in a limited, asymmetrical and imperfect manner, that is, by proportion of relation (*analogy* model). To speak of love analogically, then, is to recognize

5 Charles du Cange *et al.*, *Glossarium mediae et infimae latinitatis*, Niort: L. Favre, 1883-1887, t. 1, col. 117b. URL: http://ducange.enc.sorbonne.fr/AEQUIVOCUS1, accessed throughout June 2022.

6 Félix Gaffiot, *Dictionnaire Illustré Latin-Français* (Paris: Hachette, 1934), 76. URL: http://micmap.org/dicfro/search/gaffiot/aequivocus, accessed throughout June 2022.

7 Charlton T. Lewis and Charles Short, *A Latin Dictionary* (Oxford: Claredon Press, 1879). URL: http://www.perseus.tufts.edu/hopper/text?doc=Perseus:text:1999.04.0059:entry=a equivocus, accessed throughout June 2022.

8 Ibid.

9 Ibid.

10 See, Geoffrey Lloyd, *Polarity and Analogy: Two Types of Argumentation in Early Greek Thought* (Cambridge: Cambridge University Press, 1966).

11 Félix Gaffiot, *Dictionnaire Illustré*, 122. URL: http://micmap.org/dicfro/search/gaffiot/analogus, accessed throughout June 2022.

that only some aspects of resemblance between *agape* and *eros* may be transferable, while also recognizing that *eros* and *agape* always remain fundamentally divergent realities. In short, according to these models, *eros* and *agape* may be either (1) identical (*univocity*) or (2) distinct (*equivocity*), but not both (1) and (2); or (3) similar in some respects, but never the same (*analogy*). Models (1), (2) and (3) are indicative and descriptive only, as opposed to prescriptive. In other words, they simply describe how or what reality *is*, whereas a prescriptive model would indicate what reality *should* be. There is a fourth model, this time a prescriptive one, which may be termed the model of (4) *metamorphosis*. Metamorphosis (or transfiguration) combines the first three models thanks to its prescriptive framework. Accordingly, *eros* is different from *agape* (*equivocity*), but only initially, because *eros* finds its fullness in *agape* (*univocity*). The process unfolds through corresponding proportionality of human experience (*analogy*) and achieves a new and prescriptive reality in transformation (*metamorphosis*). The term for metamorphosis (*μεταμορφόω*), generally rendered in English translations of the New Testament as transfiguration or transformation (for instance at Matt 7.2, Mark 9.2 and Rm 12.2) or as conformation (at 2 Cor 3.18) – interestingly rarely as metamorphosis – denotes change or transformation: physical, spiritual or substantial. The *metamorphosis* model prescribes, consequently, the process whereby describing differences and similarities (*analogy*) between *eros* and *agape* is the initial moment towards realizing fulfillment in the outcome of relation, which is transfiguration, while recognizing that perfect unity (*univocity*) is unattainable. Furthermore, as an intricate organic yet spiritual process, the *metamorphosis* model identifies similarities based not in speculative discourse of onto-theology, but in the experience of the manifestation and expression of human experience by means of metaphorical language.[12] The poetics of finitude and of the body is the source of experience and the point of departure in the *metamorphosis* model, and not disincarnate ideas of speculation, as was the case with the *analogy* model. The *metamorphosis* model attempts to embed the abstract model of *analogy* within the fabric of the body's finitude. Before explicating the notion of metamorphosis, its etymology, early Christian sources, and its rough reception in contemporary discussions in French phenomenology of religion, what follows first illustrates a historical, chronological and textual synopsis of the four models as evidenced in the Christian tradition.

The four models of love – univocity, equivocity, analogy and metamorphosis – are recognizable in different ways from early Christian sources up to their lively

12 Paul Ricœur, *The Rule of Metaphor: The Creation of Meaning in Language* (London: Routledge, 2004), 255-302 and 322-9.

revival in contemporary circles of French phenomenology. An ambiguous sentence in a letter by Ignatius Theophorus (d. 108), who is usually better known as Ignatius of Antioch, inaugurates the problem of love, which is the question of the problematic relationship between *eros* and *agape* for the Christian tradition and which the four models of love above seek to address from early centuries. On the road to martyrdom, Ignatius movingly pleads for the Christian community in Rome not to hinder the opportunity to imitate Jesus unto death as a witness or martyr. "[T]hough I am alive while I write to you, I am eager to die," Ignatius writes, because, he then explains, "my love has been crucified [*ὁ ἐμὸς ἔρως ἐσταύρωται*]."[13] The complete passage from the *Epistle to the Romans* is this:

> The prince of this world would fain carry me away and corrupt my disposition towards God. Let none of you, therefore, who are [in Rome] help him; rather be on my side, that is, on the side of God. Do not speak of Jesus Christ, and yet set your desires on the world. Let not envy find a dwelling-place among you; nor even should I, when present with you, exhort you to it, be persuaded to listen to me, but rather give credit to those things which I now write to you. For though I am alive while I write to you, yet I am eager to die. *My love has been crucified* [*ὁ ἐμὸς ἔρως ἐσταύρωται*] and there is no fire in me desiring to be fed; but there is within me a water that lives and speaks, saying to me inwardly, 'come to the Father'. I have no delight in corruptible food, nor in the pleasures of this life. I desire the bread of God, the heavenly bread, the bread of life, which is *the flesh* of Jesus Christ, the Son of God, who became afterwards of the seed of David and Abraham; and I desire the drink of God, namely His blood, which is *incorruptible love* and eternal life.[14]

Ignatius wishes to model his death after the death of Jesus. Strikingly, Ignatius uses the name *eros* (*ὁ ἐμὸς*) with reference to Jesus. In other words, Ignatius is inspired to persevere onwards, with his journey to martyrdom, because of Jesus, because of *eros*, and because of this Jesus-*eros* crucified on the cross. Upon close inspection, some questions arise. Whom does Ignatius have in mind when he writes "my love [*ὁ ἐμὸς ἔρως*]", what does the crucifixion of love, considered as *eros* represent and what does it imply? Is Christ *eros* on the cross or, rather, does the crucifixion of Christ represent the purification, and therefore, the partial rejection of human *eros* in the place of a novel heavenly love, namely *agape*? The response to the problem of love unfolds according to two

---

13 Ignatius of Antioch, *Ep. Rom.* 7. In *Ante-Nicene Fathers, Vol. 1*, ed. and trans. Alexander Roberts, James Donaldson, and Cleveland Coxe (Buffalo: Christian Literature Publishing Co., 1885). Revised and edited for *New Advent* by Kevin Knight, URL: http://www.newadvent.org/fathers/0107.htm, accessed throughout June 2022.

14 Ibid.

broad strands of interpretation. According to the first line of interpretation, Christ, who is also God, and therefore *agape*, is the crucified *eros*. In this case, *eros* and *agape* are interchangeable, thereby yielding a *univocity* thesis. The second interpretation is complex: *eros* is neither Christ, nor Christ's; it is a representation of the *eros* of Ignatius, which is a symbol for the *eros* of human experience. Therefore, here, *eros* is crucified, either in Christ (*equivocity*) or through Christ (*analogy*), or alternatively, *eros* is crucified as Christ (*metamorphosis*). The ambiguity of the Ignatian *Epistle to the Romans* shaped the debate for centuries to come. Early Christian interpreters passionately engaged with this question because suddenly the uniqueness of Christianity in the recognition that "God is love [*ὁ θεὸς ἀγάπη ἐστίν*]" at 1 Jn 4.8 was, if not put into question, at least thenceforth requiring some nuance vis-à-vis the role of *eros* in Christian life. If God is *agape*, and if Jesus – God crucified[15] – is *eros*, is not God somehow, both *agape* and *eros*? Origen of Alexandria (d. 253) explicitly addresses this question in his *Commentary on the Song of Songs*, this time with reference to, and in light of, the influential Johannine expression "God is love" (1 Jn 4.8). The passage, worth citing at length, considers how and *that* God is *agape* (John) and *eros* (Ignatius). Origen writes:

> It makes no difference, therefore, whether the Sacred Scripture speak of love, or of charity, or of affection; except that the word 'charity' is so highly exalted that even God Himself is called Charity, as John says: *Dearly beloved, let us love one another, for charity is of God; and everyone that loveth is born of God and knoweth God; but he that loveth not knoweth not God, for God is Charity.* And although some other time might be more suitable in which to say something about these words that, by way of example, we have cited from John's Epistle, it seems not unreasonable to touch briefly on the matter in this context too. *Let us love one another*, he says, *for charity is of God*; and a little later: *God is Charity*. In saying this, he shows us both that God Himself is Charity, and that He who of God Himself is Charity […] Thus, then, the name of charity belongs first to God; and for that reason we are bidden to love God with all our hearts and all our souls and all our strength-Him, that is, from whom we have the very power of loving. And this command undoubtedly implies that we should also love wisdom and right-doing and piety and truth and all the other virtues; for to love God and to love good things is one and the same thing. In the second place, we are bidden also to love our neighbour as ourselves by a use of the word that is, as it were, derived and secondary. And the third usage is that by which 'loving' money, or pleasure, or anything that is connected with corruption and error, is called charity by a misnomer. So it makes no difference whether we speak of having a passion for

---

15 Origenes, *Cels.* 7.16. In *Ante-Nicene Fathers, Vol. 4*, ed. and trans. Alexander Roberts, James Donaldson, and Cleveland Coxe (Buffalo: Christian Literature Publishing Co., 1885). Revised and edited for *New Advent* by Kevin Knight, URL: http://www.newadvent.org/fathers/0416.htm, accessed throughout June 2022.

God, or of loving Him; and I do not think one could be blamed if one called God Passionate Love [*Amorem*], just as John calls Him Charity [*Caritatem*]. Indeed I remember that one of the saints, by name Ignatius, said of Christ: 'My Love [*Amor*] is crucified,' and I do not consider him worthy of censure on this account. [*Nec pato quod culpari possit, si quis Deum, sicut Joannis, charitatur, ita ipse amorem nominit. Denejire memini, aliquem sanctorum dixisse Ignatium nomine de Christo: Mens autem amor crucifixus est: nec reprehendi eum per hoc dignum judico*]. We have discussed these matters at length because we wanted to distinguish more clearly and carefully between the nature of passionate love and that of charity; lest perhaps, because Scripture says that God is Charity, the charity and love that is of God should be esteemed to be in our every attachment, even to corruptible things.[16]

Adopting the *univocity* model, albeit implicitly, Origen assuredly reads Ignatius to mean that Christ is the *eros* on the cross and, consequently, that God is unequivocally *eros* and *agape*. Via the Latin translations from the Greek by Rufinus of Aquileia (d. 410) and by Jerome of Stridon (d. 420), early and subsequent Latin Christian writers inherited a wide-ranging vocabulary – including words like *dilectio, caritas, amor, affectus* and *affectio* – to articulate, reframe, and address the problem of love.[17] Through these translations, and consequently thanks to the semantic range that these concepts afforded – and at times lost, unnecessary expanded or simply narrowed – Augustine of Hippo (d. 430), who *also* was versed in Greek, contrary to common misconception, was able to achieve the severance of the hitherto Origenian integral approach to *eros* and *agape*. Augustine stressed the dynamic, moral quality of human (*not* divine) desire in his great and arduous (*magnum opus et arduum*) masterpiece, *City of God*. Augustine writes,

And if any one fancy that *amor* is no doubt used both of good and bad loves, but that *dilectio* is reserved for the good only, let him remember what the psalm says, He that loves (*diligit*) iniquity hates_his own soul; and the words of the Apostle John, If any man love (*diligere*) the world, the love (*dilectio*) of the Father is not in him (1 Jn 2.15). Here you have in one passage *dilectio* used both in a good and a bad sense. And if any one demands an instance of *amor* being used in a bad sense (for we have already shown its use in a good sense), let him read the words, For men shall be lovers (*amantes*) of their own selves, lovers (*amatores*) of money (2 Tm 3.2).[18]

---

16 Origenes, *The Song of Songs: Commentary and Homilies*, trans. R. P. Lawson (London: Longmans, 1957), 33-6.

17 Damien Boquet and Piroska Nagy, *Medieval Sensibilities: A History of Emotions in the Middle Ages*, trans. Robert Shaw (New York: John Wiley & Sons, 2018), 9-30.

18 Augustine, *civ.*, 14.7. In *Nicene and Post-Nicene Fathers, Vol. 2*, ed. Philip Schaff (Buffalo: Christian Literature Publishing Co., 1885). Revised and edited for *New Advent* by Kevin

According to Augustine, desire does not have an inherently negative, or positive, moral quality. On the contrary, the quality or modality of desire, and its corresponding directionality, qualifies whether or not *eros* can be(come) *agape* at any given moment. Augustine's ensuing dynamic understanding of desire introduces an (inclusive) *equivocity* model, wherein *eros* (*amor*), if rightly oriented, as desire, towards the use of creation (*uti*) and the enjoyment of God alone (*frui*), may attain the rank of *agape* (*caritas*), albeit as an altogether new reality, while remaining fundamentally different, therefore, from *eros*. For human beings, who are *in* time, and *of* time, *eros* and *agape* never coincide, except through Christ, in whom *eros* is *agape* and because, at a metaphysical level, Christ is the eternal *logos* incarnate, thus embodying the perfect synthesis of time-eternity and *eros-agape*, only at the end of times. Thus, in his *Homilies on First John*, particularly *Homily* 9, Augustine playfully inverses, and not without consequence, the Johannine line "God is love", to read, instead, "love is God", and to mean, thenceforth, at once that God is *amor* (or *eros*) and *caritas* (or *agape*). While the *amor-eros* and *caritas-agape* approximation is dubious, notwithstanding the terminological superposition, Augustine's rhetorical inversion achieves an elegant reorientation on the problem of love whereby *amor-eros* and *caritas-agape* are synonymous names of God's manifestation in human life through Christ. However, and the caveat is monumental, human beings, *of* time and *in* time, may only aspire to such unity of *loves* as exemplified in Christ's humanity and divinity. Thus, Augustine combines two models: while the human experience of love is fragmented, hence the need to navigate according to an *equivocity* model in the moral life, all loves converge in God alone, in whom, under the species of eternity (*sub specie aeternitatis*), *eros* is *agape*. In essence, Augustine remains consistent with Origen's interpretation of Ignatius in attributing the *univocity* model to God alone, particularly in Christ on the cross. Augustine also expands the analysis, beyond Origen's interpretation, by framing the transformative itinerary of human love in terms of the *equivocity* model.

In *The Divine Names*, Dionysius the Areopagite, who live and wrote in the 5th or 6th century, returning to Origen, adopts a strict *univocity* model to predicate love of God. He writes,

> Indeed some of our writers on sacred matters have thought the title "yearning" to be more divine than "love", The divine Ignatius writes: "He for whom I yearn has been crucified" (Rom 7.2). In the introductory scriptures you will note the following said about the divine wisdom: "I yearned for her beauty" (Wis 8.2). So let

Knight, URL: http://www.newadvent.org/fathers/120114.htm, accessed throughout June 2022.

> us not fear this title of "yearning" nor be upset by what anyone has to say about these two names, for, in my opinion, *the sacred writers regard "yearning" and "love" as having one and the same meaning*. They added "real" to the use of "yearning" regarding divine things because of the unseemly nature such a word has for men. The title "real yearning" is praised by us and by the scriptures themselves as being appropriate to God. Others, however, tended naturally to think of a partial, *physical*, and *divided* yearning. *This is not true yearning but an empty image or, rather, a lapse from real yearning*. The fact is that men are unable to grasp the *simplicity* of the one divine yearning, and, hence, the term is quite offensive to most of them. So it is left to the divine Wisdom to lift them and to raise them up to a knowledge of what yearning really is, after which they no longer take offense. And it is clear to us that many lowly men think there is something absurd in the lovely verse.[19]

Here, Dionysius departs from Augustine in one important point. While Dionysius has no problem referring to yearning or desire for God in terms of human *eros*, because *eros* is interchangeable with *agape*, he does not base the distinction between human and divine love upon the difference between *eros* and *agape* or their orientation, as had done Augustine, but rather, on their *modality*. Dionysius distinguishes between 'real *eros*', which is God's proper, in whom all attributes are one by divine simplicity, and the 'not real' yearning, which is but a lapse from 'real *eros*'. For Dionysius, the *univocity* model applies consistently across the spectrum, for humans *and* for God.

Throughout the medieval period, concurrent strands of reflection occur in the epistolary, scholastic and monastic traditions, often organized in response to, or in conversation with, the emerging literature of courtly love. Drawing inspiration from Ovid's *The Art of Love*, composed in the 2nd century AD, Andreas Capellanus (d. 1220) sets the stage of the discussion around the problem of love by insisting, in his own *On Love* (*De Amore*), written sometime around 1190, on the value of romantic love outside of marriage. Andreas organizes the practice of extramarital romantic love, or courtly love (*fin'amor*), around rules, which eventually serve in the medieval period as a code for the highly appraised practice of courtly love. Courtly love is an exaltation of *eros*, for which reason its extrapolation in theological reflection uncovered unprecedented trajectories. In the epistolary tradition, for instance, Peter Abelard (d. 1142), a priest, exhibits the troubadour *equivocity* model of courtly literature, also known as *fin'amor*, in his passionate correspondence with Héloïse, who was a nun. For Abelard and Héloïse, the rules of courtly love (*amor*) suddenly rendered an otherwise forbidden expression of *eros* an acceptable, albeit

---

19 Pseudo-Dionysius, *The Divine Names*, 4.11. In *The Complete Works: Dionysius Areopagita*, trans. Colm Luibheid (New York: Paulist, 1987), 55.

regulated, practice, without much concern for the place of *agape* therein. The foreground of the question of love, which contributes to the development of courtly literature in religious reflection, as Gilson later notes, is a debate over the nature of love, and, in the foreground, a question of models to construe love. Is *fin'amor* a genuine expression of God through neighbour (*univocity* model), or is it, rather, legitimate within specific constraints dictated by divine love (*equivocity* model)?

The scholastic tradition developed concurrently with the question of romance and courtly love. In the *Four Books of Sentences*, the scholastic and influential (later) Bishop of Paris, Peter Lombard (d. 1160), addresses the question of love in considering pneumatology – the study on the nature of the Holy Spirit, the second person of the divine Trinity – and in its relation to marriage, to marriage's sacramental status, and to the role of canonical consent therein. In a decisive reorientation of theological discourse on the problem of love, Peter Lombard identifies *agape* with the Holy Spirit, and recognizes the experientiablity of God through the Holy Spirit *as* gift, given *by* God, *in* and *through* love of neighbor.[20] In this interpretation, which marks an important shift away from Augustine's analysis and from earlier theologians, the *univocity* of love is restricted to *agape* and applies not to God, but only to the Holy Spirit and, accordingly, only to human beings, in the context of neighborly *relations*, for which marriage functions as a paradigm of divine and triune *relationship*. Moreover, by situating the Father-Son relation as the neighbor-neighbor relation, expressed as *agape* in the Holy Spirit, Peter Lombard effectively anchors any semblance of *eros* in *agape* and only as *agape*. Peter Lombard's (seemingly) strict *univocity* decisively supplants *eros* and reduces all *agape* to *relation*, and therefore restricts *agape* to an experience of gift (or grace?) in the Holy Spirit. In Peter Lombard's appropriation of the *univocity* model, the Trinitarian God is no longer *agape* strictly speaking, and the experience of *agape* is an experience of the Holy Spirit in and as *relation*.

In parallel to its important early scholastic developments and other courtly love literature, yet a third, programmatic and dynamic approach on the relationship between *eros* and *agape* emerges in the monastic and mendicant theology of the 11th and 12th century. Ample evidence for this is found, for example, in the writings of William of Saint-Thierry (d. 1148), Bernard of Clairvaux (d. 1153) and Richard of Saint Victor (d. 1173). Particularly for Bernard of Clairvaux, who knew Peter Lombard, the question of love is not, at least not

20 Peter Lombard, *Book of Sentences*, Book I, *The Mystery of the Trinity*, distinction 17, p. 1, ch. 1-3. In *The Sentences*, trans. Giulio Silano (Toronto: Pontifical Institute of Medieval Studies, 2007).

primarily, a theological problem or as a theoretical paradox. In preaching and writing *On the Song of Songs*, a commentary on the *Song of Songs*, which Bernard calls *the book of experience*, love is for Bernard primarily an experiential phenomenon: experience is the judge of the veracity of love's predicaments and demands. The experience of *eros* and *agape* intertwine inseparably in the practice of life. In the rhythms of habitual monastic experience, in the midst of labour, liturgy and fellowship, arises the experience of God in neighbour and of God *as* love through neighbour. The aim of monastic discipline, far from aiming to discard *eros* aimed, on the contrary, to reorient *eros* towards *agape*, through degrees of perfection, and to transform *eros*, and purify it, in the *agape* of God. Operative herein is an integration of Augustine's views on the *univocity* model, applicable to God only, and the *equivocity* model, pertaining to human beings primarily – after all, the monastic theologians were close readers of Augustine. In the context of monastic and mendicant asceticism, liturgical and communal life, however, monastic theologians emphasized the transformative or metamorphosing dimension of human experience, for *eros*, into *agape*, thus anticipating, while never systematizing, the *metamorphosis* model, for such systematization would have been antithetical to their monastic project.

Among the mendicant friars, important figures in the development of the *analogy* model included Francis of Assisi (d. 1226), Bonaventure (d. 1274) and, later, more decisively through the theoretical notion of an analogy of being (*analogia entis*), Thomas Aquinas (d. 1274). By focusing on the metaphysical underpinnings of love, and not on the phenomenology of experience, as did their monastic counterparts concurrently, the Dominicans in Paris and the Franciscans at Oxford developed and championed a systematization of the model of *analogy*. Thomas Aquinas retrieves the Christian tradition and, deploying mainly Aristotle, at times Augustine and other early Christian writers, and often strands of Platonism, Aquinas fully and decisively develops the *analogy* model.[21] To do this, he specifically draws from Augustine and pseudo-Dionysius, who appear to embrace incompatible models, and aims for harmonization in the *Summa Theologicae*. The contribution of Aquinas therefore represents an important transformative synthesis of the *univocity* and the *equivocity* models into the *analogy* model. He does this systematically,

21 Jennifer Ashworth and Domenic D'Ettore, "Medieval Theories of Analogy," *The Stanford Encyclopedia of Philosophy* (Winter 2021 Edition), ed. Edward N. Zalta, URL = https://plato.stanford.edu/archives/win2021/entries/analogy-medieval/, accessed throughout June 2022.

in elegant scholastic fashion, and in various texts.[22] In his *Commentary on the Sentences* (of Peter Lombard) Aquinas instructively notes:

> The Creator and the creature are reduced to unity not by a univocal commonality but by analogy. Now, such a commonality can be twofold. It can either be because certain things participate in something according to an order of priority and posteriority, as potency and act participate in the concept of being as also substance and accident do; or this commonality can be because a thing receives its being and its concept from another, and such is the analogy between creature and Creator. In fact, the creature only has being insofar as it descends from the first being [i.e., God]. Thus, it is only called being because it imitates the first being. And the same must be said of wisdom and everything else that is said of creatures.[23]

For Aquinas, human love is love, as the being of human beings is being proper, only by analogy to the love of God, which is absolute love, and only by analogy to the being of God, which is absolute being by precedence; human love is, therefore, analogously relatively to God's absolute, *and* inevitably temporal, in contrast to divine eternity. Moreover, in the model of *analogy* of love, following Aquinas and the *analogia entis*, the love of human beings comes from God, is an imitation thereof, and is to the love of God, in terms of posteriority, what potency is to act: human love is the (imitative) act of God's being.

In his *Treatise on the Love of God*, Francis de Sales (d. 1622) – Bishop of Geneva, who lived in exile because of confessional disputes of the time – relies on the scholastic-Aristotelian concepts and distinctions between habit (*habitus*) and act (*actus*) to frame the relationship between *eros* and *agape*, which he remarkably traces back to Ignatius of Antioch and later interpretations, in support of *eros*, by Origen and Denys. Francis de Sales writes:

> Origin says somewhere that in his opinion the Divine Scripture wishing to hinder the word love from giving occasion of evil thoughts to the weak, as being more proper to signify a carnal passion than a spiritual affection, instead of this name of love has used the words charity and dilection, which are more honest. But S. Augustine having deeply weighed the use of God's word clearly shows that the name love is no less sacred than the word dilection, and that the one and the other signify sometimes a holy affection and sometimes also a depraved

22 See, for instance, Thomas Aquinas, *On Love and Charity: Readings from the* Commentary on the Sentences *of Peter Lombard*, trans. Peter A. Kwasniewski, Thomas Bolin and Joseph Bolin (Washington: The Catholic University of America Press, 2008).

23 Thomas Aquinas, *Commentary on the* Book of Sentences, Prol. q. 1, a. 2, ad 2. In Thomas Aquinas, *On Love and Charity: Readings from the* Commentary on the Sentences *of Peter Lombard*, trans. Peter A. Kwasniewski, Thomas Bolin and Joseph Bolin (Washington: The Catholic University of America Press, 2008).

> passion, alleging to this purpose different passages of Holy Scripture. But the great S. Denis, as excelling doctor of the proper use of the divine names, goes much further in favour of the word love, teaching that theologians, that is, the Apostles and their first disciples (for this saint knew no other theologians) to disabuse the common people, and break down their error in taking the word love in a profane and carnal sense, more willingly employed it in divine things than that of dilection; and, though they considered that both might be used for the same thing, yet some of them were of opinion that the word love was more proper and suitable to God than the word dilection. Hence the divine Ignatius wrote these words: "My love is crucified." And as these ancient theologians made use of the word love in divine things to free it from the taint of impurity of which it was suspected according to the imagination of the world, so to express human affections they liked to use the word dilection as exempt from all suspicion of impropriety. Wherefore one of them, as S. Denis reports, said: "Thy dilection has entered into my soul like the dilection of women." In fine the word love signifies more fervour, efficacy, and activity than that of dilection, so that amongst the Latins dilection is much less significative than love: "Clodius," says their great orator, "bears me dilection, and to say it more excellently, he loves me." Therefore the word love, as the most excellent, has justly been given to charity, as to the chief and most eminent of all loves; so that for all these reasons, and because I intend to speak of the acts of charity rather than of its habit, I have entitled this little work, *A Treatise of the Love of God*.[24]

Instead of *caritas*, Francis de Sales is concerned mainly with *dilectio*, which he roughly extrapolates with the Greek *eros*. Whereas *dilectio* is a habit (*habitus*) of the soul, explains the Bishop of Geneva, *caritas* or *agape* is the act (*actus*) thereof. Thus, *dilectio* and *caritas* pertain to love in the soul, one human, as habit, the other divine, in act; the act of love is inseparable from its habit, and its expression is a manifestation of participation in the divine life. Moreover, the love of God is the highest form of love and (perhaps when) it takes the form of act. Francis de Sales seems, though this is unclear, to adopts, therefore, the *equivocity* model, when appreciating that both loves can coexist, albeit as different realities, in human life. Although Francis of Sales does not offer an innovative contribution to the debate, his citation of Aquinas centuries after Aquinas is of interest because it shows, firstly, the prevalence and endurance of the *analogy* model after Aquinas and, secondly, because this is the last major trace of the problem of love, at least in the Catholic tradition, for many centuries. Indeed, in the wake of the Protestant Reformation, and the Catholic counter-reformation in the wake and aftermath of the Council of Trent (1545-1563), responses to the problem of love follow confessional lines, with Protestant

24 Francis de Sales, *On the Love of God*, ch. 14, trans. Henry Benedict Mackey (London: Burns & Oates, 1884), URL: https://ccel.org/ccel/desales/love/love.i.html, accessed throughout June 2022.

groups widely adopting *equivocity* model and with mainstream Catholics opting, instead, for the *analogy* model, following the *analogia entis* of the scholastics and, specially, of Thomas Aquinas. It was in this climate that Francis de Sales retrieves Aquinas. Moreover, it was because of this climate that some models, besides the *equivocity* model and the *analogy* model, blurred into the foreground of the Catholic intellectual tradition thereafter. Finally, the undeveloped habit-act distinction in the *analogia entis*, which relies on Aristotelian homomorphism and on participation, may constitute a rough precedent to the model of *metamorphosis*.

From the time of the Protestant Reformation, the confessional dimension of responses to the Christian problem of love, though observable in immediately ensuing discussions, like that of Francis de Sales, is only revisited centuries later with the re-emergence of the problem of love in French circles. There was an important though rather quiet initial revival of the problem of love in French circles of phenomenology at the turn of the 21st century which traces its genealogy not to (the Protestant and more influential) Anders Nygren, but to the (Catholic and little known) Jesuit priest Pierre Rousselot (d. 1915), an important influence of Henri de Lubac (d. 1991). In his doctoral dissertation of 1908, later published with the title *Pour l'histoire du problème de l'amour au Moyen Âge*, Rousselot offers a steadfast Thomistic analysis of love. Partly because of his Thomistic and Catholic commitments, and partly also because of his short tenure as a professor, given that he perished at a young age during WWII at the Battle of Éaprges in 1915, Rousselot's reconsideration on the problem of love, though lacking originality, witness to a renewed interest in a largely dormant debate for centuries which went largely unnoticed.

Credit for the full-fledged revival and reorientation of the contemporary question of love is usually accorded to the Swedish Lutheran Bishop of Lund, Anders Nygren (d. 1978). Through his influential work, the model of *equivocity* dominated the discourse throughout the 20th century. Relying on a forceful *motif research* reading of Augustine, largely shaped by *reformation theology*, Nygren proposes agape as the "transvaluation of all ancient values."[25] In his *magnum opus* entitled *Agape and Eros*, Nygren maintains that the injection of *eros* in Christian discourse about *agape*, mainly in the work of Augustine, compromised the integrity of the kernel of the Gospel message, which is the

---

25 Anders Nygren, *Agape and Eros*, trans. P. S. Watson (London: The Westminster Press, 1953), 31. Cited in Torstein T. Tollefsen, *Eros and agape – a critique of Anders Nygren*, in *Love – ancient perspectives*, ed. K. Grødum, H. F. Hägg, J. Kaufman & T. T. Tollefsen (Oslo: Cappelen Damm Akademisk, 2021), 17-29. URL: https://doi.org/10.23865/noasp.133.ch01, accessed throughout June 2022.

unprecedented notion of *agapaic* love. For Nygren, *eros* is antagonistic to *agape*, so *agape* does not integrate or sanitize *eros*, but supplants it altogether. His thesis is thus: "There cannot actually be any doubt that Eros and Agape belong originally to two entirely separate spiritual worlds, between which no direct communication is possible."[26] More than mere linguistic or conceptual distinctions, Nygren contraposes *eros* and *agape* as "different general attitudes to life."[27] Nygren defines *eros* thus:

> Eros is acquisitive desire and longing. It is man's way to God. It is man's own effort and assumes that his salvation is his own work. Eros is egoistic love, a form of self-assertion. It seeks to gain its life as a kind of divine and immortalized life. It is man's love and it is motivated by the worth or quality of its object.[28]

There is no continuity, in other words, between erotic love and altruistic love. Nygren thus proposes *equivocity* as the true reading of Christian love. From the time of its publication, Nygren's thesis has stimulated much debate. His problematic reading of Augustine aside, the textual, linguistic and historical method of analysis he employs emerged in phenomenological circles in the early 2000s as the fundamental flaw of his study and consequently as a challenge to his thesis of *equivocity*. For how is it possible, the phenomenologists probed, to talk about the content of the experience of *eros* and of *agape* by relying on concepts and terms, motifs or even history, and without first considering and describing the phenomena in question? In its reception among the phenomenologists, the debate on the problem of love shifted, therefore, from defending a position according to confessional lines, to reconsidering method. The method of the phenomenologists prioritized descriptive expression over (and perhaps to the detriment of) conceptual analysis.

Phenomenological concerns in the 21st century thus afforded a hospitable and fruitful method and platform to revisit, revive and expand the debate over the ancient Christian problem of love. In the 1960s, the young Karol Wojtyła (d. 2005), later John Paul II, drawing from scholasticism and from phenomenology, adopted a reformulation of the *analogy* model in *Love and Responsibility*, where he proposes that the *eros* of human sexuality, particularly in the body, reveals the divine *agape* in becoming: "love is becoming".[29] Although closely related, a series of interpretations of the biblical book of Genesis – later compiled as the *Theology of the Body* – eclipsed the importance of Wojtyła's

26 Nygren, *Agape and eros*, 31; cited by Tollefsen, *Eros and agape*, 20.
27 Nygren, *Agape and eros*, 34; cited by Tollefsen, *Eros and agape*, 20.
28 Nygren, *Agape and eros*, 210; cited by Tollefsen, *Eros and agape*, 22.
29 Karol Wojtyła, *Love and Responsibility* (Dedham: Pauline Books & Media, 2003).

originality in applying the phenomenological method in addressing the problem of love. In 2006, the French philosopher Jean-Luc Marion (b. 1946) published a series of meditations on the phenomenon of *eros* under the title *The Erotic Phenomenon* (2006), published in French three years earlier. Marion revisits the bifurcation of flesh (*chair*) and body (*corps*) in the Christian tradition, from whence ensues a correspondingly bifurcated appreciation or denigration of *eros*, attributed to the flesh, and *agape*, attributed to the body (of Christ).[30] Through the erotic reduction, by a revalorization of the flesh and body, Marion aims to overcome the bifurcation of *eros* and *agape*. Since auto-affection expressed in the clasping of hands, of flesh, following Michel-Henry, is the point of departure for Marion's erotic reduction against the objectifying gaze of a Cartesian *cogito ergo sum*, where subject and object are indistinguishable, therefore in the erotic reduction *eros* and *agape* are one as saturated phenomenon, and the basis of hetero-affection. Marion writes, "auto-affection alone makes possible hetero-affection."[31] All love, in this view, emerges from the erotic reduction that renders love as *eros-agape*. In the erotic reduction, Marion is therefore a proponent of the *univocity* model. In expounding a *univocity* model, whereby *eros* and *agape* are the same reality manifested in phenomenological reduction of the given, Marion effectively retrieves and presents a long-forgotten tradition traceable to Origen's *Commentary on the Song of Songs*, passing through the *Letter to the Romans* by Ignatius of Antioch, and systematized in the Neoplatonic thought of Pseudo-Dionysius in *The Divine Names*. This tradition, which Marion adopts, considers God as *eros*. Thus, God is *eros* and *agape*; these are two manifestations of the same, otherwise unnameable divine reality; by famously stating that God is without being, Marion presupposes, mainly, that God is beyond being, which is to say that God is, better, *eros-agape*. In response, soon thereafter, Emmanuel Falque (b. 1963), a student of Marion, writing also in the phenomenological tradition, subtly and in passing takes issue with Marion's position in *The Wedding Feast of the Lamb* (2011) and *The Metamorphosis of Finitude* (2012) – which was originally published in French in 2004. Revisiting the question of the flesh, and its relationship to the body, Falque vouches for the dynamism and complexity of love, beyond Marion's erotic and unifying reduction, and proposes, instead, a preliminary model of transformation, not yet the *metamorphosis of love*. For Falque, *agape* is a performative and transformative force that elevates,

30 Jean-Luc Marion, *The Erotic Phenomenon*, trans. Stephen E. Lewis (Chicago: University of Chicago Press, 2006), 143-4. Cited by Sandra Wynands, "Book Reeview: *The Erotic Phenomenon* by Jean Luc-Marion," *Christianity and Literature* 57, no. 1 (2007): 143-4.

31 Marion, *The Erotic Phenomenon*, 114.

purifies and changes *eros*, and this, by means of not one, but two *metamorphoses*, which are not easily reconcilable, and the relationship of which relies on Falque's understanding of flesh. The first *metamorphosis*, that of *finitude*, is eschatological and considers the continuity of the body (or the discontinuity thereof?), from death to resurrection, in terms of flesh, not simply as another modality of corporeal manifestation, but "also a disqualification, or rather a *withdrawal*, of the substantiality of the body."[32] The passage from death to resurrection is, in other words, the complete actualization of the *agape* inherent in the *eros* characteristic, with the Eucharist, of the "fleshly modality of the present."[33] Notably, for Falque, though ontologically oriented towards insubstantial manifestation in *agape* through resurrection, *eros* need not be denigrated; *eros* is simply the "the love of mankind", which stands in contrast with *agape*, which Falque defines simply as "the love of God."[34] In a sense, love's *metamorphosis* in finitude through resurrection maintains an element of *univocity*, wherein all *eros* veils traces of *agape*, and an element of *equivocity*, where the insubstantiality of the flesh, achieved in resurrection, leaves no recognizable traces of *eros* in the body. Herein arises a tension in Falque's notion of flesh and therefore, in Falque's understanding of *eros* and *agape*, in the first *metamorphosis*. On the one hand, the flesh is a continuity principle for *eros* and *agape* in and *through* the modality of the present's continuum, whereas, on the other hand, in resurrection there is not, at least not obviously so, any trace of *eros* in *agape*'s transformation, implying a failure of the present's ability to maintain continuity through the flesh. The flesh is interrupted, and, accordingly, it is discontinued, in the fist metamorphosis, through the passage of resurrection. In the second metamorphosis, that of transubstantiation in the Eucharist, where "the eucharist is *eros* converted into *agape* in the gift of embodiness,"[35] God transforms everything in the gift of the Eucharist, in the gift of Christ's body, given to his apostles, to the Church, and in the signification of nuptial love, by means of incorporation. However, insists Falque, transformation, this time in Eucharistic incorporation, not resurrection, need not supplant *eros* by *agape*. For Falque, "the carnal embrace (*eros*) is part of the most spiritual gift (*agape*)."[36] Again, Falque insists upon an inclusion "of

32 Emmanuel Falque, *The Metamorphosis of Finitude: An Essay on Birth and Resurrection*, trans. George Hughes (New York: Fordham University Press, 2012), 144.

33 Ibid, 178.

34 Ibid, 120.

35 Emmanuel Falque, *The Wedding Feast of the Lamb: Eros, the Body, and the Eucharist*, trans. George Hughes (New York: Fordham University Press, 2017), 8.

36 Ibid, 133.

the conjugal *eros* into the Eucharistic *agape*."[37] The transformation through "'the body donated' in the Eucharist is neither a simple eroticization, nor an abstraction in pure charity; it is a transformation and integration of the erotic into the *agapeic*."[38] Moreover, in this integrative transformation, Falque insists, Eucharistic transformation retrieves the animality and organicity of experiential love in *eros*. He adds, in further explaining the process of incorporation through Eucharist:

> I should like to emphasize that animality (the eucharistic legacy), embodiedness (the content of the eucharist), and eros (the modality of the eucharist) wait for and hope for their *translation* in the act of transubstantiation, so that the response to the appeal of a transformed humanity (the simple proclamation of humanism) will be echoed in a filiation that has been acknowledged (difficult but necessary in Christianity).[39]

As with the *eschatological* metamorphosis, the metamorphosis of transubstantiation purports a discontinuity, not between *agape* and *eros* in resurrection, but this time, beyond *agape* and *eros* in transubstantiation. There is, therefore, an *equivocity* model at play, which disintegrates through metamorphosis, no longer to value *agape* over *eros*, but rather, to retrieve the underlying animality and organicity of *eros* in an altogether new unity, or incorporation, of the Eucharist in *eucharistization*. In either case, Falque's metamorphosis is *not* one of continuity between *eros* and *agape* but either only of equivocation *between* or incorporation *beyond* differences. Falque explicitly adopts an *integrative* metamorphosis (against an unequivocal one like Nygren's) in a passage exploring *embrace and differentiation*,

> I have already underlined with regard to a *charitable* God that we cannot be satisfied with the total "equivocity" of the eros and agape (Nygren), nor accept simple "univocity" (Marion). The former risks separating divine charity from human love to such a degree that nothing remains in common between the two; the latter considers the modalities of divine love on the model of human love so comprehensively that nothing remains that is particular to God. The excesses of the one or the other do not prevent us, however, from linking them; far from it. The metamorphosis of eros by agape has as its role not simply to sustain the experience of the agape (eucharist) on the model of eros (sexuality), but also and above all to integrate the eros (sexuality at the heart of its conversion by the

37 Ibid, 166.
38 Ibid, 135.
39 Ibid, 175.

> agape). As I pointed out earlier, the erotic is not fulfilled for a couple unless God contains and transforms them in his agape. Auguste Rodin's sculpture *The Hand of God* shows us a couple in one another's arms but also, significantly, within the hand of God.[40]

Falque's position has a direct precedent in *God is Love* (*Deus caritas est*), an encyclical letter by Pope Emeritus Benedict XVI, previously Joseph Ratzinger (b. 1927), which was promulgated in 2006. For Benedict XVI, *eros* and *agape* are distinct loves but related. He describes the first love as ascending, and the second one, in contrast, as descending. Set apart by their opposing directionality, these loves share a single vertical movement. Left in isolation, the two remain incomplete and must therefore become a unified and harmonized love through a process of purification, whereby *eros* is transfigured into a higher form of love in *agape*, which is note yet *metamorphosis*. While moving away from Nygren's exclusive *equivocity* model, phenomenologists adopted, particularly within Catholic circles, the model of *analogy, univocity* and inclusive *equivocity*. Moreover, although the model of the *metamorphosis of love* remains underdeveloped, a constructive extrapolation between Falque's notion of love and his idea on the *metamorphosis of finitude* may form the basis for a constructive retrieval, which the present study seeks to offer. Thus, in response to Nygren – who remains in the foreground, albeit implicitly – phenomenology and its intellectual French landscape has renewed a long-neglected line of interpretative models on the problem of love.

As the historical survey shows, all four models – *equivocity, univocity, analogy* and *metamorphosis* – have had proponents by important Christian authors. Of these, though briefly and only nominally – by *metamorphosis* he means *equivocity* and *analogy* – discussed by Falque, the model of *metamorphosis* remains scattered, and underdeveloped, in history and contemporary discussion. This is likely so because the speculative discourse of scholasticism eclipsed the poetic and lived approach of the Cistercians and other monastic traditions, particularly as passed down in the genre of commentaries on the *Song of Songs*, beginning with Origen, and which Bernard of Clarivaux calls the *book of experience* (*libro experientiae*).[41] The import of Bernard's writings on love are not to be underestimated. Martin Heidegger (d. 1976) tellingly cites Bernard's expression (*libro experientiae*) to underscore the primacy of

40 Ibid, 134.

41 Bernard of Clairvaux, On the *Song of Songs I*, p. 16. Leclercq (*SC* 441), SCC 3.1, l. 1-13: "Hodie legimus in libro experientiae."

experience and, indeed, the concreteness of the mystical phenomenon in his *Phenomenology of Religious Experience*.[42] Can an exploration of *experience* in the monastic theology of Bernard contribute to the contemporary phenomenological debate on the problem of love? This book answers affirmatively. For Bernard, experience *tout court* presupposes mystical love, which, in turn, *metamorphosizes* erotic desire. That the *metamorphosis* model only returns decisively in the 21st century in French phenomenology constitutes a creative and fruitful engagement with early and medieval Christian sources ripe for further elaboration. In contemporary French phenomenology, at stake in responding to the problem of love, be it with the *univocal* model, like Marion, or the model of *metamorphosis*, such as Falque, is a disagreement over the nature of love as *given*. For Marion, love is a passive, disincarnate manifestation in human experience, whereas for Falque, love is mainly an active and fundamentally corporeal force. Thus, the debate on the problem of love oscillates today between *univocity* and *equivocity*.

Seeking to elaborate the model of *metamorphosis*, and therefore contributing a comprehensive approach to the current debate in French phenomenology, the present study turns to 12th century monastic theology and presents the first explicit and systematic exposition of the unprecedented *metamorphosis* model. In *On the Song of Songs* by Bernard of Clairvaux, the point of departure for the analysis of the *metamorphosis of love* is not speculation, or ideas, and even less syllogistic argumentation. Rather, following Bernard's method, love begins in the *book of experience*, i.e., the incarnate experience of community life, where the love of self, the love of God and the love of neighbour intersect. Community is the locus where the *book of experience* unfolds. Throughout the centuries, starting with Origen's interpretation of Ignatius, commentators have recognized in the *Song of Songs* a rich tapestry of metaphors that gracefully describe the relationship between *eros* and *agape*. The tradition of commentaries on the *Song of Songs*, dating back to fragments attributed to the Roman theologian Hippolytus (d. 235), and leading up to Bernard of Clairvaux, predominantly interpret the text as an allegory of the passionate love of Christ, the groom, for his bride, the Church. The passionate death of Christ for the Church remained faithful to the martyr witness of Ignatius, whose blood gave life to the Church. However, throughout the centuries allegory approximates, but always falls short, of the demands for a literal sense. Commentators usually shied away from mixing the sacred *agape* and the profane *eros*, an approach that betrays the *equivocity* model. Thus, in *The Mystical Theology of Saint Bernard*, Gilson argues that Bernard's writings remain free from the *eros*

42 See, Bento Silva Santos, "*Hodie legimus in libro experientiae*: Heidegger's Appropriation of Bernard of Clairvaux's Formula," *Trans-Form-Acao* 39, no. 3 (2016): 101-20.

abundantly present in the courtly literature of the period. In Gilson's view, the *amour courtois* of Chrétien de Troyes (1160-1189) was to Bernard's *ordo caritas* what Jerusalem was to Athens in Tertullian's estimation: an unholy and indeed sacrilegious marriage of the sacred and profane. At the opposite extreme, Jean-Pierre Sonnet notes the presence of *eros* in the *Song of Songs* and argues that the metaphorical language of the poem veils the erotic subtext, thereby rendering theologically acceptable what would otherwise count as profane. Bernard's *On the Song of Songs* is neither just about *agape*, for which Gilson argues, nor does it restrict love to *eros*, as Sonnet maintains. In the theology of Bernard, love encompasses *eros* and *agape*, and the monastic project consists in *fusing* without *confusing* the two into a creative *metamorphosis of love*.

Carefully charting this process of *fusion* of *loves*, human and divine, and sketching thereby the contours for Bernard's *metamorphosis of love*, is the concrete aim of the present study. The book proceeds by elucidating the *metamorphosis of love* in three parts, following a chronological-systematic phenomenological study of select sermons in Bernard's *On the Song of Songs*. The first part studies selected sermons, particularly from *s.* 1 to *s.* 60, and considers the relationship between desire and the *body*. It shows that for Bernard the body is the locus of desire and therefore the starting point of his reflection on love. By considering experience, desire and the body, part one argues that for Bernard, desire is constitutive of the body. In other words, there is no dichotomy between desire and the body, for desire emerges from the body in the beginning of *experience* (1.), *desire* then affects bodies (2.), and finally, embodied desire produces *bodies* (3.). In the *metamorphosis of love*, desire as body emerge as the very fabric on which the transformation or reconfiguration of finitude takes place, from *eros* into *agape*. Although body is desire, desire extends beyond the body. For Bernard, desire overcomes the limits of the body in the word. Therefore, the second part of the study explores the relation between *desire and the word* in a threefold movement, beginning with word as *extension* (4.) of the body, then turning to word in the *attraction* (5.) of bodies, and concluding with word as the principle of bodily *order* (6.). This second part draws from a selection of *sermons*, ranging from *s.* 60 to *s.* 85. This section argues thus: the human word, considered as the incorporeal extension of bodily desire in the divine Word, reorders desire through a reconfiguration of the body. In the great second moment of the *metamorphosis of love*, word orients desire towards divine fulfillment. Word, construed as an extension of the body's desire culminates in performativity of the incarnation, which for Bernard is the paradigm of free will or aperity. There is, therefore, a seamless continuum from desire, through the body, in the word, and to the manifestation of the body's aperity as free will. This is the topic of part three, which analyzes, from selected *sermons*, particularly *s.* 82 to *s.* 85, the relation between *desire and free will*, by considering the body as pure act or aperity and by describing the process of the free will's disclosure in *limits* (7.), in *resistance* (8.) and, finally, in and as *aperity* (9.). The cumulative argument of this part is that in *desire as free will* the word is efficient as the generative aperity of bodies.

Overall, in the *metamorphosis of love* in *On the Song of Songs* by Bernard of Clairvaux, body is localized desire, word is its incorporeal extension and free will is desire's efficacious and creative aperity. The *metamorphosis of love* is, then, a *metamorphosis of desire*, which finds expression in love, or better, as love, in the creative and therefore efficient action of free will. The closing remarks of the study revisit the structure of the *metamorphosis of love* and suggest, beyond debates on the problem of Christian love, considering it as the paradigm of Bernard's hermeneutics for a phenomenology of love, or a guide to navigate, to read, the book of experience as eternity's Trinitarian vestiges, the divine imprint in the *analogia amoris*, which unfold in a tripartite manner, according to a Trinitarian *ontological reduction*: first, body [*experience* (1.), *desire* (2.), *bodies* (3.)]; second, Word [*extension* (4.), *attraction* (5.), *order* (6.)]; third, free will [*limits* (7.), *resistance* (8.), *aperity* (9.)]. From desire, through the word and in free will, the structure and process of the *metamorphosis of love* shows that *eros* and *agape* progressively unfold and unite into a seamless whole – ascending, descending, creative and transformative – as the fabric of finitude, beginning in experience, and returning to experience, in aperity. Thus, concerning models of love, Bernard's *On the Song of Songs* offers a compelling and sophisticated account of the *metamorphosis of love*, which embraces, unites and compliments *eros* in *agape*.[43] In the panorama of contemporary French phenomenology, Bernard shows that love is neither *univocity* (Marion) or *equivocity* and *analogy* (Falque), but, rather, in the mystical theology of Bernard, love is *metamorphosis*. Finally, in terms of method, Bernard's *metamorphosis of love* maintains a close relationship between phenomenology and hermeneutics. The present contribution offers a systematic presentation of the model of the *metamorphosis of love*, with special focus on the exposition of its mechanics and the role of hermeneutics therein, with the hope that future examinations may test and either validate or refute, compliment or nuance, in Medieval texts or elsewhere, the hypothesis presented on *the metamorphosis of love*, partly or wholly.

43 Mark W. Elliot, *The* Song of Songs *and Christology in the Early Church* (Tübingen: Mohr Siebeck, 2000); Ann W. Astell, *The* Song of Songs *in the Middle Ages* (London: Cornell University Press, 1990).

PART I

Body

CHAPTER 1

Experience

Where does desire begin and *how* does it begin? In the mystical theology of Bernard of Clairvaux (1090-1153), love begins in experience, and *as* experience. More precisely, in his *On the Song of Songs* – a lengthy commentary on the biblical book entitled *Song of Songs* – the body is the locus of experience *par excellence*.[1] There is no experience without the body because the body is constitutive of experience. For this reason, Bernard astutely calls the *Song of Songs* – a recital of love, human and divine – the *book of experience*.[2] In the *book of experience*, experience, expressed mainly by means of *affects*[3], is the locus of divine manifestation and the vehicle for experience *in* and *through* the desire of the body; the body navigates and *constitutes* the field of experience henceforth. Experience of the body is the entry portal leading to the dynamic *metamorphosis* of desire and, ultimately, to the *metamorphosis of love*. However, how is the body the beginning of divine experience if God, the Ineffable One, following the apophatic theologians, is beyond body and time and even beyond being? For Bernard, God is *without beginning*. Desire of the body emerges thus in the field of experience as *the beginning without beginning* (*principium sine principio*).[4] God reveals and is revealed as the originary, generative and extemporal beginning-source. Bernard grounds his monastic theology upon experience by postulating an unprecedented beginning, considered as a beginning-source, *the beginning without beginning*. There are originary, cosmogonic beginnings, like the eternal chaos of differentiated opposites

---

1 The consulted texts on Bernard's *Sermons on the Song of Songs* are, in French and Latin, Jean Leclercq, *Sermons sur le Cantique: Sermons (1-15)*, *Sources Chrétiennes* 414 (Paris: Cerf, 2006) and, in English, Bernard of Clairvaux, On the *Song of Songs* I (Sermons 1-20), trans. Kilian Walsh (Kalamazoo: Cistercian Publications, 1971).

2 Emmanuel Falque, *Le livre de l'expérience: d'Anselme de Cantorbéry à Bernard de Clairvaux* (Paris: Cerf, 2017); Emmanuel Falque, "Expérience et empathie chez Bernard de Clairvaux," *Revue des Sciences philosophiques et théologiques* 89, no. 4 (2005): 655-96.

3 Jean Leclercq, "Voir le monde par les affects: Bernard de Clairvaux et la voie monas-[illegible]ue," *Revue des Sciences philosophiques et theologiques* 95, no. 2 (2011): 323-41; Damien [illegible]oquet, *L'ordre de l'affect au Moyen Âge: autour de l'anthropologie affective d'Aelred de Rievaulx* (Caen: CRAHM, 2005); Philip Liston-Kraft, "Bernard's Belching Bride: The *Affectus* that Words Cannot Express," *Medieval Mystical Theology* 26, no. 1 (2017): 54-72; Pacificus Delfgaauw, *Saint Bernard, maître de l'amour divin* (Paris: FAC-éditions, 1994).

4 Bernard of Clairvaux, On the *Song of Songs I*, pp. 3-4. Leclercq (*SC* 441), SCC 1.5, l. 19: "principium sine principio."

 | DOI:10.30965/9783846767504_003

in Hesiod's *Theogony*. Other beginnings are metaphysical, like the form of the *arche* (*ἀρχή*) which Anaximander evokes early on in the history of Western thought. Early Christian writers superposed the *arche* of Anaximander with the *logos* of Heraclitus. From there, with a final manoeuver, Origen locates the *arche-logos* in the Wisdom of God.[5] Thenceforth, Christian speculation, like that of the Valentians, attempted to integrate the *arche*-Wisdom by somehow temporalizing manifestation "in the beginning" according to a tripartite series of consecutive beginnings corresponding to God-father, Son-beginning and Spirit-logos.[6] Yet temporalizing the Father, insisted Augustine later, considered as source-beginning, resists all partial manifestation of God.[7] Moreover, through the Son, according the Christian doctrine of the incarnation, the body is introduced to the source-beginning, thus rendering the *arche-logos* into a *logos-sarx* in the Christology of Maximus the Confessor. Beforehand, however, an unnecessary pre-Nicaean and mainly Arian concern would locate a tension reminiscent in the Son's incarnation at odds with a seemingly necessary temporality of sequence in the manifestation of the Father and Spirit. This tension, later wrongly attributed to Augustine and Origin, was crystalized, commentators have wrongly noted, in the Thomistic synthesis of the Trinity.[8] Prior to Bernard, therefore, according to various considerations, the basic axes to conceptualize beginnings are time and place. In contrast, the Bernardine experiential (not conceptual) source-beginning is *a-temporal*, thereby resisting the before-after dichotomy of early Christological debates, and yet through the incarnation, the *logos*-beginning warrants the body as the locus of divine manifestation and of experience *tout court*. Experience of incarnation conditions the intersection of time and place in the *beginning without beginning*. In *the beginning without beginning*, the body is simultaneously manifested as infinite *saturation* and fragmented *regression*: as saturation the body arises in the ever-flowing river of experience – Heraclitus writes, "everything is in a

5 Josep Rius-Camps, *El dinamismo trinitario en la divinización de los seres racionales según Orígenes* (Roma: *Pont. Institutum orientalium studiorum*, 1970), 113-5 and 117-8; José María Rovira Belloso, "Palabra y Sacramento como signos de la Iglesia," *Diálogo ecuménico* 18, no. 61 (1983): 426.

6 Josep Rius-Camps, *El dinamismo trinitario en la divinización de los seres racionales según Orígenes*, (Roma: *Pont. Institutum orientalium studiorum*, 1970), 115.

7 For Augustine, only the Father is the 'beginning': "principium sine principio solus Pater est"; cf. *de Gen. ad literam*: 3.6 and *de trin.* 4.2.3. See, Josep Rius-Camps, *El dinamismo trinitario en la divinización de los seres racionales según Orígenes*, (Roma: *Pont. Institutum orientalium studiorum*, 1970), 115.

8 Cf. *Super Evangelium S. Ioannis*, nn. 35-39.

state of flow (πάντα ῥεῖ)"[9] – and as regression, the body unfolds in the infinite reduction of stagnation – (Zeno writes, "there is no change").[10] Therein, the Bernardine hermeneutic of the body, situated at the juncture of *flow* (*a*beginning) and *stagnation* (*without* beginning), in *a* source-beginning, which produce the paradoxical tension in which the desire of the body is transformed as a *beginning without beginning* according to the epithet, "desire impels me, not reason (*desiderio feror, non ratione*)."[11] Already, in the experience of the

9 Heraclitus writes, "As they step into the same rivers, others and still other waters flow upon them" (L, D. 12) and "One cannot step twice into the same river, nor can one grasp any mortal substance in a stable condition, but it scatters and again gathers; it forms (endures) and dissolves, and approaches and departs" (LI, D. 91). Plato cites Heraclitus in *Cratylus*, 402a: "Heraclitus says somewhere that 'everything gives way and nothing stands fast', and, likening the things that are to the flowing of a river, he says that you cannot step into the same river twice." Also in Aristotle, *On the Heavens*, 298b29: "They held that in general everything is in a state of becoming and flux, and nothing is stable"; and in *Physics*, 253b9: "And in fact some thinkers maintain not that some things are in motion and some not, but all things are in motion always, though this escapes our senses." Heraclitus writes of the *logos*: "Although this account (*logos*) holds forever, men ever fail to comprehend, both before hearing it and once they have heard. Although all things come to pass in accordance with this account (*logos*), men are like the untried when they try such words and works as I set forth, distinguishing each according to its nature and telling how it is. But other men are oblivious of what they do awake, just as they are forgetful of what they do asleep" (I, D. 1) and "although the account (*logos*) is shared, most men live as though their thinking (phronesis) were a private possession" (III, D. 2). As cited in Ajit Nayak, "Heraclitus (540-480 BC)," in *The Oxford Handbook of Process Philosophy and Organization Studies*, ed. Jenny Helin, Tor Hernes, Daniel Hjorth and Robin Holt (Oxford: Oxford University Press, 2014), 32-47.

10 Aristotle presents four paradoxes by Zeno for *a*beginning or *stagnation*: "First, there is the argument about its being impossible to move because what moves must reach the half-way point earlier than the end" (*Ph.* 6.9, 239b11-13); "Therefore the argument of Zeno falsely presumes that it is not possible to traverse or make contact with unlimited things individually in a limited time" (*Ph.* 6.2, 233a21-3). "Second is the one called 'Achilles': this is that the slowest runner never will be overtaken by the fastest; for it is necessary for the one chasing to come first to where the one fleeing started from, so that it is necessary for the slower runner always to be ahead some" (*Ph.* 6.9, 239b14-18). Third, "Zeno reasons fallaciously; for he says that if every thing always is resting whenever it is against what is equal, and what moves is always in the now, then the moving arrow is motionless" (*Ph.* 6.9, 239b5-7). "Fourth is the one about the things in the stadium moving from opposite directions, being of equal bulk, alongside things of equal size, with some moving from the end of the stadium and some from the middle, at equal speed, in which case he supposes it turns out that half the time is equal to its double" (*Ph.* 6.9, 239b3-240a1). These passages come from John Palmer, "Zeno of Elea," *The Stanford Encyclopedia of Philosophy*, ed. Edward N. Zalta (Spring 2017 Edition).

11 Bernard of Clairvaux, On the *Song of Songs I*, pp. 54-55. Leclercq (*SC* 441), SCC 9.2, l. 7: "Desiderio feror, non ratione."

beginning, at the source-beginning, manifestation is metamorphosis of desire, and revelation is reconfiguration of the matrix of finitude, by means of desire, in three moments: the beginning of desire (1.1), the exercise of the senses (1.2) and experience in the beginning (1.3).

1.1 The Beginning of Desire

Desire is originary *of* the *beginning without beginning*. However, how does desire pierce through and, in so doing, generate the location (space and time) of *the beginning without beginning* in the fabric and texture of incarnate experience where the paradox of desire activates the *metamorphosis of love*? In other words, how does the aperity of desire *flow*, from the source-beginning, as *flow*, into the experience of desire as becoming?[12] Bernard's response is this, "desire impels me, not reason".[13] Herein lies concealed the Bernardine synthesis for a hermeneutics of the body.[14] The translocation of desire by desire shows the body is constituted by desire[15] such that desire, not reason, but not in spite of reason nevertheless, is the principal (*principio*) momentum impelling human desire towards God.[16] An exploration of the Bernardine understanding of the body as the point of departure *in the beginning* is thus warranted in the body, the vehicle of desire and functions as the driving force of human love and divine knowledge through experience. The body as a way of experience

12 Jacques Blanpain, *S'ouvrir au désir : En lisant le* Cantique des cantiques *avec Bernard de Clairvaux* (Scourmont: Veilleux, 2003).

13 Bernard of Clairvaux, On the *Song of Songs I*, pp. 54-55. Leclercq (*SC* 441), SCC 9.2, l. 7: "desiderio feror, non ratione."

14 Richard Kearney, "What Is Carnal Hermeneutics?" *New Literary History: A Journal of Theory and Interpretation* 46, no. 1 (2015): 99-124; Emmanuel Falque, "The Hidden Source of Hermeneutics: The Art of Reading in Hugh of St. Victor," *Journal of French and Francophone Philosophy* 25, no. 1 (2017): 121-31; Richard Kearney, "Thinking the Flesh with Paul Ricoeur," in *Hermeneutics and Phenomenology in Paul Ricoeur: Between Text and Phenomenon. Contributions to Hermeneutics*, ed. Scott Davidson and Marc-Antoine Vallée (Cham: Springer, 2016), 31-40; Marja Schuster, "Hermeneutics as Embodied Existence," *International Journal of Qualitative Methods* 12, no. 1 (2013): 195-206.

15 Pyong-Gwan Pak, "St. Bernard of Clairvaux on the Riddle of Human Desire: The Necessity of a Reversal of Priorities in the Human Life of Desire," *Logos: A Journal of Catholic Thought and Culture* 21, no. 4 (2018): 126-50; Paul Moyaert, "Mysticism: The Transformation of a Love Consumed by Desire into a Love without Desire," *Ethical Perspectives* 7, no.4 (2000): 269-78.

16 Hubert Debbasch, *L'homme de désir, icône de Dieu* (Paris: Beauchesne, 2001); Michael Casey, *Athirst for God: Spiritual Desire in Bernard of Clairvaux's Sermons on the Song of Songs* (Collegeville: Cistercian Publications, 1988).

is revolutionary among other *ways* (*viae*) to God. To the primacy of faith over reason, inherent to the Augustinian imperative to "believe that you may understand (*crede ut intelligas*),"[17] and as reformulated in the Anselmian "faith seeking understanding (*fides quaerens intellectum*),"[18] the Bernardine *modus operandis* marks an experiential turn, in the form of a return to the experience *in the beginning* as source-beginning, wherein for Bernard "I believe that I may experience (*credo ut experiar*)".[19] To experience is to understand, yet to understand is possible only by presupposing faith. Therefore, a double gnoseological thrust embeds Bernard's journey whereby experience yields understanding and understanding unwraps the field of experience. Difficult to phantom and paradoxical to understand, for Bernard belief is a condition for experience and experience is a condition for belief in *the book of experience*. This paradox is the puzzle of desire as manifested in *the beginning without beginning*. Only a hermeneutics of the body stated, or better yet, imagined as a hermeneutics of desire presupposing faith can unlock the portal to the horizon of the experience *experienced* as metamorphosing finitude.

Experience, desire and body interlace in Bernard's *On the Song of Songs*. Bernard begins the experience (life) of experience (text) – experience twice removed from the text adds a hermeneutic distance to a hermeneutic circle – when confronting *the book of experience*, with the body. The body as the locus of experience is at the source of a hermeneutics of desire because meaning saturates the body in the tumultuous *milieu* in which Bernard lived, wrote and

17 Augustine, *Tract. Ev. Jo.*, 29.6: "Therefore *do not seek to understand in order to believe, but believe that thou mayest understand*," *Nicene and Post-Nicene Fathers*, ed. Philip Schaff (Peabody, MS: 1995), 184.

18 Anselm, *Pros.* 1: "Man cannot seek God, unless God himself teaches him; nor find him, unless he reveals himself. God created man in his image, that he might be mindful of him, think of him, and love him. *The believer does not seek to understand, that he may believe, but he believes that he may understand: for unless he believed he would not understand* [...] I do not endeavor, O Lord, to penetrate your sublimity, for in no wise do I compare my understanding with that; *but I long to understand in some degree your truth, which my heart believes and loves. For I do not seek to understand that I may believe, but I believe in order to understand. For this also I believe, that unless I believed, I should not understand*," *Monologion and Proslogion: with the Replies of Gaunilo and Anselm*, trans. Thomas Williams (Indianapolis: Hackett Publishing, 1996), 4-6.

19 Jean Leclercq, *The Love of Learning and the Desire for God: A Study of Monastic Culture* (New York: Fordham University Press, 1962), 7, 263; Kilian McDonnell, "Spirit and Experience in Bernard of Clairvaux," *Theological Studies* 58, no. 1 (1997): 4. Also, Lode Van Hecke, *Le désir dans l'expérience religieuse: l'homme réunifié – relecture de Saint Bernard* (Paris: Cerf, 1990).

preached.[20] There is more. Bernard's own experience of the body is at the origin of the text's *experience* (*On the Song of Songs*) *on* the text *of* experience (*Song of Songs*). The experience of the *Song of Songs* is, according to a hermeneutics of desire, an experience of text *on* text, with a movement from text to the desire of the body, then to desire in the body of the text. The fold upon fold of sense is a source of life requiring the labour of unfolding (*dépliage*) from whence the meaning of meaning arises through the risk of experience. Indeed, the body is the basis for Bernard's revolutionary literal reading of the biblical text precisely as *the book of experience* where the body allows Bernard to maintain unity beyond the tension of difference constitutive of human experience. Finally, the body is the vehicle for the individualization and the embodiment of the universal experience of the interplay of desire, human and divine, in *On the Song of Songs*. Therefore, desire of the body provides the hermeneutic key, in the hermeneutics of desire, to read Bernard's *On the Song of Songs*, because the body is the driving force of divine knowledge and the true motor of love impelling, compelling and propelling desire beyond reason.[21] To "believe that I may experience (*credo ut experiar*)," following Bernard, is to recognize that in the *book of experience* (*liber experientia*) "desire impels me, not reason." The hermeneutics of desire thus construed give way to *experience*.

Word, text and life seamlessly interweave in the *book of experience*, where the echoes of crystalized desire *metamorphose finitude*. It is not differently in the life of Bernard, where the body is the locus of experience, *the beginning without beginning*. The body is at the origin of *On the Song of Songs* because a twofold experience of the body rooted simultaneously in ecstasy and suffering, motivates Bernard to seek meaning and transformation in the biblical *Song of Songs*. The first of these experiential events is recorded in the biographical account of the Abbot's life, *The First Life of Bernard of Clairvaux*, or simply *First Life* (*Vita prima*),[22] composed by the French Benedictine Abbot William of Saint-Thierry (c. 1075-1148), who met and developed a close friendship with the Abbot of Clairvaux as of 1118.[23] Bernard began composing his *On the Song*

20 Jennifer Harris, "The Fate of Place in the Twelfth Century: Creation, Restoration and Body in the Writings of Bernard of Clairvaux," *Viator* 39, no. 2 (2008): 119-41; Dominic Montserrat, *Changing Bodies, Changing Meanings: Studies on the Human Body in Antiquity* (London: Routledge, 1998).

21 Bernard of Clairvaux, On the *Song of Songs I*, pp. 54-55. Leclercq (*SC* 441), SCC 9.2, l. 7: "desiderio feror, non ratione."

22 The text was begun by William of Saint-Thierry, who left it unfinished. Thereafter, Arnold of Bonneval continued it, and Geoffrey of Auxerre completed it.

23 For a biography on William of Saint-Thiery, see Jean-Marie Déchanet, *William of Saint-Thierry: The Man and His Work*, trans. R. Strachan (Kalamazoo: Cistercian Publications, 1972).

of Songs during the Advent Season of 1135, possibly echoing a formative personal dream, or mystical vision rather, which the Bernard reportedly received years earlier while in Châtillon, as an infant – an *infans*, one without speech – on Christmas night. Geoffrey of Auxerre (d. 1188) narrates this formative vision in the *First Life*.[24] The first experience is a vision of the child Jesus, wherein the speechless (*infans*) child is also, mystically and paradoxically, *the* Word of God incarnate, in the flesh, spoken from all ages unto the ages. Bernard's vision is an experience of birth and nativity (*natus*), it is an experience of beginning(s), precedes faith, and echoing the epithet, "I believe that I may experience (*credo ut experiar*)."[25] The focal point of the narrative on the nativity of the "Word-child" or rather the "wordless Word" or "pre-linguistic Word" even, which Bernard identified with the birth of Christ, is later complimented by the revelation of certain mysteries concerning the child's birth. The mystery in question is likely what Bernard calls the third coming of Christ in the soul of the faithful in the fifth sermon on Advent, the coming (*advenire*).[26] Within the context of the liturgical feast where Advent is a preparation for the *coming towards* (*ad + ventus*), that is, of an ongoing beginning already begun numerous times and which will begin numerous times again till the fulfillment of the third coming, the mystery revealed to Bernard is about *how* God is incarnated

24 William of Saint-Thierry, Arnold of Bonneval, and Geoffrey of Auxerre, *The First Life of Bernard of Clairvaux*, trans. and ed. Hilary Costello (Kalamazoo: Cistersian Publications, 2015), 7: "On the solemnity of the Lord's Nativity, when at night they were all getting ready, as was the custom, for solemn Vigils, *the Lord came to him*. Since the hour for celebrating the Night Office was put off a little, Bernard was sitting there waiting with everyone else, and his head drooped in sleep. Then it happened that *the child Jesus revealed himself in his Holy Nativity to the little boy, awakening in him the beginnings of divine contemplation and increasing his tender faith*. Jesus appeared to him *like the spouse coming forth from his chamber*. He appeared to him before his very eyes as *the wordless Word* was being born from his mother's womb, *more beautiful in form than all the children of men*. Bernard was taken out of himself so that his child-like love was transformed by the holy boy. So persuasive to his mind was this moment that from then on, as he confesses, *he believed he was at the very moment of the Lord's birth*. From those who often listened to him it is obvious that the Lord showered him with blessings at that time, since he has spoken about this mystery more frequently and delved into its meaning more profoundly." For a philosophical commentary on the passage, see Emmanuel Falque, "Saint Bernard et le champ de l'expérience," in *Expérience phiosophique et experience mystique*, ed. P. Capelle (Cerf, Paris, 2005); Emmanuel Falque, *Le livre de l'expérience: d'Anselme de Cantorbéry à Bernard de Clairvaux* (Paris: Cerf, 2017).

25 Jean Leclerq, *The Love of Learning and the Desire for God: A Study of Monastic Culture* (New York: Fordham University Press, 1962), 7, 263; Kilian McDonnell, "Spirit and Experience in Bernard of Clairvaux," *Theological Studies* 58, no. 1 (1997): 4. Also, Lode Van Hecke, *Le désir dans l'expérience religieuse: l'homme réunifié – relecture de saint Bernard* (Paris: Cerf, 1990).

26 *SBO* IV, 188-190.

in the soul. The second coming, the coming of Christ in experience, arises in incarnate desire for God. For this reason, when narrating Bernard's vision, William of Saint-Thierry[27] deploys nuptial imagery to express the creative relationship of the body, desire and the divine. William of Saint-Thierry sees the incarnation as a paradigm for romantic union and romantic love. Thus, nuptial images describe Bernard's vision, such as the image of "the beloved exiting the chamber" (cf. Ps 18.6 and Cant 1.4), and these are articulated using sensual turns of phrases directly extracted from *Song of Songs*, like "gathering all affective powers to himself." Unsurprisingly, the body offers a hermeneutic key to read the *Song of Songs* or *the book of experience*. Bernard reads the *Song of Songs* through the lenses of the desire of the body because the language of the *Song of Songs* resonates and articulates Bernard's personal experience. In short, the vision centers on the Word manifested in body as body, and about the soul's disposition as Word *towards* (*ad*) God in the body. Bernard would later find suitable vocabulary in the *Song of Songs* to articulate the experience of divine love in terms of incarnation, or as "wordless Word." In the beginning, therefore, there is an experience of the body as body in the body, even before speech, or rather, as the first form of speech. "I believe that I may experience (*credo ut experiar*)" is therefore the Bernardine appropriation of the Pauline formula, "I believed, therefore I have speak" (2 Cor 4.13), echoing similarly the Psalm, "I believed, therefore I said, 'I am greatly afflicted'" (Ps 116.10). Belief precludes *all* experience, always, wherein desire, not reason, drives life.

Years later, a second experience of the body compels Bernard to turn to the *Song of Songs*. This time, the experience is not ecstasy, but affliction, the recognition of which also depends upon belief. Around the year 1128, Bernard and William of Saint-Thierry lied ill, side by side, at the infirmary.[28] William of Saint-Thierry's account of the event focuses on the limits of the suffering body. The body is not only the receptacle of divine ecstasy but is now also the receptacle of disintegration and pathos. The limits of the body gave the friends with an occasion to turn to experience the limits of the body and then draw from the *Song of Songs* for consolation. The *Song of Songs* gives a universal body to affliction in particular bodies. In this, the contemplatives found consolation. Performative speech joins individual suffering to the deposit of universal suffering. So, what are the limits of the body in suffering? First,

27 William of Saint-Thierry, Arnold of Bonneval, and Geoffrey of Auxerre, *The First Life of Bernard of Clairvaux*, trans. and ed. Hilary Costello (Kalamazoo: Cistersian Publications, 2015); *Vita prima* 1, II, 4, cf. PL 185, 229 A.

28 Paul Verdeyen, "A Theologian of Experience," *BdC*, p. 570-71 and *SC* p. 25. Also, Emmanuel Falque, *Le livre de l'expérience: d'Anselme de Cantorbéry à Bernard de Clairvaux* (Paris: Cerf, 2017).

the sick body: "There was a time when [Bernard] was sick and there flowed from his mouth something like a stream of phlegm."[29] The sick body offers the experience of limits where an encounter with God arises. "When he seemed to be almost on the point of drawing his last breath, he *fell into an ecstasy of mind* (Acts 10.10)."[30] The encounter with God at the limits of the body is thus an experience of struggle, akin to the struggle between Jacob and the angel. Yet, as *the dissolution of the body* was imminent, at the limit of life and death, Bernard reaffirms life: "Because of this vision Bernard expected that *the dissolution of his body was imminent*, but a quite different one followed. He was placed on a certain seashore, and it seemed to him that he was waiting for a ship to carry him across. When the ship pulled in to the shore, he quickly made to board it, but withdrawing from him, it moved off into the water. *This happened three times*, and then the ship sailed off, leaving him there, and did not return. From this he understood that his *departure from this life was not yet to be*."[31] The limits of the body, fragily oscillating between decay and dissolution, produce utmost pain for which not even death is a consolation, for, taken *ad litteram*, "strong as death is love" (Cant 8.6).[32] In this vision, the divine favor is transmitted by means of the body (the hands), within an experience of communal empathy (the brothers) and is manifested in the restoration of the body (the pain disappears); the experience of God at the limits of the body occurs in sickness, struggle, pain, compassion and healing. These intense experiences of the body's depth, coupled with the visitation of the Word-child, is the lens by which Bernard is compelled to turn to the *Song of Songs* for consolation and which conditions any reading able to unlock the divine experience which is safeguarded in *the book of experience*. This is well illustrated in William of Saint-Thierry's personal illness from which he recovered by Bernard's side.[33]

---

29 *The First Life of Bernard of Clairvaux*, 1.57. Cf. *Fragm.* I.29 (VP 289; Notes 128-131); as cited in p. 59, n. 66.

30 *Ibid.* 1.57, p. 60.

31 *Ibid.* 1.58, p. 60.

32 *Ibid.* 1.58, p. 60-61: "*The pain still increased, however, and it became so grievous that the hope of imminent death did not now comfort him.* He was so *afflicted with intense pain*, which increased *beyond his strength*, that he called one of the two brothers and ordered him to go quickly and pray for him. [...] *Laying their hands on him* (Acts 13.3), they soothed the painful place *by their gentle touch*, and from that moment they removed all his sickness. Then the river of phlegm *dried up* (Mk 5.29), and all his pain disappeared."

33 *Ibid.* 1.59, pp. 61-62: "Once I myself was sick in our own house and completely drained. The sickness was prolonged and went on and on for a very long time. Hearing about it, Bernard sent to me his brother Gerard, a man of happy memory. He pressed me to come to Clairvaux, and he promised me that I would either be soon cured or die. [...] I do not know which I preferred, either dying close to him or being with him for some time. I made

The shared experience of the limits of the body, which include empathy and compassion, turn Bernard and William to *the book of experience.* Conversely, Bernard draws from experience to elucidate the meaning of *the book of experience.* Experience is thus the prerequisite for reading the *Song of Songs* and reading the *Song of Songs* is the prerequisite for understanding experience. This hermeneutic circle is the core of *the beginning without beginning* which gives rise to the Bernardine *hermeneutics of desire*, where "desire impels me, not reason."[34]

Just as William of Saint-Thierry thought himself well on the road to full recovery, he relapses into excruciating pain, which, by his own account, was the consequence for having disobeyed Bernard's prohibition from fasting in the state of illness.[35] The narrative's primary concern is not to vouch for

that journey, even though the task was very burdensome and *I was in great pain.* Once I got there, it was as he had promised me and, I confess, what I had wanted. *My health returned to me from that very alarming sickness, but my physical strength came back only gradually.* O good God, how good was that sickness for me, that time of rest, that time of prayer, which was mainly just what I wanted. *For during the time he himself was confined by his sickness, he helped me with my needs in my sickness for the whole time that I was with him.* Both of us, sick though we were, discussed for the whole day the soul's spiritual well-being, that is, the remedies of the virtues against the flagging of vices. He then commented on the *Song of Songs* to me, explaining the moral meaning to me during the time of my infirmity, leaving on one side the deeper mysteries of that part of Scripture, since that is what I wanted and what I asked of him. Each day whatever I heard on this subject I used to put it down in writing so that it might help me to remember what God had given me through him. *He used to expound it to me kindly and without any envy, to communicate his understanding of the text and his own meaning drawn from experience.* He brought light to his teaching in many ways, which could usually be discerned *only through experience.* And even though I could not as yet comprehend what he put before me, he made me understand what I had failed to grasp. But let that be enough about these things I have talked about."

34 Bernard of Clairvaux, On the *Song of Songs I*, pp. 54-55. Leclercq (*SC* 441), SCC 9.2, l. 7: "desiderio feror, non ratione."

35 *Ibid.* 1.60, pp. 63-64: "This attack came upon me with such ferocity and violence that I was tortured all night and devastated with such malice that I believed I would be overcome by it, despairing of life itself since it was *beyond my strength and beyond the limit of my endurance* that I might not still have a final word with the man of God. But after I had spent the whole night in pain, late in the morning he came at my bidding, offering me *not so much the expression of his sympathy that I was used to, but rather a rebuke.* Nevertheless he said with a chuckle, "What do you want to eat today?" Now I quickly interpreted the real cause of my affliction to be his silence at yesterday's disobedience, so I said, "Whatever you order." "Be at rest," he said; "you are not going to die yet." Then he went off. What can I say? *All the pain went away at once, except that I felt drained after the pain I had had during the night.* So for the whole day I hardly had enough energy left to get up from the bed. What about the pain or its severity? *I do not remember ever having suffered the like.* The next day

punishment to deter from disobedience, nor is this a sadistic celebration of pain. Rather, the story underscores the importance of nourishment in the experience of the limits of the body. The same imagery of nourishment and strength brings the reader to the opening lines of the *On the Song of Songs*, where Bernard lays out the regime of experience. The nourishment imagery takes full effect in the anecdote of William's disobedience. The experience of the limits of the body is a testament to the body's fragility and its inherent intimate transformative potential in and through the experience of the divine in *the book of experience*. The experience of the body is therefore the condition for reading and ultimately for experiencing the divine in the *Song of Songs*. Moreover, the body, as the locus of an experience of divine manifestation and the motor of individual experience, offers a hermeneutic framework to live the *Song of Songs*. Identifying the defining characteristics of these experiences with desire, prove Bernard a close reader of Origen's masterful *On the Song of Songs*, written nearly one thousand years earlier. Following Origen, the desire of the body is for Bernard the source of experience and ultimately the compass to navigate experience in the *Song of Songs*.

The limits of the body are experienced as an incarnate reality saturated with meaning within a social context not only in the monastic community, but also at large also within the tumultuousness and harsh conditions of the 11th century. Life itself was experienced as a limit – for instance, life expectancy caped at 30 years of age. Worship was also experienced within the confines of sacred space, the space of divine experience in the liturgy and architecture, the aesthetic life of the Cistercian reform spearheaded by Bernard. Furthermore, at the turn of the 12th century, there was a growing emphasis in thinking of the Church as the body of Christ, as advanced by the Second Lateran Council in 1139. The body fends not only from the ideological threat of heresy, but also from other kinds of disease (Peter Lombard). The body safeguards its integrity – modelled by the integrity of Virgin Mary and the growing Marian devotions at the turn of the century – and avoids schismatic breakdown – especially after the death of Pope Honorius II in 1130. At the turn of the millennia there was heightened sense that the Church as the body of Christ was fragile at the limit, as it stood in constant threat from not only within, but also from outside. Hence, the preaching of the Second Crusade and the drafting of the infamous crusading Order of the Knights Templar. The common imagination of the body as the vehicle of experience of movement, prayer, limits and pain, is a chief task for the Abbot of Clairvaux in devising *On the Song of Songs*. The work becomes

I felt *healed once more* (Jn 5.14), and my strength returned. After a few days, with the blessing and kindness of my good host, I returned home."

a true crystallization of experience at the limit – *the book of experience* – and not merely a spiritual exercise. Gestures are performative and efficient in the monastic thought of Bernard: they constitute space and place within confines, within limits. Hence, the language of the *Song of Songs* allows for the articulation of common and universal experience of the body and is deeply ingrained in the imagination of the divine (mostly mystical) experience. The epithet "I believe that I may experience" (*credo ut experiar*),[36] is therefore fittingly joined to the epithet, "I want desire, not reason"[37], because the experience of the desire of the body leads to the knowledge of God.[38] Without desire, there is no knowledge or love of God, just as without the body, there is no desire.

Thus, a number of themes recurring throughout Bernard's *On the Song of Songs* are already implicitly present or *in uovo* in Bernard's own experience, as recorded in the *First Life*. Furthermore, experience, the body and divine manifestation create the hermeneutic circle of desire which is the lens by which Bernard reads the *Song of Songs, the book of experience*[39], where one experiences to understand and must understand to experience. Finally, an embodied point of departure, which is the desire of the body, replaces the metaphor of the body in the *Song of Songs*: "Desire impels me, not reason". The desire of the body weaves the pages of *the book of experience* and gives them life in *the beginning without beginning*. Such a beginning is possible only through what Bernard calls *the exercise of the senses*.[40]

1.2 The Exercise of the Senses

Who can enjoy the experience of experience? Not all. For this, a careful training of the senses is necessary to learn about the intricacy of desire. "Be ready then to feed on bread rather than milk."[41] This line finely captures the aes-

36 Kilian McDonnell, "Spirit and Experience in Bernard of Clairvaux," *Theological Studies* 58, no. 1 (1997): 3-18.

37 Bernard of Clairvaux, On the *Song of Songs I*, pp. 54-55. Leclercq (*SC* 441), SCC 9.2, l. 7: "Desiderio feror, non ratione."

38 See SCC 14.6 l. 1-18 and SCC 9.2, l. 5-22; Brigitte Saouma, "Bernard de Clairvaux: du prêche à la croisade au baiser mystique," *Caligrama: Revista De Estudos Românicos* 10, no. 0 (2011): 209-18.

39 C. Bodard, "La Bible, expression d'une expérience religieuse chez S. Bernard," *Analecta Sacri Ordinis Cisterciensis* 9, no. 3-4 (1953), 24-45.

40 On reading as an aesthetic exercise, see Emmanuel Falque, *Le livre de l'expérience: d'Anselme de Cantorbéry à Bernard de Clairvaux* (Paris: Cerf, 2017).

41 Bernard of Clairvaux, On the *Song of Songs I*, p. 1. Leclercq (*SC* 441), SCC 1.3, l. 1-3: "itaque parate fauces non lacti, sed panis."

thetic dimension of the bodily experience of desire. In the opening lines of *On the Song of Songs*, Bernard states the purpose of his words: to "water hearts."[42] Aware of the intended audience of the sermons, that is to say the monks, Bernard compares the act of preaching to the act of nourishing. Depending on who is being nourished, different kinds of food can be offered, be they liquid (*lac potum dat*), for babies, or solids (*non escam/solida*), for toddlers.[43] Whereas those living in the world (*saeculo*) drink for spiritual nourishment like infants, the spiritual or the perfect are able to eat solid food (*solida*).[44] The aim is not to disparage the world but to emphasize a specific kind of experience which conditions the capacity to be nourished in the way Bernard is about to nourish the monks. The experience in question is what Bernard calls *the exercise of the senses* (*excercitati sensibus*). Only those who have experienced the exercise of the senses are able to profit from the solid nourishment, which the *Song of Songs* provides. Bernard invites the listener to prepare the palate to taste the splendid bread of Salomon's *Song of Songs*: "*Be ready then to feed on bread rather than milk*. Solomon has bread to give that is splendid and delicious, the *bread of that book called 'The Song of Songs.'* Let us *bring it forth* then if you please, and *break it*."[45] Therefore, entering the banquet, which is the *Song of Songs* – a true feast of delight –, presupposes prior training, a discipline in *the exercise of the senses*. In this case, the sense of taste learns to appreciate the feast of the *Song of Songs* through a gradual process, from bringing forward the bread, which is the *Song of Songs*, to breaking it for consumption. However, importantly, this discipline includes a sense of pleasure or satisfaction (*placere*) in the transition from breaking the bread (*proferare*) to consuming it (*frangere*). The desire of the senses, the body's longing for food, is the driving force precluding the preparation of the senses to be able to experience the divine banquet offered by the bread of the *Song of Songs.* Desire is what impels the listener to find delight in the banquet, yet desire impels only because it has been predisposed to do so by prior experience.

If experience is only possible by the exercise of the senses, how then are the senses prepared? The expression *the exercise of the senses* bears strong ascetic connotations. Bernard here offers a gradual regime for the monks by

---

42 Bernard of Clairvaux, On the *Song of Songs I*, p. 2. Leclercq (*SC* 441), SCC 1.3, l. 1-3: "nec stadium tam esse mii ut exponam verba, quam ut imbuam corda."

43 Bernard of Clairvaux, On the *Song of Songs I*, p. 1. Leclercq (*SC* 441), SCC 1.1, l. 1-3.

44 Bernard of Clairvaux, On the *Song of Songs I*, p. 2. Leclercq (*SC* 441), SCC 1.1, l. 9-11.

45 Bernard of Clairvaux, On the *Song of Songs I*, p. 1. Leclercq (*SC* 441), SCC 1.1, l. 10-14: "Itaque parate fauces non lacti, sed pani. Est panis apud Salomonem, isque admodum splendibus sapidusque, librum dico, qui Cantica canticorum inscribitur : proferatur, si placet, et frangatur."

a 'bodily exercise' corresponding to the 'spiritual exercises' developed elsewhere but mostly absent in the *On the Song of Songs*: the body is the point of departure and the aim is the transformation of desire through the body. The gradual regime prescribed by *the exercise of the senses* which enables the monk to advance from the gulping of liquid food to the mastication of solid food (the *Song of Songs*) is achieved by tasting the instruction (*instructere*) found in Ecclesiastes and the admonition and shaping (*emendare et informare*) contained in Proverbs.[46] What are the aims and contents of instruction, admonition and formation? The food offered by Ecclesiastes and Proverbs aim respectively to eradicate the central illnesses of human existence: love of the world and excessive love of self. Thus, *the book of experience* is the antidote to inexperience, "Since there are two evils that comprise the only, or at least the main, enemies of the soul: *a misguided love of the world and an excessive love of self, the two books previously mentioned can provide an antidote to each of these infections*."[47] As antidotes, these books prepare the right dispositions of desire by means of discipline (*disciplina*) and reason (*rationis*). They inform experience through experience. The book of Ecclesiastes has the effect of weeding out by means of discipline (*sarculo disciplinae*) all ill disposed habits as well as the superfluous pretentions of the flesh, whereas through the light of reason (*luce rationis*) the book of Proverbs equips the experiencer to discern worldly desires from the desire for solid truth. Bernard writes, "[o]ne *uproots pernicious habits of mind and body with the hoe of self-control*. The other, by *the use of enlightened reason*, quickly *perceives a delusive tinge in all that the world holds glorious*, truly distinguishing between it and *deeper truth*."[48] The aim of discipline and the stress on reason is not to extinguish the fire and the impulse of desire. Quite on the contrary, wisdom is the outcome of the fear of God, which in turn purifies desire for God.[49] Driven by desire, the instruction, admonition and formation of the senses, shaped through discipline and reason, prepares

46 Bernard of Clairvaux, On the *Song of Songs I*, pp. 1-2. Leclercq (*SC* 441), SCC 1.2, l. 1-5: "Quid et Parabolas? Annon vita et mores vestry, iuxta eam quae in ipsis invenitur doctirnam, sufficienter emendati et informati sunt?"

47 Bernard of Clairvaux, On the *Song of Songs I*, pp. 1-2. Leclercq (*SC* 441), SCC 1.2, l. 8-11: "Cum enim duo sint mala quae vel sola vel maxime militant adversus animam, vanus scilicet amor mundi, et superfluous sui, pesti utrique illi duo libri obviare noscuntur."

48 Bernard of Clairvaux, On the *Song of Songs I*, pp. 1-2. Leclercq (*SC* 441), SCC 1.2, l. 11-14: "alter sarculo disciplinae prava quaeque in moribus et carnis superflua resecans, alter luce rationais in omni gloria mundi fucum vanitatis sagaciter deprehendens veraciterque distinguens a solido veritatis."

49 Bernard of Clairvaux, On the *Song of Songs I*, pp. 1-2. Leclercq (*SC* 441), SCC 1.2, l. 16-17: "Nam de verbis Ecclesiastes mundi huius cognoscere et contemnere vanitatem, satis, ni fallor, per Dei gratiam instructi estis."

the reader of the *Song of Songs* to overcome love of the world and love of self to exercise desire in the field of experience *as* experience. The *exercise of the senses* then gradually prepares the desire of the reader's palate to taste and find nourishment not only in liquid but now also in solid food (*parate fauces non lacti, sed pani*). Together with the solid food, constituted by the bread of discipline (*Ecclesiastes*) and the bread of reason (*Proverbs*), Bernard prescribes a complimentary third bread (*tertium panem*) as the *Song of Songs* itself. The *book of experience* is bread, which nourishes, gives life and, through assimilation, becomes life.

What kind of bread is this third bread and what is its purpose? Bernard invokes those who have exercised the senses: "Now approach for this third loaf that, if possible, you may always recognize what is best."[50] Unlike the previous breads, which have as aim to exercise the senses in order to obtain nourishment from solid food, the third bread has no other aim than to delight the pleasure of the senses, for there is nothing better than this. A rightful, holy delight is the goal of discipline. With it, by means of experience, the monk may finally have access (*accedere*) to sacred words. Bernard explains, "Taking it then these two evils have been warded off by the reading of choice books, we may suitably proceed with this holy and contemplative discourse which, as the fruit of the other two, may be delivered only to *well-prepared ears and minds*."[51] Here, the asceticism of *the exercise of the senses* seeks not the eradication of desire. On the contrary, *the exercise of the senses* predisposes the senses towards the right experience of desire, according to an experiential mode of delight. Trained by experience, the senses constitute the hermeneutic key to crack open the code of divine desire crystalized in the sacred language of the third bread and accessible by means of the fruit of an experience guided and transformed by *the book of experience*. The third bread is the heart of Bernard's hermeneutic of desire.

Importantly, Bernard's hermeneutic of desire seamlessly transitions from the metaphor of bread signifying spiritual nourishment, to the literal expression to convey eating, ruminating, and assimilating the words of the text. To do this, Bernard introduces a further aspect to the metaphor of taste which allows to bridge experience and desire to apply literally (and not only by analogy)

---

50 Bernard of Clairvaux, On the *Song of Songs I*, pp. 1-2. Leclercq (*SC* 441), SCC 1.2, l. 5-8: "Proinde illis ambobus praelibatis, quos nihilominus de amici arca praestitos accepistis, accedite et ad tertium hunc panem, ut probetis forsitan potiora."

51 Bernard of Clairvaux, On the *Song of Songs I*, pp. 2-3. Leclercq (*SC* 441), SCC 1.3, l. 1-5: "Depulsis ergo duobus malis duorum lectione librorum, competenter iam acceditur ad hunc sacrum theoricumque sermonem qui, cum sit amborum fructus, non nisi sobriis mentibus et auribus omnino credendus est."

to the search for God in the *Song of Songs*. Desire is a way to encounter God and to experience God through encounter. To achieve this encounter, Bernard insists, at length and by way of warning, upon the need to accompany a holy reading (*lectio sancta*) of the *Song of Songs*, with a rigorous *exercise of the senses*. He writes, "Before the *flesh has been tamed* and the spirit set free by zeal for truth, before the world's glamour and *entanglements have been firmly repudiated*, it is a rash enterprise on any man's part *to presume to study spiritual doctrines*."[52] The *exercise of the senses* functions as an antidote to ease the tension between the body and the nourishment of the *Song of Songs*, which prepares the answer to the question: "How can there be harmony between *the wisdom that comes down from above and the wisdom of the world*, which is foolishness to God, or the *wisdom of the flesh which is at enmity with God*?"[53] By juxtaposing the odds of the wisdom from heaven (*Spiritus Dei*) and earthly wisdom (*sapientiae carnis*), Bernard attempt to avoid the suspicion and murmurs (*adversum nos murmuret*) of perhaps an overly erotized or sensualized reading of the *Song of Songs*.[54] Such a warning may strike as disdaining the flesh (*caro*) which would confine the reader of the *Song of Songs* to a purely spiritualized and analogical reading of the text. However, the opposite is true for Bernard. The purpose of the warning is not to do away with the body and the world, but rather to underscore the importance of a proper bodily and experiential disposition, achieved through discipline and the exercise of the senses, necessary for a proper reading of the *Song of Songs*. For this reason, Bernard is confident that while adversaries fail to understand how a disciplined and exercised life experience can operate as a formidable hermeneutic tool to access divine desire, those who have trodden down the journey (*de via venit*) will have no difficulty understanding once they taste the third bread: "I am sure that the friend who comes to us on his travels will have no reason to murmur against us after he has shared in this third loaf."[55] Bernard's logic of desire – "desire impels me, not

52 Bernard of Clairvaux, On the *Song of Songs I*, pp. 2-3. Leclercq (*SC* 441), SCC 1.3, l. 6-20: "Alioquin ante carnem disciplinae studiis edomitam et spiritui mancipatam, ante spretam et abiectam saeculi pompam et sarcinam, indigne ab impuris lectio sancta praesumitur."

53 Bernard of Clairvaux, On the *Song of Songs I*, pp. 2-3. Leclercq (*SC* 441), SCC 1.3, l. 6-20: "Quae enim societas ei quae desursum est sapientiae et sapientiae mundi, quae stultitia est apud Deum, aut sapientiae carnis, quae et ipsa est inimical Deo?"

54 Etienne Gilson, *La théologie mystique de saint Bernard* (Paris: Vrin, 1986); Ann W. Astell, "Telling Tales of Love: Julia Kristeva and Bernard of Clairvaux," *Christianity and Literature* 50, no. 1 (2000): 125-48. J.-P. Sonnet, "Le Cantique, entre érotique et mystique: sanctuaire de la parole échangée," *Nouvelle Revue Théologique* 119, n. 4 (1997): 481-502.

55 Bernard of Clairvaux, On the *Song of Songs I*, pp. 2-3. Leclercq (*SC* 441), SCC 1.3, l. 17-19: "Puto autem quod iam non habebit unde adversum nos murmuret is qui nobis de via venit amicus, cum et tergium istum insumpserit panem."

reason" – thus pierces and cracks open the paradoxical circle of the hermeneutics of bodily experience, whereby experience produces understanding and understanding produces experience. The discipline and the warning Bernard heeds is therefore not a condemnation of the body but rather a preparatory condition to appreciate and taste the depth of divine desire by means of a continuity across understanding and experience.

Bernard's hermeneutic of the body depends upon securing the continuity across understanding (thought) and experience (life), which he attains by stretching the metaphor of tasting and eating to express what language cannot express, namely the collapse of signifier and signified in the performativity of *the one*, for gestures communicate what words fail to grasp.[56] After warning against the flesh and just before plunging into the feast of the *Song of Songs*, Bernard introduces the final element of the hermeneutics of desire. Bernard elicits the answer when he rhetorically asks of the third bread: "But who is going to divide this loaf?"[57] With this question an important shift occurs. To the attitude required for tasting the *Song of Songs*, namely the predisposition of exercised senses and prior experience, is now added the importance of *the one* (*quis*) breaking the third bread. Here, the importance of the *exercise of the senses* is clear in the recognition of *the one* (*quis*), perhaps the only one, able to break the bread. Indeed, the various senses to which Bernard appeals, in this case mainly hearing (*franere*) and sight (*oculos*) swiftly turn to the recognition of the Lord: "it is the Lord you must see in the breaking of the bread. For who else could more fittingly do it? It is a task that I would not dare to arrogate to myself. [...] I myself am one of the seekers."[58] The word (*sermo*) of Bernard is lifted by the Word (*verbum*) who is the Lord and whose dignity alone is worthy of breaking the third bread *as* the *Song of Songs*. The metaphor of taste is not lost, but exacerbated because in the time of Bernard, language is part of the sense of taste. "Poor and needy [...] Little children go begging for bread [...] they await it from your merciful love. O God most kind, break your bread for this hungering flock, *through my hands indeed if it should please you*, but *with an efficacy that is all your own*."[59] The senses function to provide a form of non-linguistic communication. Contrary to Liston-Kraft's thesis that senses express

56 Philip Liston-Kraft, "Bernard's Belching Bride: The Affectus That Words Cannot Express," *Medieval Mystical Theology* 26, no. 1 (2017): 54-72.

57 Bernard of Clairvaux, On the *Song of Songs I*, p. 3. Leclercq (*SC* 441), SCC 1.4, l. 1-12: "Sed quis franget?"

58 Bernard of Clairvaux, On the *Song of Songs I*, p. 3. Leclercq (*SC* 441), SCC 1.4, l. 1-12.

59 Bernard of Clairvaux, On the *Song of Songs I*, p. 3. Leclercq (*SC* 441), SCC 1.4, l. 1-12: "Revera pauper et inops pulso ad eum, qui aperit et nemo claudit, super sermonis hujus profundissimo sacramento. Oculi omnium in te sperant, Domine. Parvuli petierunt panem; non est

what language cannot express, the senses rather communicate, as also do gestures, while escaping (verbal-temporal) language and this, because all senses derive within the regulation of divine language.[60] The taste of human words (*sermo*) is appreciated by experience of the exercise of the senses to the extent that these pass by or are broken and reframed using the divine language of the Word (*verbum*). Bernard thus articulates divine desire in corporeal terms. The Word as *the one* comes to break the bread and to feed the hungry (*frange esurientibus*). Just as hunger creates desire for food, so too the longing soul searches for a desire to be fed in turning to the third bread. Remarkably, the identification of the Word with *the one* (*quis*) who breaks (*frangere*) is what allows Bernard to disintegrate metaphor and to open the possibility for a poetics of divine desire. The Word is not only desired and tasted metaphorically because in Christ the Word, sign and signified united, *words* of in the *book of experience* are literally consumed, not only with the obvious allusion to the Eucharist, but also *as* part (the lover) of the third bread in the field of the *Song of Songs*.

To reiterate, by way of summary, Bernard lays down the foundations for reading the *Song of Songs* in the guise of a hermeneutics of desire, and this by stretching the metaphor of eating and tasting. The desire of the body is prepared (*preparare*) by the desire of experience in order to read about the experience of the body's desires. This is because desire and not reason is what gives access to the content of the *Song of Songs* in the beginning. Through *the exercise of the senses* (*excercitati sensibus*), by means of discipline (*disciplina*) and reason (*ratio*), the body is prepared to *experience* gradually in the replacement of milk for solid bread. The solid food, which is the most nourishing yet the most challenging, is brought forth and then broken. By bringing forth the third bread, the exercised senses are able to move on to feast on the broken bread with the condition, or by the instigation, of the pleasure (*placere*) which this third bread offers. A well-disposed or disciplined desire for nourishment and pleasure is the condition for reading the *Song of Songs*. The conditional "if it is pleasing" (*si placet*) is what holds together the preparation of the senses and the consumption of the bread. Bernard thus ascribes the desire of the body

---

qui frangat eis; speratur id a benignitate tua. O piissime, frange esurientibus panem tuum, meis quidem, si dignaris, manibus, sed tuis viribus."

60 Philip Liston-Kraft, "Bernard's Belching Bride: The Affectus that Words Cannot Express," *Medieval Mystical Theology* 26, no. 1 (2017): 54-72; Mette B. Bruun, "Wandering Eyes, Muttering, and Frowns: Bernard of Clairvaux and the Communicative Implications of Gesture," in *Understanding Monastic Practices of Oral Communication* (Turnhout: Brepols, 2011), 337-63. J. Le Goff, "Les gestes symboliques dans la vie sociale. Les gestes de la vassalité," in *Simboli et simbologia nell'Alto Medioevo* (Spoleto: CISAM, 1976): 679-780; Jean-Louis Chrétien, *Symbolique du corps: la tradition Chrétienne du* Cantique des Cantiques (Paris: PUF, 2005).

a capital role, in a well-defined hermeneutics of the desire to taste the Word (*Verbum*) who as *the one* breaks the bread (*quis franget*) in and through the words (*sermo*) of the *Song of Songs*. It is precisely when the metaphor of eating and tasting disintegrates that desire of the body (quite literally) takes center stage as the privileged means to access God in the Bernardine hermeneutics of desire, for then, and only then, can an exercised experience of desire gives rise to a desire for experience. The hermeneutics of desire constitute the preamble for plunging into a reading of the *Song of Songs* where the longing of the body, conveyed by "the kiss of the mouth" (Cant 1.2), reveals divine desire. The lover demands of the beloved: "kiss me with the kiss of his mouth".[61] Thereafter, the "kiss of the mouth" becomes the paradigmatic source-beginning of experience where desire and body interact. This marks a return by way of origin to *experience in the beginning.*

1.3 Experience in the Beginning

The beginning (*principio*) of the landscape of experience in the *Song of Songs* is navigated through an engagement with the body's delight, the paradigm for which is the experience of the third kiss, which Bernard identifies with Christ, the Word incarnate. Experience begins with the process of the Word's incarnation in the delight of the third kiss. Bernard thus invites the listener to savor the third bread with a question as provocative as the opening lines of the *Song of Songs*: "Tell us, I beg you, *by whom, about whom and to whom it is said*: 'Let him kiss me with the kiss of his mouth.'"[62] The body engenders delight in *the beginning without beginning*[63] from the moment the reader is abruptly plunged into the field of experience, this time construed as an *experience in the beginning*: "How shall I explain *so abrupt a beginning, this sudden irruption as from a speech in mid-course*? For *the words spring upon* us as if indicating one speaker to whom another is replying as she demands a kiss— *whoever she may be*."[64] The breaking of the third bread is first experienced as the breaking of the word and as an attempt to find orientation within the complex dynamic

61 Bernard of Clairvaux, On the *Song of Songs I*, pp. 3-4. Leclercq (*SC* 441), SCC 1.5, l. 2: "Osculetur me osculo oris sui."

62 Bernard of Clairvaux, On the *Song of Songs I*, pp. 3-4. Leclercq (*SC* 441), SCC 1.5, l. 1-3: "Dic, quaeso, nobis, a quo, de quo, ad quemve dicitur: Osculetur me osculo oris sui? (Cant. I, 1.)."

63 Bernard of Clairvaux, On the *Song of Songs I*, pp. 3-4. Leclercq (*SC* 441), SCC 1.5, l. 18: "principium sine principium."

64 Bernard of Clairvaux, On the *Song of Songs I*, pp. 3-4. Leclercq (*SC* 441), SCC 1.5, l. 2-7: "Sic quippe in verba prorumpit, quasi quempiam loquentem praemiserit, cui consequenter respondentem et hanc introducat personam, quaecunque est ipsa quae osculum flagitat."

of the kiss which is the manifestation of the body's desire in *the beginning without beginning*. Immediately, therefore, the questions concerning the kiss arise: 'by whom' (*a quo*), 'of whom' (*de quo*) and 'to whom' (*ad quem*)? Rather than rushing to elaborate answers, as if to resist immediate gratification, the rhetorical eloquence of the language at the beginning is sufficient to savor the text, which conveys the lover's delight in the longing for the kiss.[65] The text functions in this way as a springboard of experience, for the body of the word extends beyond the body, thereby closing the distance from the mouth to the palate of the ear. In the beginning is the Word; in the beginning is the third kiss.

The longing for the kiss is the longing for the Word as word incarnate as *beginning*. In the third kiss, desire's delight emerges as a demand, which the lover claims from the beloved. On this point, Bernard comments upon the modality of the kiss, as a kiss *of* the mouth. He notes, "But if she *asks for or demands a kiss from somebody*, why does she distinctly and expressly say *with the mouth*, and even *with his own mouth*, as if lovers should kiss by means other than the mouth, or with mouths other than their own?"[66] The precise articulation of the demand, the prompting of desire, is inspired by the love of the beloved combined with the fatigue of unfulfilled expectation. "But yet she *does not say*: 'Let him kiss me *with his mouth*'; what she says is still *more intimate*: '*with the kiss of his mouth*.' How delightful a ploy of speech this, *prompted into life by the kiss*, with Scripture's own engaging countenance *inspiring the reader and enticing him on*, that he may *find pleasure even in the laborious pursuit of what lies hidden*, with a *fascinating theme to sweeten the fatigue of research*.'"[67] Desire is manifest at the beginning, pours forth from the beginning, and returns ultimately to the beginning. This gives rise to a triadic, perhaps Trinitarian even, sequence of beginnings, generating forth as *experience* in the *beginning without beginning*, the receptacle for which is the Word, the kiss. In the *first* beginning God creates (Gn 1), in the *second* beginning God as Word takes flesh

65 Elizabeth Howe, "The Mystical Kiss, and the *Canticle of Canticles*. Three Interpretations," *American Benedictine Review*, 33 (1982): 302-11.

66 Bernard of Clairvaux, On the *Song of Songs I*, pp. 3-4. Leclercq (*SC* 441), SCC 1.5, l. 7-22: "Deinde si se osculari a nescio quo vel petit, vel praecipit; cur signanter et nominatim ore, et ore suo; quasi aliud quam os, aut alienum, et non potius suum, exhibere sibi soleant osculantes?"

67 Bernard of Clairvaux, On the *Song of Songs I*, pp. 3-4. Leclercq (*SC* 441), SCC 1.5, l. 7-22: "Quanquam ne hoc quidem dicit: Osculetur me ore suo: sed aliud profecto inusitatius: Osculo, inquit, oris sui. Et quidem jucundum eloquium, quod ab osculo principium sumit, et blanda ipsa quaedam Scripturae facies facile afficit et allicit ad legendum, ita ut quod in ea latet, delectet etiam cum labore investigare, nec fatiget inquirendi forte difficultas, ubi eloquii suavitas mulcet."

(Jn 1), and in yet a *third* beginning humanity delights in God's kiss through the incarnation of the Word, i.e., through the kiss. This *third* beginning is peculiar, for it best represents a *beginning without beginning* (*principium sine principio*), and so the mystery of its paradoxical redundancy produces curiosity and stimulates further desire from desire's delight (*delectare*). The kiss as a *beginning without beginning* is modal, not temporal. Bernard exquisitely observes, "Surely this *mode of beginning that is not a beginning*, this novelty of diction in a book so old, cannot but *increase the reader's attention*. It must follow too that this work was composed, not by any human skill but by the artistry of the Spirit, *difficult to understand indeed, yet an enticing one to investigate*."[68] The Spirit is the mode of the *beginning without beginning* as longing for God's Word awaiting (temporal) incarnation. Since, moreover, the Spirit is at the origin of the eloquent *beginning without beginning* in the encounter of the kiss,[69] God therefore enters the field of experience in the body's delight as *origin* in the paradox manifested in and through anonymous bodily desire. God is the origin of the delight driving the experience of the breaking of the third bread in the kiss of the mouth, whereby delight emerges from within the spiral of a *beginning without beginning*, inversely also plunging the reader deeper into the field of body's experience and divine desire. Desire is originary *metamorphosis* in the *beginning without beginning*, first as generative (metaphysical) beginning, then as incarnate (temporal) beginning, and finally as modal (creative) beginning.

The *beginning without beginning* is in reality a beginning with many beginnings, the unifying thread for which is desire, the *metamorphosing* matrix of the field of experience. Desire is experience in the beginning and thereafter. Bernard avidly invites the reader to savour the multiplicity of sense-filled beginnings of experience, for the possibilities of beginnings are as varied as there are readers and as delightful as there are words in the *Song of Songs*, the book of experience, against whose echoes experience becomes life. Thus, Bernard bring attention to the peculiarity of experience of the beginning and to the importance of the title of this particular canticle or song (*canticum*), which is one song among many found in scripture, and insists accordingly that nothing about the *Song of Songs* should go by unnoticed. Meaning generatively saturates the beginning through desire and so the reader should savor every

---

68 Bernard of Clairvaux, On the *Song of Songs I*, pp. 3-4. Leclercq (*SC* 441), SCC 1.5, l. 7-22: "Verum quem non valde attentum faciat istiusmodi *principium sine principio*. et novitas locutionis in veteri libro? Unde constat hoc opus non humano ingenio, sed Spiritus arte ita compositum, ut quamvis difficile intellectu, sit tamen inquisitu delectabile."

69 Kilian McDonnell, "Spirit and Experience in Bernard of Clairvaux," *Theological Studies* 58, no. 1 (1997): 3-18.

word. Bernard writes, "*So now what shall we do? Shall we by-pass the title? No, not even one iota may be omitted, since we are commanded to gather up the tiniest fragments lest they be lost.*"[70] One such important element is the title of the text. "The title runs: 'The beginning of Solomon's Song of Songs.' First of all, take note of the *appropriateness of the name* 'Peaceful,' that is, Solomon, at the head of a book which opens with *the token of peace, with a kiss*."[71] The token of peace, a consequence of *the exercise of the senses*, defines the modality of experience in the beginning. Bernard continues, "Take note too that by this kind of opening *only men of peaceful minds, men who can achieve mastery over the turmoil of the passions and the distracting burden of daily chores, are invited to the study of this book*."[72] The *exercise of the senses* is once again present at the beginning (*incipio*) as the kiss or a sign of peace. The peace from vicious perturbations is a condition for understanding the text, and therefore, a condition to experience *experience*. Peace *is* experience at the beginning. The presupposition of rightfully ordered desire as peace at the beginning (*incipio*), achieved by the discipline of the senses, breaks forth from the indeterminacy of *the beginning without beginning* (*principio*), wherein the kiss pleases (*libet*) and appeases. The singularity of the *Song of Songs*, personified in Salomon's wisdom, lies precisely in the ability to harmonize pleasure and peace. Bernard comments, therefore, of Solomon: "[…] *unique as* [Solomon] *was in wisdom, renowned above all men, abounding in wealth, secure in his peace*, stood in no need of any particular benefit that would have inspired him to sing those songs. Nor does Scripture in any place attribute such a motive to him."[73] Desire is desire's own delight; it is the labour of love and love's reward manifested *as* experience. In this sense, the *Song of Songs* is *the* song *par excellence* because, by divine inspiration (*divinitus inspiratus*), Solomon was able to *see* God face to

70 Bernard of Clairvaux, On the *Song of Songs I*, p. 4. Leclercq (*SC* 441), SCC 1.6, l. 1-10: "Sed quid? titulum praeterimus? Non oportet ne unum quidem iota (Matth. V, 18), quando et minutias jubemur colligere fragmentorum, ne pereant (Joan. VI, 12)."

71 Bernard of Clairvaux, On the *Song of Songs I*, p. 4. Leclercq (*SC* 441), SCC 1.6, l. 1-10: "Titulus talis est: Incipiunt Cantica canticorum Salomonis. Observa in primis Pacifici nomen, quod est Salomon, convenire principio libri, qui incipit a signo pacis, id est ab osculo."

72 Bernard of Clairvaux, On the *Song of Songs I*, p. 4. Leclercq (*SC* 441), SCC 1.6, l. 1-10: "simulque adverte hujuscemodi principiis solas ad hanc intelligendam scripturam mentes invitari pacificas, quae sese jam a vitiorum vindicare perturbationibus et curarum tumultibus praevalent."

73 Bernard of Clairvaux, On the *Song of Songs I*, pp. 4-5. Leclercq (*SC* 441), SCC 1.7, l. 18-22: "At vero rex iste Salomon, sapientia singularis, sublimis gloria, rebus affluens, pace securus, nullius talium eguisse cognoscitur, pro quo accepto ista decantare libuerit. Sed nec Scriptura ipsa sui uspiam tale aliquid significare videtur."

face in a way in which not even Moses was able to see God, for Moses only saw the back of God. The content of this vision of God is experience in the beginning in the form of access to a divine impulse. Bernard writes, "[…] because of its *excellence, I consider this nuptial song to be well deserving of the title that so remarkably designates it, the Song of Songs*."[74] He continues, "[…] it was a *special divine impulse that inspired these songs* of his that now celebrate the praises of Christ and his Church, *the gift of holy love*, the sacrament of endless union with God."[75] The aspects of divine inspiration (*divinitus inspiratus*), crystalized as the backbone of the experiential itinerary of the *Song of Songs*, are the compartments which the kiss unseals. These compartments are the praise of Christ and the praise of community as Church (*Christi et ecclesiae laudes*), the grace of their sacred love (*sacri amoris gratiam*), the sacred link of the eternal sacrament (*aeterni connubii cecinit sacramenta*), and the expression of a holy soul's desire (*sanctae desiderium animae*). The *Song of Songs* is a figurative (*figurato*) praise (*elogio*). The figuration is in fact an invitation to desire because what the divine inspiration, which it describes, makes sense only when it resonates in the echo of the individual soul's experience and desire.[76] In other words, desire is what makes the *Song of Songs* different from say the works of Moses who could not see the veiled face of God. The *Song of Songs* expresses "[…] *the mounting desires of the soul, its marriage song, an exultation of spirit poured forth in figurative language pregnant with delight*"[77] and "[…] *like Moses he put a veil on his face*, equally resplendent as it must have been in this encounter, *because in those days few if any could sustain the bright vision of God's glory*."[78] The suggestion is that unlike in the Moses, the face of God is now visible. The visible form of God is generative desire in experience *as* experience. The sight of God is the experience of the kiss, the beginning (*incipio*), which instantiates

---

74 Bernard of Clairvaux, *On the Song of Songs I*, p. 5. Leclercq (*SC* 441), SCC 1.8, l. 1-14: "Igitur pro sui excellentia reor nuptiale hoc carmen hujusmodi titulo praesignitum, ut merito Cantica canticorum singulariter appelletur, (I Tim. VI, 15)."

75 Bernard of Clairvaux, *On the Song of Songs I*, p. 5. Leclercq (*SC* 441), SCC 1.8, l. 1-14: "Itaque divinitus inspiratus, Christi et Ecclesiae laudes, et sacri amoris gratiam, et aeterni connubii cecinit sacramenta."

76 Bernard of Clairvaux, *On the Song of Songs II*, pp. 110-11. Leclercq (*SC* 441), SCC 29.9, l. 9-10: "Ecclesia seu studiosa quaevis anima."

77 Bernard of Clairvaux, *On the Song of Songs I*, p. 5. Leclercq (*SC* 441), SCC 1.8, l. 1-14: "simulque expressit sanctae desiderium animae, et epithalamii carmen, exsultans in spiritu, jucundo composuit eulogio, figurato tamen."

78 Bernard of Clairvaux, *On the Song of Songs I*, p. 5. Leclercq (*SC* 441), SCC 1.8, l. 1-14: "Nimirum velabat et ipse instar Moysi faciem suam (Exod. III, 6), non minus forsitan in hac parte fulgentem, eo quod illo adhuc in tempore nemo, aut rarus erat, qui revelata facie gloriam istam speculari sufficeret."

the generative circle of the *beginning without beginning* (*principium sine principium*) and which governs the hermeneutic circle of desire in the beginning, according to the logic surpassing reason, where "desire impels me, not reason". Following Augustine, then, Bernard presents touch or experience as the intimation of knowledge. Therefore, desire is the key to see God in the beginning of experience and, accordingly, desire too becomes the condition of experience in the *Song of Songs*, the crystalized testament to human longing for the divine, the book of experience.

Experience in the beginning is accessible only through desire in experience. The centrality of the experience of desire as a hermeneutic key for reading *On the Song of Songs*, which has rightly earned Bernard the title of "theologian of experience" (*théologien de l'expérience*),[79] cannot be overstressed. When explaining the superiority of the *Song of Songs* over other songs, Bernard invites the listener to turn to her own experience (*experientiam*) and to consider in what occasion she has previously praised in song: "[… .] a song to our God for his *gracious renewal of your life*."[80] The first content of experience is gratefulness. He continues, "When you repented he not only forgave your sins but even promised rewards, so that rejoicing in the *hope* of benefits to come, you sing of the Lord's ways […]"[81] The second content of experience is prospective, in the expectation of hope's fulfillment. "*In the daily trials and combats* […] you *learn by what you experience*."[82] The third content of experience is reflective. Bernard exhorts a constructive attitude to integrate the findings of experience. The final moment is again gratefulness, and so a return to the beginning, this time in the form of praise: "*For every benefit conferred, God is to be praised in his gifts*."[83] Experience culminates in singing or chanting (*canto*)

79 Paul Verdeyen, "Un theologien de l'experience," in *BdC*, p. 557-577: "Bernard est le premier théologien de l'expérience spirituelle."

80 Bernard of Clairvaux, *On the Song of Songs I*, pp. 5-6. Leclercq (*SC* 441), SCC 1.8, l. 23-25; SCC 1.9, l. 1-16: "Rursus cum adjecit primum supra petram statuere pedes vestros, et dirigere gressus vestros; puto quod et tunc nihilominus pro indulta novitate vitae immissum sit in os vestrum canticum novum, carmen Deo nostro."

81 Bernard of Clairvaux, *On the Song of Songs I*, pp. 5-6. Leclercq (*SC* 441), SCC 1.8, l. 23-25; SCC 1.9, l. 1-16: "Quid cum poenitentibus vobis non solum peccata dimisit, sed insuper promisit et praemia; non multo magis spe gaudentes futurorum bonorum, cantastis in viis Domini, quoniam magna est gloria Domini?"

82 Bernard of Clairvaux, *On the Song of Songs I*, pp. 5-6. Leclercq (*SC* 441), SCC 1.8, l. 23-25; SCC 1.9, l. 1-16: "Sed et in quotidianis exercitiis et bellis, quae nulla hora pie in Christo viventibus desunt a carne, a mundo, a diabolo, sicut militiam esse vitam hominis super terram (Job VII, 1) incessanter experimini in vobismetipsis, quotidiana necesse est cantica pro assecutis victoriis innovari."

83 Bernard of Clairvaux, *On the Song of Songs I*, pp. 5-6. Leclercq (*SC* 441), SCC 1.8, l. 23-25; SCC 1.9, l. 1-16: "et ad singula quaeque beneficia benedicitur Deus in donis suis."

praise, which results from the victory of the faith over the world, from escaping misery from the gift of a new life and so on: "*if you look back on your own experience*, is it not in that victory by which *your faith overcomes the world* [...] *that you yourselves sing a new song*?"[84] Irrespective of the specific kinds of experiences, which inspire chanting, Bernard draws attention to a more general kind of experience inherent in the *Song of Songs*. The dynamism between personal experience and universal experience is of great consequence because the listener only understands the *Song of Songs* by framing it against the echo of personal experience and this in turn presupposes rich experience. To experience is to remember and to remember is to learn. This process (experience, memory, and learning) is most evident in the *Song of Songs*, a song superior to all others: "[...] I think that your own experience reveals to you the meaning of those psalms."[85] Herein, the *Song of Songs* is superior to all other forms of song because it is the fruit of all others. The implication is of capital importance: learning the *Song of Songs* only happens through experience. Bernard writes, "[...] only personal experience can unfold its meaning (*sola addiscit experientia*)."[86] For this reason, the Abbot of Clairvaux reserve the name of *the book of experience* (*liber experientia*) to the *Song of Songs*.[87]

Moreover, Bernard's notion of experience in the beginning is intricately weaved with the divine since the *Song of Songs* is a sacred text. In other words, the *Song of Songs* does not only echo in the individual experience of listeners as a precondition for understanding. Perhaps more important is the divine source of the experience recounted in the sacred text. "But there is *that other song*, writes Bernard, which, by its *unique dignity and sweetness*, excels all those I have mentioned and any others there might be [...] *It stands at a point where all the others culminate. Only the couch of the Spirit can inspire a song like this,*

---

84 Bernard of Clairvaux, *On the Song of Songs I*, pp. 5-6. Leclercq (*SC* 441), SCC 1.8, l. 23-25; SCC 1.9, l. 1-16: "Caeterum vos, si vestram experientiam advertatis, nonne in victoria, qua vicit mundum fides vestra, et in exitu vestro de lacu miseriae et de luto faecis, cantastis et ipsi Domino canticum novum, quia mirabilia fecit?"

85 Bernard of Clairvaux, *On the Song of Songs I*, p. 6. Leclercq (*SC* 441), SCC 1.10, l. 1: "[...] arbitror vos in vobismetipsis illa iam recognoscere [...]."

86 Bernard of Clairvaux, *On the Song of Songs I*, p. 6. Leclercq (*SC* 441), SCC 1.10.

87 See also, Emmanuel Falque, "Saint Bernard et le champ de l'expérience," in *Expérience phiosophique et experience mystique*, ed. P. Capelle, *Philosophie et théologie* (Cerf, Paris, 2005); Renato Kirchner, "A intimidade da experiência religiosa: uma aproximação fenomenológica da mística de Bernardo de Claraval," *Revista Pistis Praxis* 8, no. 738 (2016): 307; Bento Silva Santos, "*Hodie legimus in libro experientiae*: Heidegger's Appropriation of Bernard of Clairvaux's Formula," *Trans-Form-Acao* 39, no. 3 (2016): 101-20; F. Gastaldelli, "Ricerca ed esperienza di Dio secondo san Bernardo," *Rivista cistercense* 8 (1991): 133-54.

and only personal experience can unfold its meaning."[88] The couch of the spirit refers to unction. The unction is a reference to Psalm 119.1, but also to Mary of Bethany who puts the fragrance of ointments on the feet of Jesus in Jn 12. In *On the Song of Songs*, Bernard uses the image of anointment to illustrate how after Christ, the Spirit is the new ointment which anoints the Church. The term experience, therefore, refers to more than to simply collecting and committing to pen a series of vague memories, although such a sense is not excluded but rather incorporated into a larger sense. The revolutionary, and for now preliminary sense of experience is, in the Bernardine reflection, something which comes from God and which is taught by God. God teaches experience and experience teaches God. There is no God without experience and there is no experience without God, and the intimate union of these constitutes the content of the *Song of Songs*. Furthermore, the term unction (*unctio*) which has inescapable sacramental connotations, some have suggested that for Bernard experience is accessible only to members of the Church. Strictly then, and this is a challenging claim, experience is only *experienced* within the confines of Church membership. The term experts (*experti*), for Bernard, is a synonym for believer, while the term inexpert (*inexperto*) refers to a non-believer. The observation is not to demark the boundaries of experience. Rater, by restricting experience to the confines of Church membership, Bernard focuses on the importance of desire (*desiderio*) in community for divine experience. The boundaries of experience may be restricted but the natural call, the movement of desire, remains universal. All are called to experience, because all desire experience, and all experience is experience of God in community. This is Bernard's teaching. He writes, "Let those who are versed in the mystery *revel in it*; let all others *burn with desire rather to attain to this experience than merely to learn about it* [...] *the very music of the heart*, not a trilling on the lips but *an inward pulsing of delight, a harmony not of voices but of wills*."[89] Inward harmony of wills fulfills the purpose of experience.

Various attitudes and responses compliment the universal call to experience. These attitudes, which Bernard presents according to experience and

88 Bernard of Clairvaux, *On the Song of Songs I*, pp. 6-7. Leclercq (*SC* 441), SCC 1.11, l. 1-14: "Sed est canticum, quod sui singulari dignitate et suavitate cunctis merito quae memoravimus, et si qua sunt alia, antecellit: et jure hoc appellaverim Canticum canticorum, quia caeterorum omnium ipsum est fructus. Istiusmodi canticum sola unction docet, sola addiscit experientia."

89 Bernard of Clairvaux, On the *Song of Songs I*, pp. 6-7. Leclercq (*SC* 441), SCC 1.11, l. 1-14: "Experti recognoscant, inexperti inardescant desiderio, non tam cognoscendi, quam experiendi. Non est enim strepitus oris, sed jubilus cordis; non sonus labiorum, sed motus gaudiorum; voluntatum, non vocum consonantia."

inexperience, are as follows. The expert or the one who is experienced recognizes, whereas the amateur, or more specifically, the inexpert or the inexperienced (*inexperto*), burns with desire. The inexpert burns with desire not for the sake of burning with desire, nor does the inexpert desire knowledge of the *Song of Songs*. The desire in question is a desire for experience. Experience is knowledge, not of voice but of common will. The *Song of Songs* is not *just* a song heard when chanted like all others. Alone those who not only listen but also chant and to whom the song is chanted understand the *Song of Songs*: "[...] *only the singer hears it and the one to whom he sings – the lover and the beloved.* It is pre-eminently a marriage song telling of chaste souls *in loving embrace*, of their *wills in sweet concord*, of the *mutual exchange of the heart's affections*."[90] The desire to experience burns even within those who are incapable of experiencing as of yet. Desire burns for experience just as experience remains athirst with desire. Moreover, here, as the first sermon ends, Bernard elegantly brings the discussion full circle, back to the beginning, *the beginning without beginning*. By warning against a certain destructive state of *burning desire*, Bernard briefly states yet again that the celestial wedding (*nuptiis caelestis*) is only for those who are advanced and for those who have mastered the *exercise of the senses*. The monks or the neophytes of experience, in the early stages, should first by means of burning desire aspire to experience and, accordingly, they must undergo rigorous discipline, in order that they may experience. To summarize, Bernard writes, "The novices, *the immature*, those but recently converted from a worldly life, do not normally sing this song or hear it sung."[91] He goes on, "Only the mind *disciplined by persevering study, only the man whose efforts have borne fruit under God's inspiration*."[92] The work of the novice is crucial, for the mature is "*measured out not in time but in merits*."[93] Concluding for the day, Bernard aptly exhorts the labour of experience, "But

---

90 Bernard of Clairvaux, On the *Song of Songs I*, pp. 6-7. Leclercq (*SC* 441), SCC 1.11, l. 1-14: "Non auditur foris, nec enim in publico personat: sola quae cantat audit, et cui cantatur, id est sponsa et sponsus. Est quippe nuptiale carmen, exprimens castos jucundosque complexus animorum, morum concordiam, affectuumque consentaneam ad alterutrum charitatem."

91 Bernard of Clairvaux, On the *Song of Songs I*, pp. 6-7. Leclercq (*SC* 441), SCC 1.11, l. 1-10: "Caeterum non est illud cantare seu audire animae puerilis et neophytae adhuc, et recens conversae de saeculo, sed provectae jam et eruditae mentis."

92 Bernard of Clairvaux, On the *Song of Songs I*, pp. 6-7. Leclercq (*SC* 441), SCC 1.11, l. 1-10: "quae suis nimirum profectibus, facta nuptiis coelestis sponsi idonea, qualis denique suo loco plenius describetur."

93 Bernard of Clairvaux, On the *Song of Songs I*, pp. 6-7. Leclercq (*SC* 441), SCC 1.11, l. 1-10: "Deo promovente, in tantum jam creverit, quatenus ad perfectam aetatem, et ad nubiles quodam modo pervenerit annos, annos dico meritorum, non temporum."

the hour has come when both our rule and the poverty of our state *demand that we go out to work.*"[94] In the closing of the sermon, as he promises to carry on with the explanation the following day, the very discipline, which is a pre-requisite to the *Song of Songs*, redirects the listener from the words (*uerbo*) to the act of the will (*voluntas*). As Bernard concludes the opening pages on *the book of experience*, the reader is launched back (*expedire*) to experience. The circle is complete: from experience, through *the book of experience*, and back again to *the beginning without beginning*. "Tomorrow, with God's help, we shall continue to speak about the kiss, because today's discourse on the title sets us free *to resume where we had begun.*"[95]

Conclusion

By locating the beginning of desire in the experience of the body in his *On the Song of Songs*, Bernard masterfully conjures a paradox for a hermeneutics of aestheticism, namely, how is it possible to experience *experience* as experience, and to recognize it thus? By way of response, and developing a hermeneutics of aestheticism accordingly, Bernard postulates *the beginning without beginning* (*principium sine principio*), i.e., an originary, self-generating, and endless beginning, on which the experience of *experience* depends. The layers of paradoxes illustrate the hermeneutic circle as *the beginning without beginning* (*principium sine principio*) corresponding to the kiss, which exemplifies desire in the *Song of Songs*. Alternatively framed, *the beginning without beginning* is the dependence of understanding on the experience to understand or, again, *the beginning of desire* and *experience in the beginning*. Far from pointing to either some incoherent or merely rhetorical play of words, Bernard inaugurates the hermeneutic circle of *the book of experience* by appealing to the expression of desire: "Desire impels me, not reason."[96] Desire, which is at the heart of what waters hearts in and through *the book of experience* accesses the portal of *the beginning without beginning* as *a* beginning (*incipio*) common to all: the paradox of desire – athirst for experience, is full only in experience. *The beginning without*

---

94 Bernard of Clairvaux, On the *Song of Songs I*, pp. 6-7. Leclercq (*SC* 441), SCC 1.11, l. 1-10: "Sed praeterit hora, qua nos exire urget ad opera manuum et paupertas et institutio regularis."

95 Bernard of Clairvaux, On the *Song of Songs I*, pp. 6-7. Leclercq (*SC* 441), SCC 1.11, l. 10-12: "Cras in nomine Domini quod coeperamus prosequemur de osculo, quia de titulo hodiernus sermo nos expedivit."

96 Bernard of Clairvaux, On the *Song of Songs I*, pp. 54-5. Leclercq (*SC* 441), SCC 9.2, l. 7: "Desiderio feror, non ratione."

beginning at the beginning (*incipio*) inaugurates the order of desire. Desire is therefore the point of departure (*incipio*) for experience. The desire of the body in *the book of experience* drives the experienced (*experti*) and the inexperienced (*inexperti*) alike towards God. Desire for God in the kiss makes experience available to the experienced (*experti*) in *the beginning without beginning* while it brings the inexperienced to the beginning (*incipio*) of divine experience. Therein, the founding moment in the *metamorphosis of love* unfolds *as* experience, preliminarily, in three moments. First, Bernard locates *the beginning of desire* in the body: the body, the originary beginning of desire, is the locus of experience. Moreover, since experience is not a given, but rather the fruit of discipline, Bernard then prescribes *the exercise of the senses* as a preamble for plunging into the experience of experience. Third, Bernard frames *the experience in the beginning* as consisting essentially in the transformation of the desire of the body. In the desire of the body, the body transforms desire in the source-beginning, the beginning without beginning, of the *metamorphosis of love*. In the first instance, body is manifested as the locus of desire. What of the body *of* desire or the body composed as desire? Does desire, too, transform the body in its constitutive role? In the counter-blow (*choc en retour*) of desire, Bernard postulates the fleshing of desire into body. Considering the body as constitutive *desire* is the subject matter of the next chapter, and the second great moment in the *metamorphosis of love*, wherein experience is desire.

CHAPTER 2

Desire

How does desire affect the body? In *the beginning without beginning*, experience begins *as* experience with desire of the body for God and through God in the Word incarnate. In the manifestation of the body in the beginning, the counter-blow (*choc en retour*) of desire affects the body, whereby desire is a modality of body. The *metamorphosis of love* begins with experience in the beginning, only to also reveal the beginning as generative of body in desire. Charting the transformative and generative itinerary of desire in the counter-blow of body's manifestation occurs first in the desire of the body (2.1), then in the manifestation of transformation as production in the production of a body (2.2), and finally in the body's modality of generation in desiring-production as body (2.3). As the *metamorphosis of love* unfolds in the Bernard's *On the Song of Songs*, desire affects body and body is production of desire in transformative generation. Therefore, in the second moment of the *metamorphosis of love*, as this chapter shows, the dynamism of love consists in the complimentary production of bodies by desire and in the desire of bodies by production.

2.1 The Desire of the Body

Having briefly expounded the kiss of *Song of Songs* in experience of *the beginning without beginning*, Bernard returns to describe it in terms of longing and body, in the desire of the body. Desire transforms and ultimately produces the body in *the kiss of the mouth*.[1] The centrality accorded to the body in experience enables Bernard to construe the desire for God in terms of the longing for the kiss by the lover.[2] The body of Christ, the one who breaks the bread,

1 Paul Moyaert, "Mysticism: The Transformation of a Love Consumed by Desire into a Love without Desire," *Ethical Perspectives* 7, no. 4 (2000): 269-278; Michael Casey, *Athirst for God: Spiritual Desire in Bernard of Clairvaux's* Sermons on the Song of Songs (Collegeville: Cistercian Publications, 1988); Pyong-Gwan Pak, "St. Bernard of Clairvaux on the Riddle of Human Desire: The Necessity of a Reversal of Priorities in the Human Life of Desire," *Logos: A Journal of Catholic Thought and Culture* 21, no. 4 (2018): 126-50; Jason Alvis, *Marion and Derrida on the Gift and Desire: Debating the Generosity of Things* (Cham: Springer, 2016); Antonio Montanari, "*Desiderium sine anxietate: Désir infini et béatitude de l'homme d'après les sermons* 84-86 *super cantica de saint Bernard*," *Collectanea cisterciensia* 70, no. 1 (2008): 4-20.

2 Elizabeth Howe, "The mystical Kiss, and the *Canticle of Canticles*: Three Interpretations," *American Benedictine Review*, 33 (1982): 302-11.

 DOI:10.30965/9783846767504_004

conditions desire for God according to the mode of the incarnation. Bernard then charts the progression of the incarnation, both historical and individual, in function of the four-fold meanings of the kiss (*osculum*) in the encounter of the lovers in *Song of Songs*. These symbolic meanings, then, indicate the dynamic structure of the manifestation of desire. The first kiss is longing for Christ, the second kiss is the unique kiss of Christ, and the third kiss is the revelation of God's sacrament (*sacramentum*)[3] as Christ. Of these, the fourth and final kiss is the highest, for through it, which presupposes all others, God is present in the flesh as efficient Word, in Christ. In the multilayered Bernardine analysis of the kiss, then, the *body* of Christ is essential for the human experience of desire for God. Bernard frames the kisses in terms of *desire and the body*. These various kisses and their relation illustrate how desire transforms bodies and also generates bodies.

The first kiss is the longing (*suspirantium*) of the fathers (*paters*) for the presence of Christ in the flesh (*caro*). Christ is promised by word and longed *as* Word. Therefore, in the absence of the Word's body, prior to its manifestation, the body *longs*. At this stage, desire is expectation due to absence or privation. How does expectation come about and how does expectation configure longing? The Abbot of Clairvaux passionately explains the reason for the longing of the fathers within the framework of prophetic expectation and the awaiting of fulfillment.[4] Bernard recounts the "great rejoicing as we *celebrate the feast of Christ's birth*. [...] I pray that *the intense longing of those men of old, their heartfelt expectation, may be enkindled in me by these words*: '*Let him kiss me with the kiss of his mouth.*'"[5] In these lines is found Bernard's logic of desire. First, the

3 Leclercq (*SC* 441), SCC 2, p. 80, n. 1: "Christi sacramento" of the ms. Bruges, Sém., 21-68 preferred instead of "Christi mysterio". Cf. ibid., p. 56 of the *Sources Chretiennes* in notes by the author. José María Rovira Belloso, "Palabra y Sacramento como signos de la Iglesia," *Diálogo ecuménico* 18, no. 61 (1983): 417-34. Hans Boersma and Matthew Levering, eds. *The Oxford Handbook of Sacramental Theology* (Oxford: Oxford University Press, 2015).

4 Brian Fitzgerald, *Inspiration and Authority in the Middle Ages: Prophets and their Critics from Scholasticism to Humanism* (Oxford: Oxford University Press, 2017); Marjorie Reeves, *The Influence of Prophecy in the Later Middle Ages: a Study in Joachimism* (Oxford: Oxford University Press, 1969); Eric Alan Constant, *Concepts of Prophecy in the Middle Ages: Inspired Exegesis, Visions from God, and the Interaction of Theories and Practice* (East Lansing: Michigan State University Press, 2016).

5 Bernard of Clairvaux, On the *Song of Songs I*, p. 8. Leclercq (*SC* 441), SCC 2.1, l. 1-16: "Ecce enim quam multi in hac ejus, quae proxime celebranda est, Nativitate gaudebunt! sed utinam de nativitate, non de vanitate! Illorum ergo desiderium flagrans et piae exspectationis affectum spirat mihi vox ista: Osculetur me osculo oris sui (Cantic. I, 1)."

flesh of Christ (*Christi a carne*) is the object of longing (*suspirare*).[6] Bernard writes, "During my frequent *ponderings on the burning desire* with which *the patriarchs longed for the incarnation* of Christ, I am stung with sorrow and shame. Even now I *can scarcely restrain my tears* [...] For which of us does the consummation of that event fill with as much joy as *the mere promise of it inflamed the desires* of the holy men of pre-Christian times?"[7] The absence of the flesh of Christ is at least one of the factors producing the longing for Christ. Furthermore, the longing for Christ in the flesh is transmitted collectively in the form of an accessible expectation or hope (*accenderant desiderium promissio*). That is to say, the desires of others (*desiderii Patrum*) is integrated into a personal desire *now* (*et nunc vix contineo lacrymas*), through the expectation of hope. Finally, the fulfillment of the desire in the coming (similar to the personal visit Bernard had) is a gift (*gratia*) which inspires joy, the joy of the nativity and not of vanity – Bernard here plays with the contrasting meaning of rhyming words in the Latin (*vanitas* and *nativitas*), vanity and nativity (*sed utinam de nativitate, non de vanitate!*). The longing for God in the nativity is, in all these rich senses, an experience of the body waged within the interplay of absence (longing) and presence (fulfillment). The desire for *the* body closes the space of time in the first kiss. Moreover, in the first kiss, the experience of desire for God in the flesh mysteriously encompasses *all* of human experience. Bernard writes, "Many an upright man in those far off times sensed within himself *how profuse the graciousness that would be poured upon those lips*. And *intense desire springing from that perception impelled him to utter*: '*Let him kiss me with the kiss of his mouth*,' hoping with *every fiber of his being* that he might not be deprived of *a share in a pleasure so great*."[8] The tensions, which the body of Christ *produces* within the dynamic matrix of absence (object), expectation (time), universality (experience), and possession (gift), configures desire. Bernard continues noting that Christmas is the "great rejoicing as we *celebrate the feast of Christ's birth*. [...] I pray that *the intense longing of those*

6 Later, the *figura* is the affect.

7 Bernard of Clairvaux, On the *Song of Songs I*, p. 8. Leclercq (*SC* 441), SCC 2.1, l. 1-16: "Ardorem desiderii Patrum suspirantium Christi a carne praesentiam frequentissime cogitans, compungor et confundor in memetipso; et nunc vix contineo lacrymas, ita pudet teporis torporisque miserabilium temporum horum. Cui namque nostrum tantum ingerat gaudium gratiae hujus exhibitio, quantum sanctis veteribus accenderat desiderium promissio?"

8 Bernard of Clairvaux, On the *Song of Songs I*, p. 8. Leclercq (*SC* 441), SCC 2.1, l. 1-16: "Senserat nimirum in spiritu, quisquis tunc spiritualis esse poterat, quanta foret gratia diffusa in labiis illis. Propterea loquens in desiderio animae aiebat, Osculetur me osculo oris sui; nimirum omnimodis cupiens tantae suavitatis participio non fraudari."

men of old, their heartfelt expectation, may be enkindled in me by these words: 'Let him kiss me with the kiss of his mouth.'"[9] On Christmas, the celebration of incarnation, and therefore of longing's fulfillment, in its various reconfiguring dimensions as the kiss, the desire for *a* body comes to constitute the space of time. Besides the configuration of desire framed in terms of the body, from the analysis of the first kiss also emerges the paradigmatic transformation of the body, whence the body produces desire and, in the counter-blow, the *choc en retour*, desire transforms the body. This transformation marks a transition from language (absence) to action (presence). In the fulfillment of longing for Christ, words *about* the body give way to actions *of* the body. He writes, "'*Of what use to me the wordy effusions of the prophets*?' Rather let him who is the *most handsome of the sons of men, let him kiss me with the kiss of his mouth. No longer am I satisfied to listen to Moses*, for he is a slow speaker and *not able to speak well. Isaiah is a man of unclean lips*, Jeremiah *does not know how to speak* [...] *not one of the prophets makes an impact on me with his words*."[10] The desire for *any*-body transforms the body in *the* body of the Word's manifestation. The Word's manifestation in the body is efficacious longing. On the one hand, the words expressing the longing of the prophet fall short of the experience of the kiss. Yet, on the other hand, words about the Word (*vivus et efficax*) are rendered alive and efficient through the Word alone. It is not words, but the body, the body of Christ, that speaks *of* Christ and *through* Christ in the first kiss, leading from desire, through the body, to the presence of love in the body. As Word incarnate, Christ bridges the longing of desire and the body in accomplishment. Bernard continues, "But he, *the one whom they proclaim*, let him speak to me, 'let him kiss me with the kiss of his mouth.' I have no desire that he should approach me *in their person* [...] rather *in his own person 'let him kiss me with the kiss of his mouth;'* let him whose *presence is full of love*."[11] The

9 Bernard of Clairvaux, On the *Song of Songs I*, p. 8. Leclercq (*SC* 441), SCC 2.1, l. 1-16: "Ecce enim quam multi in hac ejus, quae proxime celebranda est, Nativitate gaudebunt! sed utinam de nativitate, non de vanitate! Illorum ergo desiderium flagrans et piae exspectationis affectum spirat mihi vox ista: Osculetur me osculo oris sui (Cantic. I, 1)."

10 Bernard of Clairvaux, On the *Song of Songs I*, pp. 8-9. Leclercq (*SC* 441), SCC 2.2, l. 1-7: "Dicebat enim perfectus quisque: Quo mihi ora haec seminiverbia prophetarum? Ipse potius speciosus forma prae filiis hominum, ipse me osculetur osculo oris sui. Non audio jam Moysen: impeditioris siquidem linguae factus est mihi (Exod. IV, 10). Isaiae labia immunda sunt (Isai. VI, 5): Jeremias nescit loqui, quia puer est (Jerem. I, 6): et Prophetae omnes elingues sunt."

11 Bernard of Clairvaux, On the *Song of Songs I*, pp. 8-9. Leclercq (*SC* 441), SCC 2.2, l. 15-25: "Ipse, ipse quem loquuntur, ipse loquatur: ipse me osculetur osculo oris sui. Non in eis jam, aut per eos loquatur mihi, quoniam tenebrosa aqua in nubibus aeris: sed ipse me osculetur osculo oris sui, cujus gratiosa praesentia, et admirandae fluenta doctrinae fiant in me fons aquae salientis in vitam aeternam."

accomplishment of desire in the kiss as the presence of love is transformative because it captivates from within, in the efficacy of generative desire where word is gest and incarnate communication: "[L]et him become '*a spring inside me*, welling up to eternal life.' [...], [*f*]*or his living, active word is to me a kiss* [...] For my Jesus utterly surpasses these in his *majesty and splendor*. Therefore I ask of him what I ask of neither man nor angel: *that he kiss me with the kiss of his mouth*."[12] The transformation of the desire of the body by desire through the body of Christ in the first kiss illustrates the paradigmatic shift in the logic of desire. The trajectory covers the articulation of desire, in terms of the body, the expression of the body through the longing of the prophets, the touch of the first kiss, and ultimately in the rendering of the Word into a living and efficient body or, to appropriate and Deluze's expression, as desiring-production.[13] In the first kiss, desire seeks the body, then a body, then anybody, and finally, desire *becomes* body.

A further transformation arises in the subsequent kiss, the second kiss, the unique kiss of Christ. Bernard begins the explanation of the second kiss by noting the phrasing of the *Song of Songs*. The lover requests a kiss by *the kiss* of the mouth and not *of* the mouth. The further qualification by the introduction of the kiss as a noun avoids a direct encounter of the one kissed and the mouth of the one kissing. The kiss, not the one kissing, accomplishes the kiss; there is a distance between body and desire. Therefore, there is the kisser, the kiss and the kissed. The kiss can come either from the mouth of the kisser or from the kiss itself. Bernard uses the distance between desire and the body to trace and frame the transformation, already begun in the first kiss, which is the transformation of the desire of the body by a desire as body. Bernard writes, "I do not presume that it is with his mouth I shall be kissed, for that constitutes the unique felicity and singular privilege of the human nature he assumed. [...] I ask to be kissed with the kiss of his mouth, an experience shared by all."[14] The body produced is common and experienced by all. Word

12 Bernard of Clairvaux, On the *Song of Songs I*, pp. 8-9. Leclercq (*SC* 441), SCC 2.2, l. 15-25: "Quem unxit Pater oleo laetitiae prae consortibus suis (Psal. XLIV, 8), nunquid non ex ipso mihi uberior infunditur gratia? si tamen dignetur me osculari osculo oris sui. Cujus utique sermo vivus et efficax osculum mihi est [...] Quippe et ipsos longe superat Jesus meus specie sua et pulchritudine sua. Non ergo alium sive angelum, sive hominem, sed ipsum peto osculari me osculo oris sui."

13 The influence of Origen here is strong. Cf. Origen, *Hom. Cant.*, I, 2; SC 37 bis, p. 173; *Com. Cant.*, I, 1.7 (*SC* 375, 185); D. Farkasfalvy, *o.c.*, p. 31-32.

14 Bernard of Clairvaux, On the *Song of Songs I*, pp. 8-9. Leclercq (*SC* 441), SCC 2.2, l. 26-32: "Nec sane praesumo me osculatum iri ab ore ipsius (est enim hoc assumpti hominis unicae felicitatis et praerogativae singularis); sed humilius ab osculo oris sui peto me osculari, quod commune utique est multorum, qui dicere possunt, Et nos omnes de plenitudine ejus accepimus (Joan. I, 16)."

then, effects action and engenders body: the distance between desire and body is closed. This is evident in the second kiss in virtue of its author who is Verb (*Verbum*) or Word. This is not Christ in the body, as was the case with the first kiss, but the *logos* (source-beginning) or what is also called the pre-existent Christ. Bernard explains, "The mouth that kisses signifies *the Word who assumes human nature*; *the nature assumed receives the kiss*; the kiss however, that *takes its being both from the giver and the receiver*, is *a person that is formed by both*, none other than 'the one mediator between God and mankind, himself a man, *Christ Jesus*.'"[15] In a remarkable and unprecedented elucidation of the *Song of Songs*, the addressee of the kiss, in the second kiss, is the man assumed (*assumpti hominis*) by the Word.[16] Yet the kiss is not received until desire (Word) assumes a body (*assumpti hominis*) and by so doing, transforms the body (Christ). Bernard continues: "uniquely and in one sole instance the mouth of the word was pressed, *that moment when the fullness of the divinity yielded itself to him as the life of his body*. A *fertile kiss* therefore, a marvel of stupendous self-abasement [...] *is the uniting of God with man*."[17] The body

15 Bernard of Clairvaux, On the *Song of Songs I*, pp. 9-10. Leclercq (*SC* 441), SCC 2.3, l. 1-15: "Intendite. Sit os osculans, Verbum assumens; osculatum, caro quae assumitur: osculum vero, quod pariter ab osculante et osculato conficitur, persona ipsa scilicet ex utroque compacta, mediator Dei et hominum homo Christus Jesus."

16 Christoph Benke, *Unterscheidung der Geister bei Bernhard von Clairvaux* (Würzburg: Echter, 1991); A. Bosch, *Christus and the Christian Faith according to St Bernard*, 1961; A. Bosch, "Christologie Bernardine," *Cîteaux* 9 (1958): 5-17; A. Bosch, "*Dieu devenu connaissable dans le Christ d'après saint Bernard*," *Collectanea Ordinis Cisterciensum Reformatorum* 22 (1960): 11-20; A. Bosch, "Dieu rendu accessible dans le Christ d'après saint Bernard," *Collectanea Ordinis Cisterciensum Reformatorum* 21 (1959): 185-205; A. Bosch, "Le Christ, Dieu devenu imitable d'après S. Bernard," *Collectanea ordinis Cisterciensium Reformatorum* 22 (1959): 341-55; A. Bosch, "Le Christ, Dieu devenu imitable d'après S. Bernard," *Collectanea ordinis Cisterciensium Reformatorum* 22 (1961): 42-57; A. Bosch "Le mystère de l'Incarnation chez saint Bernard," *Cîteaux* 10 (1959): 85-92, 165-77, 245-67; A. Bosch, "Présupposés à la christologie Bernardine," *Cîteaux* 9, (1958): 85-105; Jean-Marie Déchanet, "Le mystère du salut. La christologie de saint Bernard," in *Saint Bernard théologien*, Actes du Congrès de Dijon (15-19 sept. 1953), ASOC, 9, fasc. 3-4 (1953): 78-91; R. Kereszty, "Relationship Between Anthropology and Christology. St. Bernard, a Teacher for our Age," *Analecta Cisterciensia*, 46 (1990), 271-300; B. Kienzle, "*Verbum Dei et Verba Bernardi*: The Function of Language in Bernard's Second Sermon for Peter and Paul," *Cîteaux commentarii cistercienses* 42, no. 1-4 (1991): 149-159; Pierluigi Lia, "Un'estetica Del Verbum in Bernardo Di Chiaravalle," Dissertazione Dottorale in Teologia 47, Milano: Facoltà Teologica Dell'Italia Settentrionale, 2011.

17 Bernard of Clairvaux, On the *Song of Songs I*, pp. 9-10. Leclercq (*SC* 441), SCC 2.3, l. 1-15: "Hac ergo ratione sanctorum nemo dicere praesumebat, Osculetur me ore suo; sed tantum, Osculo oris sui: ipsi sane servantes praerogativam istam, cui singulariter semelque os Verbi impressum tunc est, cum ei se corporaliter plenitudo omnis divinitatis indulsit."

of Christ (first kiss) elicits desire and the Word (second kiss) transforms it in the union of Word and body (*assumpti hominis*).[18] The explanation of how the originator and the addressee of the second kiss constitute *one* in the process of delivery is a paradigmatic Bernardine synthesis of the transformation of desire *by* desire *as* desire *in* the body: "For he is the peace between us, and has made the two into one."[19] Word makes body because desire is generative. There is no distance between the body and desire, only manifestation of body through the transformative power of desire.

The efficient, living Word transforms the body and in so doing becomes body, rendering the Word a generative force as desiring-production. The manifestation of body and desire in the *metamorphosis of love* is accessible by means of a sign. Bernard writes, "[n]ormally *the touch of lip on lip is the sign of the loving embrace of hearts*, but this *conjoining* of natures brings together the human and divine, shows God reconciling to himself all things."[20] The receptacle of the kiss or the Word (God) is *a body*. Desire seeks a body! Desire is received by a body. Desire produces a body. The *body* is here construed not just as the material aspect of the flesh,[21] but also as the *totality of unified social human experience*.[22] Humanity is the receptacle of divine desire construed as Church. However, Bernard carefully nuances such a way of framing the dynamism (*dynamos*) of the kiss by restricting it to the work of Christ alone. The kisser is

18 Cf. Apponius (c. 7th century), *In Canticum canticorum exposition* (3, l. 230): "Nunc autem, per unitionem Dei et hominis adsumpti, diuinitatis et humanitatis, aeternalis et temporalis, collegium, uetus et nouum duo testamenta, alterum quod promisit et alterum quod promissum Christum ostendit, Ecclesiae ubera cognoscuntur, quorum medio Christus commorari probatur." The Venerable Bede cites the commentary. The historical influence of Apponius on Bernard on the approximation of the Verb is plausible.

19 Bernard of Clairvaux, On the *Song of Songs I*, pp. 9-10. Leclercq (*SC* 441), SCC 2.3, l. 1-15: "Et ibi quidem contactus labiorum complexum significat animorum: hic autem confoederatio naturarum divinis humana componit, quae in terra sunt, et quae in coelis pacificans. Ipse est enim pax nostra, qui fecit utraque unum (Ephes. II, 14)."

20 Bernard of Clairvaux, On the *Song of Songs I*, pp. 9-10. Leclercq (*SC* 441), SCC 2.3, l. 1-15: "Felix osculum, ac stupenda dignatione mirabile, in quo non os ori imprimitur, sed Deus homini unitur."

21 On the body (*corps*) and flesh (*chair*) distinction, see Emmanuel Falque, "Y at-il une chair sans corps?" *Phénoménologie et Christianisme chez Michel Henry* (Paris: Les Éditions du Cerf, 2004); Emmanuel Falque, *Le combat amoureux: disputes phénoménologiques et théologiques* (Paris: Hermann, 2014); Emmanuel Falque, *Dieu, la chair et l'autre: d'Irénée à Duns Scot, Épiméthée* (Paris: Presses Universitaires de France, 2008); Cécile Blanc, "L'attitude d'Origène à l'égard du corps et de la chair," *StPatr* 17 (1982): 843. On the body and desire in the context of the Middle Ages, see Jacques Le Goff and Nicolas Truong, *Une histoire du corps au Moyen Age* (Paris: Liana Levi, 2003).

22 H. M. Diepen, "L'assumptus Homo patristique," *Revue thomiste*, 63 (1963): 225-245; 363-388 and 64 (1964), 32-52; 364-386.

the Word and the kissed is the flesh. The paradigm strongly points at the generative aspect of desire (desiring-production) whereby the desire expressed and received simultaneously compacts (*compacto*) a person (*persona*). The assumed man (*assumpti hominis*) as the compacted man transforms and in a sense (re)generates or reconfigures human existence in the matrix of a metamorphosing finitude as well as the distance or the space of time between longing and fulfilment, between desire and body. The flesh of Christ, not united to the Word previously and not pre-existent, unlike the Word (source-beginning), is generated in the act of divine desire to assume the totality of humanity (*assumpti hominis*). As such, the fullness of divinity is corporeally imprinted (*imprimere*) by the kiss of the Verb in a singular and unique manner.[23] While the transformation of the Word into body is restricted to Christ, "the mediator of God and of men" (1 Tm 2.5), the process of assumption serves, within an analogical analysis, as a paradigmatic framework to understand the logic of (human) desire as desiring-production. This logic has a phenomenological structure. First, a form of divine desire allows for the peaceful integration of the divine in human nature, i.e., the spiritual with the corporeal.[24] Furthermore, and more generally, desire is generative (*componere*) of *corporeality* or *body*, of the fullness of humanity *tout court* and as such, is performative and efficient like the Word. Generation or composition (*componere*) includes order or (re)configuration. Then, the *body* as the totality of humanity assumed, transformed and (re)generated by God in the Word (*assumpti hominis*) emerges as the receptacle of divinity and indeed the locus of divine manifestation. God is manifested in the reconfiguration or generation of desire as body. In view of all of these, the kiss of the Word, as a single event (*singulariter*) or a first coming, conditions and transforms all subsequent experiences of *a* kiss as visitations of the Word. This is because the transformation of humanity in the incarnation of the Word warrants the corporeality of the kiss. Desire as generative of *a body* is only due to the incarnation of God not only as a possibility, but also even as the source and fulfillment of desire itself. Before the incarnation, the desire (*cuperentque*) and sighing for the kiss could not find the fullness of its expression in the absence of *a body* because desire seeks a body to receive it (*accipere*). In other words, the transformation of human desire passes through the *body* of divine desire in the one single kiss of the Word. Bernard describes it thus: "This was the kiss for *which just men yearned* under the old dispensation,

23 Bernard of Clairvaux, On the *Song of Songs I*, pp. 9-10. Leclercq (*SC* 441), SCC 2.3, l. 1-15: "cum ei se corporaliter plenitudo omnis divinitatis indulsit."

24 Bernard of Clairvaux, On the *Song of Songs I*, pp. 9-10. Leclercq (*SC* 441), SCC 2.3, l. 1-15: "confoederatio naturarum divinis humana componit."

foreseeing as they did that in him they would 'find happiness and a crown of rejoicing,' because in him were hidden 'all the jewels of wisdom and knowledge'. Hence their *longing to taste* that fullness of his."[25] The reception of desire in a body and by a body is the very production of a body. Moreover, the receptacle as which it functions is constituted by the desire it receives. Hence, to receive or to compact in the process of assumption, is to transform, and to transform is to generate. The incarnation of the Word is generative of bodies. The body as receptacle of desire therefore is also efficient. From the first kiss (desire of the Fathers) to the second kiss (the incarnation of Christ), divine desire passes *from above*, from words through *the* Word, through the body, to transform human experience by rendering it efficient. The human body, like the generative desire which produces it, becomes generative as well. The desire of the body transforms desire, and then desire transforms the body into generation. The third kiss (revelation of the mystery of Christ) relies on the body as a sign of fulfillment of a desired promise in the kiss, thereby mapping the itinerary of desire *from below*. No longer is it divine desire but rather human desire passing from the pressure of a promise necessitating a fulfilment to the inevitability of experience as act. The third kiss frames human desire as entering through word, resulting in expectation, demanding fulfillment and finally producing experience. The kiss is a *shifting* sign of production.

There is a third kiss. According to another interpretation (*alium sensum*), the third kiss is a kind of reflection on the entry of God (*incipio*) in the beginning of human history, which remains for the Word a source-beginning or *the beginning without beginning* (*principium sine principio*) in the flesh. With the third kiss, the Abbot of Clairvaux outlines an entry of God in human thought (*cogitatio*) even prior to the incarnation such that the word (thought)[26] of the Word preceeds the Word in the flesh. This entry of God is a kind temporary ailment to human longing while waiting for the fulfillment of the promises in the Word made flesh. Bernard writes, "Those indeed who foreknew also *proclaimed that Christ would come as man, and with him, peace.* Enlightened from above they *confidently spread abroad the message*. John, the forerunner of

25 Bernard of Clairvaux, On the *Song of Songs I*, pp. 9-10. Leclercq (*SC* 441), SCC 2.3, l. 15-20: "Ad hoc igitur osculum sanctus quisque antiqui temporis suspirabat; eo quod jucunditatem et exsultationem thesaurizari super eum, et thesauros omnes sapientiae et scientiae in ipso absconditos praesentirent (Coloss. II, 3), cuperentque et ipsi de plenitudine ejus accipere."

26 B. M. Kienzle, "*Verbum Dei et Verba Bernardi*: The Function of Language in Bernard's Second Sermon for Peter and Paul," *Cîteaux commentarii cistercienses* 42, no. 1-4 (1991): 149-159; Umberto Eco and Costantino Marmo, eds. *On the Medieval Theory of Signs*, Vol. 21 (Amsterdam: John Benjamins Publishing, 1989).

the Lord, *recognizing the fulfillment of that prophecy in his own time*, declared: '*Grace and truth* have come through Jesus Christ.' *In our time every Christian can discover by experience that this is true*."[27] Therefore, Bernard introduces the interpretation (*sensum*) of the third kiss within the framework of an entry, *the* entry of God in thought, and admits to recognizing the pleasure (*placere*) which words produce. He writes, "'Surely the Lord *God does nothing without revealing his secret to his servants*, the prophets.' *What he did reveal however was obscure to many*. For in those days *faith was a rare thing on the earth, and hope but a faint impulse in the heart*."[28] Thought is affective word in action, and the body reveals the ideal in this way. Moreover, thought by means of words is prior to action. Just as words produce pleasure (*placere*), so too the entry of God in thought (*cogitare*), vindicated by experience, produces a satisfaction in longing expectation of the incarnation of God. The entry of God before the coming (*ante adventum*) of the Word in the third kiss, which is the kiss of peace (*osculum pacem*), consists in thinking thoughts of peace (*cogitare cogitationes pacem*).[29] The kiss of peace is a motif which Bernard develops early in *On the Song of Songs*, but only in the third kiss does its exposition reach full force.[30] In the third kiss, the kiss of peace (*osculum pacis*), thinking thoughts of peace precede the actual kiss of peace because "[s]urely the Lord God does nothing without revealing his secret to his servants, the prophets (Amos 3.7)."[31] As a

27 Bernard of Clairvaux, On the *Song of Songs I*, pp. 10-11. Leclercq (*SC* 441), SCC 2.4, l. 1-17: "Qui vero praesciebant, ipsi et praedicebant, et cum ipso pacem. Unde quidam eorum: Et pax erit, inquit, in terra nostra, cum venerit (Mich. V, 5). Imo per ipsum Dei gratiam homines recuperaturos cum omni fiducia, sicut divinitus acceperant, praedicabant. Quod et praecursor Domini Joannes suo tempore impletum agnovit, et perhibuit: Gratia, inquiens, et veritas per Jesum Christum facta est (Joan. I, 17): et ita verum esse omnis nunc Christianus populus experitur."

28 Bernard of Clairvaux, On the *Song of Songs I*, pp. 10-11. Leclercq (*SC* 441), SCC 2.4, l. 1-17: "Sentio, placet vobis quod dicitur: sed accipite et alium sensum. Non latuit sanctos et ante adventum salvatoris, Deum super mortalium genus cogitare cogitationes pacis (Jerem. XXIX, 11). Nec enim faceret verbum super terram, quod non revelaret servis suis prophetis (Amos III, 7). Erat tamen verbum hoc absconditum a multis (Luc. XVIII, 34). Fuit namque in tempore illo rara fides in terris, et tenuis admodum spes in pluribus quoque illorum qui exspectabant redemptionem Israel."

29 Kiril Petkov, *The Kiss of Peace: Ritual, Self, and Society in the High and Late Medieval West* (Leiden: Brill, 2003); Ronald G. Musto, "The Kiss of Peace: Ritual, Self, and Society in the High and Late Medieval West," *Speculum* 80, no. 2 (2005): 652-54.

30 The kiss of peace in Ch. Mohrmann, SBO II, p. XIV. Bernard of Clairvaux, On the *Song of Songs I*, p. 86. Leclercq (*SC* 441), SCC 2.3, n. 1.

31 Bernard of Clairvaux, On the *Song of Songs I*, pp. 10-11. Leclercq (*SC* 441), SCC 2.4, l. 1-17: "Sentio, placet vobis quod dicitur: sed accipite et alium sensum. Non latuit sanctos et ante adventum salvatoris, Deum super mortalium genus cogitare cogitationes pacis (Jerem. XXIX, 11). Nec enim faceret verbum super terram, quod non revelaret servis suis prophetis

maxim of divine revelation, the entry of God is effectuated first as the thinking of a thought, thinking thought, which constitutes the condition for the accomplishment (*facere*) of that thought in the Word. The thought in question is the coming of Christ in the flesh (*Christum in carne venturum*) and the peace, or appeasing of the longing fulfilled, which accompanies it. There is yet another movement in the unfolding of the third kiss. While the Word or thinking of the thought is manifested *as* word, it remains hidden from many ([*e*]*rat tamen verbum hoc absconditum a multis*). All experience the desire for peace, but only after the coming of Christ in the flesh. Thought is prior to action, and thought becomes complete with body and from thought to action, body enters through desire. An inherent dual suggestion is telling. On the one hand, Bernard seems to refer to the third kiss as an experience, such that the longing for the Word revealed in thought is the beginning of the experience of the desire fulfilled in hopeful expectation. On the other hand, the thought of experience, a first moment of revelation, is complimented subsequently with the experience of thought for which the flesh (*caro*) is fundamental as the kiss of peace (*osculum pacis*). Desire of the body and the body of desire oscillates between lack and production in the revelation of the performative Word as body. In the counter-blow of desire on the body, desire affects body and produces body. The Word or Verb preforms body through the efficacious signification of desire. The outcome of the three kisses is revelation or the *production of a body*.

2.2 The Production of a Body

The production of a body is the generative transformation of desire in the *metamorphosis of love*. From 'the thought of experience' to 'the experience of thought' – the production of the body's desire or desiring-production – the counter-blow (*choc en retour*) performs a transformation of desire from body to desire and back from desire to body, from *experience* as ex-*per*-ience.[32] That

---

(Amos III, 7). Erat tamen verbum hoc absconditum a multis (Luc. XVIII, 34). Fuit namque in tempore illo rara fides in terris, et tenuis admodum spes in pluribus quoque illorum qui exspectabant redemptionem Israel."

32 Emmanuel Falque, *Le livre le l'expérience: d'Anselme de Cantorbéry à Bernard de Clairvaux* (Paris: Cerf, 2017); Emmanuel Falque, "Saint Bernard et le champ de l'expérience," in *Expérience phiosophique et experience mystique*, ed. P. Capelle (Paris: Cerf, 2005); Hilary Knight, "Saint Bernard of Clairvaux on Experience," *Medieval Mystical Theology* 24, no. 1 (2015): 59-79; KIlian McDonnell, "Spirit and Experience in Bernard of Clairvaux," *Theological Studies* 58, no. 1 (1997): 3-18; F. Gastaldelli, "Ricerca ed esperienza di Dio secondo san Bernardo," *Rivista cistercense*, 8 (1991), 133-54.

is, the experience of the kiss in the body (the second kiss) is a *sign*[33] of peace (the third kiss). The transformation, according to the third kiss (the *sign* of peace), depends on the signification of the word (experienced in thought) and on the enacting of the Word itself in its efficiency (Augustine) and in the thought of experience.[34] Bernard describes signification as urgency, in delayed expectation for fulfillment (transition from thought to act), in the longing of the few to whom the third kiss (the *sign* of peace) is eventually revealed. What matters after initial manifestation ('entry of God' in thought)[35] is no longer or not *only* the revelation itself (content), nor the number of manifestations in various forms (quantity), nor again the source (origin), but rather the temporal and semiological *tension* of desire produced by the unfulfilled expectation (duration) of fulfillment. The body longs for spirit. What matters, succinctly put, is the resistance to transformative manifestation. The delay of an expected fulfillment is framed in terms of signification, i.e., the (in)capacity of words (promises and prophecies) to in fact reveal and *do* in experience what they signify.[36] A promise thus becomes an unbearable reminder of absence. This is so because the desire for the kiss or longing is not only complete when it is efficient by means of the body. In other words, human desire for God (*from below*) *tends towards* a body and indeed *needs* a body (*from above*) as a receptacle for the (re)generative performativity of desire, whereby transformation in the *metamorphosis of love* is desiring-production of bodies.

The logic of desire follows a transformative itinerary from desire to production to yield desiring-production. First, there is expectation. Bernard frames the *need* of the longing of desire to *take* a body in terms of *expectation*: "while the prophets *continued to foretell* the covenant, and its author continued to *delay his coming*, the faith of the people *never ceased to waver*. Hence men

33 Umberto Eco and Costantino Marmo, *On the Medieval Theory of Signs* (Amsterdam: John Benjamins Publishing, 1989).

34 G. R. Evans, *The Church in the Early Middle Ages* (London: IB Tauris, 2007); James Monti, *A Sense of the Sacred: Roman Catholic Worship in the Middle Ages* (San Francisco: Ignatius Press, 2012).

35 Emmanuel Falque, *Le Livre de l'expérience: d'Anselme de Cantorbéry à Bernard de Clairvaux* (Paris: Cerf, 2017).

36 Robert Markus, *St. Augustine on Signs* (Assen: Vangorcum, 1957); Karen Kilby, "Susannah Ticciati, *A New Apophaticism: Augustine and the Redemption of Signs*," *Augustinian Studies* 47, no. 2 (2016): 258-61; Susannah Ticciati, *A New Apophaticism: Augustine and the Redemption of Signs* (Leiden: Brill, 2013); Darrel B. Jackson, "The Theory of Signs in St. Augustine's *De doctrina christiana*," *Revue d'Etudes Augustiniennes et Patristiques* 15, no. 1-2 (1969): 9-49; John M. Rist, *Augustine: Ancient thought Baptized* (Cambridge: Cambridge University Press, 1994); Rowan Williams, "Language, Reality and Desire in Augustine's *De Doctrina*," *Literature and Theology* 3, no. 2 (1989): 138-50.

grumbled at the postponements of the coming of this Prince of Peace so often *proclaimed by the mouth* of his holy prophets."[37] Subsequently, and secondly, there is delay. Doubt is the response to the despair that results from the *delay* of fulfillment. Bernard writes, "[a]s doubts about the fulfillment of the prophecies began to recur, *all the more eagerly did they make demands for the kiss, the sign of the promised reconcilement.* It was as if a *voice from among the people* would *challenge the prophets of peace*: 'How much longer are you going to *keep us in suspense*? You are *always foretelling a peace that is never realized*; you *promise a world of good but trouble on trouble comes*.'"[38] Thirdly, desire undergoes *transmission* as transference. In the midst of the struggle to maintain hope in the face of despair, expectation is transmitted or transferred. The Abbot of Clairvaux continues: "[a]t various times in the past and in various different ways this *same hope was fostered* by angels among our ancestors, who in turn *have passed the tidings on to us*. 'Peace! Peace!' they say, 'but there is no peace. If God desires to convince me of that benevolent will of his, so often *vouched for by the prophets but not yet revealed by the event, then let him kiss me with the kiss of his mouth*, and so by this token of peace make my peace secure. For *how shall I any longer put my trust in mere words*?"[39] Fourth and lastly, there is correspondence. The authenticity of truth in embodied transformative manifestation consists in the correspondence of words and actions. The tension of hope and despair was such that at one point it was *necessary* for action to secure words: "It is necessary now that words be vindicated by action."[40] Desire produces a body in and to the extent that the transformative approximation of word to action corresponds to the ensuing desiring-production.

---

37 Bernard of Clairvaux, On the *Song of Songs I*, pp. 11-12. Leclercq (*SC* 441), SCC 2.5, l. 1-6: "Caeterum illis praenuntiantibus pacem, moram autem faciente auctore pacis, nutabat populi fides, dum non erat qui redimeret, neque qui salvum faceret. Itaque causabantur homines moras, quod ille toties nuntiatus necdum veniret princeps pacis, sicut locutus fuerat per os sanctorum, qui a saeculo sunt, prophetarum ejus."

38 Bernard of Clairvaux, On the *Song of Songs I*, pp. 11-2. Leclercq (*SC* 441), SCC 2.5, l. 6-11: "et suspectas habentes promissiones, signum promissae reconciliationis, quod est osculum, flagitabant; ac si nuntiis pacis unus quilibet de populo responderet, Quousque tollitis animas nostras? Jam olim praedicitis pacem, et non venit; promittitis bona, et adhuc turbatio."

39 Bernard of Clairvaux, On the *Song of Songs I*, pp. 11-2. Leclercq (*SC* 441), SCC 2.5, l. 11-18: "Ecce hoc ipsum multifarie, multisque modis et angeli patribus, et patres nostri annuntiarunt nobis dicentes: Pax, pax; et non est pax (Jerem. VI, 14). Si mihi vult esse persuasum Deus, quod de suae beneplacito voluntatis tam crebra jam legatione respondet, nec exhibet; osculetur me osculo oris sui, sicque in signo pacis faciat de pace securum. Nam verbis jam quomodo credam?"

40 Bernard of Clairvaux, On the *Song of Songs I*, pp. 11-2. Leclercq (*SC* 441), SCC 2.5, l. 18: "Opus magis est opere verba firmari."

Framed differently, desiring-production consists in the transformative correspondence of word (desire) to body (production). The word (as *signum*) signifies the Word (what is *signified*) efficaciously, not as symbol (description) or phenomenon (indication), but as embodied action (transformative prescription): the word (response to human desire) is *preformed* (*firmare*) through the Word (initiative of divine desire) in the entry of God in thought. For performance to occur, the role of the body and of the flesh is capital. Hence, Bernard astutely integrates the epitaph by Lactance into the account of the transition of the experience of the Word. Lactance's epithet goes, "[a]cts must declare words."[41] Bernard writes, "[*i*]*t is necessary now that words be vindicated by action.* [...] *prove the truth of their words by his own advent*, so often the keynote of their *predictions*, because *unless he comes they can do nothing*. He sent his servant *bearing a staff*, but neither *voice nor life is forthcoming. I do not rise up, I am not awakened, I am not shaken out of the dust, nor do I breathe in hope*, if the Prophet himself does not come down and kiss me with the kiss of his mouth.'"[42] Temporal succession does not, as of yet, merge desire and production. It focuses, however, on the issue at hand, namely, that desire is incomplete without a body.

Desire is complete in the body of desire. Moreover, for Bernard, desire is production only when desire is completed by a body. Returning to Lactance, acts declare and in so doing give weight to the full meaning of words. Before the Word in the flesh, the many signs (*signum*) of the object of human longing (the Word) were inefficient, thus lacking the capacity to speak and signify fully through speech (*vox*), and lacking also the capacity to signify efficaciously (*vita*). Bernard writes, "He sent his servant bearing a staff, but neither voice nor life is forthcoming."[43] Thus, just as the words of Christ become the words of humans in the expression of longed manifestation, so too, the Word becomes the flesh of all after and precisely because of the incarnation, the word in the body. Bernard beautifully expresses the union of humanity with Christ mediator (*mediatorem Dei Filium*) in the third kiss, the kiss of peace, using

41 Lactance, *Institutions divines*, 4.23.9 (*SC* 377), 194: "Superest ut factis verba firmentur (il est donc a confirmer les paroles par les actes)," as cited in Leclercq (*SC* 441), SCC 2.4, pp. 88-9, n. 2.

42 Bernard of Clairvaux, On the *Song of Songs I*, pp. 11-12. Leclercq (*SC* 441), SCC 2.5, l. 18-25: "Opus magis est opere verba firmari. Probet veridicos nuntios suos Deus (si tamen nuntii ejus sunt), et sequatur eos ipse, ut saepius promiserunt, quia sine ipso possunt facere nihil. Misit puerum, tulit baculum, et necdum est vox neque vita (IV Reg. IV, 29-31). Non surgo, non suscitor, non excutior de pulvere, non respiro in spem, si non propheta ipse descendat, et osculetur me osculo oris sui."

43 Bernard of Clairvaux, On the *Song of Songs I*, pp. 11-2. Leclercq (*SC* 441), SCC 2.5, l. 21-22: "Misit puerum, tulit baculum, et necdum est vox neque vita."

the language of the union of man and woman "in one flesh" (Gen 2.23). He writes, "When I come to *recognize that he is truly mine*, then I shall feel secure in welcoming the Son of God as mediator. Not even a shadow of mistrust can then exist, for after all he is my brother, and *my own flesh*. It is impossible that I should be spurned by him who is *bone from my bones, and flesh from my flesh*."[44] Unity signifies the completion of desire in a body. Moreover, a single body signifies *all* desire. The desire for God, transmitted through the expectation of the prophets across the space of time, is remarkably accomplished (*exigere*) in the third kiss: "We should by now have come to understand how the discontent of our ancestors displayed a need for this sacrosanct kiss, that is, the mystery of the incarnate word, for faith, hard-pressed throughout the ages with trouble upon trouble, was ever on the point of failing, [...] *yielding to discouragement*, murmured against the promises of God. I suggest that you will find it to be the teaching of the Scriptures [...]."[45] Desire gives words their signifying power only to the extent that words are rendered efficacious and therefore performative in the generative process of the Word made flesh. The *body* is efficient signification of desire in a twofold sense. First, as a fulfillment of an expectation and, second, by means of unification of *all* bodies in the *one* body of Christ through the incarnation. That is, all desire assumes a single directionality by the accomplishment (*exigere*) of manifestation (as efficient signification) in the body of Christ. The single body of Christ renders all desire efficient by means of unity. The body is the locus of signification. The presence of the body of Christ (*de carnis praesentia*) is the assurance of the longing for a sign of peace (the third kiss): the body *is* the certainty of the performative signification of the sign. Bernard continues: "Therefore because Christ was *late in coming*, and the whole human race in danger of being *lost in despair*, so convinced was it that human weakness was an object of contempt with no *hope of the reconciliation* with God through *a grace so frequently promised*, those good men whose f*aith remained strong eagerly longed for the more powerful assurance that only his human presence could convey*. They prayed intensely for a sign that the covenant was about to be restored for the sake of a spiritless,

---

44 Bernard of Clairvaux, On the *Song of Songs I*, pp. 11-2. Leclercq (*SC* 441), SCC 2.6, l. 11-4: "Securus suscipio mediatorem Dei Filium, quem agnosco et meum. Minime plane jam mihi suspectus erit: frater enim et caro mea est. Puto enim, spernere me jam non poterit, os de ossibus meis, et caro de carne mea."

45 Bernard of Clairvaux, On the *Song of Songs I*, pp. 12-3. Leclercq (*SC* 441), SCC 2.7, l. 1-6: "Ita ergo vetus querela sacrosanctum osculum, id est incarnandi Verbi mysterium, exigebat, dum longa et molesta exspectatione fatigata fides deficeret, et infidelis populus adversus promissa Dei victus taedio murmuraret. Adinventio mea est, si non hoc idem et vos recognoscitis de Scripturis."

faithless people."[46] Body makes presence the object or subject of desire. Body therefore efficiently signifies the signifier in transformative configuration. The transformation from 'the thought of experience' to 'the experience of thought' occurs in the performative and generative locus of signification where word which longs for the signifier is signified by taking a body. The sign generates the body and is manifest as the accomplishment of desire. As the discussion of the third kiss closes, Bernard appeals to the reader's experience of reading the scripture where all these things may be found. Understanding presupposes experience from whence to draw recognition (*recognoscere*) after hearing: "I suggest that you will find it to be the teaching of the Scriptures."[47] The hermeneutic circle of the 'third kiss' is thus sealed. In the "hermeneutics of desire", the 'thought of experience' and the 'experience of thought' overlap. Sign and signifier collapse: to signify is not to correspond, but to reconfigure and generate. This is the fourth kiss.

Sign and signified collapse *in* the body. The last kiss, the fourth kiss, concludes Bernard's hermeneutics of desire and advances the itinerary of transformations of desire, from the thought of experience to the experience of thought. The fourth kiss tracks the attitude towards the manifestation of the desired sign of peace, namely the incarnation of Christ. In the exposition of the fourth kiss, Bernard presents the figure of Simeon to convey the structure of divine manifestation – the entry of God at *the beginning without beginning* – and to convey the paradigmatic attitude towards the experience of the manifestation of the Word (*signum*) in the flesh as *the* Messiah. In manifestation, the figure of Simeon remains important because in its promise, expectations and embodied fulfillment coincide. The Biblical passage reads, Simeon "said to Mary his mother, 'You see this child: he is destined for the fall and for the rising of many in Israel, destined to be a sign that is rejected- and a sword will pierce your own soul too-so that the secret thoughts of many may be laid bare'."[48] This infamous

46 Bernard of Clairvaux, On the *Song of Songs I*, pp. 12-3. Leclercq (*SC* 441), SCC 2.7, l. 21-8: "Ne ergo universum genus humanum, moram faciente Christo, desperatione periret, dum se contemni suspicaretur infirma mortalitas, suaeque reconciliationis cum Deo de gratia toties repromissa diffideret; sancti qui de spiritu certi erant, certitudinem de carnis praesentia exoptabant, ac signum reformandae pacis propter pusillanimes et incredulos omni instantia requirebant."

47 Bernard of Clairvaux, On the *Song of Songs I*, pp. 12-3. Leclercq (*SC* 441), SCC 2.7, l. 5-6: "Adinventio mea est, si non hoc idem et vos recognoscitis de Scripturis."

48 Translation from the Jerusalem Bible. Cf. Luke 2.25-35, Latin Vulgate by Jerome: "Et ecce homo erat in Jerusalem, cui nomen Simeon, et homo iste justus, et timoratus, exspectans consolationem Israël : et Spiritus Sanctus erat in eo. Et responsum acceperat a Spiritu Sancto, non visurum se mortem, nisi prius videret Christum Domini. Et venit in spiritu in templum. Et cum inducerent puerum Jesum parentes ejus, ut facerent secundum

passage (*Nunc Dimittis*) is at the heart of Bernard's exposition of the fourth kiss and is the paradigm of prophetic fulfillment. The passage would have naturally echoed Bernard's own experience of the infant child's visitation on Christmas Eve. Bernard writes, "Oh root of Jesse, that stands as *a signal to the peoples*, how many prophets and kings *wanted to see what you see, and never saw it*! *Happy above them all is Simeon*, by God's mercy still bearing fruit in old age! *He rejoiced to think that he would see the long-desired sign. He saw it and was glad*; and having *received the kiss of peace he is allowed to go in peace*, but not before he had *told his audience* that Jesus was born to be *a sign that would be rejected*."[49] The figure of Simeon – the name means "God is listening" – is of capital importance for Bernard because it brings all three kisses together in the manifestation of the Christ in the flesh, the fourth kiss: the desire of the prophets (the first kiss), the incarnation (the second kiss) and the revelation of the mystery (the third kiss). Simeon sees the prophecy fulfilled: the longing of words invoke the presence of the body. Divine manifestation in the flesh follows the logic of desire. At the crossroads of Simeon's life is the desire and expectation of the prophets to see Christ (the first kiss). Furthermore, the longing resulting from the expectation of the birth of Christ is fulfilled by the incarnation (the second kiss). Finally, Simeon receives a direct revelation (in thought) of the mystery of Christ from the Holy Spirit (the third kiss). While the life of Simeon simultaneously brings the first three kisses together, these occur independently of each other in longing (the first kiss), manifestation (the third kiss), and accomplishment (the fourth kiss). Yet these come together *only for Simeon* upon beholding the presence of Christ in the flesh (the fourth kiss). The divine manifestation then is only complete when Simeon realizes that the first three kisses are contained in the fourth kiss, which constitutes longing, manifestation and accomplishment by means of the body of Christ. The body is as such the ultimate locus

---

consuetudinem legis pro eo, et ipse accepit eum in ulnas suas: et benedixit Deum, et dixit: Nunc dimittis servum tuum Domine, secundum verbum tuum in pace: quia viderunt oculi mei salutare tuum, quod parasti ante faciem omnium populorum: lumen ad revelationem gentium, et gloriam plebis tuæ Israël. Et erat pater ejus et mater mirantes super his quæ dicebantur de illo. Et benedixit illis Simeon, et dixit ad Mariam matrem ejus: Ecce positus est hic in ruinam, et in resurrectionem multorum in Israël, et in signum cui contradicetur: et tuam ipsius animam pertransibit gladius ut revelentur ex multis cordibus cogitationes."

49 Bernard of Clairvaux, On the *Song of Songs I*, pp. 13-4. Leclercq (*SC* 441), SCC 2.8, l. 1-7: "O radix Jesse, qui slas in signum populorum! (Isai. XI, 10.) Quam multi reges et prophetae voluerunt te videre, et non viderunt! Felix tamen ex omnibus Simeon, cujus senectus in misericordia uberi! Is nempe exultavit ut videret desiderii signum: et vidit, et gavisus est; acceptoque osculo pacis in pace dimittitur, ante tamen aperte pronuntians, Jesum esse natum in signum, cui contradicendum erat (Luc. II, 25-35)."

and transformative experience of human desire for God. The logic of desire, then, governs the response to the collapse of the signifier and the signified into the body. Why is this significant? How the three kisses are integrated in the fourth kiss is important because the dynamic before and after the integration governs the manifestation of the sign (*signum*) and the reaction of those who perceive Christ made manifest in the flesh (the fourth kiss) starting with, and after Simeon. Previously, in the first three kisses, the dynamic and transformation of desire with regards to the body and experience was charted, now the figure of Simeon furnishes the elements of the response to the experience of divine manifestation. The first elements are exultation (*exultare*) and rejoicing (*gavire*). For Simeon (literally meaning "he who hears"), to see (*videre*) is to rejoice (*exultare*). Simeon recognized the experience of the vision of the promise fulfilled in the presence of the body because the vision echoes the sound of the Word previously revealed. Thus, longing of the ear is transformed by the body in the recognition of experience through the desire of the eye in the fourth kiss.[50] The touch (body) of the fourth kiss joins Word (hearing) and vision (sight). The efficiency of the sign as such lies in desire itself. The second dimension of the dynamic and transformation of the sign (*signum*) is appreciated by contrasting the response of Simeon to the variety of other responses to the incarnation. Different responses are possible, in spite of the inherent efficacy of the fourth kiss, because the sign in the presence of the flesh requires the predisposition and capacity to understand the sign in experience: experience is the preamble to recognize the kiss. Since there are different personal experiences, there are also different personal responses. However, all of these responses follow the logic of desire.

A single body yields varying responses to the sign of peace (*signo pacis*) manifested in the fourth kiss. The first response, upon seeing the desired sign (*desiderii signum*), is the response of Simeon who sees (*videre*) and who, upon seeing, then rejoices (*exultare*). To see is also to receive the fourth kiss as an efficient kiss of peace. Hence, after receiving (*acceptare*) the kiss of peace, Simeon *goes* in peace.[51] As a gift, the fourth kiss transforms the desire of expectation through the mediation of the sight of Christ manifested in the flesh, into peace. The kiss of peace is therefore performative *only* for Simeon in whose experience the first three kisses are integrated. Experience is the condition for the receptacle of the transformation of human desire for God through the

50 Bernard of Clairvaux, On the *Song of Songs I*, pp. 13-4. Leclercq (*SC* 441), SCC 2.8, l. 1-7: "Is nempe exsultavit ut videret desiderii signum: et vidit, et gavisus est."

51 Bernard of Clairvaux, On the *Song of Songs I*, pp. 13-4. Leclercq (*SC* 441), SCC 2.8, l. 1-7: "acceptoque osculo pacis, in pace dimittitur."

flesh. Simeon's experience of the kiss of peace culminates in the declaration (*pronuntiare*) of Christ, also a sign, this time one of contradiction.[52] The sign of the people (*signum populorum*), which is the sign of desire (*signum desiderii*), is manifested in the body.This manifestation brings the first three kisses together in the fourth kiss, which is the sign of peace (*signum pacis*), where the word becomes efficient through the Word by giving peace, and by being peace. Paradoxically, the sign of peace for Simeon is also the sign of contradiction (*signum contradicendum*). The first response to the sign is fragmentation. The second response is the response of those who, unlike Simeon, experience the manifestation of the fourth kiss as a sign of contradiction. Bernard writes, "*Time proved how true this was.* No sooner had the sign of peace arisen than it was opposed, by those, that is, who hated peace; for his peace is with men of good-will, but for the evil-minded he is a stone to stumble over, a rock to bring men down. Herod accordingly was perturbed, and so was the whole of Jerusalem. Christ came to his own domain, and his own people did not accept him."[53] The experience of Simeon at the threshold of the first three kisses which allows for the reception (*acceptare*) of the kiss of peace is framed in terms of good will (*bonae voluntatis*). Christ is a sign of contradiction for those who have not integrated the first three kisses of experience or for those of ill will (*malevolis voluntatis*), "for the evil-minded he is 'a stone to stumble over, a rock to bring men down.'"[54] The figure of Herod represents the second attitude to the kiss of peace and illustrates the internal disposition, which accounts for the failure to recognize the kiss of peace precisely *as* a kiss of peace. The second response shifts from fragmentation to confusion. The third attitude is the attitude of the shepherds in whom the fullness of the promise of the sign of peace is accomplished in the kiss of peace in Christ: "Those shepherds [...] were fortunate for they were gladdened by *a vision of this sign*."[55] Bernard continues, "Herod, as you know, *desired to see him*, but because *his motive was not genuine he did not succeed. The sign of peace was given only to men of good-will*, hence to Herod

52 Bernard of Clairvaux, On the *Song of Songs I*, pp. 13-4. Leclercq (*SC* 441), SCC 2.8, l. 1-7: "acceptoque osculo pacis, in pace dimittitur; ante tamen aperte pronuntians Iesum esse natum in signum cui contradicendum erat."

53 Bernard of Clairvaux, On the *Song of Songs I*, pp. 13-4. Leclercq (*SC* 441), SCC 2.8, l. 8-13: "Omnino ita fuit. Contradictum est exorto signo pacis, sed ab his qui oderunt pacem: nam pax hominibus bonae voluntatis, malevolis autem petra scandali, et lapis offensionis (ibid., 14). Herodes denique turbatus est, et omnis Jerosolyma eum illo (Matth. II, 3): siquidem in propria venit, et sui eum non receperunt (Joan. I, 11)."

54 Bernard of Clairvaux, On the *Song of Songs I*, pp. 13-4. Leclercq (*SC* 441), SCC 2.8, l. 8-13: "malevolis autem petra scandali et lapis offensionis."

55 Bernard of Clairvaux, On the *Song of Songs I*, pp. 13-4. Leclercq (*SC* 441), SCC 2.8, l. 12-13: "Felices illi in sua pernoctatione pastores, qui signi hujus visione digni habiti sunt."

and others like him was given the sign of the prophet Jonah."[56] Then, "The angel said to the shepherds: '*Here is a sign for you,' What sign?* The sign *promised* by the angels, *sought* after by the people, *foretold* by the prophets."[57] He continues, "this is the sign that the *Lord Jesus has now brought into existence and revealed to you*, a sign by which the *incredulous are made believers*, the *dispirited are made hopeful* and the *fervent achieve security*."[58] Finally, the content of signification: "This therefore is the sign for you. But as a sign what does it signify? It reveals mercy, grace, peace, the peace that has no end."[59] Moreover, "the sign is this: 'You will find a baby [...] lying in a manger. God himself, however, is in this baby, reconciling the world to himself."[60] The narrative continues, "He will be put to death for your sins and raised to life to justify you, so that made righteous by faith you may be at peace with God. This was the sign of peace."[61] Then, "His wretched state blinded him to the belief that in this sign the highest things above would be joined to the lowest things below in peace."[62] The third response is a slow unfolding of recognition. Through these three responses to the body – fragmentation, confusion and recognition – the body of desire is either unification or dissolution. Hence, even among those of good will, the sign of peace either strengthens the faith of the weak or satisfies the desire of the perfect. Bernard concludes the sermon thus: "I must end this sermon. But let me sum up briefly the points we have raised. It would seem

56 Bernard of Clairvaux, On the *Song of Songs I*, pp. 13-4. Leclercq (*SC* 441), SCC 2.8, l. 16-20: "Et Herodes videre voluit; sed quia non bona voluntate, non meruit, pacis siquidem signum erat, datum tantum hominibus bonae voluntatis; Herodi vero et similibus ejus non dabitur nisi signum Jonae prophetae."

57 Bernard of Clairvaux, On the *Song of Songs I*, pp. 13-4. Leclercq (*SC* 441), SCC 2.8, l. 24-25: "Quod? Quod angeli promittebant, quod populi requirebant, quod prophetae praedixerant."

58 Bernard of Clairvaux, On the *Song of Songs I*, pp. 13-4. Leclercq (*SC* 441), SCC 2.8, l. 25-27: "hoc fecit Dominus nunc, et ostendit vobis, in quo recipiant increduli fidem, pusillanimes spem, perfecti securitatem."

59 Bernard of Clairvaux, On the *Song of Songs I*, pp. 13-4. Leclercq (*SC* 441), SCC 2.8, l. 27-29: "Hoc ergo vobis signum. Cujus rei signum? Indulgentiae, gratiae, pacis, et pacis cujus non erit finis."

60 Bernard of Clairvaux, On the *Song of Songs I*, pp. 13-4. Leclercq (*SC* 441), SCC 2.8, l. 29-32: "Hoc est ergo signum: Invenietis infantem pannis quidem involutum, et positum in praesepio (Luc. II, 12). Deus est tamen in ipso mundum reconcilians sibi (II Cor. V, 19)."

61 Bernard of Clairvaux, On the *Song of Songs I*, pp. 13-4. Leclercq (*SC* 441), SCC 2.8, l. 32-34: "Morietur propter peccata vestra, et resurget propter justificationem vestram, uta justificati per fidem, pacem habeatis ad Deum (Rom. IV, 25; V, 1)."

62 Bernard of Clairvaux, On the *Song of Songs I*, pp. 13-4. Leclercq (*SC* 441), SCC 2.8, l. 34-36: "Hoc signum pacis propheta quondam regi Achaz proponebat petendum a Domino Deo suo, sive in excelso supra, sive in inferno deorsum."

that *this holy kiss was of necessity bestowed on the world* for two reasons."[63] First, there is *the desire of the body*: "*Without* [*the kiss*] *the faith of those who wavered* would not have been strengthened, nor the *desires of the fervent appeased*."[64] Then, Bernard covers *the production of a body*: "Moreover, this kiss is no other than *the Mediator between God and man, himself a man*, Christ Jesus."[65] The three kisses, culminating in the fourth kiss or the kiss of peace, bring to the fore the full force of the consequences of the manifestation of Christ through the transformation of desire as sign (*signum*) by means of the body within the confines of *exercised* experience. Desire and body, when configured to correspond, become desiring-production, for wherein the signifier and the signified collapse, bodies are produced. In the Bernardine *metamorphosis of love*, manifestation is production in the presupposition of *desiring-production as body*.

2.3 Desiring-Production as Body

Body produces desire and desire transforms the body. Then, in the next moment of *desire and the body* in the *metamorphosis of love*, the transformation of desire becomes generation of bodies. This last moment is *desiring-production as body*. Whereas the desire of the body is *primarily* transformative at first, progressively in addition, the desire of the body becomes *exclusively* generative, and so, body is generation or production. As such, the transformation of the body by the desire of the body results in desiring-production – Deluze's formulation in French is *production désirante*. The transformation of desire from

63 Bernard of Clairvaux, On the *Song of Songs I*, p. 15. Leclercq (*SC* 441), SCC 2.9, l. 1-8: "Sermo finiendus est: sed ut quod in eo disputatum est, brevi recolligam summa, patet hoc sanctum osculum duabus ex causis necessarie indultum mundo, ut et infirmis faceret fidem, et desiderio satisfaceret perfectorum: porro ipsum osculum esse non aliud quam mediatorem Dei et hominum, hominem Jesum Christum, qui cum Patre et Spiritu sancto vivit et regnat Deus per omnia saecula saeculorum, Amen."

64 Bernard of Clairvaux, On the *Song of Songs I*, p. 15. Leclercq (*SC* 441), SCC 2.9, l. 1-8: "Sermo finiendus est: sed ut quod in eo disputatum est, brevi recolligam summa, patet hoc sanctum osculum duabus ex causis necessarie indultum mundo, ut et infirmis faceret fidem, et desiderio satisfaceret perfectorum: porro ipsum osculum esse non aliud quam mediatorem Dei et hominum, hominem Jesum Christum, qui cum Patre et Spiritu sancto vivit et regnat Deus per omnia saecula saeculorum, Amen."

65 Bernard of Clairvaux, On the *Song of Songs I*, p. 15. Leclercq (*SC* 441), SCC 2.9, l. 1-8: "Sermo finiendus est: sed ut quod in eo disputatum est, brevi recolligam summa, patet hoc sanctum osculum duabus ex causis necessarie indultum mundo, ut et infirmis faceret fidem, et desiderio satisfaceret perfectorum: porro ipsum osculum esse non aliud quam mediatorem Dei et hominum, hominem Jesum Christum, qui cum Patre et Spiritu sancto vivit et regnat Deus per omnia saecula saeculorum, Amen."

Word (*signum*) to the manifestation of the flesh in the kiss of the mouth is preceded and conditioned by experience of *the beginning without beginning* available through the hermeneutics of desire: the exercise of the sense and the disposition of good will exercised by experience is what allows for the recognition of the kiss of the mouth in its ultimate form as the fourth kiss or the kiss of peace – namely, as Christ manifested in the body.

As the counter-blow of the body's desire, in production desire returns as desire. The hermeneutics of desire thus return to experience where the kiss gradually progresses, according to a moral exegesis, from the first kiss (the kiss of the feet), through the second kiss (the kiss of the hands), only to return to the point of departure in yet another *beginning without beginning*, namely the third kiss, also called the kiss of the mouth. The four-fold sense of the kiss of the mouth is hence precluded by the three-fold sense of the kiss according to the moral exegesis as a return to the exercise of the senses. Thus, on a first moment, the hermeneutics of desire tracks the transformation of desire from Word through body, with the book of scripture as the point of departure, in longing, sings and accomplishments. On a second moment, the hermeneutics of the desire echo back to individual experience where the transformation of desire is tracked, within the framework of the book of scripture, but this time as *the book of experience*. The return to desire as generation of a body is authentic experience. Desire is authentic experience in three senses. First, experience is at the origin of desire. "Today the text we are to study is *the book of our own experience*."[66] The circle of desire at *the beginning without beginning* has an *origin* in experience. Second, experience goes in hand with desire: "I am attempting to *discover* if any of you has been privileged to say from his heart: 'Let him kiss me with the kiss of his mouth.'"[67] Third, and final, experience is its own condition and end because experience presupposes experience for the possibility of experience. Bernard writes, "Those to whom *it is given to utter these words* sincerely are comparatively few, but anyone *who has received this mystical kiss from the mouth of Christ* at least once, *seeks again that intimate*

---

66 Bernard of Clairvaux, On the *Song of Songs I*, p. 16. Leclercq (*SC* 441), SCC 3.1, l. 1-13: "Hodie legimus in libro experientiae"; Emmanuel Falque, "Saint Bernard et le champ de l'expérience," in *Expérience phiosophique et experience mystique*, ed. P. Capelle (Paris: Cerf, 2005); Emmanuel Falque, *Le Livre de l'expérience: d'Anselme de Cantorbéry à Bernard de Clairvaux* (Paris: Cerf, 2017); Emmanuel Falque, "Expérience et empathie chez Bernard de Clairvaux," *Revue des sciences philosophiques et théologiques* 89, no. 4 (2005): 655-96.

67 Bernard of Clairvaux, On the *Song of Songs I*, p. 16. Leclercq (*SC* 441), SCC 3.1, l. 1-13: "Explorare velim, si cui unquam vestrum ex sententia dicere datum sit: Osculetur me osculo oris sui (Cantic. I, 1)."

experience, and eagerly looks for its frequent renewal."[68] As such, Bernard situates the study of the kiss in the exhortation to turn to the interior well of personal experience following *the exercise of the senses*, "You must therefore *turn your attention inwards*, each one must take note of his own *particular awareness of the things I am about to discuss.*"[69] The exercised senses *transform* whereas the inward attention *preforms*. Transformation and performance, which constitute the structure of experience, are manifestations of desiring-production.

Experience reveals desire. Having described the nature of the kiss, Bernard appeals to the experience of the listener to discover whether the listener may meaningfully say, by herself, "let him kiss me with the kiss of his mouth." The spiritual kiss (*spiritual osculum*) is possible only when the senses have been exercised sufficiently to recognize *the* kiss in personal experience: personal experience echoes in the book of experience and the book of experience offers meaning to personal experience. Experience is, as was the case before, the condition for recognition: recognition of the subject of desire in the flesh.[70] For this reason, Bernard urges the listener to pry into personal experience, the locus of the spiritual kiss. What does the turn to experience reveal about the kiss? Remarkably, experience of the kiss reveals a fundamental dimension of human desire for God and the divine desire for humanity. The personal experience of the kiss does not satiate human longing (perhaps because of the absence of the body of Christ?): "I think that *nobody can grasp what it is except the one who receives it.* For it is 'a hidden manna,' and *only he who eats it still hungers for more.* It is '*a sealed fountain*' to which *no stranger has access*; only he who drinks still thirsts for more. Listen *to one who has had the experience.*"[71] Experience reveals desire and shows it unfulfilled. However, precisely in that it is unfulfilled, desire proves generative, not as lack, but as production. Desire is the origin of human experience. Experience reveals that the human desire for God in 'the kiss' generates desire and, more radically, is

---

68 Bernard of Clairvaux, On the *Song of Songs I*, p. 16. Leclercq (*SC* 441), SCC 3.1, l. 1-13: "Non est enim cujusvis hominum ex affectu hoc dicere; sed si quis ex ore Christi spirituale osculum vel semel accepit, hunc proprium experimentum profecto sollicitat, et repetit libens."

69 Bernard of Clairvaux, On the *Song of Songs I*, p. 16. Leclercq (*SC* 441), SCC 3.1, l. 1-13: "Convertimini ad vos ipsos, et attendat unusquisque conscientiam suam super his quae dicenda sunt."

70 Bernard of Clairvaux, On the *Song of Songs I*, p. 16. Leclercq (*SC* 441), SCC 3.1, l. 1-13: "Ego arbitror neminem vel scire posse quid sit, nisi qui accipit."

71 Bernard of Clairvaux, On the *Song of Songs I*, p. 16. Leclercq (*SC* 441), SCC 3.1, l. 1-13: "Ego arbitror neminem vel scire posse quid sit, nisi qui accipit: est quippe manna absconditum; et solus qui edit, adhuc esuriet. Est fons signatus, cui non communicat alienus; sed solus qui bibit, adhuc sitiet. Audi expertum, quomodo requirit. Redde mihi, inquit, laetitiam salutaris tui (Psal. L, 14)."

the very source of human experience. There is no experience outside of the experience of the kiss, which the Spirit mediates.[72] There is no experience outside the Spirit. What prevents the experience of the kiss? Whereas in the kiss of peace Simeon's longing is fulfilled in the presence of the body of Christ manifest, in the absence of such body, human longing is generative of further insatiable longing but is prevented from experiencing the kiss and from experience *tout court* by the weight of human flesh. "But a soul like mine, burdened with sins, still subject to carnal passions, devoid of any knowledge of spiritual delights, *may not presume to make such a request, almost totally unacquainted* as it is with the joys of the supernatural life."[73] The ascent from the kiss of the feet to the kiss of the hands and ultimately back to the kiss of the mouth is, from the insatiable longing for God as found in personal experience, no longer an ascent *of* the *body* (of Christ), as was the case with the four kisses, but an ascent *against* the flesh (of humanity). Desire produces experience in the two-fold complimentary movement of generation of body and resistance of flesh. Desire is preformed. This is so, for instance, in the kiss of the feet. The kiss of the feet, at the feet of the Lord, is not in *Song of Songs*, but is rooted in the liturgical practice of the washing of the feet in the office of Holy Thursday.[74] The kiss of the feet is therefore not *only* moral, but also liturgical. Unfortunately, the moral exegesis of the kiss of the feet often, and unfortunately, eclipses its liturgical embedding. In the kiss of the feet, interpreted as liturgical action, the ascent *against* the flesh occurs progressively as transformation through the *body* of Christ in Word. While the liturgical transformation, or better, metamorphosis of desire begins here, only later does it come to the fore in the body of Christ as Church, which is the extension of preformed desire. Liturgy purifies desire. The kiss of the feet as the *purgative way* (*la voie purgative*)[75] is a place (*locum*) of fear (*timore*), weeping (*flevit*) and change (*mutare*). Bernard

72 Bernard of Clairvaux, On the *Song of Songs I*, p. 16. Leclercq (*SC* 441), SCC 3.1, l. 16-17: "internorum ignara atque inexperta penitus gaudiorum." Kilian McDonnell, "Spirit and Experience in Bernard of Clairvaux," *Theological Studies* 58, no. 1 (1997): 3-18; R. Fassetta, "Le rôle de l'Esprit-Saint dans la vie spirituelle selon saint Bernard de Clairvaux," *Analecta Cisterciensia* 46 (1990), 349-90.

73 Bernard of Clairvaux, On the *Song of Songs I*, p. 16. Leclercq (*SC* 441), SCC 3.1, l. 13-17: "Minime ergo id sibi arroget mei similis anima, onerata peccatis, suaeque adhuc carnis obnoxia passionibus, quae suavitatem spiritus necdum senserit, internorum ignara atque inexperta penitus gaudiorum."

74 Bernard of Clairvaux, On the *Song of Songs I*, p. 16-18. Leclercq (*SC* 441), SCC 3.2, l. 2-4: "ad pedes severissimi Domini."

75 Pacificus Delfgaauw, "An Approach to St Bernard's *Sermons on the Song of Songs*," *COCR* 23 (1961): 152, as cited in Bernard of Clairvaux, On the *Song of Songs I*, pp. 102-3; Leclercq (*SC* 441), SCC 3.2, n. 3.

writes: "They *may not rashly aspire to the lips* [...] but let them prostrate with me in fear at the feet [...] on what grounds did she merit it? I can tell you in a few words. *She wept bitterly, she sighed deeply from her heart, she sobbed with a repentance that shook her very being*, till *the evil that inflamed her passions was cleansed away*."[76] Desires preforms essentially a reconfiguration (*purgatio*) of the matrix of finitude.

Not all desire however is reconfigured, for the matrix of finitude is not concomitant with lack but is rather the condition for the possibility of change. In the kiss of the feet, the *purgation* of desire is the transformation of the flesh through words. Not everything *of* the flesh undergoes transformation. The kiss of the mouth begins with the purgation of desire through good works in the liturgical kiss of the feet and then ascends through the kiss of the hands before finally reaching the kiss of the mouth. The second kiss in the moral exegesis is the kiss of the hand. Like the kiss of the feet, the kiss of the hands is not in the *Song of Songs*. Again, like the kiss of the feet, the kiss of the hands is likely liturgical, referring probably to the sacrament of the anointing of the hands. The kiss of the hands, following purgation, opens the ascent (*gradus*) to the illuminative stage. Bernard notes: "Though you have made *a beginning* by kissing the feet, you may not presume to *rise at once by impulse* to the kiss of the mouth; *there is a step to be surmounted in between*, an intervening kiss on the hand."[77] Change by degrees of transformation opens and conditions the horizon of generative manifestation. Such conditions regulate the origin and manifestation of desire. At this point the kiss of the hand still requires reasons (*accipe rationem*) throughout the degrees of ascent (*gradus*). Later, by the time the kiss of the mouth is reached, desire surpasses reason. These reasons

76 Bernard of Clairvaux, On the *Song of Songs I*, pp. 16-8. Leclercq (*SC* 441), SCC 3.2, l. 1-17: "Ostendo tamen ei quae hujusmodi est, locum in salutari sibi congruentem. Non temere assurgat ad os serenissimi sponsi, sed ad pedes severissimi Domini mecum pavida jaceat, et cum publicano terram tremens non coelum aspiciat (Luc. XVIII, 13), ne confusa in luminaribus coeli facies assueta tenebris opprimatur a gloria, atque insolitis reverberata splendoribus majestatis, densioris rursum caecitate caliginis obvolvatur. Non tibi, o quaecunque es talis anima, non tibi ille locus vilis aut despicabilis videatur, ubi sancta peccatrix peccata deposuit, induit sanctitatem. Ibi Aethiopissa mutavit pellem, et in novum restituta candorem, jam tunc fiducialiter veraciterque respondebat exprobrantibus sibi verbum: Nigra sum, sed formosa, filiae Jerusalem (Cant. I, 4). Miraris quanam id arte potuerit, vel quibus obtinuerit meritis? Paucis accipe. Flevit amare, et de intimis visceribus longa suspiria trahens, salutaribus intra se succussa singultibus, felleos humores evomuit."

77 Bernard of Clairvaux, On the *Song of Songs I*, p. 18. Leclercq (*SC* 441), SCC 3.3, l. 1-5: "Sumpto itaque ad pedes primo osculo, nec sic quidem praesumes statim ad osculum oris assurgere, sed erit tibi gradus ad ipsum medium quoddam aliud osculum, quod secundo loco ad manum accipies: de quo et talem accipe rationem."

concern the transformation of desire, the origin of the said transformation and its manifestation. The antidote of the Word in the kiss of the feet is effective (*Denique sermo Dei vivus et efficax*) and achieves an initial repentance. However, the effectiveness is stale if the repentance results in falling back or lapsing to the point of departure (*sine dubio recidenti quam iacenti deterius*). In the kiss of the hands the gift of repentance (*dedit voluntatem paenitendi*) goes in hand with the force of continence (*opus est ut addat et continendi virtutem*). The efficacy of the Word as such remains active as gift and in perseverance. What changes is the stage (*gradus*) of the transformation of desire (*peccare desiderio*). Desire is manifest in stages and the limit is constitutive of generation.

Desire has a directionality in the process of transformation by degrees. The directionality is upwards in the ascent. First, ascent begins with *repentance*. "If Jesus says to me: "Your sins are forgiven," what will it profit me if I do not cease from sinning? [...] he who healed me said to me as he exercised his mercy: 'Now you are well again, be sure not to sin any more, or something worse may happen to you.'"[78] Second, ascent requires *perseverance*: "He, however, who *gave me the grace to repent, must also give me the power to persevere*, lest by repeating my sins I should end up by being worse than I was before."[79] Perseverance comes with the *power* not to return to a previous stage. Third, ascent demands *humility* or the realization of insufficiency: "I really mean nothing; of myself I can achieve *neither repentance nor perseverance*."[80] Fourth, there is *confession* in ascent: "I muse confess that *I am not entirely satisfied with the first grace* by which I am enabled to repent of my sins; *I must have the second as well* [...] that I may not return like the dog to its vomit."[81] Overall, grace damps ascent. *Grace* is the inevitability of the Spirit as God in the possibility of *experience*. As such, the framework of ascent in the transformation of desire as production of *a* body returns to the generative *origin*: God or source-beginning.

78 Bernard of Clairvaux, On the *Song of Songs I*, p. 18. Leclercq (*SC* 441), SCC 3.3, l. 1-5: "Vae enim mihi etiam poenitenti, si statim subtraxerit manum, sine quo nihil possum facere."

79 Bernard of Clairvaux, On the *Song of Songs I*, p. 18. Leclercq (*SC* 441), SCC 3.3, l. 1-5: "Qui autem dedit voluntatem poenitendi, opus est ut addat et continendi virtutem; ne iterem poenitenda, faciamque novissima mea pejora prioribus."

80 Bernard of Clairvaux, On the *Song of Songs I*, p. 18. Leclercq (*SC* 441), SCC 3.3, l. 1-5: "Nihil inquam, quia nec poenitere, nec continere."

81 Bernard of Clairvaux, On the *Song of Songs I*, p. 18. Leclercq (*SC* 441), SCC 3.3, l. 1-5: "Audio proinde, quod consulit Sapiens: Verbum, inquit, in oratione ne iteres (Eccli. VII, 15). Paveo et quod judex intentat arbori non facienti fructum bonum (Matth. III, 10). Fateor pro hujusmodi non sum omnino contentus priori gratia, qua jam malorum sum poenitens, nisi et secundam accepero, ut videlicet dignos faciam poenitentiae fructus; et deinceps non revertar ad vomitum."

Desire thus begins (act) at the beginning (locus), wherein act and locus coincide. The process of repentance (penance) and perseverance (good acts), which transforms the desire for sin, has God at its origin in *the beginning without beginning* and is revealed as gift through the efficiency of the Word in *the book of experience*. However, what about human actions? Does the dependence on God for righteous moral action and the condemnation of presumption in the ascent from the kiss of the feet to the kiss of the mouth without passing through the kiss of the hands leave any room for the human free will?[82] "'*The Word of God is something alive and active*. It cuts like any double-edged sword but more finely. It can *slip through the place where the soul is divided from the spirit*, or the joints from the marrow: it can judge the secret thoughts.'"[83] In other words, from the Word (*verbum*), through the body (actions), does the transformation of desire pass through human will in the accomplishment of good actions in spite of grace? Bernard writes, "I am now able to see what *I must seek for and receive* before I may hope to attain to a higher and holier state. *I do not wish to be suddenly on the heights, my desire is to advance by degrees*."[84] Where act and locus coincide, specific modes manifest desire. Generation is thus *modal*. A mode may be conceptualized and preformed simultaneously as an attitude or a stance. In the generation of the body, even before the question of will surfaces, Bernard exhorts an attitude, a *mode*. Before the insufficiency of human will, an awareness of humility arises: "The *impudence* of the sinner

82 Bernard of Clairvaux, On the *Song of Songs I*, p. 18. Leclercq (*SC* 441), SCC 3.3, l. 1-5: "Sumpto itaque ad pedes primo osculo, nec sic quidem praesumes statim ad osculum oris assurgere, sed erit tibi gradus ad ipsum medium quoddam aliud osculum, quod secundo loco ad manum accipies: de quo et talem accipe rationem."

83 Bernard of Clairvaux, On the *Song of Songs I*, pp. 16-18. Leclercq (*SC* 441), SCC 3.2, l. 17-32: "Coelestis medicus celerrime subvenit: quia velociter currit sermo ejus (Psal. CXLVII, 15). Nunquid non potio est sermo Dei? Est utique, et fortis et vehemens, et scrutans corda et renes (Psal. VII, 10). Denique sermo Dei vivus et efficax, et penetrabilior omni gladio ancipiti, pertingens usque ad divisionem animae ac spiritus, compagum auoque ac medullarum, et discretor cogitationum (Hebr. IV, 12). Hujus ergo beatae poenitentis exemplo prosternere et tu, o misera, ut desinas esse misera; prosternere et tu in terram; amplectere pedes, placa osculis, riga lacrymis, quibus tamen non illum laves, sed te, ei fias una de grege tonsarum quae ascendunt de lavacro (Cant. IV, 2); ita sane tu suffusum pudore ac moerore vultum non ante sustollere audeas quam audias, et ipsa: Dimittuntur tibi peccata tua (Luc. VII, 37-48); quam audias: Consurge, consurge, captiva filia Sion; consurge, excutere de pulvere (Isai. LII, 1, 2)."

84 Bernard of Clairvaux, On the *Song of Songs I*, pp. 18-9. Leclercq (*SC* 441), SCC 3.4, l. 1-20: "Hoc ergo restat mihi prius petendum et accipiendum, quam praesumam altiora et sacratiora contingere. Nolo repente fieri summus; paulatim proficere volo."

displeases God as much as the *modesty* of the penitent gives him pleasure."[85] The insufficiency or sin is not however, to be confused with the limits of human ability – that being said, sin does in fact help recognize limits. Bernard goes on, "[y]ou will please him more readily *if you live within the limits proper to you, and do not set your sights at things beyond you*. It is a long and formidable leap from the foot to the mouth, *a manner of approach that is not commendable*."[86] From the recognition of insufficiency and the drawing of limits arises the realization of dependence: "still tarnished as you are with the dust of sin, *would you dare touch those sacred lips*? Yesterday you were *lifted from the mud*, today you wish to encounter *the glory of his face*?"[87] Finally, dependence leads to gratitude. "*What do you have that was not given to you? And if it was given; how can you boast as though it were not*?"[88] The *mode* of the process of generation emerges within the dialectic of request and reception, gift and merit. Mode also reveals dependence. The purpose of the request and the reception (*petendum et accipendum*) dialectic in the second kiss certainly has a dimension of dependence which underscores the gratuitous dimension of divine experience as 'grace' such that, again, there is no experience *outside* God.[89] The will is *in* God. Bernard emphasizes this point, however, without either undermining or discarding the will (*voluntate*) and its autonomy. In the ascent (*gradus*) towards the kiss of the mouth, repentance of the first kiss requires daring (*praesumere*). Daring, which emphasizes the role of human will, however, is empowered and conditioned by the request and the acceptance of a gift. Hence, the raising of the will (*erigere*) is accomplished, as a gift, by giving a reason or a motivation for daring to not fall back into negative habits of sin.[90] The motivation for dar-

85 Bernard of Clairvaux, On the *Song of Songs I*, pp. 18-9. Leclercq (*SC* 441), SCC 3.4, l. 1-20: "Quantum displicet Deo impudentia peccatoris, tantum poenitentis verecundia placet."

86 Bernard of Clairvaux, On the *Song of Songs I*, pp. 18-9. Leclercq (*SC* 441), SCC 3.4, l. 1-20: "Citius placas eum, si mensuram tuam servaveris, et altiora te non quaesieris. Longus saltus et arduus est de pede ad os, sed nec accessus conveniens."

87 Bernard of Clairvaux, On the *Song of Songs I*, pp. 18-9. Leclercq (*SC* 441), SCC 3.4, l. 1-20: Quid istud? Decor continentiae, et digni poenitentiae fructus, quae sunt opera pietatis. Haec te de stercore erigent in spem audendi potiora. Sane accipiendo donum, osculare manum: hoc est, non tibi, sed nomini ejus da gloriam. Da semel, et da iterum, tum pro donatis criminibus, tum pro collatis virtutibus. Aut certe videto unde munias frontem contra ictus istos."

88 Bernard of Clairvaux, On the *Song of Songs I*, pp. 18-19. Leclercq (*SC* 441), SCC 3.4, l. 1-20: "Quid habes quod non accepisti? Si autem accepisti, quid gloriaris quasi non acceperis? (I Cor. IV, 7.)."

89 Bernard of Clairvaux, On the *Song of Songs I*, pp. 18-9. Leclercq (*SC* 441), SCC 3.4, l. 1: "Hoc ergo restat mihi prius *petendum et accipendum*."

90 Bernard of Clairvaux, On the *Song of Songs I*, pp. 18-9. Leclercq (SC 441), SCC 3.4, l. 1: "Quomodo erigat? Dando unde praesumas."

ing which results from the gift of perseverance is thus alone the transitional source for the transformation of desire in the experience of the body in order to ascend from the kiss of the feet to the kiss of the mouth. The ascent of the will in the transformation of desire is as such a gift (external element) the recognition of which is activated in the experience of the gift *as* gift (internal element). Therefore, Bernard writes (earlier), "He, however, who gave me the grace to repent, must also give me the power to persevere, lest by repeating my sins I should end up by being worse than I was before."[91] The transformation of desire in a sense also transforms the will from a gift (*dedit voluntatem*) in terms of mode, as a power (*virtutem*), and in terms of quality, as growth (*addere*). Summarily, the kiss of the hand expresses the gratitude for a gift, which does not thwart the will.[92] Rather, in transforming desire, and in the recognition of experience, the will identifies daring (*praesumere*) and, with it, will empowers act as a power in greater degrees. In short, the will is actively involved in generation *as one* with the efficiency of divine action through the *efficient Word*. The dependant mode of desire is the union to the efficient Word. There is no performative language outside of the Word's efficiency.

The manifestation of the Word's efficiency is the outcome of the degrees. The efficient Word (Heb 4.12) accomplishes the (liturgical) transformation of desire from the depths of the rupture of soul and spirit in the kiss of the feet and then of the will into power in the kiss of the hands.[93] These preliminary kisses, leading to the supreme kiss, the kiss of the mouth, are paved within transformation of desire as recognized in the field of experience (*experimentum*), ultimately as production of experience itself. The Abbot of Clairvaux writes, "[o]nce you have had *this twofold experience of God's benevolence in these two kisses*, you need no longer feel abashed *in aspiring to a holier intimacy*."[94] In these kisses, leading up to the lover's mouth, Bernard makes of experience, construed as the generative outcome of desire, a method or "the way, the order" (*haec via, hic ordo*) of ascent (*gradus*): "*the order of procedure*: first, *we cast ourselves* at his feet, *we weep before* the Lord who made us [...] *Then we reach out* for the hand

91 Bernard of Clairvaux, On the *Song of Songs I*, p. 18. Leclercq (*SC* 441), SCC 3.3, l. 13-16: "Qui autem dedit voluntatem paenitendi, opus est ut addat et continendi virtutem, ne iterem paenitenda faciamque novissima mea peiora prioribus."

92 Bernard of Clairvaux, On the *Song of Songs I*, pp. 18-9. Leclercq (*SC* 441), SCC 3.4, l. 1-20: "Sane accipiendo donum, osculare manum."

93 Bernard of Clairvaux, On the *Song of Songs I*, pp. 8-9. Leclercq (*SC* 441), SCC 2.2, l. 15: "Sermo vivus et efficax."

94 Bernard of Clairvaux, On the *Song of Songs I*, pp. 19-20. Leclercq (*SC* 441), SCC 3.5, l. 1-17: "Jam tandem in osculis duobus geminum habens divinae dignationis experimentum, forsan non confunderis praesumere sanctiora."

that will lift us up."[95] The outcome of such procedure is the reception of desire: "finally, when we shall have obtained these favors through many prayers and tears, we humbly dare to *raise our eyes to his mouth*, so *divinely beautiful* [...] to receive its kiss."[96] The outcome of transformation is therefore autonomous generation.

Transformative ascent follows closely the way (*via*) of experience. The hermeneutics of desire is ultimately a hermeneutics of experience. These are not dissociated, because the generative transformation of desire is at the core of the process. As such, the body is also at the forefront of the hermeneutics of experience. The ascent is expressed in corporeal terms (feet, hands and mouth) and the aim is not merely contemplation (*speculare*) but ultimately to kiss (*osculandum*). Again, using vivid conjugal imagery, the kiss of the mouth joins the lovers into a single spirit: "'*Christ the Lord is a Spirit before our face*' [...] *he who is joined to him in a holy kiss becomes through his good pleasure, one spirit with him*."[97] The efficacy of the Word (the kiss of the feet), passing through the transformation of the will into power by means of daring (*praesumere*), culminates in the union of spirits as expressed by the body. Bernard beautifully summarizes the progress of the kisses leading up to the mouth in the closing of the sermon. He writes, "In the *dawn* you brought me *proof of your love, in my first approach to kiss your revered feet* [...] With the *advancement of the day* you gave your servant reason to *rejoice* when, in *the kiss of the hand*, you imparted the *grace to live rightly*."[98] Desire is desire's proof and assurance. "And now [...] I am with the fullness of your light, and while my spirit is fervent, *you would graciously bestow on me the kiss of your mouth and give me unbounded*

95 Bernard of Clairvaux, On the *Song of Songs I*, pp. 19-20. Leclercq (*SC* 441), SCC 3.5, l. 1-17: "Haec via, hic ordo. Primo ad pedes procidimus, et ploramus coram Domino qui fecit nos, ea quae fecimus nos. Secundo manum quaerimus sublevantis, et roborantis genua dissoluta."

96 Bernard of Clairvaux, On the *Song of Songs I*, pp. 19-20. Leclercq (*SC* 441), SCC 3.5, l. 1-17: "Postremo cum ista multis precibus et lacrymis obtinemus, tum demum audemus forsitan ad ipsum os gloriae caput attollere, pavens et tremens dico, non solum speculandum, sed etiam osculandum."

97 Bernard of Clairvaux, On the *Song of Songs I*, pp. 19-20. Leclercq (*SC* 441), SCC 3.5, l. 1-17: "quia spiritus ante faciem nostram Christus Dominus, cui adhaerentes in osculo sancto, unus spiritus ipsius dignatione efficimur."

98 Bernard of Clairvaux, On the *Song of Songs I*, pp. 19-20. Leclercq (*SC* 441), SCC 3.6, l. 1-12: "Tibi, Domine Jesu, tibi merito dixit cor meum: Exquisivit te facies mea; faciem tuam, Domine, requiram. Nempe auditam fecisti mihi mane misericordiam tuam, cum jacenti primum in pulvere, tuaque deosculanti reverenda vestigia, quod male vixeram remisisti. Porro in progressu diei laetificasti animam servi tui, cum deinde in osculo manus etiam bene vivendi gratiam indulsisti."

joy in your presence [...] where will you rest it at *noon*?"[99] The generation is the presence of desire. The reading of *the book of experience* through a hermeneutics of desire begins with a turn to experience where the divine transformation of desire is recognized and culminates with the transformation of the body in the kiss of the mouth, only to return to experience at *the beginning without beginning*. Once again, the hermeneutic circle is opened, and closed, through the key of desire, from understanding by reason to understanding by desire. From the experience of the body, Bernard brings the listener back to the body of experience thereby sealing the intimate intertwining of *the book of experience* with the hermeneutics of desire where the desire for experience becomes the experience of efficient desire (desiring production): "*the burden of the day calls us elsewhere*. These guests [...] *compel me to break off rather than to conclude a talk that I enjoy so much*. So, I go to meet the guests, *to make sure that the duty of charity, of which we have been speaking, may not suffer neglect*, that we may not hear it said of us: 'They do not *practice what they preach*.'"[100] The correspondence of words and actions, generative signification by the signifier, is what ensures authentic experience.

Conclusion

How does desire of the body affect the body, through the body, in the second moment of the *metamorphosis of love*? The desire of the body produces *bodies*. The *metamorphosis of love* begins with the body as the locus of desire and then reveals a generative interaction between body and desire. The desire of the body results in the transformation of desire and ultimately in generation for which the incarnation is the governing principle and the paradigmatic model. And so, the generation of desire (desiring-production) in the efficient

---

99 Bernard of Clairvaux, On the *Song of Songs I*, p. 20. Leclercq (*SC* 441), SCC 3.6, l. 1-12: "Et nunc quid restat, o bone Domine, nisi ut jam in plenitudine lucis, in fervore spiritus ad oris quoque osculum dignanter admittens, adimpleas me laetitia cum vultu tuo? Indica mihi, o suavissime, o serenissime, indica mihi ubi pascis, ubi cubas in meridie."

100 Bernard of Clairvaux, On the *Song of Songs I*, p. 20. Leclercq (*SC* 441), SCC 3.6, l. 12-20: "Fratres, bonum est nos hic esse; sed ecce avocat nos diei malitia. Hi siquidem, qui modo supervenisse nuntiantur, gratum cogunt rumpere magis quam finire sermonem. Ego exibo ad hospites, ne quid desit officiis ejus, de qua loquimur, charitatis, ne forte et de nobis audire contingat: Dicunt enim, et non faciunt (Matth. XXIII, 3). Vos orate interim, ut voluntaria oris mei beneplacita faciat Deus ad vestram ipsorum aedificationem, et laudem et gloriam nominis sui."

"hermeneutics of desire"[101] at *the beginning without beginning*, passing through desire of the body in *the kiss of the mouth* and transformation of the body by desire in *the book of experience* is the basis for the Bernardine construal of generated and efficient bodies of desiring-production in bodies. Thus, the *metamorphosis of love* develops from desire of the body through the interaction of desire and the body and yields the generation or the production of bodies. Now the question arises, what *bodies* does desire produce? By way of hypothesis, it is suggested that a multiplicity of bodily manifestations or productions is possible as modes of a unified body. This is the subject matter of inquiry in the following chapter on *bodies*, which elucidates *the body of God* and *the body of man*, and which explores the symbiotic difference and dependence between the two.

101 Bernard of Clairvaux, On the *Song of Songs I*, pp. 54-5. Leclercq (*SC* 441), SCC 9.2, l. 7: "Desiderio feror, non rationes."

CHAPTER 3

Bodies

How do bodies inter-act? Desiring-production engenders *the body of God* and *the body of man*. These bodies are *grafted* onto each other and are as such organically united *in* action and *as* action. The *metamorphosis of love* thus enters an important third moment, for while the body produces and transforms desire in a first moment, and desire in turn transforms the body in a second moment, now the body emerges as transformation of body into *action*. Body is action. The production of desire is desire itself transformed or desiring-production, and this is body. The desire of the body produces bodies of desire. The semeiotic desire of the body as body of desire, which is manifested in the desiring-production of a functioning whole through the (dis)order of the parts, lies at the intersection of "the body without organs" (Deluze)[1] and "the organs without bodies" (Žižek)[2] – possibly as "the flesh without body" (Falque). The "spread body" or "le corps épandu" (Falque),[3] considered not only at the intersection of spatial and temporal extension (Descartes)[4] and embodiment (phenomenology),[5] but rather in terms of desiring-production and order (Bernard), simultaneously becomes "a body (with)out organs" and "an organ with(out) bodies" or a semiotic body. The semiotic body is the synthesis of an organic process (sign/signified) of generation or *grafting* encompassing transformation and (dis)order of *the body of God* and *the body of man*. Alone in the organic mechanisms of parts (organs) relating to the whole (body), and vice-versa, simultaneously as resistance and striving to become (Spinoza), is the desiring-production of bodies alone adequately framed within the horizon of finitude in which "no one knows what a body is capable of."[6] As action,

1 Gilles Deleuze and Félix Guattari, *Anti-Oedipus* (London : A & C Black, 2004).

2 Slavoj Zizek, *Organs Without Bodies: Deleuze and Consequences* (London: Routledge, 2016).

3 Emmanuel Falque, "Ceci est mon corps," *Études*, no. 4 (2012): 6.

4 *Princ.* II.3-4, IV.203: extension is the essence of matter. Tad M. Schmaltz, "Descartes on the Extensions of Space and Time," *Analytica* 13, no. 2 (2009): 113-47. There is no space without matter. "We attribute a generic *unity to the extension of the space* [of a body], so that *when the body which fills the space has been changed, the extension of the space itself is not considered to have been changed or transported but to remain one and the same*; as long as it remains of the same size and shape and maintains the same situation among certain external bodies by means of which we specify that space (Pr II 10F)."

5 Emmanuel Falque, "Ceci est mon corps," *Études*, no. 4 (2012): 6.

6 Baruch Spinoza, *Ethics*, Part II, proposition 2, schol, 64 in *The Essential Spinoza: Ethics and Related Writings*, trans. Samuel Shirley, ed. Michael L. Morgan (Indianapolis: Hacket Publishing Company, 2006).

 | DOI:10.30965/9783846767504_005

bodies are bundles of performative desire. What are bodies, construed as bundles of desire, from the vantage point of the *metamorphosis of love*? In the *metamorphosis of* love, transformative production is manifested according to the efficiency of the Word, which is preformed through desire in the body. Between "love without being" (Marion)[7] and the "being without love" (onto-theology) is found the Bernardine "love of being" and the "being of love". Just as *the beginning without beginning* focuses on the entry of desire into the body, the production of the body by desire becomes manifest in *the body of God*. In *the book of experience*, production begins where desire ends, for the two merge in a continuum of action: in *the body of God* and then in *the body of man*. The desire of the body, which produces bodies, now transforms the body. The transformation or *metamorphosis of the body* occurs first in *the beginning of production* (3.1), then in *action and bodies* (3.2) and finally, it reveals *the body as action* (3.3).

3.1 The Beginning of Production

Desire produces bodies. How are bodies produced? There are three stages in the production of *bodies*. These stages correspond to the "three stages of the soul's progress under the figure of the three kisses [...] given to *the feet, the hand* and *the mouth*, in that order. The first is the sign of a genuine conversion of life, the second is accorded to those making progress, *the third is the experience of only a few of the more perfect*."[8] The backward order of the kisses suggests that in the beginning is the end: the last kiss is first, the first kiss is last. Bernard notes: "The *book of Scripture* that we have undertaken to expound *begins with this last kiss*, but I have added the other two in the hope that you will attain a better understanding of the last."[9] The transformation is growth of love and

7 Derek J. Morrow, "The Love 'Without Being' That Opens (To) Distance Part One: Exploring the Giveneness of the Erotic Phenomenon With J-L. Marion," *Heythrop Journal* 46, no. 3 (2005): 281-98.

8 Bernard of Clairvaux, On the *Song of Songs I*, pp. 21-3. Leclercq (*SC* 441), SCC 4.1, l. 1-9: "Triplicem quemdam animae profectum sub nomine trium osculorum sermo hesternus complexus est. Nunquid excidit vobis? Is mihi hodierna disputatione prosequendus erit, prout parare dignabitur in dulcedine sua pauperi Deus. Diximus, si recolitis, illa oscula sumi ad pedes, ad manum, ad os, singula singulis referentes. In primo sane primordia dedicantur nostrae conversionis; secundum autem proficientibus indulgetur: porro tertium sola experitur, et rara perfectio."

9 Bernard of Clairvaux, On the *Song of Songs I*, pp. 21-3. Leclercq (*SC* 441), SCC 4.1, l. 9-12: "Ab hoc solo, quod ultimum positum est, sumpsit exordium Scriptura ista quam tractare suscepimus, et ipsius causa reliqua duo a nobis adjuncta sunt. An vero necessarie vos judicabitis."

becomes intelligible only in the light of experience. Bernard continues: "We have here *three stages of the soul's growth in love*, three stages of its *advance toward perfection* that are sufficiently known and intelligible *to those who have experienced them*."[10] The process of transformation is a sequence from word to deed, which reveals the limits of finitude as the frailty of the body. There is "*forgiveness of sins*, then the *grace that follows on good deeds*, and finally that *contemplative gift* by which a kind and beneficent Lord shows himself to the soul with *as much clarity as bodily frailty can endure*."[11] The progression as preambles to the production of *a* body culminate in the final step opening to the question of God's body in the kiss of God's hand. The production of bodies is progressive. The need of a body for experience prompts Bernard to postulate also a divine body in which all bodies *are* bodies. The "phrase quite properly said to be kissing God's hand"[12] lays the transition and problematic for the interpretations which follow. These last remarks on the kiss of the hands prompt Bernard to develop a literal interpretation of the kiss of the hand, which does not include a body for God. This opens a sustained reflection on the body before resuming the supreme kiss as knowledge of God and love. The apparent diversion is in fact central to the hermeneutics of desire elucidated and applied in *On the Song of Songs*. In these passages, the body is at the heart of human experience and of human desire for God. How does human desire pass and undergoes transformation through the experience of touching the divine body? How is this experience accessible and what is the touch of the divine body? In Bernard's *On the Song of Songs*, the body (*corpus*) attains an unprecedented status in the account of spiritual experience and in the mediation of divine desire.[13] To experience, the divine body must be touched, as it were, and touch necessitates, calls upon, conjures a body.

However, the image of a body demands a *real* body. The (for the moment) metaphorical *touch* of the kiss is located in the equally metaphorical hands of

10 Bernard of Clairvaux, On the *Song of Songs I*, pp. 21-3. Leclercq (*SC* 441), SCC 4.1, l. 29-31: "Sunt ergo hi tres animarum affectus, sive profectus, expertis duntaxat satis noti et manifesti."

11 Bernard of Clairvaux, On the *Song of Songs I*, pp. 21-3. Leclercq (*SC* 441), SCC 4.1, l. 31-34: "cum aut de actis malis indulgentiam, aut de bonis agendis gratiam, aut ipsius etiam indultoris et benefactoris sui praesentiam, eo quidem modo quo in corpore fragili possibile est, obtinent intueri. Caeterum primum et secundum qua ratione oscula nominaverim, manifestius accipite."

12 Bernard of Clairvaux, On the *Song of Songs I*, pp. 22-3. Leclercq (*SC* 441), SCC 4.3, l. 13: "Dei dicitur non incongrue manum osculari."

13 Sean McGrath and Andrzej Wierciński, *A Companion to Heidegger's Phenomenology of Religious Life* (Amsterdam: Rodopi, 2010); Mette Birkedal Bruun, *Parables: Bernard of Clairvaux's Mapping of Spiritual Topography* (Leiden: Brill, 2007).

God. The challenge for Bernard consists in harmonizing the material (God has hands) and immaterial (God is Spirit) predications of God. He asks, "This poses a problem for you? *God is spirit, his simple substance* cannot be considered to have *bodily members*, so then, you say, show us what you mean by the hands and feet of God; explain to us the kiss of these hands and feet."[14] Furthermore, because the divine substance is simple (*simplex*),[15] it cannot be "taken into another" (*recipiat tale aliquid*). However, Bernard insists on not discarding the divine body but rather hopes to show *how* and *why* "God has a body", not only metaphorically, but also a real body, a body in the *Song of Songs*, where there is a transformation from body to spirit and from spirit to body. After all, if God has a mouth, reasons Bernard, why would God not also, and by implication, have a body? Either God has (*pertinere*) a mouth as Scripture suggests, in which case God has also other hands and feet; or else God does not have any of these members: "Surely *if we attribute a mouth to God, we may also attribute hands and feet*, for, if he lacks these latter he must lack the former too."[16] What to make of this *touch*? Is it a real body? Alternatively, is it an altogether different body in light of which what a real body is must be determined? The body of God is real yet remains quite unlike human bodies. The revolutionary interpretation of *touch* marks a daring transition from the metaphor to the literal sense of *the body of God*. God *has* a body. Concerning its members (*membris*), *the body of God* reaches out to human beings as members of *that* body. In fact, Bernard suggests, *all* these members belong to God, for God has it all (*habet Deus omnia*), surely on the basis of their Scriptural origin, but also based upon how these members reach out to human beings. Thus, the mouth of God teaches humanity.[17] The hand of God, on the other hand, nourishes the flesh.[18] The feet of God, moreover, lay on the earth as its footstool to forgive sinners.[19] Hence, because the mouth, hand and feet *of God* teach, feed and

14 Bernard of Clairvaux, On the *Song of Songs I*, pp. 23-24. Leclercq (*SC* 441), SCC 4.4, l. 1-13: "Verum quia spiritus est Deus (Joan. IV, 24), et nullis simplex illa substantia membris distincta corporeis; erit forsan qui nullatenus de illo recipiat tale aliquid sed a me sibi Dei manus vel pedes flagitet demonstrari, sicque probari quod de osculo pedum manusve definio."

15 This passage echoes the notion of a condensed verb.

16 Bernard of Clairvaux, On the *Song of Songs I*, pp. 23-4. Leclercq (*SC* 441), SCC 4.4, l. 1-13: "Nempe aut cum isto simul et illa habet, aut cum illis pariter et isto caret."

17 Bernard of Clairvaux, On the *Song of Songs I*, pp. 23-4. Leclercq (*SC* 441), SCC 4.4, l. 1-13: "os habet Deus quo docet hominem scientiam."

18 Bernard of Clairvaux, On the *Song of Songs I*, pp. 23-4. Leclercq (*SC* 441), SCC 4.4, l. 1-13: "et manum habet qua date scam omni carni."

19 Bernard of Clairvaux, On the *Song of Songs I*, pp. 23-4. Leclercq (*SC* 441), SCC 4.4, l. 1-13: "et pedes habet quorum terra scabellum est."

forgive humanity, therefore God, in a strong sense, not just metaphorically, but quite literally, has (*habere*) a body *with* real members. This is *the body of God*. In other words, the action of God for humanity is recognisable in experience as written in Scripture, and from there it follows that God has a sort of body. The *desire of God* for human beings is, as it were, the originator of *the body of God* which humanity recognizes in experience. This much is also supported by the centrality of desire in the three kisses of the moral exegesis, which coincide with the members of God. Clearly, Bernard has something more in mind than merely an ordinary human body when he says that God has members such as a mouth, hands and feet. Thus, what exactly is this *body of God* and what is its relationship to *members*? The *body* of God is fundamentally *extension* in action which is, for now, production and, eventually, aperity.

Another way of conceptualizing extension is action. Thus, the body of God *is* action. The central Bernardine contention with regards to the kiss is the postulation of a divine body, perhaps generated by desire, but fundamentally construed *by means of effects* or simply as action (*per effectum*)[20] and not by nature (*per naturam*): "I allow of course that *God does not have these members by his nature*, they represent *certain modes of our encounter with him*."[21] In fact, according to a literal rendering of the Latin, it can be stated that, for Bernard, "God *has* all by effect, not by nature." God thus *possesses* by means of action in an ongoing process of extension. In this process, human desire for God undergoes productive transformation of and through the human body and its expression in experience as *will*, which is simultaneously individual and collective in the members of the body, as well as by means of the collective experience of body and desire. The body is the extension of action. God fundamentally acts as body in affect and by effect. What is the effect of God or how does God affect? In other words, what is *the body of God*? That is, what does it mean to say, *God has all by effect, not by nature*? For the Abbot of Clairvaux, *the body of God* is most fundamentally an instantiation of divine governance. Bernard writes, "*God does not have these members by his nature*, they represent certain *modes of our encounter with him* [...] Because his *providence rules over all*, he is *all things to all*, yet, to speak with accuracy, *he is in no way what these*

---

20 Avicenna, *Liber de philosophia prima siue scientia diuina*, tract. 4, cap. 2, pag. 211, l. 24. "Pone me super cor tuum per affectum amoris; pone me super brachium per effectum operationis." The expression is about signs/sacrament. The question is, what kind of signification?

21 Bernard of Clairvaux, On the *Song of Songs I*, pp. 23-4. Leclercq (*SC* 441), SCC 4.4, l. 13-14: "Haec, inquam, habet Deus omnia per effectum, non per naturam."

things are. If we *consider him in himself* [he has] no bounds."[22] The governance of *the body of God* and its organizing principles remain intimate to the members, which God governs. Bernard writes, "[y]et he who by his very nature *is the principle* through whom all creatures *spring into being, cannot be far from any of us*, since *without him all are nothing* [...] *no one can be more intimately present to us than he, no one is more incomprehensible*."[23] Bernard thus gives *an external body* to what Augustine says of the internally intimate God, echoing thereby Augustine's characterization of God, who is "more intimate to myself than I am to myself."[24] God is intimate in the body (Bernard) and not in spite of it (Augustine). God's action is embodied presence.

The action of *the body of God* as embodied presence or extension is on a first moment possession. Bernard understands *the body of God* primarily and initially not in terms of corporeality but in terms of possession of a whole (*omnia habet*), as reaching out (effects), or as *tending towards*. *The body of God* is dynamism, extension and generation. Hence, in *the body of God* the underlying concern is to have a God who is at once intimately close to humanity while remaining infinitely beyond it. To articulate this paradox of simultaneous divine proximity and remoteness, Bernard draws a distinction between effect (*effectum*) and nature (*naturam*): "'All that exists comes from him, all is by him and in him.' He is the *creator, the efficient cause, not the material*, of every creature."[25] On the one hand, as effect, God "is all for all" (*omnia omnibus*) and God "administers" (*administare*) all.[26] On the other hand, as nature, God "is not

22 Bernard of Clairvaux, On the *Song of Songs I*, pp. 23-4. Leclercq (*SC* 441), SCC 4.4, l. 13-14: "Nam, quod in se est, lucem habitat inaccessibilem (I Tim. VI, 16), et pax ejus exsuperat omnem sensum (Philipp. IV, 7); et sapientiae ejus non est numerus (Psal. CXLVI, 5), et magnitudinis ejus non est finis (Psal. CXLIV, 3); nec potest eum videre homo ut vivat (Exod. XXXIII, 20). Non quod longe ab unoquoque sit qui esse omnium est, sine quo omnia nihil: sed, ut tu plus mireris, et nil eo praesentius, et nil incomprehensibilius."

23 Bernard of Clairvaux, On the *Song of Songs I*, pp. 23-4. Leclercq (*SC* 441), SCC 4.4, l. 13-34: "Haec, inquam, habet Deus omnia per effectum, non per naturam. Invenit profecto apud Deum et verecunda confessio, quo se humiliando dejiciat; et prompta devotio, ubi se innovando reficiat; et jucunda contemplatio, ubi excedendo quiescat. Omnia omnibus est qui omnia administrat, nec quidquam est omnium proprie."

24 Augustine, *Confessions*, 3.6: "tu autem eras interior intimo meo et superior summo meo!"

25 Bernard of Clairvaux, On the *Song of Songs I*, pp. 23-4. Leclercq (*SC* 441), SCC 4.4, l. 13-34: "Esse est ergo omnium quae facta sunt ipse factor eorum, sed causale, non materiale. Tali proinde modo dignatur illa majestas suis esse creaturis, omnibus quidem quod sunt; animantibus autem quod et vivunt; porro ratione utentibus lux, recte vero utentibus virtus, vincentibus gloria."

26 Bernard of Clairvaux, On the *Song of Songs I*, pp. 23-4. Leclercq (*SC* 441), SCC 4.4, l. 13-34: "Omnia omnibus est qui omnia administrat."

properly any such thing."[27] The distinction between effect and nature offers a paradox. Namely, God is the most intimate, indeed the very being (*esse*) of things, yet the most remote of all creation. Bernard formulates the paradox thus: "[f]or *what is more intimate to anything than its own being*? And yet, what is *more incomprehensible* to any of us than *the being of all things*? [...] when I say that God is the being of all things, *I do not wish it to be understood in the sense that he and they are identical*."[28] God is therefore, Bernard concludes, the beginning of all things (source-beginning) in terms of cause (*casuale*) and not in terms of matter (*materiale*).[29] Hence, while *the body of God* is action or power, God remains beyond action and power. The presence of God in experience, desire and the body is fundamentally a presence of and by action.

The *body of God* affects *the body of man*. How is divine action manifested and how does affect the human body and the transformation of desire? The problematic in the Bernardine postulation of *the body of God* as action consists in determining *how* God interacts, through a body, with humanity, simultaneously as most intimate, and yet as remaining most distant. *The body of God* does not need corporeal mediation to effect action. God's will *is* God's action: *the body of God* is therefore *pure generative power*. The divine transformation from nature to effect occurs through the efficiency of the Word. God does not need *corporeality* to govern or to (dis)order. A hypothesis follows thus: the perfection of *bodies* is pure action as is the case with the Word. The Word manifests divine action. "*By his word alone* he had made all things [...] Souls have a need for bodies, and bodies in turn a need for senses, if they are *to know and influence* each other."[30] The Word is the organizing principle of God's desire in the body so that generation of desire is intricately inherent to the process of order. Because of the Word (*verbum*), which is immaterial, God creates without corporeality and therefore without mediation by means of a simple act of will. Bernard notes, "[n]ot so the omnipotent God, who *by the immediate act of*

27 Bernard of Clairvaux, On the *Song of Songs I*, pp. 23-4. Leclercq (*SC* 441), SCC 4.4, l. 13-34: "nec quidquam est omnium proprie."

28 Bernard of Clairvaux, On the *Song of Songs I*, pp. 23-4. Leclercq (*SC* 441), SCC 4.4, l. 13-34: "Quid nempe cuique rei praesentius, quam esse suum? Quid cuique tamen incomprehensibilius, quam esse omnium? Sane esse omnium dixerim Deum, non quia illa sunt quod est ille; sed quia ex ipso, et per ipsum, et in ipso sunt omnia (Rom. XI, 36)." Cf. Ps.-Denys, *Celestial Hierarchies*, 4.1 (*SC* 56, p. 93-4), as cited in Bernard of Clairvaux, On the *Song of Songs* I, Leclercq (*SC* 441), SCC 4.4, p. 118, n. 2.

29 Bernard of Clairvaux, On the *Song of Songs I*, pp. 23-4. Leclercq (*SC* 441), SCC 4.4, l. 13-34: "Esse est ergo omnium quae facta sunt ipse factor eorum, sed causale, non materiale."

30 Bernard of Clairvaux, On the *Song of Songs I*, pp. 23-4. Leclercq (*SC* 441), SCC 4.4, l. 1-17: "qui omnia solo verbo et corpora creavit, et spiritus. Animae corporibus et corporeis egent sensibus, quibus sibi invicem innotescant, et valeant."

his will, and that alone both *creates and governs*. His influence touches *whom he wills, as much as he wills*, without calling on the aid or service of bodily powers."[31] In contrast to God, human actions require the body for mediation of the bodily members. "In this work of *creation*, of *government*, of *administration*, of *imparting motion*, of steering toward *particular ends*, of *renewal* and *strengthening*, he has *no need of bodily instruments*."[32] Another hypothesis follows: action in finitude *has* body; body is a consequence of the limits of action. Body does not limit actions. Action limits bodies.[33] God affects whereas humans are affected. Body construed as act reframes the conception of desire. The discussion of *the body of God* as pure and simple act of the will through the (incorporeal) Word is not mere speculative reflection. Rather, it is rooted in the moral exegesis of *the three kisses* and ultimately functions in *On the Song of Songs* as the prelude to lay out the importance of the human body in the experience *of* and desire *for* God. Furthermore, it traces the inseparability of divine manifestation in the single stroke of Word, will and body. The ongoing reflection on the nature and purpose of *the body of God* also transforms, by means of generative order, *the body of man*, and this, not only as a product of divine desire, but also, this time, as acting *in the body of God* because in desiring-production the human body is *a* member of *the body of God*. In other words, human experience is possible only through God in *the book of experience* because the human body, as the product of divine desire, is *a* body only as effect (*per effectum*) of *the body of God* in the efficient Word. Access to the body happens therefore only by mediation through the experience of *the body of God*. Desire constitutes the body. Agency is therefore the expression of the body's desire. The ascent (*gradus*) of the three kisses of the moral exegesis (the kiss of the feet, the kiss of the hand and the kiss of the mouth) leading to the four-fold sense of the kiss of the mouth, passes through the experience of desire in *the body of man* and in *the body of God*. The passage is a transformation not only of human desire, but also an identification of the locus of the generation of the body itself. The itinerary of the ongoing transformation, or rather the production of the body as manifestation of divine desire in and

31 Bernard of Clairvaux, On the *Song of Songs I*, pp. 23-4. Leclercq (*SC* 441), SCC 4.4, l. 1-17: At non ita omnipotens Deus, qui de sola voluntate celeris suppetit efficientia tam creandis rebus, quam ordinandis prout voluerit. Valet qui vult, quantum vult, et absque corporalium officio, obsequiove membrorum."

32 Bernard of Clairvaux, On the *Song of Songs I*, pp. 23-4. Leclercq (*SC* 441), SCC 4.4, l. 1-17: "Et in his omnibus creandis, gubernandis, administrandis, movendis, promovendis, innovandis, firmandis, nullis corporeis indiget instrumentis."

33 Caroline W. Bynum, "Did the Twelfth Century Discover the Individual?" *The Journal of Ecclesiastical History* 31, no. 1 (1980): 1-17.

through the human experience of God, therefore progresses from the focused analysis of *the body of God* to that of *the body of man*: the second is produced in the first. The body is therefore not only a vehicle for desire but is indeed the product of desire passing through the experience of *the body of God*. Bodies are a consequence of action. Bodies are therefore fundamentally action. Thus far, we have shown, desire produces *the body of God* and *the body of man*. Before further exploring *the body as action* in the final section of this chapter, we now turn to the relationship between *action and bodies*.

3.2 Action and Bodies

Desire intertwines action and body. The performative mediation of the Word produces the body of divine desire, which is then transformed by human desire. Bernard opens the discussion of *the body of man* with a taxonomy of spirits and in so doing situates the latter *in the body of God*.[34] As such, the optic of the function of the human body is really a question of a blueprint, which aims at tracking the organizing modes of generation in desiring-production. Whereas for God action *is* body effectuated by Word, for human body *is* action produced by desire. The body is necessary for agency. The division of kinds of spirits (*spirtuum genera*) allows Bernard to underscore the function of the body in its various modes of generation and to expound the central maxim that *all* spirits *need* a body: "Each of these [spirits] needs a body."[35] What is the function of the body? The functions of the body arise in terms of how it manifests existence at the various levels of spirits. The body (*corpus*) or the appearance of a body (*corporisve similitude*) is necessary, for every spirit, in one of three ways: for itself (*propter se*), for others (*propter alium*), or for both for itself and for others (*propter utruquem*). Hence, the three-fold Bernardine classification of spirits: "*that of the animal, that of man, that of the angel, and that of God who created all the others.* Each of these, with one exception, needs *a body or a body's likeness, either for its own sake or for the sake of others or for both.*"[36] In all three cases, the relation of the body to spirit is relative or relational. The body

---

34 Bernard of Clairvaux, On the *Song* of Songs *I*, pp. 25-6. Leclercq (*SC* 441), SCC 5.1, l. 1-11: "quatuor sunt spirituum genera."

35 Bernard of Clairvaux, On the *Song of Songs I*, pp. 25-6. Leclercq (*SC* 441), SCC 5.1, l. 1-11: "Non est ex omnibus, cui [...] necessarium corpus non sit."

36 Bernard of Clairvaux, On the *Song of Songs I*, pp. 25-6. Leclercq (*SC* 441), SCC 5.1, l. 1-11: "Quatuor spirituum genera nota sunt vobis, pecoris, noster, angelicus, et qui condidit istos. Non est ex omnibus, cui sive propter se, sive propter alium, sive propter utrumque, necessarium corpus non sit, corporisve similitudo, excepto duntaxat illo, cui omnis tam

is predicated (*praedicare*) necessarily of the spirit as a sort of relative (*πρός τι*). Yet, this is *not* relative predication in the Aristotelian sense.[37] For Bernard, in the application of the three *relatives* (*propter se, propter alium, propter utruquem*) to the four spirits (animal, human, celestial and God), the body is not just *accidental* but necessary for the possibility of existence altogether. Where there is action, there is body. In addition, since there is no existence without action, axiomatically it follows; there is no existence without body. The body is a means of access to the very possibility of modal existence. At the extremes of the spectrum are animals and God. The kind of body needed for a specific action depends on the directionality of agency. The body is a mode of agency: animal, human, divine. Existence is the mode of animal agency. Animals cannot exist without a body whereas God does not require a body whatsoever. Writing of the animal body, Bernard writes, "If we consider the animal, we see that its spirit, its life principle, cannot even exist without a body. When the animal dies its soul ceases to live at the same moment that it ceases to impart life."[38] The animal spirit vivifies body, which engenders the animal existence quite substantially (*subsistere*), a bodily existence. In a basic sense, the animal spirit *is* not much more than the body. Conversely, without the vivification of the animal body, the animal spirit remains and cannot *enter* existence, it cannot *subsist*. The body, then, mediates animal existence. Amodality is the mode of human agency – a modeless mode or a measure without measure –, which the body's autonomy expresses in the mode of nature and grace. The second kind of spirit is the human spirit. Whereas the animal spirit cannot survive the animal body, the human spirit can survive without body, as per the principle of resurrection. This, however, does not mean the human body is not important for humans or that it is less important than the spirit. On the contrary, according to Bernard, the human body is *necessary* for two central activities of human flourishing, which are the exercise of beatitude (*beata vita*) and the search for knowledge (*cognitionem*). "All creatures that [God] has made, creatures that possess a body and are therefore visible," writes Bernard, "can be understood by our minds only through the body's instrumentality. Therefore

---

corporalis, quam spiritualis creatura merito confitetur, et dicit: Deus meus es tu, quoniam bonorum meorum non eges (Psal. XV, 2)."

37 Allan Bäck, *Aristotle's Theory of Predication* (Leiden: Brill, 2000); Pamela Michelle Hood, *Aristotle on the Category of Relation* (Lanham: University Press of America, 2004); Emmanuel Falque, *Dieu, la chair et l'autre: d'Irénée à Duns Scot* (Paris: Presses Universitaires de France, 2008).

38 Bernard of Clairvaux, On the *Song of Songs I*, pp. 25-6. Leclercq (*SC* 441), SCC 5.1, l. 1-11: "Et primum quidem ita corpore egere constat, ut nec subsistere absque illo utcunque possit. Simul quippe et vivificare desinit, et vivere ille spiritus, quando moritur pecus."

our souls have need of a body."[39] The centrality of the human body to obtain knowledge would become axiomatic later (Aquinas), following Aristotle.[40] According to the Bernardine reflection, the body is the means by which (*per corporea*) all things corporeal and visible become, in a broad sense, accessible to human beings. Humans access the world by means of the body. Bernard further underscores the importance of access to the world by means of the body by the conflation, or approximation, of knowledge and happiness. Ascent by degrees (*gradus*) to happiness occurs by means of knowledge of the happy life (*beata*) through the world and by the mediation of *a* body. "Without [the body], notes Bernard, we cannot attain to that form of knowledge [...] of truths essential to happiness."[41] The human body, unlike the animal body, extends beyond itself, as it were, so that the mode of human agency culminates in modeless agency.

God also affects human agency through grace. Grace is an external affection of human modality. However, the natural (internal) and external (grace) modes remain neatly separated. This is well illustrated in Bernard's introduction of an objection concerning baptism. If the body is necessary for knowledge of happiness, then why or how do baptized infants (*parvulis regeneratis*) have access to the happy life (*beatam vita*)? "If one of you will object that baptized infants who die before acquiring a knowledge of the material creation are believed nevertheless to enter heaven, I shall reply briefly that *this is a gift of grace, not a reward of merit*. For the moment this discussion deals *with normal processes, not with the special interventions of God*."[42] This objection draws a distinction between the order of grace and the order of nature and maintains the

39 Bernard of Clairvaux, On the *Song of Songs I*, pp. 25-6. Leclercq (*SC* 441), SCC 5.1, l. 11-20: "Verum nos vivimus quidem post corpus; sed ad ea quibus beate vivitur, nullus nobis accessus patet, nisi per corpus. Senserat hoc qui dicebat: Invisibilia Dei, per ea quae facta sunt, intellecta conspiciuntur (Rom. I, 20). Ipsa siquidem quae facta sunt, id est corporalia et visibilia ista, nonnisi per corporis instrumentum sensa, in nostram notitiam veniunt. Habet ergo necessarium corpus spiritualis creatura quae nos sumus, sine quo nimirum nequaquam illam scientiam assequitur, quam solam accepit gradum ad ea, de quorum fit cognitione beata."

40 Aquinas: "oportet ut quod est in intellectu nostro, prius in sensu fuerit", "Tout ce qui se trouve dans notre intellect doit se trouver d'abord dans nos senses" (*De veritate*, q. II, a. 3, 19), as cited in Bernard of Clairvaux, On the *Song of Songs I*, Leclercq (*SC* 441), SCC 5.1, p. 124, n. 1.

41 Bernard of Clairvaux, On the *Song of Songs I*, pp. 25-6. Leclercq (*SC* 441), SCC 5.1, l. 21-25: "sine quo nimirum nequaquam illam scientiam assequitur, quam solam accepit gradum ad ea, de quorum fit cognitione beata."

42 Bernard of Clairvaux, On the *Song of Songs I*, pp. 25-6. Leclercq (*SC* 441), SCC 5.1, l. 21-25: "Hic si mihi objicitur de parvulis regeneratis, quod absque scientia rerum corporalium exeuntes de corpore, ad beatam vitam nihilominus transire credantur; breviter respondeo

semeiological rapport governing interactions between the two. Furthermore it shows, on the one hand, that the ascent (*gradus*) to the happy life can be achieved naturally, i.e., without grace (*gratiam*). Such a position is remarkable and finds its basis in *the book of experience*: "The invisible things of God are understood through the things he has made."[43] The objection shows, on the other hand, that the same effect, namely beatitude, results from both orders. In the order of grace (*gratia*), the body gains merits.[44] The centrality of the body is, without a question, of central importance for Bernard and the reflections on the body proceed, methodologically, according to nature; the body also acquires knowledge and happiness. Bernard naturalizes what before was alone the domain of grace (Augustine): humans are fully autonomous in the realm of nature, even to the point of knowing happiness and achieving it (Aristotle). The internal mode fully expresses bodily agency. Pure agency is the mode of angelic agency. The third kind of spirit is the super celestial spirit (*supercoelestes spiritus*), which is another name for an *angel*. The interest in this kind of spirit lies in how the Bernardine analysis sheds light on the function of bodies in general, and on human bodies specifically. Angels, like humans and animals, also need bodies, yet in a very different sense. The body of the angel is not primarily for vivification (animal spirit) or for the knowledge of happiness (human spirit), but for the implementation of action (*ministerium*): bodies are inherently pure dynamism. The angel's mode of efficient manifestation is the body: "We can be absolutely sure that *these have a need of bodies* [...] How will it be possible for them to fulfill this service without a body, especially among beings who possess bodies? [...] though both animal and angelic spirits have need of bodies, *it is not for their own sakes but in order to render some service to others*."[45] This is why Bernard insists that an angel without a body is not an angel because the very action of the angel depends action, which a body

hoc illis conferre gratiam, non naturam. Et quid ad me de miraculo Dei. qui de naturalibus dissero?"

43 Bernard of Clairvaux, On the *Song of Songs I*, pp. 27-8. Leclercq (*SC* 441), SCC 5.4, l. 1-28: "invisibilia Dei, per ea quae facta sunt, intellecta conspiciuntur."

44 Bernard of Clairvaux, On the *Song of Songs I*, pp. 27-8. Leclercq (*SC* 441), SCC 5.2, n. 2, pp. 124-125.

45 Bernard of Clairvaux, On the *Song of Songs I*, p. 26. Leclercq (*SC* 441), SCC 5.2, l. 1-13: "Jam quod et supercoelestes spiritus opus corporibus habeant, illa maxime certos nos faciat vera, et vere divina sententia: Nonne omnes. ait, administratorii spiritus sunt, missi in ministerium propter eos qui haereditatem capiunt salutis? (Hebr. I, 14.) Quonam ergo modo implent ministerium suum absque corpore, praesertim apud viventes in corpore? Denique non est discurrere, nec de loco ad locum transire, nisi corporum: quod frequenter angelos facere tam indubitata, quam nota probat auctoritas. Hinc est quod et visi sunt patribus, et ad eos intraverunt, et manducaverunt, et pedes laverunt. Ita inferior

alone can produce. The body reaches therefore its closest identification with action or power (*virtus*) in the consideration of angelic bodies. Indeed, there is no action and there is no movement without a body.[46] There is no reason why the conclusion cannot also apply to human and animal bodies. Without a body, furthermore, the angels could not interact with other bodily spirits, or, literally, spirits *living corporeally* (*viventes in corpore*). Summarily, in the analysis of angelic bodies applied by extension to human and animal bodies, the body is the locus of spiritual manifestation, in terms of action, movement and relation. The modes of bodily manifestation in agency are existence (animals), amodality (humans) and pure agency (angels). The mode of the body, in short, mediates and determines manifestation.

The body is a mode of agency. What determines the distinctive features of *bodies* as modes of agency? In other words, why do specific modes of corporeality manifest agency? *Purpose* determines the mode of a body. That is, the modal manifestation akin to the degrees of love determines the particularities of concrete desiring *bodies*. The *mode* of a bodily manifestation can *be* for itself (*propter se*) *or* for others (*propter alium*), or finally, for both, for itself *and* for others (*propter utrumque*). The animal body is *for itself.* The angelic body is *for others*. The human body is *for itself* and *for others*. Again, the importance of *relatives* is at play as much as the prospects of love and the body. Modal manifestation of agency is the purpose determined by intentionality and directionality. The purpose of a body can be construed as function. The nature of bodies proper to the different kinds of spirits can be framed in terms of function: bodies have a dynamic directionality, even an intentionality *towards* (*propter*) in reference to either itself (*propter se*), others (*propter alium*) or both (*utrumque*), itself and others. Having done so, Bernard then articulates, on a second instance, the nature of bodies proper to each of the spirits (*espiritus*) based on limits. The directionality of a body determines its limits. Function and limits therefore condition the modes of bodily manifestations. The function and limits of bodies provides the locus of tension between desire and experience. Desire and experience of the human body stands between the body of animals (*propter se*) and the body of angels (*propter alium*), between pure vivification (animals) and pure action (angels). Since the functions of the body mirror the structure of the degrees of love in Bernard's *On Loving God*, it may be postulated that the body is the starting point of love; at least of the

superiorque spiritus propriis corporibus egent, sed tantum [alias tamen], quibus juvent, non etiam juventur."

46 Bernard of Clairvaux, On the *Song of Songs I*, p. 26. Leclercq (*SC* 441), SCC 5.2, l. 1-13: "Denique non est discurrere, nec de loco ad locum transire, nisi corporum."

dynamic intentionality towards (*propter*) something or other. The discussion of the body is therefore a discussion about how the body functions to mediate relations and, ultimately, to enact existence. More importantly, the body's (unlimited) modes of manifestation are ultimately manifestations and transformations of desire, i.e., desire which seeks a body. The mode of bodily functions is limitless desiring-production.

Desire also interacts with desire and bodies with bodies. The modes of bodies can also be analyzed in terms of how bodies relate to the human body. Animal bodies are servile (not free) and are useful for human beings only for temporal aims, whereas angelic bodies are free (not servile) and are useful for human beings for eternal aims. Bernard writes, "*the animal spirit or soul is limited by time, it dies with the body* [...] those who treat him well will discover that the usage of this temporal service will redound to eternal rewards."[47] Bodies function in the use (servility) of desire. Different uses corresponds to different modes of desire. The body is the condition for relation, which is in turn a mode of desire. The servile condition of the animal body renders its services useful for temporal and corporeal necessities of life alone. Animal bodies perish because of their temporal limitations. Even human beings use these bodies only by orienting them to the achievement of eternal life. "The *animal kingdom is destined by nature to serve*, and that service is fulfilled in alleviating the *temporal and physical needs of man*."[48] The angel however employs the body for action of goodness. The difference between an angel and an animal is framed in terms of freedom: the animal is servile while the angel is free. Free or not, both angel and animal need *a* body. "The angel, however, in the *freedom of his spirit*, applies himself with eagerness to the demands of his duty, which is *to bring prompt and swift assistance* to us mortals in our *striving for the blessings that are to come*."[49] Hence, the body is essential for action and for relation, and the mode of operation is, on a first instance, defined by freedom because animals are irrational, while angels are not. The fundamental human attitude is to *use* or to be *reached out* by others, animals or angels. The limits of the body emerge

47 Bernard of Clairvaux, On the *Song of Songs I*, pp. 26-7. Leclercq (*SC* 441), SCC 5.3, l. 1-14: "Servus quippe non manet in domo in aeternum, licet qui bene eo utuntur, omnem usum hujus temporalis servitutis ad quaestum referant aeternorum."

48 Bernard of Clairvaux, On the *Song of Songs I*, pp. 26-7. Leclercq (*SC* 441), SCC 5.3, l. 1-14: "At pecus quidem ex debito servitutis, et ad usus tantum temporalium corporaliumque necessitatum juvando servit; ideoque ille spiritus et cum tempore transit, et cum corpore deficit."

49 Bernard of Clairvaux, On the *Song of Songs I*, pp. 26-7. Leclercq (*SC* 441), SCC 5.3, l. 1-14: "Angelus vero curat satagitque in libertate spiritus administrare officium pietatis, futurorum bonorum promptum mortalibus alacremque ministrum sese exhibens, utpote suis in aeternum futuris civibus [alias concivibus], et cohaeredibus supernae jucunditatis."

in modal function. What, then, are the limits of the body? The first limit of the body is *functional necessity*. The function of bodies for animals and angels is service. Bernard continues, "Therefore *both the animal and the angel need bodies that they might be of help to us*, the first that he may *give us the service appropriate to his nature, the second that he may lovingly support us*."[50] Animals and angels use bodies to serve (animals) and to love (angels). However, such function reveals the first limits of the body as necessity. Animals *need* bodies to serve. Angels *need* bodies to support. The second limit of the body is *cognitive possibility*. "*The spirit of the animal can indeed perceive corporeal things by means of the body*, but is this body of such potential value to him that the material world *which he experiences through the senses* enables him to advance to a knowledge of spiritual and intellectual truths? Surely not."[51] The body is construed, more precisely, as *potentiality* for cognitive possibility. Animals *can* use their bodies but the horizon of cognitive possibility is limited to only sensual knowledge. This is because the animal body as *limited* agency cannot fully manifest the possibilities of cognitive potentiality in the same way that other *bodies* can: "*within the limits of its corporeal and temporal service*, the body does provide a gateway to a knowledge of these truths for those who *transmute* their usage of the things of time into coin of eternal reward."[52] The limits of the body vary regarding cognitive possibility. The third limit of the body is *functional utility* for the possibility of mediation. Different kinds of body condition utility. However, another difference between the bodies, besides utility, is the capacity to overcome the body. The notion of overcoming the body is framed in terms of a passage from what is corporeal to what is incorporeal or spiritual. While animals cannot overcome the body, angles can overcome the body. Moreover, while the (animal) body can overcome bodily realities, it cannot overcome itself.[53] Nevertheless, the animal body can be useful for others to overcome

50 Bernard of Clairvaux, On the *Song of Songs I*, pp. 26-7. Leclercq (*SC* 441), SCC 5.3, l. 14-22: "Ille ergo ut jure serviat, iste ut pie subveniat, ambo procul dubio suis corporibus egent ut juvent."

51 Bernard of Clairvaux, On the *Song of Songs I*, pp. 26-7. Leclercq (*SC* 441), SCC 5.3, l. 14-22: "Nam in quo ipsi eis juventur, non video, ad profectum duntaxat aeternitatis. Irrationalis nempe spiritus, etsi corporalia per corpus et ipse hauriat: nunquid tamen eousque juvatur corpore suo, ut per corporalia et sensibilia quae per illud sentit, etiam ad spiritualia et intelligibilia proficiendo pertingat?"

52 Bernard of Clairvaux, On the *Song of Songs I*, pp. 26-7. Leclercq (*SC* 441), SCC 5.3, l. 14-22: "Ad quae tamen capessenda pro suo corporali temporalique obsequio noscitur juvare illos, qui omnem usum rerum temporalium ad fructum transferunt aeternarum, utentes hoc mundo, tanquam non utentes."

53 Bernard of Clairvaux, On the *Song of Songs I*, pp. 26-7. Leclercq (*SC* 441), SCC 5.3, l. 14-22: "Ad quae tamen capessenda pro suo corporali temporalique obsequio noscitur juvare

the body. Therefore, the animal body is not able to access incorporeal or spiritual realities. The angelic bodies, however, which are *enrobed by the flesh*, can indeed access the spiritual realities without the body's mediation. The limits of mediation are stretched in the case of angels who acquire knowledge by "*nature rather than with the aid of a body*, or with *the awareness of things that bodily senses provide*."[54] The body is an *aid* therefore, which leads to nature, but which is not necessary for it. The fourth limit of the body is *process by way of degrees*: the body proceeds by degrees as it extends. "Because this is not so for the creature of heaven. For, what the spirit clothed in flesh and dwelling on the earth strives to achieve *gradually and little by little, through the knowledge it derives from the senses, that same the dweller of the heavens attains with all speed and ease*, because of the native fineness and sublime quality of its being."[55] Degrees include displacement or movement, as well as change over time or speed, and finally intensity or ease. Part of the ease depends on the source. The angelic source is not experience but life itself. "Why should they search for spiritual meanings among bodily substances when they can find them in the *book of life* without any discordance, and understand them without any hardship?"[56] Life goes beyond experience yet there is no purity of life without the body. The fifth and final limit is *accomplishment or happiness*. The body leads to fulfillment by means of cognitive acquisition. Bernard writes, "*Neither angelic nor brute spirit therefore can benefit from corporeal aids in*

---

illos, qui omnem usum rerum temporalium ad fructum transferunt aeternarum, utentes hoc mundo, tanquam non utentes."

54 Bernard of Clairvaux, On the *Song of Songs I*, pp. 27-8. Leclercq (*SC* 441), SCC 5.4, l. 1-28: "Porro autem supercoelestis spiritus absque adjutorio corporis, et absque intuitu horum quae per corpus sentiuntur, sola profecto suae vicinitate ac vivacitate naturae sufficit apprehendere summa, et intima penetrare. An non hoc Apostolus intellexit, qui cum diceret: Invisibilia Dei per ea quae facta sunt intellecta conspiciuntur; adjecit protinus, a creatura mundi?"

55 Bernard of Clairvaux, On the *Song of Songs I*, pp. 27-8. Leclercq (*SC* 441), SCC 5.4, l. 1-28: "Nimirum quoniam a creatura coeli non ita. Quo enim is involutus carne et terrae incola spiritus, ex consideratione sensibilium proficiens, gradatim quodam modo paulatimque nititur pervenire: eo ille coelestium habitator ingenita subtilitate ac sublimitate sua, in omni velocitate facilitateque pertingit, nullo utique sensus corporei adminiculo fultus, nullo corporei membri adjutus officio, nullo corporeae cujuscunque rei informatus intuitu."

56 Bernard of Clairvaux, On the *Song of Songs I*, pp. 27-8. Leclercq (*SC* 441), SCC 5.4, l. 1-28: "Cur enim inter corpora spirituales scrutetur sensus, quos in libro vitae et absque contradictione legit, et absque difficultate intelligit? cur in sudore vultus sui laboret excutere grana de paleis, de uvis vina, et de amurca oleum, qui ex omnibus satis abundeque ad manum habet? Quis mendicet victum suum per domos alienas, in sua abundans panibus? quis puteum fodere curet, et in terrae visceribus venas aquarum cum labore rimari, cui ultro affatim aquas limpidas fons vivus emanat?"

acquiring the knowledge that makes a spiritual being happy. The brute's natural stupidity renders him *incapable of that knowledge*, while the angel [...] *has no need of a bodily intermediary*."[57] Action is the fulfilment of the body, precisely where body disintegrates to *become* action. The limits of the body, revealed in action, are thus (inversely) as follows: accomplishment, process, function, cognition and necessity. Across the limits of the body arises the disintegration of limits. Where limits disintegrate, body and action collapse and body becomes action. Transformative desire constitutes and overcomes the limits of the body to produce unlimited body *as* action: action is the modeless mode of the body's desire. This raises the question of limits in the *metamorphosis of love*, which a later chapter addresses. For now, a final aspect of consideration regarding bodies is the *body as action*.

3.3 Body as Action

To consider *body as action* is to say that the body *is* action. To recapitulate the central contention of *body and action*, it can be stated that angels and animals alike do not use the body to access what is incorporeal: animals because of ability (they cannot) and angels because of necessity (they ought not). Human beings are somewhere in the middle, having simultaneously the capacity (can) and the necessity (ought) to use the body to overcome the body. Centuries later, Pascal elegantly articulates the gist of Bernard's proposal: "Man is neither angel, nor beast, and misfortune has it such that whoever wants to be an angel must be first a beast."[58] In other words, the human body frames the condition for progress by necessarily passing through the experience of the body to reach the possibility of the incorporeal. Bernard writes, "[Humanity] holds a *middle place between the extremes of bestial and angelic spirits*, manifestly has a *two-fold need of a body*: without it the soul can act neither *for its own advantage nor for the benefit of others*. [...] how, I ask, can you *instruct* the listener if you have no tongue, or *receive instruction* if you have no ear?"[59] The body is no longer

57 Bernard of Clairvaux, On the *Song of Songs I*, pp. 27-8. Leclercq (*SC* 441), SCC 5.4, l. 1-28: "Nec brutus ergo, nec angelicus spiritus ad ea capessenda, quae beatam spiritualem faciunt creaturam, suis ullo modo corporibus adjuvantur; ille quidem pro innata stoliditate non capiens, iste vero pro excellentioris gloriae praerogativa non indigens."

58 Blaise Pascal, *Pensées*, 358, 704, ed. Jacques Chevalier (Flammarion: Paris 1949), 171, as cited in Leclercq (*SC* 441), in SCC 5, n. 3, p. 129: "L'homme n'est ni ange, ni bête, et le malheur veut que qui veut faire l'ange, fait la bête." Translation is mine.

59 Bernard of Clairvaux, On the *Song of Songs I*, p. 28. Leclercq (*SC* 441), SCC 5.5, l. 1-7: "Porro hominis spiritum, qui medium quemdam inter supremum et infimum tenet locum,

overcome merely as limitation – for animals and angels, the body is *always* and *only* limitation. Experiencing the limit of the body is for humans precisely the process of transforming the *roots of human animality accessible only through the body*: from the anorganic, to the organic, the bestial and the animal, and finally the human.[60] Desire is the framework in which the *metamorphosis of the limit* unfolds. The body then *is* most truly effective action at the limit where necessity becomes possibility (modality). The modality of the body is extension. The body extends beyond limits in the passage from necessity to possibility. By embracing animality (the body), humans become fully human when they *can* operate like angels. Modality as act is change. The body is in constant becoming in the mode of extension. There is no continuum of *bodies*. Rather, each mode of the body is wholly particular. "Therefore, writes Bernard, since without the support of the body the brute spirit cannot offer the *service it owes*, nor the heavenly spirit fulfill its *labor of love*, nor the rational spirit of man succeed in *providing for its own and its neighbor's salvation*, it follows that every created spirit certainly *has a need of bodily faculties* whether it be mercy to *assist others*, or, as in the case of man, *to assist as well as being assisted*."[61] Pure extension is the modeless mode of the body. Hence, the desire of the body reaches beyond the body and transforms the confines of the body.

The body extends in the act of study, in admiration and in contemplation. In extension, the modality of the body, the body overcomes limitation because, again, extension is the modeless mode of the body. Even *useless* things, things that do not perform a function for the service of humans, are available for *study*. Bernard writes, "[w]hat then if there be *some living things whose existence seems to confer no benefit on themselves*, nor *to minister in any obvious way to the needs of humanity*? Well, are they not *good to look at, if not to use*? They are for the *mind's study* rather than the *body's utility*, there their advantage

usque adeo ad utrumque necessarium habere corpus manifestum est, ut absque eo nec ipse proficere, nec alteri prodesse possit. Nam, ut taceam membra caetera corporis, officiave membrorum; quonam modo, quaeso, aut sine lingua instruis audientem, aut sine auribus percipis instruentem?"

60 Emmanuel Falque, *Les noces de l'agneau: essai philosophique sur le corps et l'eucharistie* (Paris: Cerf, 2011); Emmanuel Falque, *Ca n'a rien à voir: lire Freud en philosophe* (Paris: Cerf, 2018).

61 Bernard of Clairvaux, On the *Song of Songs I*, pp. 28-9. Leclercq (*SC* 441), SCC 5.6, l. 1-7: "Itaque cum absque corporis adminiculo nec bestialis spiritus servilis conditionis solvere debitum, nec spiritualis coelestisque creatura implere ministerium pietatis, nec rationalis anima tam proximo, quam etiam sibi sufficiat consulere ad salutem: liquet omnem creatum spiritum, sive ut juvet, sive ut juvetur simul et juvet, corporeo prorsus indigere solatio."

lies."[62] The use of other things, furthermore, is simply *appreciation* or *admiration*. The Abbot of Clairvaux goes on, "[e]*ven if injurious, and an obstacle to human welfare in this world, their bodies still serve a purpose* [...] If these creatures do not *provide food or perform a service,* they certainly make man use *his wits in accord with that progress in understanding common to all who enjoy the use of reason,* by which the mysteries of God may be *apprehended* and *contemplated through the things he has made*."[63] The need of limits collapses in the *study* and *contemplation*: "For both the devil and his satellites [...] God forbid that they should be able to harm you. The truth rather is that in spite of themselves they benefit the good."[64] To summarize, the human body is unique in that it is inherently part of the human being (unlike angels) and yet is not constrained but can go beyond utility (unlike animals). This is evident in that extension is a condition for bodily manifestation in contemplation, admiration and study. The body is constitutive of human beings and the extension of its limits is authentic action. Amodality is the mode of (human) action in *extension. Bodies* become embedded in the fabric of finitude by action and in action. The amodal mode of *the body of man* is the *effect* of *the body of God.* God acts by effects, not by agency. These effects are the manifestation of the human body as *limit* and extension. It has been previously suggested that *the body of man* manifests *limits* as modal necessity and *extension* as modal possibility. With *the body of God,* Bernard introduces yet a fourth *kind of spirit* (in addition to the animal, the human and the celestial spirits), namely the spirit of God or *the* Spirit. The Spirit is *the body of God* and pure amodal action or unlimited over-extended omnipotence. The Spirit, in short, is power. Bernard writes, "*He alone has need of no one, he alone, by reason of his omnipotent will,*

---

62 Bernard of Clairvaux, On the *Song of Songs I*, pp. 28-9. Leclercq (*SC* 441), SCC 5.6, l. 7-11: "Quid enim si qua animantia, quantum ad usum sui, reperiantur incommoda, nullisque apta usibus humanarum necessitatum? Prosunt profecto visu, etsi non usu; utiliora cordibus intuentium, quam utentium esse corporibus possent."

63 Bernard of Clairvaux, On the *Song of Songs I*, pp. 28-9. Leclercq (*SC* 441), SCC 5.6, l. 11-19: "Etsi nociva, etsi etiam perniciosa temporali hominum constet esse saluti; non tamen deest eorum corporibus unde cooperentur in bonum his qui secundum propositum vocati sunt sancti; et si non cedendo in cibum, aut exhibendo ministerium, certe ingenium exercendo, juxta eum, qui utique omni utendi ratione praesto est, communis disciplinae profectum, quo invisibilia Dei, per ea quae facta sunt, intellecta conspiciuntur."

64 Bernard of Clairvaux, On the *Song of Songs I*, pp. 28-9. Leclercq (*SC* 441), SCC 5.6, l. 19-25: "Nam et diabolus ejusque satellites, cum sit semper eorum maligna intentio, nocere quidem semper cupiunt, sed bonis aemulatoribus, quibus dicitur: Quis vobis nocere poterit, si boni aemulatores fueritis (I Petr. III, 13)? absit ut possint; magis autem prosunt et nolentes, cooperanturque in bonum bonis."

is sufficient for himself and for all."[65] The Spirit does not need *a* body or *any* body, be it for itself *or* for others, or both for itself *and* for others. Hence, God has *no* specific function assigned, nor does God have limits and as such God is not confined to a body for *operation*. Better, where there is no function there is no limits to agency and body is manifested therein without constraints and as pure agency. Whereas the body is a kind of limited action based on function for all other spirits, for God the body is pure omnipotent will without limits. To will, then, is to act. God, therefore, does not require mediation of instruments for divine agency. *Pure action* reveals God: "[*God*] *communicates himself directly to the mind, he makes himself known directly*; a pure spirit himself, he is received by us in proportion to our rectitude."[66] The Spirit is the fabric of bodily *embeddedness* as power.

The power of the Spirit embeds by means of omnipotence and omnipresence. The agency of God therefore, as *the body of God*, is all-potent (omnipotence). God can in fact command (*imperare*) corporeal things to assume (*assumere*) the divine work. Bodies mediate the action of God. Subsequently, corporeal things are embedded in God as members of *the body of God*, which is without limits. Bernard writes, "[n]evertheless, there *are boundless and countless* achievements that he carries through *by means of his subject creatures, whether corporeal or spiritual*, but he *uses them as master rather than as suppliant*."[67] The Abbot of Clairvaux goes on to offer some examples of divine action accomplished through corporeal members: "[God] *employs my tongue for his purpose of instructing you*, when he *could certainly impart the same knowledge directly with greater facility on his part and more pleasure for you*."[68] The power of the Spirit is manifested in unifying extension by closing

65 Bernard of Clairvaux, On the *Song of Songs I*, pp. 29-30. Leclercq (*SC* 441), SCC 5.8, l. 9-14: "Sequestretur proinde praerogativa haec summo ac incircumscripto Spiritui, qui solus, cum docet angelum sive hominem scientiam, instrumentum non quaerit nostrae corporeae auris, sicut nec sibi oris. Per se infunditur, per se innotescit, purus capitur a puris. Solus nullius indiget; solus et sibi, et omnibus de sola omnipotenti voluntate sufficiens."

66 Bernard of Clairvaux, On the *Song of Songs I*, pp. 29-30. Leclercq (*SC* 441), SCC 5.8, l. 9-14: "Sequestretur proinde praerogativa haec summo ac incircumscripto Spiritui, qui solus, cum docet angelum sive hominem scientiam, instrumentum non quaerit nostrae corporeae auris, sicut nec sibi oris. Per se infunditur, per se innotescit, purus capitur a puris. Solus nullius indiget; solus et sibi, et omnibus de sola omnipotenti voluntate sufficiens."

67 Bernard of Clairvaux, On the *Song of Songs I*, p. 30. Leclercq (*SC* 441), SCC 5.9, l. 1-18: "Operatur tamen immensa et innumera per subjectam creaturam corporalem, sive spiritualem; sed quasi imperans, non quasi mendicans."

68 Bernard of Clairvaux, On the *Song of Songs I*, p. 30. Leclercq (*SC* 441), SCC 5.9, l. 1-18: "En, verbi gratia, quod linguam meam corporalem assumpsit nunc in opus suum, docere videlicet vos, cum per se absque dubio facilius suaviusque id posset."

the distance of space and limit. Desire as amodal possibility can be resistance to extension: "I know not why, *we seem to feel that the good which comes to us through an evil agent is on that account more gratifying and pleasurable.*"[69] The good, which results from evil, produces *jouissance*; as such divine action, also includes desire. God does not *need* a body but can use bodies to effect (*proferare*) or act because the divine mode of agency is kindness (production), not consumption (lack): "*This mode of acting that he has chosen represents an indulgence on his part, not indigence.*"[70] The divine *use* or governance of bodies is also the key to understanding why God can accomplish good things through bad people even if God could do otherwise. "*God makes*, notes Bernard, *use of the wicked to benefit the just; it by no means implies that he needs their help in doing good.*"[71] God is omnipotent in choice of members but also in governance over evil. The extension of the Spirit embeds also evil construed as resistance at the limits, sinful or otherwise (finitude).

There are no limits without delineation: extension requires resistance. Limits are inherent to action. What are these limits? The divine will operates (*operare*) through bodies not for itself, but for others and because of others (*per eum*): "*There is furthermore the case of the person* [...] *who performs good deeds against his will.* It is plain that *the good of which he is the agent does not benefit himself since no good can benefit one whose will is set against it.* He is therefore merely a *dispenser* of good."[72] Despite God not needing a body that is without function and limits as pure will, God can still govern or order bodies in creation. Bodies are the organizing principle of creation. The said *imposition* of limits on divine agency is the manner of operation or mode as *resistance*. Whereas extension is amodal agency, limitation is modal resistance. Bodies must resist in order to extend. Resistance is a condition for bodies to extend beyond limits in action. Resistance demarks limits. There is *resistance* in the *drive* of God (*egere*) to govern much more over things without reason

69 Bernard of Clairvaux, On the *Song of Songs I*, p. 30. Leclercq (*SC* 441), SCC 5.9, l. 1-18: "Igitur ei quidem dispensatio tantum credita est; sed nescio quomodo gratius jucundiusque sentimus bonum, quod per malum dispensatorem ministratur."

70 Bernard of Clairvaux, On the *Song of Songs I*, p. 30. Leclercq (*SC* 441), SCC 5.9, l. 1-18: "En, verbi gratia, quod linguam meam corporalem assumpsit nunc in opus suum, docere videlicet vos, cum per se absque dubio facilius suaviusque id posset; profecto indulgentia est, non indigentia."

71 Bernard of Clairvaux, On the *Song of Songs I*, p. 30. Leclercq (*SC* 441), SCC 5.9, l. 1-18: "Ipsa est ergo causa, cur et per malos Deus faciat bona bonis: non autem, quod opera eorum indigeat in benefaciendo."

72 Bernard of Clairvaux, On the *Song of Songs I*, p. 30. Leclercq (*SC* 441), SCC 5.9, l. 1-18: "Est tamen qui bonum operatur non volens, sive homo malus, sive angelus malus: et constat non fieri propter cum, quod fit per eum, cum prodesse nullum bonum possit invito."

or sense than over those that do have them. Bernard does not explain exactly why while noting that "*God has less need still of those creatures that lack sense or reason*? [...] when these do *have a share in the doing of good* we are reminded that *all creatures are the servants of that God*."[73] This statement is puzzling as there are no bodies without reason or sense. Even animal bodies have sense. *A* body does not constrain God. Rather, in *the body of God*, construed as pure will, the sense and reason of bodies in a way *resist* God. This is not a contradiction. On the contrary, it shows that "all belongs to God"[74] since even things beyond the *limits* of divine control where *resistance* arises are ultimately governed by God to the extent that they accomplish good works (*opus bonum*). And, observes Bernard with a flare of fatality, things operate God's work most of the time anyways, and so there is no reason why God would need a body to force things to act otherwise (necessity): "Granted then that *bodily agents are often and opportunely used in promoting the works of God* [...] what need has he, I ask, *for a body of his own* when *to his least desire all bodies* [...] are *equally obedient*?"[75] *Extension* (later *diffusion*) compliment the limit of bodies as *resistance* to divine agency. The operation of the universe by bodies *is* the extension of divine will. "Again, because he knows the *means* that best suit his *purpose*, he does not choose a bodily creature for the sake of *the efficacy of its action but rather for the fittingness of it*."[76] The choice of limit is not *efficacy* construed as speed of outcome but rather mode (*congruetiam*). The *extension* of *resistance* determines mode. The resistance of bodies to divine governance as pure action determines the mode of divine governance as extension. The oscillating reciprocation between the limits of God in resistance by bodies and the inevitably, or fatality of divine governance as action produces a tension: no extension without resistance, no resistance without extension. Resistance is constitutive of limits.

73 Bernard of Clairvaux, On the *Song of Songs I*, pp. 30-1. Leclercq (*SC* 441), SCC 5.10, l. 1-17: "Porro his quae ratione vel sensu carentia sunt, multo minus Deum egere quis dubitet? Sed quando in opus bonum et ipsa concurrunt, apparet quoniam omnia serviunt ei, cui merito est dicere: Meus est orbis terrae (Psal. XLIX, 12)."

74 Bernard of Clairvaux, On the *Song of Songs I*, pp. 30-1. Leclercq (*SC* 441), SCC 5.10, l. 1-17: "Meus est orbis terrae."

75 Bernard of Clairvaux, On the *Song of Songs I*, pp. 30-1. Leclercq (*SC* 441), SCC 5.10, l. 1-17: "Esto deinde quod corporum ministeria opportune plerumque divinis operibus applicentur, ut, verbi gratia, pluviae vivificandis seminibus, vel multiplicandis segetibus, vel fructibus maturandis; quid proprio, quaeso, de corpore facere habet, cui ad nutum indifferenter universa corpora coelestia atque terrestria obsequi constat?"

76 Bernard of Clairvaux, On the *Song of Songs I*, pp. 30-1. Leclercq (*SC* 441), SCC 5.10, l. 1-17: "Aut certe quia novit quae per quae convenientius fiant; de servitute corporeae creaturae non efficaciam quaerit, sed congruentiam."

Harmony orders resistance and extension in the limits. The qualitative expression of divine agency emerges within the interplay of resistence and extension. God does not need a body because other bodies accomplish the work God would have to accomplish by a body did he not have other bodies to do so. God governs bodies not only by efficient action, i.e., by acting upon things, but primarily by harmonious action, i.e., by ensuring order. Order is harmony of bodies through the will of God effectuated by means of bodies precisely as *the body of God*. All bodies act in simultaneous conjunction as orchestration by divine command. In addition, such is the measure of divine presence in the world. Presence (governance) is not identification (pantheism). God is absolute and incorporeal because God is intimate *in* the depth of bodies. Indeed, there is a deeply intimate bond between the divine governance and the harmony of *all* bodies of creation. Ultimately, God does not need a body because no *body* is alien or strange (*alienum*) to God: "*A body of his own would be superfluous to one for whom none exists outside his sway*."[77] God is not *a* body. To speak of *the body of God* is to refer to the harmony of *all* other bodies in existence, which, together, through their harmony, fulfill the good works of providence and simultaneously manifest God. God does not enter the world because God is *in* the world as *flesh of the world* (Merleau-Ponty). *The body of God* is proximity manifested in harmony of extension and resistance in the limits.

Conclusion

The present chapter has been concerned with transformative desire of the body and with explicating how it produces *bodies* in experience. Desire generates the body, the amodal mode of the body is action as desire manifested in extension beyond limits and limits are harmoniously constituted at the limits by the interplay of extension and resistance, which is Spirit. The desire of God as God's intimate governance of all bodies, moreover, is the condition for human experience. The hermeneutics of desire bring experience of the human body to *the body of God* as harmonious action. In the process, there is yet another transformation of desire, this time not as transformation of the

77 Bernard of Clairvaux, On the *Song of Songs I*, pp. 30-1. Leclercq (*SC* 441), SCC 5.10, l. 1-17: "Plane superfluo haberet suum, qui nullum sibi reperit alienum. Verum si cuncta, quae hoc loco dicenda occurrunt, praesenti volumus sermone concludere, sermo modum excedet, et vires forsitan aliquorum: propterea quae restant, sub alio servemus absolvenda principio."

body, but as transformation of the flesh through divine action. The generation of *bodies, the body of God* and *the body of man*, therefore marks a further *metamorphosis*, this time in the form of configurative generation, of the body by the body, whereby the itinerary of desire returns to the beginning as *the beginning without beginning*. In the *metamorphosis of love*, desire generates body. In the *metamorphosis of love*, desire and body emerge as the very fabric on which the transformation or reconfiguration of finitude takes place, from *eros* into *agape*. Desire of the body and the body of desire are intimately interwoven and progressively manifested in transformation, thereby constituting the framework for the possibility of the *metamorphosis of love*. In an ongoing effort to continue charting the *metamorphosis of love* as an answer to the question of the relationship between *eros* and *agape*, the next major part of this study turns attention to the relationship between *desire and word*. The third and final part focuses on *desire and free will*.

PART II

Word

CHAPTER 4

Extension

How do bodies *extend* through *the* Word? An initial approach to this question must first consider *extension* of desire *as* body, which in the *des-order* of love, arises in the *a*-rationality of desire. This ensures a transition from body to the Word, which is, precisely, a transition from *desire and the body* to *desire in the word*, or from the initial Bernardine preference of desire over reason in the *book of experience*, to desire's *metamorphosis* into the order of charity. The delightful contrast, and perhaps even contradiction, between desire and reason is engrained deeply within a historical discourse of an antagonism – albeit artificial, conceptual, and with little room for the experiential – between desire and reason. In this history, the question is thus: if truly desire impels and compels even reason, and beyond reason, perhaps even to the exclusion of reason, how then, does desire order charity, or how, in other words, does desire effectuate order *tout court*? Bernard's proposal consists in considering *des-order* as reconfiguration in the *metamorphosis of love*. *Des-order*, moreover, ensures the passage from body to word. *Des-order*, the synthesis of desire and order, is a harmonious balance, which negates and overcomes the dichotomy of reason and desire. In the *des-order* of charity, reason and desire are flawlessly incorporated without reducing or subordinating one to the other. Therefore, *des-order* avoids restricting the functions of reason to the movements of the passions (Hume)[1] or considering the passions as the 'whip' of reason (Hobbes[2] and Locke[3]). *Des-order* also renounces the quest for "rationality of the passions"

1 David Hume, *A Treatise of Human Nature* (Chelmsford: Courier Corporation, 2003), II.3.3.

2 Arrigo Pacchi, "Hobbes and the Passions," *Topoi* 6, no. 2 (1987): 111, "It is well known that the cornerstone of Hobbes' political philosophy is *the opposition between reason and the emotions*: even if the State, which provides the only guarantee of peace and welfare for mankind, is a model of rational construction, its stability is threatened not only by *ignorance but also by the disrupting influence of the passions*, which operate direction or by way of destructive doctrines or religious superstition." Only passions move passions for Hobbes (*De Corpore* 9.7) which raises the question of motivation by the opposing entities of reason and passions (*de Cive* 8.18) or "the problem of the rationality of passions," cf. Micheline Triomphe, "La rationalité de la passion chez Hobbes," *Revue de la Société d'études anglo-américaines des XVIIe et XVIIIe siècles* 7, no. 1 (1978): 49-60.

3 'The passions too have most of them, in most persons, operations on the body, and cause various changes in it; which, not being always sensible, do not make a necessary part of the *idea* of each passion.' 192; 'For whatever good is proposed, if its absence carries no displeasure nor pain with it, if a man be easy and content without it, there is no desire of it nor

 | DOI:10.30965/9783846767504_006

(Rousseau),[4] the sentimentalism of reason (Shaftesbury and Hutcheson), and the manoeuvre of the performative reduction of impulse (Butler) as well as, finally, a turn to pure divine voluntarism (Pufendorf). In *des-order*, Bernard construes desire as the governing principle, again, paradoxically, of the order of charity. Thus, the epithet "[desire] ordered charity in me"[5] refers simultaneously to order and disorder, which is *des-order*, as manifested in *extension* of Word, and, specifically, in *extension* through *words of desire* (4.1), *the extension of desire* (4.2) and *the effusion of the word* (4.3).

4.1 Words of Desire

Desire extends the body beyond the confines of limits by means of words. Desire is the extension of the body and words extend body into desire. For Bernard, *words of desire* perform the body. Differently framed, the performativity of *words* bridges the distance from body to action. Between the body and extension of desire is the word, wherefore the incarnation is the locus of the passage (metaphysics) or *metamorphosis* of pure divine action into the experience of the body *in* God. The manifestation of God in the body and in the flesh charts accordingly the inevitable transition from the efficient Word (*verbum*), through pure act (*voluntas*), to the body (*corpus*). Thus, *the body is divine action* accomplished by a single movement of divine will. The *voie* to the carnal feet of Christ are the spiritual feet of God. The entry point from *desire*

---

endeavour after it;' 190-1, Locke: 'Pleasure and pain and that which causes them, good and evil, are the hinges on which our passions turn'. (190): Of Power', Book II Chapter XXI of his *Essay Concerning Human Understanding.*

4 Jean-Jacques Rousseau, *Discourse on the Origin and the Foundations of Inequality among Men*, Boston: Bedford/St. Martins, 2011): "the human understanding is greatly indebted to the passions, which, it is universally allowed, are also much indebted to the understanding. It is by the activity of the passions that our reason is improved; for we desire knowledge only because we wish to enjoy; and it is impossible to conceive any reason why a person who has neither fears nor desires should give himself the trouble of reasoning. The passions, again, originate in our wants, and their progress depends on that of our knowledge; for we cannot desire or fear anything, except from the idea we have of it, or from the simple impulse of nature" (Part I).

5 Bernard of Clairvaux, On the *Song of Songs III*, p. 30. Verdeyen (*SC* 452), SSC 50.1, l. 1, cf. Cant. 2.4. "*ordinavit in me charitatem.*" On 'the order of charity', cf. *ordo* and *ordo caritatis* in Pierluigi Lia, *L'estetica Teologica Di Bernardo Di Chiaravalle. La Mistica Cristiana Tra Oriente E Occidente* (Firenze: Sismel, 2007), 107-131.

and the body to *desire in the Word* occurs analogously to *the beginning without beginning*, yet this time in *the body and reason*, where *the book of experience* transforms reason and the desire of the body, is now the locus of extension. Extension manifests the body as becoming. Extension is an exit from tension, or *ex*-tension. The limits of desire in the word, where "desire impels me, not reason"[6] are illustrated by the unfulfilled longing for the supreme kiss in the dialogue of the lovers. The progression and various transformations as well as manifestations and multilayered senses of the kisses culminate in an unsatisfactory expression of desire in the supreme kiss. The longing for the kiss is expressed by the dialogue which ensues between the bride and the bridegroom. Bernard writes, "It is time now for us *to return to the book* and attempt an explanation of the words of the bride and their consequence. [...] they are, *swinging precipitately out of nowhere, suspended before us*. But we must see if there is *something antecedent to them to which we may suitably connect them up*."[7] The desire between the spouses is the code for making sense (*cohereant*) of the sudden conversation, which emerges without a beginning (*principio*). The hermeneutics of desire takes the relay of a hermeneutics of the body and brings full circle the analysis of the kisses back to the motivating movement across body, word, God and experience, namely desire. Bernard plunges the hearer into the conversation without preparation and without a departure. Desire emerges out of (*ex*) a tension (*tension*) – from stretching out of the limits, later stretching is manifested as a continuum or spreading. The tension is unfulfilled desire. The bride is anxious and weary awaiting the bride with great anticipation. Bernard describes her thus: "[t]hey find her *in a state of weariness, bemoaning her condition; and wondering what the cause may be, they begin to question her*: 'What has happened? [...]' 'I cannot rest,' she said, 'unless he kisses me with the kiss of his mouth. [...] if he has genuine regard for me, let him kiss me with the kiss of his mouth. There is no question of ingratitude on

6 Bernard of Clairvaux, On the *Song of Songs I*, pp. 54-5. Leclercq (*SC* 441): SCC 9.2, l. 7. Cf. also, SCC 58.1, SCC 75.1: "Desiderio feror, non ratione." Also, cf. Augustine *Conf.* XIII, 9 and Virgil *Buocoliques*, II, 65: "trahit sua quemque voluptas", "*each one is trained by their pleasure*". Bernard also employs the expression in a negative way in SBO V 216, 4; Via 136. Cited in SCC 9.2, n. 1, p. 199.

7 Bernard of Clairvaux, On the *Song of Songs I*, pp. 53-4. Leclercq (*SC* 441), SCC 9.1, l. 1-4: "Accedamus jam ad librum, verbisque sponsae rationem demus et consequentiam. Pendent enim, et praerupta nutant absque principio. Ideoque praemittendum cui competenter cohaereant."

my part, it is simply that I am in love."[8] Confusion and a sense of unworthiness accompanies the bride. Bernard continues, "The favors I have received are far *above what I deserve, but they are less than what I long for. It is desire that drives me on, not reason.*"[9] There is also a sense of the inevitable, where the drive of desire trumps reason. Ultimately, the strength of love is the reason for the words. "Please do not accuse me of presumption *if I yield to this impulse of love.* My shame indeed rebukes me, but *love is stronger than all.* [...] love does not wait for judgment, is not chastened by advice, not shackled by shame nor subdued by reason."[10] The intriguing emphasis now shifts from longing as the driving force of desire, accomplished through God in the body and experience, to the engendering of longing *by* longing, and finally, to unfulfilled desire. For the bride, the kiss of the feet and the kiss of the hands are not enough. In this passage, the restlessness of the bride who lays claim to love as an entitlement puzzles Bernard. The tension of desire, construed in terms of generation, is failure to extend or *resistance.* From this vantage point, love is the extension of desire. The attitude of the bride is significant. At this turning point, where word reveals desire, so too love overcomes reason. What exactly does the bride want? What can be done to satisfy her? In the dialogue, the bride refuses to

---

8 Bernard of Clairvaux, On the *Song of Songs I*, pp. 53-6. Leclercq (*SC* 441), SCC 9.1, l. 8-27: "Ponamus proinde istos, quos sponsi sodales diximus, visitandi salutandique gratia, sicut heri et nudiustertius, accessisse nunc quoque ad sponsam; ipsamque submurmurantem et taedentem reperisse, mirari causam, et quasi alloqui in hunc modum. Quid novi accidit? quid te cernimus solito tristiorem? quae inopinati murmuris causa? Certe cum aversa et alienata ires post amatores tuos, cum quibus male erat tibi, compulsa tandem reverti ad virum tuum priorem, nonne ut saltem merereris tangere pedes, multis precibus et fletibus institisti? Recolo, inquit. Quid? Obtento eo, simulque accepta in osculo pedum indulgentia de offensis, nunquid non rursus facta impatiens, et tanta nequaquam dignatione contenta, sed majoris familiaritatis cupida, secundam quoque gratiam eadem qua prius instantia postulasti et impetrasti, ita ut in osculo manus adepta sis virtutes non paucas, et non parvas? Non diffiteor, ait. Et illi: Enimvero num tu es quae jurare et obtestari solebas, si unquam ad osculum manus pervenire daretur, sufficere jam tibi; nil te de caetero petituram? Ego. Quid igitur? Forte horum quae acceperas quidpiam ablatum causaberis? Nihil. An vero times repetitum iri, quod tibi de mala tua pristina conversatione indultum praesumpseras? Non."

9 Bernard of Clairvaux, On the *Song of Songs I*, pp. 54-5. Leclercq (*SC* 441), SCC 9.2, l. 7: "Desiderio feror, non ratione."

10 Bernard of Clairvaux, On the *Song of Songs I*, pp. 54-5. Leclercq (*SC* 441), SCC 9.2, l. 1-12: "Age tamen, dic unde queamus satisfacere tibi. Non quiesco, ait, nisi osculetur me osculo oris sui. Gratias de osculo pedum, gratias et de manus; sed si cura est illi ulla de me, Osculetur me osculo oris sui (Cant. I, 1). Non sum ingrata, sed amo. Accepi, fateor, meritis potiora, sed prorsus inferiora votis. Desiderio feror, non ratione. Ne, quaeso, causemini praesumptionem, ubi affectio urget. Pudor sane reclamat; sed superat amor. Nec ignoro, quod honor regis judicium diligit (Psal. XCVIII, 4); sed praeceps amor nec judicium praestolatur, nec consilio temperatur, nec pudore frenatur, nec rationi subjicitur."

find peace (*non quiesco*) with anything falling short of the supreme kiss. The attitude of such human desire for God is not a mark of ungratefulness. Rather, it is the expression of a paradigmatic shift in the logic of divine desire. The request for the kiss of the mouth testifies to the bride's love for the groom: "There is no question of ingratitude on my part, it is simply that I am in love."[11] At this point, and for the first time in *On the Song of Songs*, desire (*desiderio*) *is* framed in terms of love (*amor*). The bride does not shy away from desiring more than is merited (*merito*) because the promise (*votum*), presumably of love, goes beyond merit. Love is gratuitous because love is a gift. In other words, desire is the mark of love (*non sum ingrata, sed amo*). The unquenched expectation and demand of unmerited love in the dynamic of desire and satisfaction is *the* mark of love. A promise (*votum*) is what bridges (*merited*) desire with (unmerited) love. The phrase "*non sum ingrata, sed amo*" is a mirror alternative of "*desiderio feror, non ratione*"[12]: the logic of desire, over and against reason (*ratione*), is postulated as *the* expression of love. Love is the extension of desire which from the tension (*ex-tension*) emerges as generative and constitutive of the body. Thus, the body manifests love as metamorphosed desire. Extension is the locus where the multiplicity of the range of desire and love is waged. Are love and *desire* deployed synonymously (uinivocity) or do they maintain a singularity while overlapping somehow (equivocity)? There is a third way: the *metamorphosis of love.* The lines which follow seem to suggest that while they are related, love and desire remain distinct while exhibiting a transformative force (metamorphosis). What is the difference between desire and love, and how do they relate? The urgency (*urgere*) of desire is *not* from desire itself, but from the affect (*affectus*).[13] The affect produces a sense of urgency (*ubi affectio urget*) expressed as desire beyond reason. Though desire may be *affected* into urgency of satisfaction, the modesty or shame (*pudor*) in so demanding is overcome by love.[14] The overcoming of affect as expressed in desire beyond

11 Bernard of Clairvaux, On the *Song of Songs I*, pp. 54-5. Leclercq (*SC* 441), SCC 9.2, l. 1-12: "Non sum ingrata, sed amo."

12 Bernard of Clairvaux, On the *Song of Songs I*, pp. 54-5. Leclercq (*SC* 441), SCC 9.2, l. 7: "Desiderio feror, non ratione."

13 Damien Boquet, *L'ordre de l'affect au moyen Âge: autour de l'anthropologie affective d'Aelred de Rievaulx* (Caen: CRAHM, 2005); Pacificus Delfgaauw, *Saint Bernard : maître de l'amour divin* (Paris: FAC-éditions, 1994); Pacificus Delfgaauw, "La nature et les degrés de l'amour selon saint Bernard," in *Saint Bernard theologien: actes du congres de Dijon* (1953): 15-9; Jean Leclercq, "Voir le monde par les affects : Bernard de Clairvaux et La voie monastique," *Revue des Sciences Philosophiques et Theologiques* 95, no. 2 (2011): 323-41; Philip Liston-Kraft, "Bernard's Belching Bride: The *Affectus* That Words Cannot Express," *Medieval Mystical Theology* 26, no. 1 (2017): 54-72.

14 Bernard of Clairvaux, On the *Song of Songs I*, pp. 54-5. Leclercq (*SC* 441), SCC 9.2, l. 1-12: "Pudor sane reclamat; sed superat amor."

reason is overcome (*superare*) by love. Thus, desire is not love. Love is the cause for demanding unmerited desire. Desire is the currency of love and yet when affected (*affectus*), desire is overcome, not by reason, but by love. This overcoming (*superare*) inaugurates the transformation or metamorphosis of desire by love. Love is the generative transformation of desire, which is desired.

The proposed Bernardine generative metamorphosis of desire resulting in the manifestation of love offers an unprecedented synthesis. The weight of love in Augustine – "my love is my weight"[15] – is injected into Virgil's "drive of pleasure." Bernard harmonizes the drive of desire as love (Augustine) with the initially contrasting drive of pleasure against love (Virgil) in order to give desire a prominent place in the search for God and ultimately in loving God. On the one hand, "desire is my weight" (Augustine) and, on the other hand, "everyone is guided by their own love" (Virgil), are reconfigured in the (dis)order or metamorphosis of desire by love. What separates the equivocal *élan* of love as desire (Augustine) from the univocal desire without love (Virgil) is the experience of the body, which effects the transformation of desire into love and of love into desire (Bernard). Such is the significance of the final interpretation of the kiss progressively reached through the careful weaving of appeal to experience and the body to recognize and make desire. Specifically, Bernard recognizes the limits of language to communicate and contain desire. Desire thus becomes an extension of word in the body: desire breaks the distance between space (body) and extension (word). Desire extends limits and performs corporeality in the process. There is no extension without tension (*acedia*). Words express the limits of the body but only desire extends beyond confines. The insufficiency of words to capture desire frames the Bernardine extension of desire by love in the *metamorphosis of love*. Following the hermeneutics of desire, Bernard appeals to the experience of the hearer: "Many of you too, as I recall […]."[16] He then concludes a sustained interpretation of *the kiss* throughout the previous nine sermons, with a return to experience of the body: "Many of you too, as I recall, are *accustomed to complain* to me in our private conversations about a

15 Cf. *Conf.* XIII: "pondus meum amor meus: eo feror quocumque feror." Denis O'Brien, "*pondus meum amor meus*: Saint Augustine and Jamblique," *Revue de l'histoire des religions* (1981): 423-8; Emmanuel Falque, " Après la métaphysique ? Le "poids de la vie" selon saint Augustin ", *in* Alain de Libera (éd.), *Après la métaphysique : saint Augustin ?*, coll. " Institut d'Etudes Médiévales " (Paris: Vrin, 2013): 111-28; Jean-Luc Marion, "Substantia. Note sur l'usage de Substantia par st. Augustin et sur son appartenance à l'histoire de la métaphysique," in *Mots médiévaux offerts à Ruedi Imbach*: 691-701.

16 Bernard of Clairvaux, On the *Song of Songs I*, p. 55. Leclercq (*SC* 441), SCC 9.3, l. 1: "plurimique vestrum mihi quoque."

similar languor and dryness of soul."[17] Without movement (*acedia*), there is no extension, desire or love. Indeed, love is the driving force of extension: "*What of these, except that they yearn to be kissed?* That they yearn is indeed evident, their very *mouths are open* to inhale [...] *insight that they may attain to what they long for, wisdom in order to savor what the mind apprehends.*"[18] The longing, alone, fails to move because words are sterile without experience. Even the linguistic expression of the kiss is insufficient to capture the experience of the kiss. Desire escapes language (Liston-Kraft) and even the body.[19] Words (*expressum*) give way to the body (*impressum*). The body encounters limits through words and then gives way to action.[20] Words perform body in resistance to a-tension (*acedia*). Body is performed as experience. Experience is the precondition, the means by which and the consequence of the kiss, weaved through desire, the body and God. The experience of love as desire is therefore no longer only something that happens passively and univocally as "erotic phenomenon" (Marion).[21] Love is the proof of active manifestation *as* experience: "It is through her experience of this twofold goodness therefore, that the bride

---

17 Bernard of Clairvaux, On the *Song of Songs I*, p. 55. Leclercq (*SC* 441), SCC 9.3, l. 1-21: "Plerique vestrum mihi quoque, ut memini, in privatis confessionibus suis conqueri solent super hujuscemodi animi arentis languore atque hebetudine stolidae mentis, quod Dei scilicet alta atque subtilia penetrare nequeant, quod de suavitate spiritus aut nil, aut parum sentiant."

18 Bernard of Clairvaux, On the *Song of Songs I*, p. 55. Leclercq (*SC* 441), SCC 9.3, l. 1-21: "Quid isti, nisi ad osculum suspirant? Suspirant plane, et inhiant spiritui sapientiae et intellectus: intellectus utique quo pertingant; sapientiae, quia gustent quod intellectu apprehenderint. Ego in hoc ipso affectu sanctum puto orasse Prophetam, cum diceret: Sicut adipe et pinguedine repleatur anima mea, et labiis exsultationis laudabit os meum (Psal. LXII, 6). Osculum omnino petebat, et illud osculum, in cujus tactu perfusis labiis pinguedine gratiae specialis [alias, spiritualis], sequeretur quod alibi idem ipse precatur: Repleatur os meum laude, ut cantem gloriam tuam, tota die magnitudinem tuam (Psal. LXX, 8). Denique et eructavit ubi gustavit: Quam magna multitudo dulcedinis tuae, Domine, quam abscondisti timentibus te (Psal. XXX, 20). Satis hoc osculum detinuit nos, et necdum me illud, ut verum fatear, digne satis expressisse confido. Sed transeamus ad reliqua; quia id melius impressum, quam expressum innotescit."

19 Philip Liston-Kraft, "Bernard's Belching Bride: The *Affectus* That Words Cannot Express," *Medieval Mystical Theology* 26, no. 1 (2017): 54-72.

20 Bernard of Clairvaux, On the *Song of Songs I*, p. 60. Leclercq (SC 441), SCC 9.10, l. 21-23: "Cumulatur deinde laus uberum fragantia unguentorum, quod non solum verborum sapore pascant, sed et factorum opinion redoleant."

21 Ilona Bala, "La phénoménologie de l'amour de Jean-Luc Marion : l'expérience de la passivité en tant que dépassement de l'égologie," *Studia Litteraria Universitatis Iagellonicae Cracoviensis* 10, no. 4 (2015): 299-315.

justifies the increase of confidence that emboldened her to ask for the kiss."[22] Experience begets desire to experience love. Love generates desire and desire generates love in an endless *beginning without beginning*. What is this *proof* of experience? The experienced proof of experience is the passage, as transformation, from word to action, from desire to love, through *the* Word and *bodies*, which gaps desire and love. There is no discontinuity from desire to love or from word to action. The efficiency of the word in action, or the Verb, transforms through bodies. Hence, a new conception of desire is possible, not as lacking longing, or simply limited to unfulfilled desire, but as desiring-production. These pass through the experience of *fecundation* through the Word of God. Bernard continues, "While the bride is conversing about the Bridegroom, he, as I have said, *suddenly appears, yields to her desire by giving her a kiss*, and so brings to fulfillment those words of the psalm: '*You have granted him his heart's desire, not denied him what his lips entreated.*'"[23] The limits of words to express desire show that body is the extension of desire, which words cannot contain. Experience is active manifestation of the body. Various modes or potencies manifest the body, specifically in three moments: physical (*soma*), significatory (*sema*) and actualization. A first manifestation is physical expression of the *fullness* of joy. Desire has the physical manifestation of joy. Bernard writes, "[*t*]*he filling up of her breasts is a proof of this*. For so great is the *potency of that holy kiss*, that no sooner has the bride received it than *she conceives and her breasts grow rounded with the fruitfulness of conception* [...]. Men with an urge to frequent prayer will have experience of what I say."[24] A second mode of desire is the signification of the body as *overflowing*: "[o]ften enough when we approach the altar to pray our hearts are dry and lukewarm. But if we persevere, there comes an *unexpected infusion of grace, our breast expands as it were, and our interior is filled with an overflowing love*."[25] Finally, what is signi-

22 Bernard of Clairvaux, On the *Song of Songs I*, p. 55. Leclercq (*SC* 441), SCC 9.5, l. 23-25: "Huiius ergo geminae bonitatis experiment in eam se fiduciam excrevisse fatetur sponsa, ut auderet petere osculum."

23 Bernard of Clairvaux, On the *Song of Songs I*, pp. 58-9. Leclercq (*SC* 441), SCC 9.7, l. 1-4: "Sponsa loquente de sponso, repente, ut dixeram, adest ille, annuit voto, dat osculum, impletque in ea sermonem qui scriptus est: Desiderium cordis ejus tribuisti ei, et voluntate labiorum ejus non fraudasti eum (Psal. XX. 3)."

24 Bernard of Clairvaux, On the *Song of Songs I*, pp. 58-9. Leclercq (*SC* 441), SCC 9.7, l. 4-10: "Quod et probat ex ejus uberum repletione. Tantae nempe efficaciae osculum sanctum est, ut ex ipso mox, cum acceperit illud, sponsa concipiat, tumescentibus nimirum uberibus, et lacte quasi pinguescentibus in testimonium. Quibus studium est orare frequenter, experti sunt quod dico."

25 Bernard of Clairvaux, On the *Song of Songs I*, pp. 58-9. Leclercq (*SC* 441), SCC 9.7, l. 10-14: "Saepe corde tepido et arido accedimus ad altare, orationi incumbimus. Persistentibus

fied becomes actualized, and so, the sign of desire is the actualization of bodily reception. "'You have received, my love, what you asked for, and *here is a sign to show you,* your breasts are better than wine; henceforth *you will know that you have received the kiss because you will be conscious of having conceived.*'"[26] The body is a receptacle of desire. There is no dichotomy between language and the body because when words fail to express desire, the language of the body emerges as the extension of desire. Words perform the modes of the body as *extension of desire.*

4.2 Extension of Desire

Efficacious words, the outcome of the extension of desire, perform the body. The efficacious and holy kiss immediately conceives. Love is the *efficacious* outcome of desire. Words, which speak first about desire, reach a limit when words become desire. Words no longer communicate or frame desire, they are efficacious bearers of desire, which in expressing desire, in fact *do* what they express.[27] However, love as an outcome of desire *must* be treated in Bernard's *On the Song of Song* fundamentally as *productive transformation* or desiring-production, thereby giving way to a complimentary reading of the epithet "desire impels me, not reason."[28] Indeed, the term *feror* can signify *guidance* or *production.* Therefore, the fundamental concern at the heart of the metamorphosis of desire by love in the body and experience is not a question of tension between loves or love and desire (Augustine and Vergil), or of their collapse into a single passive phenomenon (Marion), but of *directionality* (*feror* as guidance) and of *production* (*feror* as generation). In short, desire and love relate fundamentally as *extension.* Therefore, if love is the extension of bodily desire, love is not at odds with desire but with reason. Bernard not only harmonizes love and desire but also goes beyond their dialectic (Virgil

autem repente infunditur gratia, pinguescit pectus, replet viscera inundatio pietatis; et si sit qui premat, lac conceptae dulcedinis ubertim fundere non tardabunt."

26 Bernard of Clairvaux, On the *Song of Songs I*, pp. 58-9. Leclercq (*SC* 441), SCC 9.7, l. 14-21: "Dicat ergo: Habes, sponsa, quod petiisti, et hoc tibi signum, quia meliora facta sunt ubera tua vino. Hinc te scilicet noveris osculum accepisse, quod te concepisse sentis. Unde et ubera tibi intumuerunt, facta in ubertate lactis meliora vino scientiae saecularis, quae [alias, quod] quidem inebriat, sed curiositate, non charitate; implens, non nutriens; inflans, non aedificans; ingurgitans, non confortans."

27 Hans Boersma and Matthew Levering, eds. *The Oxford Handbook of Sacramental Theology* (Oxford: Oxford University Press, 2015).

28 Bernard of Clairvaux, On the *Song of Songs I*, pp. 54-5. Leclercq (*SC* 441), SCC 9.2, l. 7: "Desiderio feror, non ratione."

and Augustine). Thus, love is the extension of desire performed as body by words. Love extends through the performative action of the Word in the body. In the hermeneutics of the body, previously charted in the paradigm of the Word in the flesh, the *assumed man* (*assumptis homino*) is now simultaneously the generator of desire (*desiderio feror*) and the desiring extension of the body. The Word as *signifier signified* extends desire into love according to a three-fold movement in the *metamorphosis of love*: reception, conception or generation and (re)order or *des-order.* On a first moment, the body is mainly considered as a receptacle of desire. The body is then considered, on a second moment, primarily as a generator of desire. Finally, a reconfigured body seems to emerge. In the second movement where "He ordered charity in me" can be read – and this is a central hypothesis of the present chapter – as: "[Desire] ordered charity in me."[29] The motor of the *metamorphosis of love* is generative desire effectuated by the Word-desire. Before turning to the question of the *force* of the Word and to the notion of order as the reconfiguration of desire or *des-order*, the centrality of the Word in the performance of desire is analyzed in *the extension of desire* and *the effusion of the word.*

First, then, *the extension of desire*. Extension is *modal*. This is illustrated by Bernard's winepress imagery which he deploys to explain the fecundity signified by the dilated breasts of the lover: "What they are really saying is: 'Your breasts are better than wine.' 'These spiritual delights,' they say, 'that *your breasts distill can conquer in us the pleasures of the flesh, that enslaved us just as drunkards are enslaved by wine*.'"[30] The transformation is *modal*. The *slavery* of love is the modal manifestation of senselessness (drunk) in pleasure and delight. He continues, "This comparison of carnal pleasures with wine is so very apt. *For the grape, once pressed, can never again exude its liquid, it is condemned to endless dryness*. So too the flesh, caught in the winepress of death, is completely drained of its co-natural pleasures, *never again to revive to the stirring of sensual passions*."[31] However, not everything in the process of pressing is earned. The liquefaction of grapes is the process of transformation with

29 Bernard of Clairvaux, On the *Song of Songs III*, p. 30. Verdeyen (*SC* 452), SSC 50.1, l. 1, cf. Cant. 2.4. "ordinavit in me charitatem."

30 Bernard of Clairvaux, On the *Song of Songs I*, pp. 59-60. Leclercq (*SC* 441), SCC 9.9, l. 9-19/10.9, l. 1-5: "Hoc ergo est quod aiunt: Quia meliora sunt ubera tua vino. Carnis, inquiunt, voluptatem, qua paulo ante, tanquam vino, ebriae tenebamur, vincunt hae, quas tua nobis ubera stillant, deliciae spirituales."

31 Bernard of Clairvaux, On the *Song of Songs I*, pp. 59-60. Leclercq (*SC* 441), SCC 9.9, l. 9-19/10.9, l. 1-5: "Et pulchre vino comparant carnalem affectum. Ut enim uva semel expressa non habet jam quod denuo fundat, sed perpetua ariditate damnatur; sic caro in pressura mortis ab omni prorsus sua delectatione siccatur, nec ultra revirescit ad libidines."

residue and product at once. This passage and imagery illustrate that the transformation of desire is not the loss of desire and that it occurs by means of the flesh. The desire which is transformed is the voluptuousness of the flesh (*carnis voluptatem*). The generation results from the transformation of affect of the flesh (*carnalem affectum*). As such, the semantic range allows framing transformation, continuity, and production at the locus of which is the flesh. Yet conceptually, the implications are far reaching. The transformation is all-encompassing, and it touches the totality of the human person and of society as a whole. This is achieved through *the body of Christ*, the locus where the generative directionality of the flesh is transformed. In short, *the body of Christ* as the actualization of the Word is the *extension* of the body as the desire towards which *bodies* tend upon encountering the limitations of desire. Extension is modal transformation. Furthermore, modal transformation is generation. The generation of desire occurs by means of the body. In fact, the body itself is a consequence of desire. The mechanism of *the body of God* intimately (*non alienum*) weaved into *the body of man* obtains a further sense of governance and autonomous efficacious expression in the body of the Word or *the body of Christ*. Hence, the generation of desire as transformation occurs through a complimentary double movement. First, God desiring humanity produces the body of the Word in the incarnation. Second, simultaneously with, and in fact because of the first, is the approximation of *the body of man* to *the body of Christ* or the desiring production transforming the body into will. The movement goes from word, through Word, by means of desire, into body, then bodies (as Church) and ultimately as the utmost expression of desire: aperity or freedom. Word desires body. The Word acts on *bodies*. The manifestation of the Word as *sign signified* in the flesh was key for laying out a hermeneutics of desire. The discussion that ensues is undoubtedly rooted in the manifestation of the promised sign in the flesh, yet goes beyond it by providing a careful analysis of *the body as action* which reveals the force of the Word on bodies. The point of convergence – and indeed the gravitational center of the *metamorphosis of love* – becomes the power of the flesh in the Word or *the body of Christ*. The Word acts on bodies by transforming human desire. The transformation is modal: human desire becomes capable of generating. The transformation or *metamorphosis* of desire into charity is rooted in the body of the Word. Bernard begins discussing *the body of Christ* in his interpretation of the three perfumes in *On the Song of Songs*.[32] The proper mode of the perfumes is *infusion*. The oils of the perfumes *infuse* the soul with the fire of charity:

32 Bernard discusses the first two in SCC 10.4, l. 12-16, and moves on to discuss the third in SCC 12.

"pouring upon them the oil of mercy and warming them with the fire of charity!"[33] The result is the waging of life at the expense of death – to live, one must die – in order to achieve a modeless mode of presence: "making yourself all things for all people."[34] It may seem that the death of desire or *my eros* crucified (Ignatius of Antioch) begets the fire of charity. On the contrary, the infusion of the fire of charity, rooted in the limits of the body (death), overcomes the limits of the body (life). The body overcomes the confines of bodily finitude (*ut vivas omnibus*) by means of the *infusion of the fire of charity* (*ardore caritatis*). Hence, charity metamorphoses, and does not supplant desire. Furthermore, charity remains deeply rooted in the body. Bernard movingly speaks of the tears of Samuel, "Joseph, after he had drawn all the Egyptians *to run after him to the odor of his ointments*, ultimately *proffered the same perfumed favor* to the very men who had sold him."[35] The body is a means of expression of desire. "He began indeed *by angrily reproaching them*, but could not for long *restrain the tears that burst forth from the fullness of his heart, tears that effaced the signs of anger and betrayed his love*."[36] The expression of desire is then *extended* or *diffused*: "Samuel mourned for Saul [...] *his heart grew warm with the fire of charity, his spirit melted within him, and love made him weep*. And because his reputation was *diffused* abroad like a perfume '[...] Samuel was *accredited as a prophet of the Lord*.'"[37] Bernard's moving account of the liquefaction of the heart prompted by the sight of loving tears illustrates the corporeal expression of the fire of charity at the heart of experience.[38] Within this

33 Bernard of Clairvaux, On the *Song of Songs I*, pp. 77-8. Leclercq (*SC* 441), SCC 12.1, l. 20-21: "infundens ea oleo misericordiae et ardore decoquens caritatis!"

34 Bernard of Clairvaux, On the *Song of Songs I*, pp. 77-8. Leclercq (*SC* 441), SCC 12.1, l. 30-31: "sic denique mortua tibi, ut vivas omnibus."

35 Bernard of Clairvaux, On the *Song of Songs I*, pp. 79-80. Leclercq (*SC* 441), SCC 12.4, l. 1-3: "Joseph postquam universam Aegyptum post se fecit currere in odore unguentorum suorum, etiam suis venditoribus eamdem demum fragrantiam propinavit."

36 Bernard of Clairvaux, On the *Song of Songs I*, pp. 79-80. Leclercq (*SC* 441), SCC 12.4, l. 3-6: "Et quidem increpatoria verba vultu proferebat irato; sed erumpebant lacrymae de pinguedine cordis (Gen. XLIII, 30; XLV, 2), non irae indices, sed gratiae proditrices."

37 Bernard of Clairvaux, On the *Song of Songs I*, pp. 79-80. Leclercq (*SC* 441), SCC 12.4, l. 6-12: "Samuel lugebat Saul (I Reg. IV, 35), qui se quaerebat occidere, et ad ignem charitatis incalescente pectore liquefactus intus, pietatis adeps foras emanabat per oculos. Ob bonum denique quem circumquaque diffuderat suae opinionis odorem, refert de eo Scriptura, quia cognoverunt omnes a Dan usque Bersabee, quod fidelis Samuel propheta esset Domini (I Reg. III, 20)."

38 Piroska Nagy, *Le don des larmes au Moyen-Âge* (Paris: Albin Michel, 2000); Damien Boquet and Nagy Piroska, "Une histoire des émotions incarnées," *Médiévales* 61, no. 2 (2012): 5-24; Damien Boquet and Nagy Piroska, "Medieval sciences of emotions during the eleventh to thirteenth centuries: an intellectual history," *Osiris* 31, no. 1 (2016): 21-45; Alix Cohen

interplay of body, experience and love, Bernard introduces the discussion of *the body of Christ* and its functions as the *diffusion* of the third perfume. The Word is the central element for the *metamorphosis of love* in terms of liquefaction. The image of *liquefaction* enables Bernard to weave seamlessly desire into the body of Christ to transform it (desire) into active charity. Liquefaction has the mode of corporeal *spreading* and of *totality*. The third perfume of the bride in *On the Song of Songs* immediately bring Bernard to the account of the anointing of Christ, which conveniently also finds a parallel in the number of perfumes (Mc 16.1).[39] The parallel offers an opportunity to develop Bernard's thoughts on *the body of Christ* with relation to the fire of charity. The symbolic action of the ointments is fundamental. First, the ointment *spreads*. "What were these ointments, so precious that they were *bought and prepared for the body of Christ, so abundant that they sufficed to anoint every part of it*? [...] *they were spread over every part of it*."[40] Then, the ointment reaches *all parts*. Bernard writes, "the ointment for his body was not bought ready made, *a totally new one was prepared*; and *not for application merely to a part of his body* such as the feet or the head [but] *'to anoint Jesus' -- to cover his whole body, not any particular part*."[41] The key insight in the Bernardine

---

and Robert Stern, *Thinking About the Emotions: a Philosophical History* (Oxford: Oxford University Press, 2017); Simo Knuuttila, *Emotions in Ancient and Medieval Philosophy* (Oxford: Clarendon, 2004); Barbara H. Rosenwein, *Generations of Feeling: A History of Emotions, 600-1700* (Cambridge: Cambridge University Press, 2016); Barbara H. Rosenwein and Riccardo Cristiani, *What Is the History of Emotions?* (Cambridge: Polity Press, 2018); Barbara H. Rosenwein, "Thinking Historically about Medieval Emotions," *History Compass* 8, no. 8 (2010): 828-42; Barbara H. Rosenwein, "Worrying about Emotions in History," *The American Historical Review* 107, no. 3 (2002): 821-45; Gordon Rudy, *Mystical Language of Sensation in the Later Middle Ages* (New York: Routledge, 2002); Charles Baladier, *Érôs au Moyen Âge : Amour, désir et délectation morose* (Paris: Cerf, 1999); William M. Reddy, *The Navigation of Feeling: a Framework for the History of Emotions* (Cambridge University Press, 2001); John L. Austin, *How to Do Things With Words* (Oxford: Oxford University Press, 1975).

39 The two previous perfumes are found in Lc 7.38, Matt 26.7 and Mc 14.3.

40 Bernard of Clairvaux, On the *Song of Songs I*, p. 82. Leclercq (*SC* 441), SCC 12.6, l. 1-18: "Sed recurramus ad Evangelium, atque aliquid, quod forte spectet et ad haec unguenta, requiramus. Maria Magdalene, et Maria Jacobi et Salome, emerunt aromata, ut venientes ungerent Jesum (Marc. XVI, 1). Quaenam ista unguenta, tam pretiosa ut Christi corpori parentur et comparentur, tam copiosa ut toti sufficiant? Neutrum quippe duorum praecedentium aut emptum, aut factum specialiter ad opus Domini, aut toto in corpore legitur fuisse diffusum. Sed desubito introducitur mulier, uno quidem in loco osculans pedes, et unguento ungens (Luc. VII, 38; Joan. XII, 3); in altero vero vel ipsa, vel altera, habens alabastrum unguenti, et illud mittens in caput (Marc. XIV, 3)."

41 Bernard of Clairvaux, On the *Song of Songs I*, p. 82. Leclercq (*SC* 441), SCC 12.6, l. 1-18: "Caeterum nunc, emerunt, ait, aromata, ut venientes ungerent Jesum. Emunt non

analysis of the ointment of Christ's body is the mer(e)ological import since it covers all of Christ and not just some parts: "[…] *to cover his whole body, not any particular part.*"[42] The totality of the anointing serves for Bernard to then prescribe doing good to *all*. By uniting all, the body of Christ is in a sense simultaneously extended to all and so any injury to the body is an injury to all. Therefore, all must do good to all. *The body of Christ spreads* and *unites the body of man* – the result is the *the spread body* in the final *extension* of the Word's effusion. The *spreading* unites in *totality* by means of *extension*. The *totality* of the anointing of the body of Christ is the basis (justification) for *extending* the practice of corporeal and spiritual good to *all* (*ad omnes*). Bernard notes, "[y]ou too, *if you are to become deeply compassionate* […] *not only to parents and relatives*, or *those from whom you have received or hope to receive a good turn* […] *you must make the effort to do good to all.* […] *you will never refuse to do an act of charity* […] to an *enemy*."[43] These anointments are manifest in one's life to the extent that good actions extend to *all*. The sharing of ointments, like Christ, by accomplishing good deeds for all, is not simply a metaphorical proposal. *Sharing* is participatory through an *extension* of *the body of Christ*. Furthermore, *the* good extends to *all*, only by uniting all (cause), quite literally incorporating *all* to *the body of Christ*. Hence, the momentum of *extension* is fundamentally unifying.

What *extends*? The *whole body* (*totum corpus*).[44] Therein, there is no space in the distance. Better yet, the distance is the by-product of *extension*. The union is in the suffering of Christ in the figure of the cross (*figura crucis*, Ep. 3.18).[45] *The body of Christ*, the *totum corpus*, is the Church: "*his whole body which is*

---

unguenta, sed aromata: et unctio in obsequium Domini non facta assumitur, sed nova conficitur; nec ad ungendam tantum aliquam corporis partem, verbi gratia pedes aut caput; sed sicut scriptum est: Ut venientes ungerent Jesum; quod est totius complexio, non partis distinctio."

42 Bernard of Clairvaux, On the *Song of Songs I*, p. 82. Leclercq (*SC* 441), SCC 12.6, l. 1-18: "quod est totius complexio, non distinctio."

43 Bernard of Clairvaux, On the *Song of Songs I*, pp. 82-3. Leclercq (*SC* 441), SCC 12.7, l. 1-7: "Tu quoque si te induas viscera misericordiae, liberalem benignumque exhibeas, non tantum parentibus sive cognatis tuis, aut quos tibi vel benefactores tenes, vel benefacturos speras: nam et ethnici hoc faciunt (Matth. V, 47); sed, juxta Pauli consilium, studeas operari bonum ad omnes (Galat. VI, 10), ita ut propter Deum nec inimico officium humanitatis corporale seu spirituale negandum, subtrahendumve existimes."

44 *De ag. Crh. 18.20. ubique totus*. Also as discussed in ep. 55.25, Robert Dodaro, *Christ and the Just Society in the Thought of Augustine* (Cambridge: Cambridge University Press, 2004): 132.

45 J-M. Prieur, *La croix chez les Pères du IIe au début du IVe siècle* (Strasbourg: *Cahiers de Biblia Patristica*, 2006).

the Church."[46] The *totum corpus* (Bernard) approximates to the *totus Christus* (Augustine). The body of Christ on the cross for Augustine is alive in Bernard. The cross is a symbol, but also, and fundamentally, a sign (Augustine). Bernard goes on, "*he wished to reserve it for his living body.* The Church, which eats the living bread, which has come down from heaven, is alive: *she is the more precious Body of Christ* that was not to taste death's bitterness, whereas *every Christian knows that his other body did suffer death. His will is that she be anointed, that she be cared for, that her sick members be restored to health with remedies that are the fruit of diligence.*"[47] Words, or more specifically *the* Word, performs the *extension* of bodies. So the body *extends.* Now, how does *extension* not only perform bodies, but also unite bodies? Bodies manifest as *united* in the process of *grafting* and in the mode of *intensity*: the *metamorphosis of love* manifests as *grafting* of *bodies* by *extension* and *intensity*. Bernard characterizes the anointing of *the body of Christ*[48] in these lines, in terms of extension, intensity and life. The *extension* of *the body of Christ* is the surface covered by the anointing, namely the whole body (of Christ). Bernard identifies this whole body (*totum corpus*) with the Church (*ecclesia*).[49] A whole body implies, inversely, an incomplete body or at least a partial body. A whole body also suggests a relation of sorts, or a principle of order, whereby parts are arranged to fit the whole; whereby *bodies* fit in *the* body. The reach of the extension of the body beyond limits as

46 Bernard of Clairvaux, On the *Song of Songs I*, pp. 82-3. Leclercq (*SC* 441), SCC 12.7, l. 1-7: "totum corpus, quod est Ecclesia."

47 Bernard of Clairvaux, On the *Song of Songs I*, pp. 82-3. Leclercq (*SC* 441), SCC 12.7, l. 8-33: "constat te quoque abundare unguentis optimis, nec caput aut pedes Domini tantum, sed passim, quantum in te est, ungere suscepisse totum corpus, quod est Ecclesia. Et forte proinde ob hoc Dominus Jesus paratam sibi confectionem expendi noluit in suo corpore mortuo, ut servaret vivo. Vivit enim Ecclesia, quae manducat panem vivum, qui de coelo descendit. Ipsa est charius corpus Christi, quod ne mortem gustaret, morti illud alterum traditum fuisse nullus Christianus ignorat. Ipsam ungi, ipsam foveri desiderat, ipsius infirma membra cupit momentis accuratioribus relevari. Ipsi ergo pretiosa unguenta retinuit, cum anticipans horam, et accelerans gloriam, mulierum devotionem non elusit, sed instruxit. Renuit ungi, sed parcens, non spernens; non recusans obsequium, sed reservans proficuum. Proficuum dico, non hujus materialis atque corporalis unguenti, sed plane spiritualis, quod in isto designatum est. In isto ergo pepercit Magister pietatis unguentis optimis pietatis, quae membris suis indigentibus tam corporaliter quam spiritualiter omnino cuperet exhiberi. Denique paulo ante, cum in caput ejus, aut etiam in pedes funderetur unguentum, ipsumque satis pretiosum, nunquid prohibuit? Imo et obstitit prohibentibus. Nam et Simoni indignanti, quod se tangi a peccatrice permitteret, longam texuit reprehensionis parabolam; et aliis perditionem unguenti causantibus respondit, dicens: Quid molesti estis huic mulieri?"

48 Yves Congar, "L'ecclésiologie de saint Bernard," *Analecta sacri. Ordinis Cistercensis* 9, n. 3-4 (1953): 148; Leclercq (*SC* 441), SCC 12.7, p. 268, n. 2.

49 Compare to *totus Christus* in Augustine: *Epistle of John* 1.2, s. 341.1.1, s. 9.1.

dynamic extension (*ferior*) and modal manifestation of the whole body rejoins the chiasm separating the body without organs (Deluze) and the organs without bodies (Žižek).[50] The united body is desire as identity (Bernard) not pain as identification (Augustine) – the Church unites by passion in Augustine, and by compassion in Bernard. As for the *intensity*, individual desire is the driving force producing the unity of the whole body through the act of anointing: "It will thus be clear that you abound with the best ointments, that you have undertaken to care not only for the head or feet of the Lord, but, as far as in you lies, for his whole body which is the Church."[51] Body extends by intensity and grafting. Bodies produce a united and living body, which extends. To the three bodies (animal, human, celestial), a fourth is added: *the body of Christ, which* is construed as a *binding body* and as a *holistic body*. The idea of a whole body is therefore not simply a metaphor for unity nor merely a description of relation, it is in fact an efficient, living and bodily expression of interwoven *bodies* in *the* body effectuated by human desire enveloping the totality of existence (*sed passim, quantum in te est*) through the Word in the flesh. Hence, *the body of Christ* mediates desire to produce the whole body as Church in *extension* and in *intensity*. It is within this totality of unity, achieved by the fabric of the desiring body that experience alone *can* happen. Thus, experience is governed not only by the spirit (Killan) – there is no experience outside of the Church, but by the mode (intensity) and the *limits* (extension) of the body as well – but also by the experiencem, both inside and outside of the Church, which remians within the potential for manifestation of the whole body.[52] The whole body, in addition, is regulated by the overcoming of *time* (duration) at *the beginning without beginning* in the assumed man. The extension of bodies conditions the possibility of modes of experience. Compassion grafts bodies. Thus far, *the body of Christ* unfolds from various complimentary vantage points. First, the Word (*verbum*) or pre-existent Christ *assumes a* body in the incarnation as the 'assumed man' (*assumptus homo*). There is, furthermore, *the body of Christ* as the *whole body* (*totum corpus*) which extends throughout the world as the Church (*ecclesia*) through desire. Other *bodies* give texture to the *assumed body* of Christ and to the *Church as body* of Christ. The *breaks* or (dis)order in desiring-production yield 'the crucified body' (*corpus crucifixum*) and the passionate body (*corpus acquisitum est passione*) as the mode of suffering or passion (*passio*). Desire as

50 Slavoj Zizek, *Organs without Bodies: Deleuze and Consequences* (London: Routledge, 2016).

51 Bernard of Clairvaux, On the *Song of Songs I*, pp. 82-3. Leclercq (*SC* 441), SCC 12.7, l. 1-7: "nec caput aut pedes Domini tantum, sed passim, quantum in te est, ungere suscepisse totum corpus, quod est Ecclesia."

52 Kilian McDonnell, "Spirit and Experience in Bernard of Clairvaux," *Theological Studies* 58, no. 1 (1997): 3-18.

suffering or passion is a very specific way in which the body reaches out with all it has (*sed passim, quantum in te est*) to produce the whole body (*totum corpus*) or the universal body of Christ (*universum Christi corpus*). *The* passion which renders *a* passion effective in desiring-production is the (com)passion of the body of Christ: the functioning (dis)order of the parts in relation to the whole, as organs are to bodies, and inversely, as bodies are to organs. To graft is to (con)figure or (re)order. Tissues join in grafting to produce a *grafted body*. The fabric of the *grafted body* is compassion. (Com)passion is what reaches the *whole* body of Christ (*et per universum Christi corpus diffunditur*). As such, compassion (*compassionem*) is the very fabric of the unifying body, i.e., *the spread body* which is the 'diffused' or 'effused' (*corpus diffusus*) body, *the body of Christ*. The Abbot of Clairvaux asks, "[d]o you not see how that ointment of merciful love, the only one that may not be wasted, is to be preferred to the others? The function of merciful love, however, is superior to both; it works for the *welfare of the afflicted and is diffused through the whole Body of Christ*."[53] Hence, Bernard distinguishes the crucified body from the passionate body: "*I do not mean the body which was crucified, but the one that he acquired by his passion* [...] for he said: 'What I want is mercy, not sacrifice.' This, more than all the other virtues, *is diffused*, like a perfume from the breasts of the bride, who desires *to conform in all things to the will of her Bridegroom*."[54] The passionate body is "the one he acquired through his passion."[55] In other words, the crucified body of Christ is transformed through the passion to produce the passionate body which in turn, by means of (com)passion, or an ongoing extension

53 Bernard of Clairvaux, On the *Song of Songs I*, pp. 85-6. Leclercq (*SC* 441), SCC 12.10, l. 1-22: "Sed redeamus ad unguenta sponsae. Videsne quam sit praeferendum caeteris istud pietatis unguentum, de quo solo permissum non est perditionem fieri? In tantum perditio de ipso non fit, ut nec aquae frigidae munus irremuneratum sinatur (Matth. X, 42). Bonum tamen contritionis unguentum, quod de recordatione peccatorum conficitur, mittiturque in pedes Domini; quia cor contritum et humiliatum Deus non despiciet (Psal. L, 19). Caeterum longe melius esse arbitror id quod dicitur devotionis, factum de recordatione beneficiorum Dei; quippe quod et capiti idoneum reputatur, ita ut perhibeat de ipso Deus: Sacrificium laudis honorificabit me (Psal. XLIX, 23)."

54 Bernard of Clairvaux, On the *Song of Songs I*, pp. 85-86. Leclercq (*SC* 441), SCC 12.10, l. 1-22: "Porro utrumque vincit unctio pietatis, quae de respectu miserorum fit, et per universum Christi corpus diffunditur. Corpus dico, non illud crucifixum, sed quod illius acquisitum est passione. Optimum revera unguentum, in cujus comparatione caetera nec respicere se ostendit, qui ait: Misericordiam volo, et non sacrificium (Matth. IX, 13). Hanc ergo potissimum inter caeteras virtutes redolere puto ubera sponsae, quae sponsi per omnia gestit congruere voluntati. An non odore misericordiae Thabita etiam in morte fragrabat? Et ideo cito de morte convaluit (Act. IX, 39-41), quia praevaluit odor vitae."

55 Bernard of Clairvaux, On the *Song of Songs I*, pp. 85-86. Leclercq (*SC* 441), SCC 12.10, l. 1-22: "acquisitum sed passionem."

of Christ's own desiring production, the crucified body ultimately becomes the whole body (*corpus totum*) or *the spread body* (*corpus difussus*). Passion *is* desiring-production from the crucified body to the whole body (*corpus totum*) in the generative interruption of desiring-production. The grafting of bodies weaves the fabric of *the spread body*.

The Word performs *the spread body*. The passion of Christ therefore becomes the paradigmatic and efficient model whereby human actions also produce, and indeed become, by re-enactment of (com)passion, 'the whole body'. The ongoing 're-enactment' of (com)passion as the production of 'the whole body' is the conformation of wills: "to conform in all things to the will."[56] The will (*voluntas*) thus enters the discourse on the passion by means of the body as aperity, where the production of desire results in conformation without boundaries (aperity) to the degree that *the spread body* is produced. In its all-encompassing and efficacious totality, *the spread body* embraces *all in all*. Again, the unifying totality of *the spread body* unfolds from word to body through the efficient word. Bernard goes on to note that the church is the bride. "The *Church's fragrance is radiated* by those who *use their money*, tainted though it be, to win themselves friends; she intoxicates by the *words of her preachers* [...] and yield a harvest through their perseverance."[57] He goes on, "and although none of us will dare arrogate for his own soul the title of bride of the Lord, *nevertheless we are members of the Church which rightly boasts of this title and of the reality that it signifies*."[58] Bernard continues, "*For what all of us simultaneously possess in a full and perfect manner, that each single one of us undoubtedly possesses by participation* [...] Thank you, Lord Jesus, for [...] *uniting us to the Church* you so dearly love.[59] The identification to *all* determines the characteristics of particular bodies. The Word achieves identification.

---

56 Bernard of Clairvaux, On the *Song of Songs I*, pp. 85-86. Leclercq (*SC* 441), SCC 12.10, l. 1-22: "quae sponsi per omnia gestit congruere voluntati."

57 Bernard of Clairvaux, On the *Song of Songs I*, p. 86. Leclercq (*SC* 441), SCC 12.11, l. 1-30: "Fragrat Ecclesia in his, qui sibi faciunt amicos de mammona iniquitatis; inebriat in ministris verbi, qui vino laetitiae spiritualis infundunt terram, et inebriant eam, et fructum referunt in patientia. Ipsa audacter secureque sese nominat sponsam, tanquam quae vere habet ubera meliora vino, et fragrantia unguentis optimis."

58 Bernard of Clairvaux, On the *Song of Songs I*, p. 86. Leclercq (*SC* 441), SCC 12.11, l. 1-30: "Quod etsi nemo nostrum sibi arrogare praesumat, ut animam suam quis audeat sponsam Domini appellare; quoniam tamen de Ecclesia sumus, quae merito hoc nomine, et re nominis gloriatur; non immerito gloriae hujus participium usurpamus."

59 Bernard of Clairvaux, On the *Song of Songs I*, p. 86. Leclercq (*SC* 441), SCC 12.11, l. 1-30: "Quod enim simul omnes plene integreque possidemus, hoc singuli sine contradictione participamus. Gratias tibi, Domine Jesu, qui nos charissimae Ecclesiae tuae aggregare dignatus es, non solum ut fideles essemus, sed ut etiam tibi vice sponsae in amplexus

The performance of *the spread body* is the manifestation of the Word. Thus, the *condensed* Word *spreads*. Christ as the abbreviated or condensed Word (*verbum abbreviatum*)[60] of God finds its fullest manifestation, as efficient sign, in the generation of the whole body (*corpus totum*) as *the spread body*. The condensed Word is the source and incarnation of the gift (*dono*). The gift is precisely the very expression of efficiency in *the* production of desire or desiring-production. The distribution or rather channelling of gifts are uneven and therefore sterile (*sterile*) individually, but become efficient in their collective action (*opera*): "Which of us can live uprightly and perfectly even for one hour, an hour free from fruitless talk and careless work?"[61] There is no entitlement to the gift in individual merit. However, collectively or universally, the harmonious order of gifts contributes to the composition of an integral whole. Bernard continues, "[s]he is the church, whose fullness is a never-ceasing fount of intoxicating joy, perpetually fragrant. For *what she lacks in one member she possesses in another according* to the measure of *Christ's gift* and *the plan of the Spirit* who *distributes to each one just as he chooses*."[62] The totality (*universitate*) of the Church as *the spread body* therefore acquires efficient agency *only* when it is a gift (*dono*) and when it is universal (*universitate*). The unity resulting as desiring-production from the spreading of the condensed Word is, again, not metaphorical but quite carnal in the copulation (*copulare*) of the members of *the spread body* acting as one flesh. For Bernard, the *condensed* Word is transformed by desire into *the spread body*. The simultaneous action suggests there is no mere identification among the parts and the whole, the members and *the body of Christ* (Augustine). Rather, identification becomes identity and

jucundos, castus, aeternosque copularemur, revelata et ipsi facie speculantes gloriam tuam, quae tibi communis pariter est cum Patre et Spiritu sancto in saecula saeculorum. Amen."

60 Cf. *Dil* 21 (*SC* 393, P. 112, note 2); Bernard of Clairvaux, On the *Song of Songs I*, Leclercq (*SC* 441), SCC 59.9, 9 (SBO II, 140, 25); 79, 2 (SBO II, 273, 9), *Nat* 1.1 (SBO IV, 244, 14-15 and *Miss* ii, 9 (SC 390, p. 144 s.). Bernard of Clairvaux, On the *Song of Songs* I, n. 1, p. 276-7. Leclercq (*SC* 441), SCC 12.11, l. 8-33. The expression is also used with *verbum coadunatum* and *verbum contractum*. Peter Cantur (ca. 1197) wrote a work called *Verbum Abbreviatum*.

61 Bernard of Clairvaux, On the *Song of Songs I*, p. 86. Leclercq (*SC* 441), SCC 12.11, l. 1-30: "Quis nostrum unum saltem horum integre perfecteque possideat, ut non videlicet interdum et in dicendo sterilior, et in operando tepidior sit?"

62 Bernard of Clairvaux, On the *Song of Songs I*, p. 86. Leclercq (*SC* 441), SCC 12.11, l. 1-30: "Sed est quae merito et non dubie hoc praeconio glorietur, Ecclesia utique, cui nunquam de universitate sua deest et unde inebriet, et unde fragret. Quod enim sibi deest in uno, habet in altero, secundum mensuram donationis Christi, ac moderationem Spiritus, dividentis singulis prout vult (Ephes. IV, 7; I Cor. XII, 11)."

the individual *is* the Church, "because we are *of* the Church."[63] Membership in the Church is fusion or copulation (*copulare*) and aggregation (*aggregare*). The Word manifests itself as unifying *gift* and *totality* in the *fusion* of bodies. The *fusion* of bodies is a (re)configuration of bodies (in)to *the* body. How do parts relate to the whole? How are organs grafted to become body? What is the process of constitution of the body of organs? That is, how does *aggregation* happen? These questions touch on the limits or confines of the Church as *the body of Christ*. Where does *the body of Christ* begin and where does it end, or is it simply a *beginning without beginning*? If so, where is the beginning? The question is difficult to answer because it is riddled with a paradox. The entry to the body is mediated by (com)passion or desire thus construed *in the body of Christ* and is achieved (*aggregare*) as gift within the overarching harmony of divine governance of bodies to efficiently become the total body or *the spread body*. However, the entry point as actualization of the efficient Word *in* the body occurs within the beginning, the source-beginning or origin (*incipio*), now the abbreviated Word (*verbum abbreviatum*),[64] and at the beginning as point of departure (*principium*). The limits of *extension cannot* and indeed *must not* be contained because such an exercise would result in closure, which is contrary to what is most defining of *the spread body*. Namely, it is a *beginning without beginning* and therefore *extension* contains without limiting, it is a confine without a confine, which is constantly producing and spreading. The efficacy of the Word ensures the process or desiring-production as unlimited aperity or freedom (*voluntas*). This is treated, furthermore, in the proximity of the Word to the soul, against the background of the soul as *the Church* or will in *the spread body* in *the effusion of the Word*.

4.3 The Effusion of the Word

The *spread body* unfolds through the Word from without as *extension* and from within as *effusion*. In the logic of desire, *desire in the word* overcomes reason in *the body of man* and is transformed and generated in *the body of Christ* to produce *the spread body*. Though the limits of *the spread body* are by definition without limits, a sort of *beginning without beginning* in desire – or pure aperity –, it remains to describe what happens within *the spread body* precisely insofar as it *spreads*. The process takes place by the spreading of the name

63 Bernard of Clairvaux, On the *Song of Songs I*, p. 86. Leclercq (*SC* 441), SCC 12.11, l. 1-30: "quoniam tamen de Ecclesia sumus."

64 Cassiadorus is the first to use the term. Aelred uses it also.

(*word*) of the Holy Spirit upon all flesh: "an outpouring of his Spirit on all mankind."[65] The effusion (*effundere*) of the effective Word, in turn as Spirit, is the motor of expansion (*diffundere*) as spread body (*corpus diffusus*). The basis for the possibility of spreading, from Word to body from within, is the double meaning, which Bernard attributes to the oil spread on the breasts of the bride in the *Song of Songs.* This is the spreading of the name together: "you emptied out the power of your name, O Beloved, and poured it on my breasts; that is why the maidens love you so much."[66] Parting from Origen, the oil spreads actively for Bernard; whereas the former prefers the passive phrase a perfume that is spread (*unguentum exinantium*), the later deploys the active spreading of the oil (*oleum effusum*).[67] The active character of the oil allows Bernard to make a smooth transition to illustrate the active Word, specifically by identifying it to the double sense of compassion (*misericordia*) and power (*potestas*). In other words, the efficient Word is manifested as (com)passion and power. This passage provides the detailed process whereby *the spread body* is actively (Bernard), not passively (Origen), and by identity, not by identification (Augustine), extended (*effundere*) from within according to the efficacious voice (the Holy Spirit) of the abbreviated word (*verbum abbreviatum*) echoing *the beginning without beginning.* Bernard writes, "Which of these therefore is poured out? In some mysterious way, the name of majesty and power transfuses into that of love and mercy, an amalgam abundantly poured out in the person of our Savior Jesus Christ. The name 'God' *liquefies and dissolves into the title 'God with us,' that is, into 'Emmanuel.'*"[68] The Word's efficiency is manifested simultaneously in the *liquefaction* of *extension* (Word) with *effusion* (Spirit). *Effusion* involves actively invoking the Spirit. The extension of *the spread body* is ongoing by the intimate presence of God in the governance of the world but also includes, from the perspective of human beings, a dimension

65 Bernard of Clairvaux, On the *Song of Songs I*, pp. 106-7. Leclercq (*SC* 441), SCC 15.2, l. 9-10: "effundente de Spiritu suo super omnem carnem."

66 Bernard of Clairvaux, On the *Song of Songs I*, p. 140. Leclercq (*SC* 431), SCC 19.1: "non strustra nec inaniter nomen tuum exinanitum est, o sponse, atque effusum in ubera mea (Cant. 1.2 and Phil 2.7)" SBO I, 108, 20. Cited in Bernard of Clairvaux, On the *Song of Songs* I, p. 334-5, n. 3. Leclercq (*SC* 441), SCC 15.4.

67 Cf. Origen, *Com. Cant.* I, 4, 1 and 4 (*SC* 375), p. 220-222.

68 Bernard of Clairvaux, On the *Song of Songs I*, pp. 105-6. Leclercq (*SC* 441), SCC 15.1, l. 1-40: "Spiritus ita dicit etiam per sibi familiarius organum: Duo haec audivi: quia potestas Dei est, et tibi, Domine, misericordia (Psal. LXI, 12, 13). Ergo secundum majestatem: Sanctum et terribile nomen ejus (Psal. CX, 9); secundum pietatem: Non est nomen aliud sub coelo datum hominibus, in quo oporteat nos salvos fieri (Act. IV, 12). Sed exemplis magis perspicuum fiet. Hoc est, inquit, nomen quod vocabunt eum, Dominus, justus noster (Jerem. XXIII, 6). Nomen potentiae est. Item: Et vocabitur nomen ejus Emmanuel (Isai. VII, 14)."

of invocation: "*Wisdom is a kindly spirit, and easy of access to those who call upon him*. Quite often he *anticipates their request* and says: '*Here I am*.' [...] I put before you a name that is rightly compared to oil [...]. You encounter *many names for the Bridegroom* [...] I sum up for you in two [...] *the gift of his love* (*potestas*) or *the power of his majesty*."[69] The Holy Spirit is already present and at work even before being invoked. What is this work? The work of the efficient Word, which the Spirit invokes, or calls upon, is comparable to the oil of the *Song of Songs*, which bears many names (*nomen*).[70] These names, however, are but synonyms of the Spirit. The main names for the Spirit are *power* and *compassion*. Bernard suggests abbreviating the many names of the Word into only two. These are, power (*potestas*) and compassion (*Misericordia*). As manifestations of the divine name constituting the very fabric of *the spread body*, these names are potencies or powers (*nomen potential est*). In the process of effusion, these power-names embrace and constantly 'teach' (*docere*) everything spiritual and corporeal.[71] The prefiguration of the sign ultimately converges in the effusion of the name of Jesus or the *signifier-signified* as the abbreviated word. Bernard explains: "[*t*]*his process is not new:* in ancient times Abram became Abraham and Sarai became Sara; and we are reminded that in these events the mystery of the communication of salvation was pre-figured and celebrated."[72]

---

69 Bernard of Clairvaux, On the *Song of Songs I*, pp. 105-6. Leclercq (*SC* 441), SCC 15.1, l. 1-40: "Benignus est Spiritus sapientiae (Sap. I, 6), et non consuevit esse difficilis se invocantibus, qui saepe et antequam invocetur, dicit: Ecce adsum (Isai. LXV, 24). Audite jam quod orantibus vobis per me indicare dignatur de eo, quod heri ad hoc ipsum distulimus, et orationum vestrarum fructum tempestivum percipite. En ostendo nomen, quod oleo merito comparatur; et quo merito, dicam."

70 Bernard of Clairvaux, On the *Song of Songs I*, pp. 105-6. Leclercq (*SC* 441), SCC 15.1, l. 1-40: "Multa quidem Sponsi vocabula sparsa per omnem divinam paginam legitis, sed in duo ea vobis universa complectar. Nullum, ut arbitror, reperietis, quod non aut pietatis gratiam, aut potentiam majestatis sonet."

71 Bernard of Clairvaux, On the *Song of Songs I*, pp. 105-6. Leclercq (*SC* 441), SCC 15.1, l. 1-40: "Non enim minus pium est docere animum scientiam, quam praebere escam corpori."

72 Bernard of Clairvaux, On the *Song of Songs I*, pp. 105-6. Leclercq (*SC* 441), SCC 15.1, l. 1-40: "pietatem insinuat. Item ipse de se: Vos vocatis me, ait, Magister et Domine (Joan. XIII, 13). Primum gratiae est, secundum majestatis. Non enim minus pium est docere animum scientiam, quam praebere escam corpori. Rursum propheta: Vocabitur, inquit, nomen ejus Admirabilis, consiliarius, Deus fortis, pater futuri saeculi, princeps pacis (Isai. IX, 6). Primum, tertium, quartum, majestatem sonant; reliqua, pietatem. Quod horum ergo effunditur? Profecto majestatis ac potentiae nomen, in id quod est pietatis et gratiae, quodam modo transfunditur, ipsumque effunditur abunde per Jesum Christum Salvatorem nostrum. Nomen, verbi causa, quod Deus est, nonne in id quod est nobiscum Deus (Matth. I, 23), hoc est in Emmanuel, liquescit et deficit? Sic Admirabilis, in id quod est consiliarius; sic Deus et fortis, in ea quae sunt pater futuri saeculi et princeps pacis; et Dominus justus noster, in misericors et miserator Dominus (Psal. CX, 4). Non dico novum

Hence, *the spread body* diffuses (*effundere*) by means of the intimate Word invoked in the Holy Spirit and construed as productive power (*potestas*) and/or compassion (*misericordiam*). The diffusion is all-encompassing, touching body and soul, and is the fulfillment of the prefigured sign-signified promise through Christ, the abbreviated word in the flesh. Bernard continues, "[n]or am I surprised if, when the time has fully come, *there is an outpouring of Jesus' name as God fulfills what he had promised* [...] *an outpouring of his Spirit on all mankind*."[73] The crux of the matter lies in the significance of the outpouring as the encounter of sign and signified: "[h]ow is it, I ask, that God's first answer to Moses' question was: 'I Am Who I Am,' and 'I Am has sent me to you'? I doubt if even Moses *himself would have grasped its import if it had not been poured out. But it was poured*, and he understood it."[74] Within the outward force of the *spread body*, (com)passion is force and force is compassion made efficiently productive through bodies in the spread body of Christ. The names of the Spirit, *power* and *compassion* motor the *effusion* of *the spread body*.

The Word is the force that pours out the body. The Word as power (*potestas*), though present, is constantly revealed as manifestation diffused in the flesh (*carnem*) – *fusum* = to spread out and *effusum* = to pour in/on/out. Bernard writes, "[...] *not only poured but poured out, for an inward pouring had already occurred* [...] Now it is *sent abroad*, and what was infused into the angels as an intimate secret was poured out upon men, so that henceforth they could justly proclaim from the earth: '*Your name is oil poured out*,' if the obstinacy of a thankless people did not prevent it. For he had said: 'I am the God of Abraham, the God of Isaac and the God of Jacob.'"[75] The measure (*quatenus*) and the quality (*qualiter*) of the effusion of Christ reaches *all* (*utrumque*) of the *body*

---

quid: quondam quoque nihilominus Abram in Abraham, et Sarai in Saram effusa sunt (Gen. XVII, 5, 15); et jam tunc salutiferae effusionis celebratum praefiguratumque mysterium recordamur."

73 Bernard of Clairvaux, On the *Song of Songs I*, pp. 106-7. Leclercq (*SC* 441), SCC 15.2, l. 7-23: "Nec miror, si cum venit plenitudo temporis, facta est effusio nominis; Deo quippe quod per Joelem promiserat adimplente, et effundente de Spiritu suo super omnem carnem (Joel. II, 28)."

74 Bernard of Clairvaux, On the *Song of Songs I*, pp. 106-7. Leclercq (*SC* 441), SCC 15.2, l. 7-23: "cum tale aliquid et apud Hebraeos olim contigisse legam. Credo vos praevolare, et scire jam quid dicere velim. Quale erat, inquam, quod sciscitanti Moysi primo responsum est: Ego sum qui sum? et: Qui est, misit me ad vos? (Exod, III, 14.) Nescio an vel ipse Moyses caperet sic, si non videlicet effunderetur."

75 Bernard of Clairvaux, On the *Song of Songs I*, pp. 106-7. Leclercq (*SC* 441), SCC 15.2, l. 7-23: "Sed fusum est, et captum est; nec modo fusum, sed et effusum: nam infusum jam erat. Jam coeli habebant illud, jam angelis innotuerat. Est autem foris missum; et quod angelis ita erat infusum ut esset et privatum, effusum et in homines est, ita ut jam tunc merito clamaretur de terra: Oleum effusum nomen tuum (Cant. I, 2): si non ingratae plebis exosa

and as power (*potentia*) unifies it. Bernard continues by exhorting to "*Take the name Christ, take the name Jesus*; both were infused into the angels, both were *poured out upon men* [...] How precious your name, and yet how cheap! Cheap, but the instrument of salvation."[76] The body pour out everywhere. Word, finally, *is* extended power, for "if [the name of Jesus] lacked saving power, it would not have won me. Made *a sharer in the name*, I share too in its inheritance. For I am a Christian, Christ's own brother. If I am what I say, I am the heir of God, co-heir with Christ."[77] Bernard continues, "[*a*]*nd what wonder if the name of the Bridegroom is poured out, since he himself is poured out? For he emptied himself to assume the condition of a slave*. Did he not even say: '*I am poured out like water*'?"[78] And again, "[t]he fullness of *the divine life* was poured out and *lived on earth in bodily form*, that all of us who live in this body doomed to death may receive from that fullness and being filled with its life-giving odor *say*: '*Your name is oil poured out*.' Such is what is meant by *the outpouring of the name*, such its *manner*, such its *extent*."[79] The body of Christ has two further expressions: the body of death and the closely related crucified Christ: "he brought the good news of Jesus, and him crucified."[80] Word as power generates the body. Word, as extended power, generates extended and effused body.

---

pervicacia obstitisset. Ait enim: Ego sum Deus Abraham, et Deus Isaac, et Deus Jacob (Exod. III, 6, 15)."

76 Bernard of Clairvaux, On the *Song of Songs I*, pp. 108-9. Leclercq (*SC* 441), SCC 15.4, l. 11-27: "Ecce Christus, ecce Jesus, utrumque infusum angelis, utrumque effusum in homines, et illos homines qui computruerant tanquam jumenta in stercore suo, homines et jumenta salvans, quemadmodum multiplicavit misericordiam suam Deus. Quam charum, quam vile! vile, sed salubre."

77 Bernard of Clairvaux, On the *Song of Songs I*, pp. 108-9. Leclercq (*SC* 441), SCC 15.4, l. 11-27: "Si vile non esset, non mihi effunderetur; si salubre non esset, non me lucraretur. Particeps nominis sum, sum et haereditatis, Christianus sum; frater Christi sum. Si sum quod dicor, haeres sum Dei, cohaeres autem Christi (Rom. VIII, 17)."

78 Bernard of Clairvaux, On the *Song of Songs I*, pp. 108-9. Leclercq (*SC* 441), SCC 15.4, l. 11-27: "Et quid mirum, si sponsi effusum est nomen, cum ipse quoque effusus sit? Nam semetipsum exinanivit, formam servi accipiens (Philipp. II, 7). Denique ait: Sicut aqua effusus sum (Psal. XXI, 15)."

79 Bernard of Clairvaux, On the *Song of Songs I*, pp. 108-9. Leclercq (*SC* 441), SCC 15.4, l. 11-27: "Effusa est plenitudo Divinitatis, habitans super terram corporaliter, ut de illa plenitudine omnes, qui corpus mortis gestamus, caperemus, ac vitali odore repleti diceremus: Oleum effusum nomen tuum. En quod nomen effusum, et qualiter, et quatenus."

80 Bernard of Clairvaux, On the *Song of Songs I*, pp. 109-10. Leclercq (*SC* 441), SCC 15.6, l. 12-3: "[...] annuntians in omni colo Iesum, et hunc crucifixum."

Conclusion

So how do bodies *extend*? In the *metamorphosis of love*, bodies *extend*, first, in *words of desire*, secondly, in *the extension of desire*, and thirdly, in *the effusion of the word*. Body is produced in *extension* within the (re)configuration of the *metamorphosis of finitude* by desire over reason. In the process of the *metamorphosis of love*, *extension* is the desiring-production of bodies. The *mere(o)logy of the body* is composed based upon an understanding of desire as production (*desiring-production*) which in its resistance produces order of love vis-à-vis desire in the mode of *the spread body* as diffusion in intensity, duration and extension in which parts become identified through the whole body through Christ. A *mer(o)logy of the body* yields an *aesthetics of the body* where desire for *the flesh of the word* leads to the desiring-production, as (dis)order this time, of *the beauty of a grotesque body*. The process of generational extension of *bodies* is fundamentally *fusion* and *fusion* in turn is possible only by means of *attraction*. Having considered *extension*, the subject matter of *attraction* is the point of inquiry in the chapter that follows. The question to be addressed is, how do bodies *attract* in order to then *fuse* in the process of *extension* and *effusion*, that is, how do bodies *fuse* through the power of the Word?

CHAPTER 5

Attraction

There is no *extension* of bodies or in bodies without *attraction*. Extension is the counterblow of attraction. From considering *extension*, reflecting on the dynamism of *attraction* follows. How, then, do bodies *attract*? There is *fusion* in *attraction*. Therefore, *attraction* in the *metamorphosis of love* is about how bodies *fuse*, because of *attraction*, in the process of *extension*. In the *metamorphosis of love*, the question of the *attraction* of bodies is this, how does *attraction* achieve the *fusion* of bodies? Attraction inevitably demands considering the *metamorphosis of love* or the transformation of desire, from the vantage point of aesthetics, so that bodies relate by fusion and repulsion. And so, this chapter primarily treats *attraction* in terms of the (re)configuration of desire (in the fabric of finitude) in generative ex-*tension*, which is the foundation for a *mer(e)ological aesthetics*, or an aesthetics of parthood relation in organic determination. A preamble to a *mer(e)ological aesthetics*, the subject-matter of the next chapter, must consider first the consequences of the body's *extension* construed as performative Word. Accordingly, the central contention of the discussion on *attraction* is that *fusion* of bodies results from the performative Word, which gives bodies a gravity, and which in turn manifests the body as action. Therefore, the *attraction* of body manifests the force of the Word in the *metamorphosis of love*. This central moment in the *metamorphosis of love*, whereby *Word becomes body*, is the centerpiece of *attraction*. Attraction, then, in the *metamorphosis of love*, occurs first in the *word as force* (5.1), secondly in *the weight of the body* (5.2), and finally, in *the body as force* (5.3). With *attraction*, whereby *Word becomes body*, the foundation is ready for a *mer(e)ological aesthetics*.

5.1 Word as Force

Desire is the force of the Word. The force of the Word extends the body. The force of the Word generates desire. What are these forces, where do they come from and what is their dynamism? By means of an inner motion, the body is outwardly propelled and so it is *extended*. By means of an outward pressure, the body undergoes *effusion*, because other bodies propel it. The force of the Word therefore generates desire by *extension* and by *attraction*. Body is thus manifested *as* power. The manifestation of *flesh of the word* as power

 | DOI:10.30965/9783846767504_007

(*vir*) or force in the mode of love (*dilectio/caritas*) juxtaposes desire and reason and inverses them such that desire is force while reason is fragility. Within the inherent union and desiring-production of *the body of Christ* in *the spread body*, the questions of the flesh (*caro*) and love (*amor*) arise as constitutive qualities in the resistance of desiring-production in *the spread body*, and as the very force of generation (*virtus*) and diffusion (*effusion*) in production and resistance. Desire impels *bodies*: *the body of man* in *the* body, *the body of God*, through *the flesh of the word* as transformative generation, then as transformative resistance. Desire as love is the force or power of the Word. What, then, is the *power* of love? Is it reason? Reasonable love is fragile because love is always powerful. Bernard writes, "[l]ove without power (*virtutis*) is reasonable, but fragile."[1] According to the view of love as power (*virtus*), love *is* nothing other than a specific manifestation of the Word's efficiency in the whole body (*totum corpum*). Furthermore, love as power *is* also close to desire. In fact, love is desire in the mode of power (*virtus*) or as desiring-production. Granted, love has the power-manifestations in the Word (*potentia*) and in human beings (*virtus*). Thus, love, allowing for various modes, in the mode of power (*virtus*) *is* unreasonable yet efficient, whereas love in the mode of reasonability remains fragile. The unreasonable power (*virtus*) of love as desire over reason returns full circle to *the beginning without beginning* where "[d]esire impels me, not reason."[2] The texture of desire is body and body extends and attracts as power. The power of love is body, not reason. Love is not opposed to reason. Rather, love exceeds reason with desire or, better yet, *as* desire. The production of desire as love is the excess of reason. Excess is not saturation but transformation or metamorphosis. Like desiring-production resulting in the generation of *bodies*, so too love becomes productive in the mode of desire beyond reason. The power of love is generation. Where *is* love generated? The body is the locus of generation. The paradigmatic body is the body of Christ. Christ is the locus of human love for Bernard. Christ generates love in the suffering of the cross, in the love of neighbour, in the Church as *the spread body* because Christ is the true wisdom of the philosopher, everywhere and always.[3] The human love for Christ and the love of Christ for humans in the body is the prelude and grounding for the discussion on the love of the soul for the Word. Hence, Bernard cites the Pauline injunction to love Christ (1 Cor 16.22).

1 Bernard of Clairvaux, On the *Song of Songs I*, pp. 149-50. Leclercq (*SC* 431), SCC 20.4, l. 36-37: "illo qui virtutis est, rationabilem esse, sed fragilem."

2 Bernard of Clairvaux, On the *Song of Songs I*, pp. 55-7. Leclercq (*SC* 414), SCC 9.2, l. 7: "Desiderio feror, non rationes."

3 Augustine, *Soliloquy*, 2.1.

Why must Christ be loved and what is the love of Christ? Bernard responds, "*I ought to love* the one through whom I have *my being, my life, my understanding*. If I am ungrateful, I am unworthy too. Lord Jesus, whoever refuses to live for you [...] is in fact dead already."[4] Love is generated in the attraction of the body towards Christ. Insufficiency and absence produce *attraction*. The love of Christ begins with a reflection on the experience of absence and insufficiency. Humans are *naturally* attracted to the love of Christ because besides Christ humans revert to their origin, which is nothingness. Indeed, outside of human beings there is nothing: "And whoever wants to become something without you, without doubt that man is considered nothing and is just that. *You have made all things for yourself, O God, and whoever wants to live for himself and not for you, in all that he does, is nothing*."[5] Love generates outwardly in Christ. Humans are attracted to Christ by the force of the word, which pulls humanity out of absence into existence. Where love *is*, the body *is*. *Attraction* gives the Word a body. Distance separates bodies. The possibility of *attraction* between bodies depends on distance. Since bodies are ever in *attraction*, an infinite distance separates bodies. What then overcomes the distance of bodies? The Word. However, the Word and the body are not of the same order. How can body and word interact at all? Are they not of different orders of which Pascal wrote? "The infinite distance between body and mind symbolizes the infinitely more infinite distance between mind and charity, for charity is supernatural. Out of all bodies together we could not succeed in creating one little thought. It is impossible, and of a different order. Out of all bodies and minds we could not extract one impulse of true charity. It is impossible, and of a different, supernatural, order."[6] Pascal does not include the distance between bodies because the movement from the body to a body produces distance. Distance separates bodies by the body and not because of the body. The word is not a bridge between bodies therefore, but rather the impetus of bodies.

How to construe the aforementioned distance? What is the *fabric* of distance? The word, as impetus of the body, is the chiasm of difference or what, following the Neoplatonist tradition, Augustine and later Bernard call

4 Bernard of Clairvaux, On the *Song of Songs I*, pp. 147-8. Leclercq (*SC* 431), SCC 20.1, l. 1-26: "Valde omnino mihi amandus est, per quem sum, vivo et sapio. Si ingratus sum; et indignus. Dignus plane est morte, qui tibi, Domine Jesu, recusat vivere, et mortuus est."

5 Bernard of Clairvaux, On the *Song of Songs I*, pp. 147-8. Leclercq (*SC* 431), SCC 20.1, l. 1-26: "Propter temetipsum, Deus, fecisti omnia; et qui esse vult sibi et non tibi, nihil esse incipit inter omnia: Deum time, et mandata ejus observa; hoc est, inquit, omnis homo (Eccle. XII, 13). Ergo si hoc est omnis homo, absque hoc nihil omnis homo."

6 Bernard of Clairvaux, On the *Song of Songs I*, pp. 147-8. Leclercq (*SC* 431), SCC 20.1, l. 1-26.

dissimilitude or dissemblance.[7] Distance is not only absence. Certainly, there is absence in distance, but distance also has positive qualities. Distance has space, texture and mode. In one word, presence. Distance is the power of the body. However, more on this later. For now, word is the *fabric* of distance. Therefore, the question becomes, how does word gain a body? Differently stated, how can humans turn to the love of Christ without external recourse and how is the love of God (the Word) manifested in the attraction of bodies? Undoubtedly, these questions anticipate the question of *order* in *attraction* and ultimately the Bernardine paradox concerning the (*dis*)*order of charity*. Suffice it to note for the time being, that these questions bring to the fore a tension in desire's resistance to *order* and to the relation between orders. This is not because desire has no order but because desire reconfigures all order. The *fabric* of distance emerges as presence only in the order of desire. Still, what is this texture? The *texture* of distance is found in order. In the *Pensées*, Pascal identifies three orders. The highest is the order of grace, which is infinitely more distant than the distance between all other orders. The order of grace governs the relation between grace and free will which here emerges analogously in terms of what *the body of man can* love (possibility) and what it *must* love (necessity). Bernard lays out the development from possibility to necessity as follows. *First*, desire is center-stage: desire longs for what is absent. He writes, "*my every desire and intention is before you* [...] *I am eager for what is lacking. For all these things, and as much as I am able, I love you.*"[8] The capacity of desire is limited by the quantity (*modus*) of love (*servire*) and has not yet reached the mode (*modus*) of love (*amor*). The mode of love is therefore capacity or possibility when it is quantified and becomes modeless or necessity when it is qualified – *love of order*. *Second*, the *texture* of desire in the distance is presence, not absence, as tension. Desire is at odds with reason at the limit where possibility must become necessity, i.e., where distance is no longer lack but production or *texture*. The distance or limit is constitutive of the possibility-necessity complex in which quantity and quality, desire and reason, servitude and love, all coexist in unresolved tension. What matter is that the tension of desire and order is a defining feature of humans which arises even before the love of Christ and before humans fail to love. Third, the *texture* is

7 François Chatillon, "Regio dissimilitudinis," in *Mélanges E. Podechard* (Lyon: Facultés Catholiques, 1954): 85-102.

8 Bernard of Clairvaux, On the *Song of Songs I*, pp. 147-8. Leclercq (*SC* 431), SCC 20.1, l. 1-26: "ante te est omne desiderium meum, et propositum cordis mei; si qua esset in me, servarem ad te. Sed, Deus, tu scis insipientiam meam; nisi quod hoc ipsum fortasse sapere est, quod et ego agnosco eam, et quidem ex munere tuo. Auge illud mihi, minime quidem ingrato pro munusculo; sed sollicito pro eo quod deest. Pro his ergo ita sum amans te, quantum possum."

presence as gift: the gift of presence. Gift is not lack. Gift is pure presence in the *texture* of desire's distance. Love is a gift that comes from the exterior and it is what makes love possible.[9] Love falls short, in the experience of limits, of its intended and original momentum marked by desire and confined to nothingness besides Christ. This is love, not ungratefulness. The experience of love is the result of a prior love given as gift (*munere tuo*). Hence, human desire is propelled towards the love of Christ in the experience of lack or nothingness (*nihil*) as presence. In the experience, love is revealed as gift in the face of the insufficiency or sterility of human desire. Therefore, desire, presence and gift form the texture of the distance in the Word as body to body. There is no texture in a body, but only in bodies. Body attracts body as an extension of the Word. Body is the gift of the Word. The distance is therefore pure presence. The presence of the body is at once so present and strange, that it is experienced as absence. Augustine's words can be restated, whereby body is "more present to myself than I am to myself."[10] Body *is* the texture of distance and is the result of the Word's order.

What is the order of the Word? Disorder is prior to order. The *texture* of distance, presence of absence, or disorder, is suffering. The *metamorphosis* of desire in the passage (*meta-physics*) of limits into (dis)order undergoes three stages: first, *suffering* at the limit; then *resistance* to reconfiguration as freedom; and finally *delimitation* in constitutive order. First, suffering. Suffering *attracts* bodies. The space of distance is the *texture* of the Word, the love of Christ. Bernard writes: "[b]ut there is *something else that moves me, arouses and enflames me even more* [...] *the price of our redemption*, makes me love you more than all the rest. *This alone would be enough to claim our love*. This, I say, is what *wins our love* so sweetly, *justly demands* it, firmly *binds it*, deeply *affects it*."[11] The disorder of suffering leads to the love of the Word. He continues, "[o] ur Savior had to toil so hard in this, in fact in making the whole world the Creator did not labor so much. Then he *spoke and they were made*; he *commanded and they were created*. But in saving us *he had to endure men who contradicted his words, criticized his actions, ridiculed his sufferings, and mocked his*

9 Bernard of Clairvaux, On the *Song of Songs I*, pp. 147-8. Leclercq (*SC* 431), SCC 20.1, l. 1-26: "Auge illud mihi, minime quidem ingrato pro munusculo; sed sollicito pro eo quod deest. Pro his ergo ita sum amans te, quantum possum."

10 Augustine, *Confessions* 3.6.

11 Bernard of Clairvaux, On the *Song of Songs I*, p. 148. Leclercq (*SC* 431), SCC 20.2, l. 1-26: "Sed est quod me plus movet, plus urget, plus accendit. Super omnia, inquam, reddit amabilem te mihi, Jesu bone, calix quem bibisti, opus nostrae redemptionis. Hoc omnino amorem nostrum facile vindicat totum sibi. Hoc, inquam, est quod nostram devotionem et blandius allicit, et justius exigit, et arctius stringit, et afficit vehementius."

death."[12] In suffering, love is born freely: the free love for the Word conditions the possibility for love. Bernard writes, "[s]*ee how much he loved us.* [...] *he was not returning love but freely offering it.* For who *had given him anything first,* that it *should be returned to him*?"[13] Furthermore, the unconditional love which engenders love is *resisted* in the process of attraction. "As St John said: 'Not that we had loved him, but that *he first loved us.' He loved us even before we existed, and in addition he loved us when we resisted him.*"[14] Third, *delimitation.* The love of Christ pours out even beyond the limits of existence; it encompasses what *is* and what is not. Bernard writes, "[i]f he had not loved his enemies, he could not have had any friends, just as he would have had no one *to love if he had not loved those who were not* [*nondum*]."[15] The limits of love are existential and modal. The love of enemy, who *is*, constitutes *resistance.* Inherent in the love of what *is*, even as resistance, is the possibility for the love of what is *not yet* (*nondum*). The *delimitation* of love is not, therefore, simply an existential distinction between what *is* and what *is not.* It is that, but it is also more. Love extends to what is not yet also, or to what will become. Hence love is manifest within the tension of temporal *resistance* between what is (friends and enemies) as a condition for the possibility of what is to become (what is not yet). The temporal delimiting *texture* of love is the Word itself. In brief, the limit, first experienced as suffering, is then reconfigured through resistance to achieve *delimitation. Delimitation* is nothing other than the constitution of limits in the *metamorphosis* of finitude in attraction as resistance. Bodies *attract* in the distance because in the Word lies the matrix or the texture of finitude where possibility and necessity are but the signposts of manifestation. The order of

---

12 Bernard of Clairvaux, On the *Song of Songs I*, p. 148. Leclercq (*SC* 431), SCC 20.2, l. 1-26: "Multum quippe laboravit in eo Salvator, nec in omni mundi fabrica tantum fatigationis auctor assumpsit. Illa denique dixit, et facta sunt; mandavit, et creata sunt (Psal. XXXII, 9). At vero hic et in dictis suis sustinuit contradictores, et in factis observatores, et in tormentis illusores, et in morte exprobratores."

13 Bernard of Clairvaux, On the *Song of Songs I*, p. 148. Leclercq (*SC* 431), SCC 20.2, l. 1-26: "Ecce quomodo dilexit. Adde quod hanc ipsam dilectionem non reddidit, sed addidit. Nam quis prior dedit ei, et retribuetur ei? (Rom. XI, 35.)."

14 Bernard of Clairvaux, On the *Song of Songs I*, p. 148. Leclercq (*SC* 431), SCC 20.2, l. 1-26: "Sed ut sanctus Joannes evangelista ait: Non quia nos dilexerimus Deum, sed quia ipse prior dilexit nos (I Joan. IV, 10). Denique dilexit etiam non existentes; sed adjicit et resistentes diligere, juxta Pauli testimonium dicentis: Quoniam cum adhuc inimici essemus, reconciliati sumus Deo per sanguinem Filii ejus (Rom. V, 10)."

15 Bernard of Clairvaux, On the *Song of Songs I*, p. 148. Leclercq (*SC* 431), SCC 20.2, l. 1-26: "Alioquin si non dilexisset inimicos, nondum possedisset amicos, sicut necdum quos sic diligeret essent, si non dilexisset qui nondum essent."

the Word is the very texture of *attraction*. Word is a generative *metamorphosis* of ordering *attraction*.

Thus far, the *word as force* has been considered in terms of the generative *attraction* of the Word which, by reconfiguring the matrix of finitude as love also orders the *extension* of the body. Now, since the suffering Christ is the origin (*incipio*) and beginning (*principium*), the beginning without beginning (*principium sine principium*), how does the grotesque of the body attract in resistance? In other words, what is the gravity of the crucified Christ? How does the body on the cross, fix those who stare? By way of hypothesis: the flesh of the Word is the weight of finitude – a weight too easily and too often confused with sin – and the weight of finitude is the gravity of love. This hypothesis is fully fleshed out in the following section entitled *the weight of the body*. What remains of this section focuses on the laws of order of *attraction* when considered from the lens of suffering or the repulsion of the grotesque body on the Cross. Love begins in suffering flesh of the Word, namely, in the grotesque. Love is not subject to the law of reason, or of desire, but to the grotesque. Love begins, it has been argued, above all, in suffering: suffering, which *attracts* by the Word. Furthermore, love in the flesh conceals a tension. In the suffering Christ on the cross, the grotesque *attracts* but also *repels*. Therefore, to will to love is not alone sufficient to love. In the reduction of the love of Christ, gravity (*gravitas*) of love is suffering in its entire dimension. The suffering of Christ *is* the attractive power of love. What is this attraction? The bitter chalice and the work of redemption refer to the suffering of Christ, the passion of Christ. The suffering on the cross, without beauty or decor, later treated in terms of aesthetics of desire, is here considered only as the verso of nothingness, which is the gravitational point of the weight of love, to use the Augustinian epithet, "my love is my weight."[16] The love that *is* and the love of what *is not yet* or what is to become, is governed by an *a*temporal weight of the suffering Word in the flesh. The suffering of Christ as Word made flesh alone vindicates (*vindicare*) the totality of human love.[17] The suffering flesh is the weight of finitude on the Word's body. The double sense of 'to vindicate' binds the intentionality of desire towards Christ with the suffering which vindicates humanity brings with the passion of Christ. What is the difference between attraction by lack (from nothing) and attraction by suffering? The first is accomplished by a simple word, the second by a Word which takes flesh and is thus able to suffer. Hence, the love for God passes through the suffering body of Christ.

16 Augustine, *Confessions*, 13.10: "pondus meum amor meus; eo feror, quocumque feror."

17 Bernard of Clairvaux, On the *Song of Songs I*, p. 148. Leclercq (*SC* 431), SCC 20.2, l. 1-26: "Hoc omnino amorem nostrum facile vindicat totum sibi."

In either case, humans love because they are loved; love begets love. Bernard writes, "[n]ot that we had loved him, but that he first loved us."[18] Yet, a tension, a resistance (*resistentes*), remains between *willing* to love God and the *ability* to love God. This tension conditions the ways in which Jesus is loved, for "[h]e loved us even before we existed, and in addition he loved us when we resisted him."[19] The interior conflict brings back to the conflicted desire of the will at the heart of experience in the desire of the flesh. The constitutive limits of human beings (*nihil*) and the resistance (*resistentes*) manifested in human suffering, underscore the importance of the gravity of love in the grotesque. The grotesque is a law unto itself, which governs how Christ can be loved and how Christ must be loved. How is Christ to be loved? Love results in love. Encounter empowers love, produces love, and engenders love. Yet the encounter with the grotesque flesh of the Word is mostly indirectly codified in the law. The Apostle Paul provides the guidelines for loving Christ.[20] Not only is Christ to be loved, Christ teaches *how* to love because the love of God makes love possible in the first place (cf. 1 Jn 4.10). The gravity of love on the Cross provides the model, the means and the possibility for love. Citing Paul, Bernard writes, "*Christian, learn from Christ how you ought to love Christ.* Learn a *love that is tender, wise, strong*; love with tenderness, *not passion*, wisdom, *not foolishness, and strength*, lest you *become weary* and *turn away* from the love of the Lord."[21] The mode of love is *action*: Christ is the power of God (*virtus Dei Christus*). Bernard continues, "Christ as the strength of God should support you so that you may not be worn down by difficulties. *Let love enkindle your zeal, let knowledge inform it*, let *constancy strengthen it. Keep it fervent, discreet, courageous.*"[22] The encounter

18 Bernard of Clairvaux, On the *Song of Songs I*, p. 148. Leclercq (*SC* 431), SCC 20.2, l. 1-26: "Non quia nos dilexerimus Deum, sed quia ipse prior dilexit nos (I Joan. IV, 10)."

19 Bernard of Clairvaux, On the *Song of* Songs *I*, p. 148. Leclercq (*SC* 431), SCC 20.2, l. 1-26: "Denique dilexit etiam non existentes; sed adjicit et resistentes diligere."

20 Bernard of Clairvaux, On the *Song of Songs I*, pp. 147-8. Leclercq (*SC* 431), SCC 20.1, l. 1-26: "Qui non amat Dominum Jesum, anathemata sit."

21 Bernard of Clairvaux, On the *Song of Songs I*, pp. 149-50. Leclercq (*SC* 431), SCC 20.4, l. 1-11: "Disce, o Christiane, a Christo, quemadmodum diligas Christum. Disce amare dulciter, amare prudenter, amare fortiter. Dulciter, ne illecti; prudenter, ne decepti; fortiter, ne oppressi ab amore Domini avertamur."

22 Bernard of Clairvaux, On the *Song of Songs I*, pp. 149-50. Leclercq (*SC* 431), SCC 20.4, l. 1-11: "Ne mundi gloria seu carnis voluptatibus abducaris, dulcescat tibi prae his sapientia Christus; ne seducaris spiritu mendacii et erroris, lucescat tibi veritas Christus; ne adversitatibus fatigeris, confortet te virtus Dei Christus. Zelum tuum inflammet charitas, informet scientia, firmet constantia. Sit fervidus, sit circumspectus, sit invictus. Nec teporem habeat, nec careat discretione, nec timidus sit."

with the grotesque resistance-attraction complex enkindles, informs and strengthens love.

A paradox: love has a law. The law teaches the love of God, especially in the Great Commandment (cf. Deut 6.5). The Bernardine three-fold analysis of how Christ teaches how us how he is to be loved has an immediately striking feature: the Great Commandment or the law passes down the teaching, even prior to the incarnation. The Word is a precursor and anticipation of the grotesque flesh. But how can Christ be loved before the incarnation? In other words, what manifestation of Christ, or rather the Word, is present in the law, such that Christ is revealed in the Word? Furthermore, the conscription of love (*amor*) to the law (*legem*) in light of the tension between desire (love) and reason (law), and especially in view of the hermeneutics of desire,[23] suggests either love is bound to reason in the law, or else that love overcomes the fragility of reason in the flesh, beyond the law. In addition, if so, how does love overcome reason in the law? Either way, reason and love seem at odds. Furthermore, since the love of Christ (not the Word, in Bernard's estimation) can be taught, and indeed practiced, in the absence of the incarnation, what is the role of the body, if any at all? Finally, if love is a gift, why is it commanded? Is not a gift gratuitous or is rather love given because it is commanded? And if so, what to say about free will of love within the necessity of the law? In short, how can love have a law? The law is love. Though separated by time, the law and Christ are not at odds because Christ *is* the very power of the law, hence the law is no different from love. The answer to all these questions revolves around the Pauline identification, which Bernard adopts, of Christ with the power of God (*virtus Dei Christus*) in 1 Cor 1. The alternative use of *your power* (*virtute tua*), rather than the Vulgate's original *your force* (*fortitudine tua*) suggests Bernard intentionally introduces Christ in the Great Command's exhortation to "love with all your power (*dilige et totat virtute*)." Christ teaches love in the law before the incarnation. The power of God is human freedom as aperity in self-imposed necessity. This is one of the passages where the power of God is closest to *desire* in the flesh and ultimately to *free will*. The command to love God "with all your heart, with all your soul, and with all your power,"[24] acquires a revolutionary meaning when Christ as the power of God is a substitute of "with all your power (*ex tota virtute tua*)," yielding, *with all your Christ*. Love of God is conditioned on Christ: Christ loves in all; all love through Christ in *the spread body*. Hence,

---

23 Bernard of Clairvaux, On the *Song of Songs I*, pp. 54-5. Leclercq (*SC* 441), SCC 9.2, l. 5: "Desiderio feror, non ratione."

24 *Vulgata*, Deut 4.5: "Diliges Dominum Deum tuum ex toto corde tuo, et ex tota anima tua, et ex tota virtute tua."

the Great Commandment can be re-framed: "[love God] with all your heart, with all your soul, and with all *your* Christ." The love of God through *our* Christ depends on Christ becoming *ours*. Bernard proposes three ways in which the (natural) law teaches,[25] within the Great Commandment, how to achieve the qualities of love to love God through Christ. The teaching of the law, however, is rooted in experience and is not meant to contain desire. On the contrary, by channelling desire, the law turns desire into corporeal aperity: "[s]ee it is not tepid, or temerarious, or timid. See for yourself if those three commands are not prescribed in the law when God says: '*You shall love the Lord your God with your whole heart, your whole soul and your whole strength.*'"[26] The *power of God* is modal aperity. Modal aperity, for now, can be treated in terms of modal love: *with all heart, soul and mind.* Bernard characterizes the 'three loves' of the Great Commandment in terms of their dynamic aim (*ad*). These are *affection, action* and *intensity*. First, *affection.* The love of the heart is the love of *affection* aimed towards zeal or emulation: "the *love of the heart* relates to a certain *warmth of affection, the love of the soul* to energy or *judgment of reason*, and the *love of strength* can refer to *constancy and vigor of spirit*."[27] Second, *action.* The love of the soul is the love directed towards the activity of judgement and reason. Third, *intensity*. The love of force is the love aimed at procuring the constancy and the intensity of love. The immediate aim of love is Christ: "[s]o love the Lord your God with the full and *deep affection of your heart*, love him with your mind wholly awake and discreet, love him with all your strength, so much so that you would *not even fear to die for love* of him. '*For love is strong as death, jealousy is bitter as hell.*'"[28] The *power* of love has the mode of intensity and constancy: "Let your love *be strong and constant*, neither yielding to fear

25 Simo Knuuttila, *Emotions in Ancient and Medieval Philosophy* (Oxford: Clarendon, 2004); John R. Sommerfeldt, *Bernard of Clairvaux on the Life of the Mind* (Mahwah: Paulist Press, 2004), 6, 50; G. R. Evans, *Bernard of Clairvaux. Great Medieval Thinkers* (New York: Oxford University Press, 2000), 139.

26 Bernard of Clairvaux, On the *Song of Songs I*, pp. 149-50. Leclercq (*SC* 431), SCC 20.4, l. 11-19: "Et vide ne forte tria ista tibi et in lege tradita fuerint, dicente Deo: Diliges Dominum Deum tuum ex toto corde tuo, et ex tota anima tua, et ex tota virtute tua (Deut. VI, 5)."

27 Bernard of Clairvaux, On the *Song of Songs I*, pp. 149-50. Leclercq (*SC* 431), SCC 20.4, l. 11-19: "Mihi videtur (si alius competentior sensus in hac trina distinctione non occurrit) amor quidem cordis ad zelum quemdam pertinere affectionis; animae vero amor ad industriam seu judicium rationis; virtutis autem dilectio ad animi posse referri constantiam vel vigorem."

28 Bernard of Clairvaux, On the *Song of Songs I*, pp. 149-50. Leclercq (*SC* 431), SCC 20.4, l. 19-37: "Dilige ergo Dominum Deum tuum toto et pleno cordis affectu; dilige tota rationis vigilantia et circumspectione; dilige et tota virtute, ut nec mori pro ejus amore pertimescas, sicut scriptum est in consequentibus: Quoniam fortis est ut mors dilectio, dura sicut infernus aemulatio (Cant. VIII, 6)."

nor cowering at hard work. Let us love *affectionately, discreetly, intensely*."[29] The ultimate strength of love is desire as extension: "*the love of the soul is wise indeed, but fragile without that love which is called the love of strength*."[30] Thus, the extension of desire is the power of love in the force of the Word. The modal aperity of the Word is expressed in body and as body through *affection, action* and intensity. Word and body *fuse* in the *attraction* of the *metamorphosis of love*. The *word as force attracts* and *fuses* in the process by *the weight of the body*.

5.2 The Weight of the Body

The body undergoes metamorphosis in love. This is the weight (*pondus*) of the body: the body is capable of becoming more than what it is and the body expresses God (Spinoza) as gravitating love (Augustine). The *extension* of the body as the force of Christ also bears a weight on the body in *attraction*. The Word and the flesh are united in the suffering Christ. Suffering weights down the body and in so doing *attracts*. The attraction of the body is the force of the Word. With Christ as its ultimate aim, the law teaches a love therefore that is fundamentally *spread* by emulation, judgement and intensity. Through Christ, Christ is loved with all the heart, soul and force.[31] As if by degrees, the love of Christ rises from the heart to the soul and culminates in the bodily force of God on the cross of Christ, even to the point of death. The force of Christ is the suffering body, which overcomes even the fear of death.[32] The force (*virtus*) of God on the cross as "my eros crucified" (Ignatius of Antioch) is in the *Song of Songs* transformed into the force (*fortis*) of love, strong as death, "as strong

---

29 Bernard of Clairvaux, On the *Song of Songs I*, pp. 149-50. Leclercq (*SC* 431), SCC 20.4, l. 19-37: "Sit etiam fortis et constans amor tuus, nec cedens terroribus, nec succumbens laboribus. Ergo amemus affectuose, circumspecte et valide, scientes amorem cordis, quem affectuosum dicimus, absque eo qui dicitur animae, dulcem quidem, sed seducibilem; istum vero absque illo qui virtutis est, rationabilem esse, sed fragilem."

30 Bernard of Clairvaux, On the *Song of Songs I*, pp. 149-50. Leclercq (*SC* 431), SCC 20.4, l. 19-37: "istum vero absque illo qui virtutis est, rationabilem esse, sed fragilem."

31 Bernard of Clairvaux, On the *Song of Songs I*, pp. 149-50. Leclercq (*SC* 431), SCC 20.4, l. 19-37: "Dilige ergo Dominum Deum tuum toto et pleno cordis affectu; dilige tota rationis vigilantia et circumspectione; dilige et tota virtute."

32 Bernard of Clairvaux, On the *Song of Songs I*, pp. 149-50. Leclercq (*SC* 431), SCC 20.4, l. 19-37: "dilige et tota virtute, ut nec mori pro ejus amore pertimescas, sicut scriptum est in consequentibus: Quoniam fortis est ut mors dilectio, dura sicut infernus aemulatio Cant. VIII, 6.)"

as death is love" (Cant 8.6).[33] Again, in "[He] ordered charity in me," desire as force becomes a substitute for *he*, resulting in "[Desire] ordered charity in me." The force of God crucified in the most vice real expression of bodily suffering, indeed to the point of death as the strength of love, is different from a presumed rejection of the body and desire. Rather than rejection (of the body) and suppression (of desire), the strength of love by "my eros crucified" is *metamorphosis*. The desire of love in the transformation of force (from *virtus* to *fortis*) is manifest ultimately as incarnate love on the cross in the *spreading* of *the spread body* inversely, transformation is rejection (not of the body, but of the flesh); rejection (*expello*) of an old love in preference for a new love: "[y]our affection for your Lord Jesus should be both tender and intimate, to oppose the sweet enticements of sensual life. Sweetness conquers sweetness as *one nail drives out another*. No less than this, keep him as a *strong light for your mind* and a *guide for your intellect*."[34] Desire and desire alone drives out desire in the totality of the human directionality towards God, in heart, mind and force, through Christ. While indeed in the order of love the primacy of reason trumps the force of desire, in an inversed order of love, desire, as "my crucified eros,"[35] is *the* force of love: "[...] *the love of the soul is wise indeed, but fragile without that love which is called the love of strength*."[36] The body is metamorphosed into the force of love. The transformative impetus of the body *towards* another body is the weight of love. The metamorphosis of love in the body occurs in the transition of desiring love to charitable love. The force of love is bifurcated in the body. The force of love is waged at the intersection of love as desire (*dilegere*) and charitable love (*caritas*). In the force of love crucified, transformed love is desire and transformed desire is love. Bernard frames the transformation of the intensity of love for God with all force, from *virtus* to *fortis*, in terms of the problem of love as *dilectio* and as *caritas*.[37] The intensity

33 Bernard of Clairvaux, On the *Song of Songs I*, pp. 149-50. Leclercq (*SC* 431), SCC 20.4, l. 19-37: "quoniam fortis est ut mors dilectio."

34 Bernard of Clairvaux, On the *Song of Songs I*, pp. 149-50. Leclercq (*SC* 431), SCC 20.4, I. 24-27; p. 133, n. 3: "Sit suavis et dulcis affectui tuo Dominus Jesus, contra male utique dulces vitae carnalis illecebras; et vincat dulcedo dulcedinem, quemadmodum clavum clavus expellit. Sed sit nihilominus intellectui praevia lux et dux rationi, non solum ob cavendas haereticae fraudis decipulas, et fidei puritatem ab eorum versutiis custodiendam, verum et cautus quoque sis nimiam et indiscretam vehementiam in tua conversatione [alias, conversione] vitare." Also, cf. *Epist.* 125, 14 (*CSEL* 54, 132, l. 14).

35 *Ep. Rom.* Ignatius of Antioch.

36 Bernard of Clairvaux, On the *Song of Songs I*, pp. 149-50. Leclercq (*SC* 431), SCC 20.4, l. 19-37: "istum vero absque illo qui virtutis est, rationabilem esse, sed fragilem."

37 On the *dilectio/caritas* couplet, cf. Bernard of Clairvaux, On the *Song of Songs I*, pp. 149-50. Leclercq (*SC* 431), SCC 20.4, p. 136, n. 1. Also, SCC 18.6 and DDD 1, n. 1, SC 393, 64.

of love (*dilectio*) on the cross is transformed into charity (*caritas*) by desire on the cross: the gift of life for the sake of others.[38] What is rejected in the transformation of the love of the heart to the love of force? Not desire; not the flesh. Indeed, the force of love, the force of Christ, is carnal.

Love as desire (*diligere*) becomes charitable love (*caritas*) when it is oriented towards the flesh of Christ: "*the love of the heart is, in a certain sense, carnal, because our hearts are attracted most toward the humanity of Christ* and *the things he did* or commanded *while in the flesh*."[39] Specifically, the affective orientation of the heart towards the flesh looks at the actions and teachings of Christ, i.e. the experience of Christ. "The heart that is *filled with this love is quickly* touched by *every word* on this subject. Nothing else *is as pleasant to listen to*, or is read with as much interest, *nothing is as frequently in remembrance or as sweet in reflection*."[40] In other words, the purpose of the incarnation is fundamentally to re-order the orientation of human affectivity, and in so doing, to synthesize love (*dilegere/caritas*) through the desire strong as death, in my crucified eros. Therefore, to love is not to give up carnal love, but to transform its modality. Love in affection, action and intensity must be wholly (*ex toto*) directed towards God, which is only possible through embodied experience of God in the incarnation. The flesh is thus a gift of love, and so too is the love for the *flesh of Christ*: "[t]his is why Christ said to them: 'Because I have said this to you, sadness has filled your hearts.' So i*t was only by his physical presence that their hearts were detached from carnal loves*."[41] Longing then turns into action of the spirit in *the spread body* as the constitution, in desiring-production, of the *body* in spirit. The body is metamorphosed from desiring love to charitable love in two degrees. These are *first*, the spirit and *second*, action. First degree: *spirit*. The process in the first degree is the spirit. "Afterwards he showed them a higher degree of love when he said, '[*i*]*t is the Spirit who gives life, the flesh profits nothing*.' I think Paul had reached this level when he said: '*Even if we*

38 Bernard of Clairvaux, On the *Song of Songs I*, pp. 151-2. Leclercq (*SC* 431), SCC 20.5, l. 32-33: *maiorem siquidem caritatem nemo habet, quam si animam suam ponat quis pro amicis suis.*

39 Bernard of Clairvaux, On the *Song of Songs I*, p. 152. Leclercq (*SC* 431), SCC 20.6, l. 1-27: "Et nota amorem cordis quodam modo esse carnalem, quod magis erga carnem Christi, et quae in carne Christus gessit vel jussit, cor humanum afficiat."

40 Bernard of Clairvaux, On the *Song of Songs I*, p. 152. Leclercq (*SC* 431), SCC 20.6, l. 1-27: "Hoc repletus amore, facile ad omnem de hujusmodi sermonem compungitur. Nihil audit libentius, nihil legit studiosius, nihil frequentius recolit, nihil suavius meditatur."

41 Bernard of Clairvaux, On the *Song of Songs I*, p. 152. Leclercq (*SC* 431), SCC 20.6, l. 1-27: "Hoc enim est quod eis dicebat: Quia haec locutus sum vobis, tristitia implevit cor vestrum (Joan. XVI, 6). Itaque in sola interim gratia praesentis suae carnis eos ab amore omnis carnis suspenderat."

once knew Christ in the body, we know him thus no longer.'"[42] Bernard continues, "They may be nourished by the *sweetness of his humanity* since they are *not yet able to perceive* the things which *are of the Spirit of God*."[43] What is this shade? "*The shade of Christ,* I suggest, *is his flesh.* Therefore in this human devotion there is in the meantime consolation for whomever does not as yet have the Spirit which gives life, at least who do not have him in the same way as those who say: '[a] Spirit before our face is Christ the Lord,' and again: '[*i*]*f we once knew Christ in the flesh we know him thus no longer*.'"[44] Bernard continues, "*there is no love of Christ at all without the Holy Spirit,* even if this love is in the flesh, and without its fullness. *The measure of such love* is this: *its sweetness seizes the whole heart and draws it completely* from the love of all flesh and every sensual pleasure. Really this is what it means to love with the whole heart."[45] There is no alternative between flesh and spirit; they go together by *feeling* precisely the weight of the body. Bernard goes on: "If I prefer to the humanity of my Lord someone joined to me by ties of blood, or some sensual pleasure, this would obviously prove that I do not love with my whole heart since it is divided between its own interests and the *love of the one who taught me as a man, both by his words and examples*. Would I not seem to give my love partly to him and partly to my own?"[46] There is action when the union is achieved, because words follow example. Thus, "to love *with the whole heart* means to put *the love of his*

---

42 Bernard of Clairvaux, On the *Song of Songs I*, pp. 152-3. Leclercq (*SC* 431), SCC 20.7, l. 1-38: "Monstrabat autem postea eis altiorem amoris gradum, cum diceret: Spiritus est qui vivificat, caro non prodest quidquam (Joan. VI, 64). Puto, hunc ascenderat jam qui dicebat: Etsi cognovimus Christum secundum carnem, sed nunc jam non novimus (II Cor. V, 16)."

43 Bernard of Clairvaux, On the *Song of Songs I*, pp. 152-3. Leclercq (*SC* 431), SCC 20.7, l. 1-38: "et carnis dulcedine nutriantur, dum necdum valent ea percipere quae sunt Spiritus Dei."

44 Bernard of Clairvaux, On the *Song of Songs I*, pp. 152-3. Leclercq (*SC* 431), SCC 20.7, l. 1-38: Umbram siquidem Christi, carnem reor esse ipsius, de qua obumbratum est et Mariae (Luc. I, 35), ut ejus objectu fervor splendorque Spiritus illi temperaretur. In carnis ergo devotione interim consoletur, qui vivificantem Spiritum necdum habet, eo duntaxat modo, quo habent illi qui aiunt: Spiritus ante faciem nostram Christus Dominus; et item: Etsi cognovimus Christum secundum carnem, sed nunc jam non novimus."

45 Bernard of Clairvaux, On the *Song of Songs I*, pp. 152-3. Leclercq (*SC* 431), SCC 20.7, l. 1-38: Nam alias quidem nequaquam sine Spiritu sancto vel in carne diligitur Christus, etsi non in illa plenitudine. Cujus tamen mensura devotionis haec est, ut totum cor illa suavitas occupet, totum sibi ab amore universae carnis ac carnalis illecebrae vindicet. Hoc quippe toto corde diligere est."

46 Bernard of Clairvaux, On the *Song of Songs I*, pp. 152-3. Leclercq (*SC* 431), SCC 20.7, 1-38: Alioquin si carnis meae quamlibet consanguinitatem vel voluptatem forte praefero carni Domini mei, per quod me videlicet minus ea implere contingat, quae in carne manens verbo et exemplo me docuit; nonne liquido constat, quod toto nequaquam diligo corde, cum id divisum habens, partem impendere videar carni ejus, partem intorquere ad propriam?"

sacred humanity before everything [...] *from within or without*."[47] Action ensues only after there is unification. The second degree is *action*. Second degree is the passage from flesh to Spirit (action). Action is the flesh of Christ: the shadow of Christ is his flesh (not body). Like the Shadow of the spirit. Love between the flesh of Christ and one's own flesh. The efficiency of the flesh is a gift. "Of course *this devotion to the humanity of Christ is a gift, a great gift of the Spirit*. I have called it carnal with comparison to that other love which does not know the *Word as flesh* so much as the *Word as wisdom, as justice, truth, holiness, loyalty, strength, and whatever else could be said in this manner. Christ is truly all these things*."[48] The gift takes the shape of compassion. "[The man who] *feels a share in Christ's sufferings*, is *affected and easily moved at the thought of all that he suffered*; he is nourished and strengthened by the sweetness of this devotion to good and honest and worthy actions."[49] The carnal love is part of action. "But that *carnal love is worthwhile since through it, sensual love is excluded*, and the world is condemned and conquered. It becomes better when it is rational and becomes perfect when it is spiritual."[50] Finally, the manifestation of action

47 Bernard of Clairvaux, On the *Song of Songs I*, pp. 152-3. Leclercq (*SC* 431), SCC 20.7, 1-38: "Denique ait: Qui amat patrem aut matrem plus quam me, non est me dignus; et qui amat filium aut filiam plus quam me, non est me dignus (Matth. X, 37). Ergo, ut breviter dicam, toto corde diligere, est omne quod blanditur de carne propria vel aliena, sacrosanctae carnis ejus amori postponere. In quo et mundi aeque gloriam comprehendo, quia gloria mundi gloria est carnis, et qui ea delectantur, carnales esse non dubium est."

48 Bernard of Clairvaux, On the *Song of Songs I*, p. 154. Leclercq (*SC* 431), SCC 20.8, l. 1-24: "Licet vero donum, et magnum donum Spiritus sit istiusmodi erga carnem Christi devotio; carnalem tamen dixerim hunc amorem, illius utique amoris respectu, quo non tam Verbum caro jam sapit, quam Verbum sapientia, Verbum justitia, Verbum veritas, Verbum sanctitas, pietas, virtus; et si quid aliud quod sit, hujusmodi dici potest. Et haec nempe omnia Christus, qui factus est nobis sapientia a Deo, et justitia, et sanctificatio, et redemptio (I Cor. I, 30)."

49 Bernard of Clairvaux, On the *Song of Songs I*, p. 154. Leclercq (*SC* 431), SCC 20.8, l. 1-24: "An tibi aeque et uno modo affecti videntur, is quidem qui Christo passo pie compatitur, compungitur, et movetur facile ad memoriam honorum quae pertulit, atque istius devotionis suavitate pascitur, et confortatur ad quaeque salubria, honesta, pia: itemque ille, qui justitiae zelo semper est accensus, qui veritatem ubique zelat, qui sapientiae fervet studiis; cui amica sanctitas vitae, et morum disciplina; cujus mores erubescunt jactantiam, abhorrent detractionem, invidiam nesciunt, superbiam detestantur, omnem humanam gloriam non solum fugiunt, sed et fastidiunt et contemnunt; omnem in se carnis et cordis impuritatem vehementissime abominantur et persequuntur; omne denique tanquam naturaliter et malum respuunt, et quod bonum est amplectuntur? Nonne si compares utriusque affectiones, constat quodam modo illum superiorem, respectu quidem hujus, amare quasi carnaliter?"

50 Bernard of Clairvaux, On the *Song of Songs I*, pp. 154-5. Leclercq (*SC* 431), SCC 20.9, l. 1-23: "Bonus tamen amor iste carnalis, per quem vita carnalis excluditur, contemnitur

is the fullness of the Spirit. "I think the name is very fitting for this special love because of the *special fullness of the Spirit in which it excels*."[51] The mediation of the self with the self by the word becomes externalized through the mediation of the self to the other, and vice-versa, through the body. However, the abyss between word and flesh can only be possibly mediated by the Word in the flesh through the incarnation analogous to the word mediated in the self, the Word mediates with others. Why? Because the access to the body occurs only through *the spread body*, the body of Christ on the first instance, later the body of the Church, *the body of God*. What is the mechanism of such mediation? What triggers it, what are its conditions and what are the outcomes? In short, the weight of the body reaches a new moment where body is the force of action. This is further explored in *the body as force*.

5.3 The Body as Force

The core of *attraction* is *the force of the body*. The force of the body is the grotesque or repulsion. The question is how can repulsion attract? The question of the beauty of the crucified body has a long tradition and is rooted in the emblematic words of the prophet Isaiah (Is 53.2) which, in Christian tradition, are often thought of as foreshadowing the suffering Christ, "[h]e had no beauty or majesty to attract us to him, nothing in his appearance that we should desire him (*non erat ei species neque decor*)." On the one hand, the incarnate Word, Christ, is beautiful, "the fairest among all sons of men" (Ps 45.2). On the other hand, the crucified state of the Christ exemplifies the grotesque, for in the crucified body, Christ is hardly recognizable as human and the suffering body is repulsive.[52] How then, is the suffering Christ simultaneously beautiful and grotesque and, more importantly, attracting yet repelling or, better yet, attracting while repelling.[53] The words of Augustine are fitting: "How can we love

---

et vincitur mundus. Proficitur autem in eo, cum fit et rationalis; perficitur, cum efficitur etiam spiritualis."

51 Bernard of Clairvaux, On the *Song of Songs I*, pp. 154-5. Leclercq (*SC* 431), SCC 20.9, l. 1-23: "Itemque cum in propria conversatione illa cautela servatur, ut discretionis meta nulla superstitione vel levitate, vel spiritus quasi ferventioris vehementia excedatur."

52 István Czachesz, *The Grotesque Body in Early Christian Discourse: Hell, Scatology, and Metamorphosis* (Abingdon: Routledge, 2014); Mary Carruthers, *The Experience of Beauty in the Middle Ages* (Oxford: Oxford University Press, 2013); Anthony N. S. Lane, *Bernard of Clairvaux, Theologian of the Cross* (Collegeville: Liturgical Press, 2013), 143, 152-6, 172-197, 203, 225.

53 Rosario Assunto, "Sulle idee estetiche di Bernardo di Chiaravalle," *Rivista di Estetica* 4 (1959): 240-68; Fiona C. Black, *The Artifice of Love: Grotesque Bodies in the* Song of Songs

anything but the beautiful? What, then is a beautiful thing? Can anything compel us that is not beautiful and fitting?"[54] In the Christian tradition, the usual response consists in (re)localizing true, lasting and wholesome beauty in the interior, not the exterior (Plotinus). The exterior bears a semblance of beauty, but remains transitory, incomplete, and ultimately illusory. The exterior is a sign (*signum*) of the beauty of things (*res*). Though this historically provided Christian thinkers with a simple and elegant strategy for harmonizing the coexistence of the (externally) grotesque and the (interiorly) beautiful of the crucified body, the suffering Christ, it remains that the approach bypasses and even rejects the significance of the suffering body and grotesque flesh of the passion. As such, the bifurcation of the internal/external failed to appreciate the grotesque as resistance (*conatus essendi*), reducing it rather to lack – the flesh is more than sin at the limit – rather than privation (cf. *privatio*, Augustine) in desiring-production. Beauty, which *attracts* in *repulsion* of bodies, is manifestation as production. The grotesque is production. Bernard's revolutionary contribution in dealing with the aesthetics of the cross lies in his having framed positively the generative power of the grotesque. Bernard's point of departure is his ongoing emphasis on the intimate connection between the body and desire: even the grotesque body of the suffering Christ *must* function, not only as a sign of the interior beauty, but also as the *very* presence of beauty, just as conversely, the body of the resurrection signifies performative and efficient desire. The sign of the cross is not sterile, but just like the resurrection, it is productive. Efficient desire is not only attraction but also transformation in process and production. Concisely stated, as in the inversion effectuated in the order of charity, so too in the reconciliation of the grotesque and the beautiful, or the grotesque as the beautiful, the hermeneutics of desire offer the key to the portal of generation. The fundamental Bernardine thesis on this point is as follows: the body, experienced in the suffering of the flesh, is the locus of desire and the locus of divine manifestation. Hence, *the spread body* is the vehicle to access to the mystery of divine pathos at the heart of experience: desiring-production. For Bernard, desire is productive and generative: the body is the force of the Word. The *extension* of *the spread body* occurs within *attraction* – and the *force* of the body's *weight* reconfigures the matrix of finitude in tended *order*. The weight of the body in *extension* with *attraction*

(London: Clark, 2009); M. Kilian Hufgard, *Saint Bernard of Clairvaux: A Theory of Art Formulated from His Writings and Illustrated in Twelfth-century Works of Art* (Lewiston: Mellen, 1989); Janet Martin Soskice, "Being and Love: Schleiermacher, Aquinas and Augustine," *Modern Theology* 34, no. 3 (2018): 480-91.

54 Augustine, *Confessions* 3.20.

(beauty) and *repulsion* (grotesque) – later *resistance* – is a complimentary dimension of production. Now, *the weight of the body* most distinctly shows *the body as force*. The body's production is the force of the body.

The body is force. The force of the body is beauty and the grotesque. The desire for the body and of the body begins with beholding the crucified (a question of aesthetics). However, there is more. The gaze demands a response, a response that inevitably conjures a plethora of moral questions. The gaze of the crucified gives way, therefore, to normativity. And this is the case in two senses. First, if the ugly (descriptive) should be beautiful (prescriptive), then how is the ugly desired and should it be desired at all? Second, the shock of the grotesque *must* produce an often-neglected counter-blow (*choque-en-retour*), a counter-blow that does not negate beauty, but rather confronts conditions and transforms it. What is the counter-blow and what is the beauty it produces? The twofold sense merges into a single concern: what is the force of the body (prescription) in response to the gaze (description) or how to bridge what *is* with what *must be* – or better yet, become? Indeed, the force of the body is not absolute nor void of moral texture. The moral texture begins in the gaze because from the gaze ensues a response, a transformative experience: *first*, the gaze impels; *then*, the gaze compels. First, the gaze impels: "*Behold, you are beautiful!*"[55] The point of departure is the gaze of the grotesque. *Behold* the beauty of the bride, *behold* the grotesque of the crucified – "behold the one whom they have pierced." This poses difficulties. How can *nothing* (*nihil*) attract or repel? Indeed, for Augustine the grotesque is desired by a disordered desire (*concupiscence*) or by a *love of love* (*amor amoris*) because the grotesque is, if not convertible with, at least indicatory of evil (*privatio*). The grotesque is an illusory image of the beautiful, much like time is a passing image of eternity, or humanity an approximate semblance to the image of the perfect divine image who is Christ. The difficulty is pressing: how is privation or the *nihil* desired? By a gravitation towards the beginning of human origin (*de nihilo*) from whence creation pours forth (*ex nihilo*). While Bernard maintains the core elements of the discourse on desire and the grotesque ('disordered desire', evil as 'privation'), the desire for the grotesque as *love of love* is not wholly evil as such because it is construed in affirmative terms, and not merely in terms of lack or absence. In the Bernardine discourse, the desire for the agony of Christ in the flesh is not displaced into an internal beauty but is rather a kind of desired ugliness, which escapes the *nihil*. This is the central Bernardine thesis on the aesthetics of the desiring body: the flesh in agony is the source of desire not as fulfillment of lack, but as creative production manifested in the

55 Cf. Cant 1.14-15.

resistance of the free will's willed necessity. The passage from word to body (incarnation) is complete in the mediation of the soul's desire for the suffering body of Christ: experience of the incarnate divine pathos is the hermeneutic condition for the possibility of desire of the flesh. Desire constitutes the passage from the experience of the body to the Word (incarnate). Paradoxically, body and word collapse and indeed metamorphose, in the desired grotesque of divine pathos. The desire of the gaze touches the grotesque body, and in so doing, is transformed in and by the force of the body.

"Behold, you are beautiful!"[56] Bernard uses the dialogue between the lovers of the *Song of Songs* to chart the structure of beauty, which ultimately emerges as desiring-production. The lovers in question are the soul (*anima*) and Christ. How and why does Christ desire the soul? How and why does the soul desire Christ? On the one hand, what can be beautiful and therefore desirable about the soul in the eyes of Christ? On the other hand, how can the suffering Christ on the grotesque cross be desired at all? What is not beautiful can be desirable, as the grotesque, just as the sublime, not being beautiful, is desired as well (Burke). The grotesque is the awe-inspiring wonder inverse of the sublime. The difficulty is accentuated, therefore. There is no way around it. The road to beauty is the way of the cross from whence follows love. Love is knowledge of Christ, Christ crucified: "I was resolved that the only knowledge I would have while I was with you was knowledge of Jesus, and of him as the crucified Christ."[57] Knowledge is not sight, for Bernard, but touch. There is a rift, therefore, between the body and the gaze, between knowledge and love. To behold beauty, is to touch it. The gaze touches the body and savors beauty through the Word. Between gaze and the body is the Word. Christ desires the soul irrespective of the soul's beauty. But what is the love's beauty and what is the effect of love on the relation between the soul and Christ? Love is between equals. The transformation from the greatness of Christ to the lowliness of the soul, which enables the mutual love, is triggered by language, in the conversation between the lover and the beloved. The Word mediates the touch of the gaze upon the body and of the body upon the gaze. The Word is the force of the body. *Second*, the gaze compels. The gaze compels when the Word, as force of the body, and indeed of bodies, produces generative reciprocity of love (*ex amore*). Love (*amore*) and beauty (*pulcher*) give way to the bride's presumption (*praesumption*) and to the groom's indignation (*indignatio*). Presumption and indignation constitute the moral poles, the texture, of the exchange of touch

56 Cf. Cant 1.14-15: "ecce tu pulchra es."

57 Bernard of Clairvaux, On the *Song of Songs II*, pp. 234-5. Leclercq (*SC* 452), SCC 45.3: "Sufficit mihi, nolo jam scire nisi Jesum, et hunc crucifixum. Magna humilitas!"

by Words. The force of the weight of bodies first impels (gaze) and then compels (Word). In the gaze, there is admiration: "Behold, *how beautiful you are, my dearest, O how beautiful* [...] How beautifully said, how excellent."[58] Admiration arises from love. Love (*ex amore*) is the origin of desire, which springs from within the funnel of loving reciprocity between lover and beloved, from the beauty of the body to Words and ultimately actions: "The bride's *presumption springs from her love*, the Bridegroom's *anger from his love*."[59] The beginning of the circle of desire comes from love (*ex amore*). What is the outcome? The presumption produces correction, the correction results in amend, and amend in reward, "For correction followed the presumption, amendment the correction, and reward the amendment."[60] The beauty of the bride, in other words, on the one hand produces the frustration of the groom, but on the other hand is the very reward of the bride. The bride's dependence on the groom is helplessness based on beauty alone and love simply creates a circle, the circle of desire (*principium sine principium*). The circle is generative. The bride depends on it for love, but because of it, the bride must also return love. Love is at the origin (*ex amore*) of the circle of desire but it is also at the point where self-love or idolatrous love of beauty, the love of love (*amor amoris*), is overcome. The production of self-love overcome is the affect (*affectus*).[61] The tension between love and beauty and the desire for beauty is fragile, for it risks collapsing into vanity. Generative affect emerges shortly, if but only to disappear. In short, the generative power of the gaze compels and demands a response: the affect. The gaze *impels* (to behold is to touch) and *compels* (to behold is to affect) through the Word and by the Word: the force of the gaze, which touches the body, is the weight of the body in the Word. The process occurs at the juncture where the body communicates desire as affect through language, just as Moses spoke with God *almost* (*quasi*) like a friend.[62] The affect of friendship (*amicitia*), or the love of friends (*philia*) is not enough to mediate the force of the gaze in touch and affect. The focus is not on friendship, but in the intimacy of

58 Bernard of Clairvaux, On the *Song of Songs II*, p. 232. Leclercq (*SC* 452), SCC 45.1, l. 1-8: "Ecce tu pulchra es, amica mea, ecce tu pulchra; oculi tui columbarum (Cantic. I, 14)."

59 Bernard of Clairvaux, On the *Song of Songs II*, p. 232. Leclercq (*SC* 452), SCC 45.1, l. 1-8: "Pulchre, optime, ex amore, sponsae praesumptio; ex amore, indignatio sponsi."

60 Bernard of Clairvaux, On the *Song of Songs II*, p. 232. Leclercq (*SC* 452), SCC 45.1, l. 1-8: "Etenim praesumptionem correptio, correptionem emendatio, emendationem remuneratio secuta est."

61 Bernard of Clairvaux, On the *Song of Songs II*, p. 232. Leclercq (*SC* 452), SCC 45.1, l. 1-8: "Cedit quippe fastus, ubi invalescit affectus."

62 Bernard of Clairvaux, On the *Song of Songs II*, p. 232. Leclercq (*SC* 452), SCC 45.1, l. 1-8: "Et sicut quondam quasi amicus ad amicum Moyses loquebatur (Exod. XXXIII, 11), et Dominus respondebat."

conversation (*confabulatio*). Through language, the soul gains familiarity with the Word, "And just as Moses once spoke to God as a friend to a friend and God answered him, so now the Word and the soul converse with mutual enjoyment, like two friends."[63] Words are no longer simply the tool to mediate the self with the self; there is no longer a tension between beauty and love.[64] Rather, the vehicle for overcoming the difference between interlocutors in the tension of love and beauty is the levelling force of desire, not only out of love this time (*ex amore*) but as the generative outcome of *love of love* (*amor amoris*), i.e., affect (*affectus*): "Winged words honey-sweet fly to and fro between them, and their eyes like heralds of holy love, betray to each other their fullness of delight."[65] The wings of words weigh down upon the body with the sweetness of delight. Language is thus, specifically the divine language of the Word (*verbum*), the bridge that allows for communication between the Word and the soul beyond the circle of desire. The Word acts; the Word impels in touch and acts in affect.

The force of the body is the Word. By Word we understand more than linguistic communication, more than sound. Beauty is known by the touch of the Word because the Word is an embodied force. Language, and to be precise, embodied language in word, in the form of voice (elocution), *is* the condition and cause of love. The body is communicated through the Word. That the engagement of beauty and love find their source in the embodiment of language (word/voice), and not automatically in desire, also opens the possibility of conceiving a relation of desire and the grotesque in the absence of beauty, and by means of embodied language in the embodiment of suffering language "to know Christ and him crucified" (*scire nisi Iesum, et hunc crucifixum*).[66] The Word is the force of the body. Language announces embodied beauty: "*The two streams of their love have but a single source from which they are equally sustained. Winged words honey-sweet fly to and fro between them*, and their eyes

63 Bernard of Clairvaux, On the *Song of Songs II*, p. 232. Leclercq (*SC* 452), SCC 45.1, l. 1-8: "Et sicut quondam quasi amicus ad amicum Moyses loquebatur (Exod. XXXIII, 11), et Dominus respondebat: ita et nunc inter Verbum et animam, ac si inter duos vicinos, familiaris admodum celebratur confabulatio."

64 cf. SD 110.

65 Bernard of Clairvaux, On the *Song of Songs II*, p. 232. Leclercq (*SC* 452), SCC 45.1, l. 1-8: "Ergo dulciora melle volant hinc inde verba, mutui in se totius suavitatis feruntur aspectus, sancti indices amoris."

66 Bernard of Clairvaux, On the *Song of Songs II*, pp. 234-5. Leclercq (*SC* 452), SCC 45.3: "Et tamen increpata poenitentiam agit, et dicit: Fasciculus myrrhae dilectus meus mihi, inter ubera mea commo rabitur (Cantic. I, 12): hoc est: Sufficit mihi, nolo jam scire nisi Jesum, et hunc crucifixum. Magna humilitas!"

like heralds of holy love, betray to each other *their fullness of delight*."[67] What is that beauty and how does the elocution of beauty not only produce love but also transform it? "*He calls her his dearest one, proclaims her beauty, repeats that proclamation, only to win a like response from her*."[68] Bernard identifies a two-fold beauty of the soul worthy of desire. Love is attracted to beauty and love beautifies. The soul is lovable if and when it is humble and simple. Humility and simplicity, together, make up for the ugliness of the soul (sin) and render the soul lovable for transformation.[69] The beauty of the soul, humility and simplicity, allows the soul to contemplate the humility of the groom: the incarnation and the passion.[70] The force of the gaze is the Word and the Word communicates the body in unconditioned *attraction*, both of and to beauty and of and to the grotesque. The Word, as force of the body, *beholds beauty* (impelling/compelling) – "*O how beautiful*"[71] and *knows the grotesque* (in touch) – "to know Christ and him crucified (*scire nisi Iesum, et hunc crucifixum*)." The weight of the Word's touch *metamorphoses* the body and the *metamorphosis* of the body *extends* and *attracts* in Word. By compelling through the Word, the gaze obtains its moral texture. Moral texture is a twofold normative mode: *humility* and *simplicity*. In the mutual gaze of the lovers, the true beauty of the bride is humility and simplicity and it encounters the great beauty of the grotesque on the cross: the humility of the cross (*Magna humilitas*): "As much as to say, it is enough for me. *I desire to know* nothing any longer except *Jesus and him crucified*. What great humility!"[72] All is in simplicity and humility: the gaze, the touch, knowledge and love. The frailty of the body on the cross is the frailty of humility: "For I believe that in this vision images of his flesh, or of

67 Bernard of Clairvaux, On the *Song of Songs II*, p. 232. Leclercq (*SC* 452), SCC 45.1, l. 8-18: "Nec mirum. Ex uno amoris fonte utrique influit diligere invicem, confoveri pariter. Ergo dulciora melle volant hinc inde verba, mutui in se totius suavitatis feruntur aspectus, sancti indices amoris."

68 Bernard of Clairvaux, On the *Song of Songs II*, p. 232. Leclercq (*SC* 452), SCC 45.1, l. 8-18: "Denique is iilam amicam nuncupat, pulchram pronuntiat, pulchram iterat, eadem ab illa vicissim recipiens. Nec otiosa iteratio, quae amoris confirmatio est, et fortassis aliquid innuit requirendum."

69 Bernard of Clairvaux, On the *Song of Songs II*, pp. 234-5. Leclercq (*SC* 452), SCC 45.3, l. 27-29: "non solum ex meo amore, sed etiam ex tua humilitate."

70 Bernard of Clairvaux, On the *Song of Songs II*, pp. 234-5. Leclercq (*SC* 452), SCC 45.3, l. 12: "dumtaxat incarnato et passo."

71 Bernard of Clairvaux, On the *Song of Songs II*, p. 232. Leclercq (*SC* 452), SCC 45.1, l. 1-8: "Ecce tu pulchra es, amica mea, ecce tu pulchra; oculi tui columbarum (Cantic. I, 14)."

72 Bernard of Clairvaux, On the *Song of Songs II*, pp. 234-5. Leclercq (*SC* 452), SCC 45.3: Et tamen increpata poenitentiam agit, et dicit: Fasciculus myrrhae dilectus meus mihi, inter ubera mea commo rabitur (Cantic. I, 12): hoc est: Sufficit mihi, nolo jam scire nisi Jesum, et hunc crucifixum. Magna humilitas!"

the cross, or in any way suggestive of physical frailty, were not imprinted on her imagination, since the Prophet tells us that under these forms, *he possessed neither beauty nor majesty*."[73] In this passage, Bernard brings together for the first time the beauty of the bride and the grotesque of the cross. The gaze proclaims in word the Word's beauty and majesty which is none other than the body's fragility or humility. "But as she now contemplates him, *she declares him both beautiful and majestic*, making it clear that *her present vision transcended all others*. He speaks to her face to face as once he spoke to Moses, and she for her part *sees God plainly, not through riddles and symbols*."[74] The gaze of the vision transcends. The moral texture is thus the purity of the gaze and, in the counter-blow, the transformation, indeed the *metamorphosis* of the gaze in the fragility of the body.

The rest of this section focuses on articulating the question of the relation between the interior and the exterior, beauty and the grotesque, when the body is construed as force. The fundamental hypothesis is: the Word as the force of the body unifies, rather than reject or polarize, the interior and exterior through the presence of signification. The conclusion, which will be discussed later is, Word is *force* indeed, and, as such, Word is performative. In short, the force of the body is the Word because Word is embodied. Bernard thinks of beauty (the bride in her chamber) and the grotesque (the groom on the cross) in terms of the force of the body: the Word. There is no need to bifurcate the interior and the exterior as there is no need to negate them. Bernard unites interior and exterior through the Word. Bernard may seem to adopt the mainstream distinction between the exterior ugliness and the interior beauty of Christ on the cross in order to explain how Christ is at once repulsive on the cross, yet desirable in the passion of the flesh. However, the true Bernardine concern is not to merely displace the locus of beauty (outside to inside) but rather, in so doing, to show how the grotesque opens to the beautiful. The transition is achieved by the special emphasis on the role of language in the vision of God.[75] The spouse gazes upon the images of the flesh (*imagines carnis*) where there is neither beauty nor decorum (*non erat ei species neque decor*).

---

73 Bernard of Clairvaux, On the *Song of Songs II*, pp. 236-7. Leclercq (*SC* 452), SCC 45.6.

74 Bernard of Clairvaux, On the *Song of Songs II*, pp. 236-7. Leclercq (*SC* 452), SCC 45.6, l. 12-20: "Existimo enim nequaquam hac vice ejus sensibus importatas imagines carnis, aut crucis, aut alias quascunque corporearum similitudines infirmitatum. In his namque, juxta prophetam, non erat ei species neque decor (Isai. LIII, 2). Haec autem eum intuita, nunc pulchrum decorumque pronuntiat, in visione meliori illum sibi apparuisse significans. Ore enim ad os, sicut quondam cum sancto Moyse (Exod. XXXIII, 11), loquitur cum sponsa; et palam, non per aenigmata et figuras, Deum videt."

75 Augustine, *Confessions* 9.24.

The contemplation (*intueri*) of the suffering Christ utters (*pronuntiare*) the beauty of Christ. The vision (*intueri*) and the expression (*pronuntiare*) coincide where the eyes *touch* the flesh of Christ. Bernard illustrates the *touch* in the image "from mouth to mouth" (Num 12.8). A transformation occurs from the vision to the utterance. The transformation is remarkably framed. The vision of speech in the transformation is akin, according to a Bernard, to the direct conversation of Moses and God culminating in a complete vision, face to face. The centrality of language in procuring the possibility for the sight of God on earth is appreciated when the position is compared to overwhelmingly opposing mainstream views on the issue.[76] Indeed, Bernard parts ways not only with the precedents, but is exceptionally inconsistent with his own views on the topic. In short, the Word as the force of the body functions as an efficient sign, which at once manifests and transforms, indeed *metamorphoses* the beauty of love and the love of beauty in the body. Upon first gaze, beauty is not easily recognized. The gaze, we have said it, touches the body. The force of the gaze's touch is not without response: *extension* is the counter-blow of *attraction* and vise-versa. The responses to the gaze of the grotesque are fear, awe and distance. In the beauty of the (grotesque), Word is love.[77] Love is manifested and transmitted in the transition from body (word/vision) to embodied Word (voice) in language. The ugliness is the sight of suffering, yet such sight communicates love. In other words, Christ communicates love as the beauty of the Verb through the ugliness of the passion. The embodied Word, the voice, as efficient love in the incarnation, is what mediates the grotesque of the cross and the beautiful of the Verb's love. Suffering alone is the portal to beauty and love in the human experience of the divine pathos. Hence, language is not only a vehicle for overcoming the circle of desire; it is also the very key to access the beauty of the Word beyond the ugly suffering of the flesh. Language is the means by which the soul and the Verb communicate love passing through experience of the love transformed in the suffering flesh of Christ on the cross. The utterance, "how beautiful you are, my love, and how you delight me (*ecce tu pulcher es, dilecte mi, et decorus*)" is transformative and bridges word with vision, because it is accompanied, even propelled and motivated, by the sentiments in the manifestation. God can be manifested in the experience of beauty as love and in the experience of the grotesque as fear. "One text runs, 'I saw the Lord seated on a high and lofty throne,' another, 'I have seen God face to face and yet my life

---

76 Bernard of Clairvaux, On the *Song of Songs II*, pp. 236-7. Leclercq (*SC* 452), SCC 45.6, p. 266, n. 1, *De Genesi ad litteram* XII, 26 (CSEL 28.420, 2-9).

77 Bernard of Clairvaux, On the *Song of Songs II*, pp. 237-8. Leclercq (*SC* 452), SCC 45.7, l. 6-7: "siquidem pulchritude illius dilectio eius."

is preserved.' But he says, 'If I am a master, where is my fear?' If the revelation accorded to them was accompanied by fear, since where the Lord is there too is fear of him, I for my part, given the choice, should embrace with greater willingness and love the vision seen by the bride, because it comes about through a *more wonderful passion, that of love*. For to fear is to expect punishment, *but perfect love casts out fear*."[78] Love and fear come together: 'There is a vast difference between him who appears so terrible in his deeds among men, and *him who surpasses men in beauty of form*. 'Behold, you are beautiful, my beloved, truly lovely.' *These words are vibrating with love, not fear*."[79] The first gaze is fear because there is no love without fear, as there is no sublimity in the absence of wonder. The force of fear results in action or love. The aesthetic manifestation of God – theological aesthetics[80] – is mediated through the desire of affections (*affectione*) as embodied through the language of the Word. "*It is not the word that speaks, it is we who speak the word*. So too, the soul has no means of *uttering speech unless the body's mouth forms and speaks the words*.' [...] *it is the Spirit who speaks*."[81] In the aesthetic manifestation of beauty and ugliness as love, a difficulty remains. How to move from the description of the utterance to the performance? Is the embodied word as expression of love efficient? In short, yes. Love is efficient because love is the *aperity*. Love is, to borrow Falque's phrase, "the word of the body."[82] Having described the beauty of the soul and the ugliness of the Word on the cross, Bernard illustrates the efficiency of love

---

78 Bernard of Clairvaux, On the *Song of Songs II*, pp. 236-7. Leclercq (*SC* 452), SCC 45.6, l. 31-40: "Sic enim habes: Vidi Dominum sedentem super solium excelsum, et elevatum (Isai. VI, 1); et item: Vidi Dominum facie ad faciem, et salva facta est anima mea (Gen. XXXII, 30). Sed si ego Dominus, inquit, ubi est timor meus? (Malach. I, 6.) Quod si illis facta est revelatio cum timore; quia ubi Dominus, ibi timor: ego profecto, si optio daretur, tanto libentius, tantoque charius sponsae amplecterer visionem, quanto in meliori affectione, quae est amor, factam adverto. Nam timor poenam habet, perfecta autem charitas foras mittit timorem (I Joan. IV, 18)."

79 Bernard of Clairvaux, On the *Song of Songs II*, pp. 236-7. Leclercq (*SC* 452), SCC 45.6, l. 31-40: "Multum sane interest apparere terribilem in consiliis super filios hominum (Psal. LXV, 15), et apparere speciosum forma prae filiis hominum (Psal. XLIV, 5). Ecce tu pulcher es, dilecte mi, et decorus. Verba ista plane amorem resonant, non timorem."

80 Richard Viladesau, *Theological Aesthetics: God in Imagination, Beauty, and Art* (New York: Oxford University Press, 1999).

81 Bernard of Clairvaux, On the *Song of Songs II*, pp. 236-7. Leclercq (*SC* 452), SCC 45.7, l. 1-20: "Nam verbo loquimur, non verbum loquitur. Itemque anima non habet unde loquatur, nisi os corporis sibi verba formaverit ad loquendum. Bene quaeris: sed attende spiritum loqui, et spiritualiter oportere intelligi quae dicuntur."

82 Emmanuel Falque, "Christ doesn't save us by his Words First of all, but by his body," interview with Arthur Rossman, 7 June 2018, *Church Life Journal*, University of Notrea Dame. URL: https://churchlifejournal.nd.edu/articles/christ-doesnt-save-us-by-words-first-of-all-but-by-his-body/, accessed throughout July 2022.

as the channel and impulsion of desire in language by looking at the reciprocal communication of language between the beauty of the soul and the Word wherein description becomes action through the flesh. Gaze produces act. The action of love unfolds as progressive (*gradus*) and modal (*modus*) manifestation. In love's mode (*modus*) of manifestation, the beautiful and the grotesque are intertwined. The question of the efficacy of embodied love can be articulated in terms of the conditions for the possibility of communication between the soul and the Word. This is fundamentally *resistance*: "*The Word is a spirit, the soul is a spirit, and they possess their own mode of speech and mode of presence in accord with their nature*. The *speech of the Word is loving kindness*, that of the soul, the *fervor of devotion*. The soul without devotion is a *speechless infant* that *can never enjoy such intercourse with the Word*."[83] How is the reciprocal communication possible? Bernard anticipates the problem, "But perhaps you are thinking and asking yourselves with increasing doubt, 'How can the words of the *Word be spoken to the soul and those of the soul to the Word*, so that *she hears his voice telling her that she is beautiful*, and she in return offers a similar compliment to him? How can this happen?"[84] The question of the function of the word in communication, between self through words by the Word is fully laid out elsewhere.[85] While following key aspects of the Augustinian

83 Bernard of Clairvaux, On the *Song of Songs II*, pp. 237-8. Leclercq (*SC* 452), SCC 45.7, l. 1-20: "Quoties proinde audis vel legis, Verbum atque animam pariter colloqui, et se invicem intueri; noli tibi imaginari quasi corporeas intercurrere voces, sicut nec corporeas colloquentium apparere imagines. Audi potius quid tibi sit in hujusmodi cogitandum. Spiritus est Verbum, spiritusque anima, et habent linguas suas, quibus se alterutrum alloquantur, praesentesque indicent. Et Verbi quidem lingua favor dignationis ejus: animae vero, devotionis fervor. Elinguis est anima atque infans quae hanc non habet, et non potest ipsi ullatenus sermocinatio esse cum Verbo."

84 Bernard of Clairvaux, On the *Song of Songs II*, pp. 237-8. Leclercq (*SC* 452), SCC 45.7, l. 1-20: "Sed forte ascendunt cogitationes in corde tuo, et quaeris dubius apud te, dicens: Qua ratione verba Verbi facta ad animam referuntur, et rursum animae ad Verbum, ut illa audierit vocem loquentis sibi, et perhibentis quod pulchra sit, vicissimque idem praeconium suo mox reddiderit laudatori? Quomodo possunt haec fieri?"

85 cf. SDD 110, *SC* 384 Bernard of Clairvaux, On the *Song of Songs II*, pp. 237-8. Leclercq (*SC* 452), SCC 45.7, l. 1-20: "Quanta est miseria nostra, et indigentia nostra quam multiplex! Etiam verbis opus habemus. Et cum utrumque sit miserum, non jam mirum quod inter nos; mirum magis, quod etiam ad nos ipsos. Nemo scit quae sunt in homine, nisi spiritus hominis qui est in ipso (I Cor. II, 11). Chaos magnum inter nos firmatum est, nisi interveniente quasi instrumento verborum fiat ad invicem transitus quidam cordium in communicatione cogitationum. Hac necessitate inventa sunt verba: quis nesciat? Verumtamen et nos ipsos verbis jam alloqui necesse est. Nonne Deo subjecta eris, anima mea? Propheta ait, ab ipso enim salutare meum (Psal. LXI, I). Et cui non frequenter necesse est animam revocare suam, advocare rationem suam, suos convocare affectus? Cui non opus est crebro se ipsum convenire verbis, increpare minis, sollicitare monitis, urgere accusationibus?

theory of words as signs, as laid out in *De magistro* and in *De doctrina christiana*, Bernard does not shy away from emphasizing the role of the body, and by extension the implications of desire on communication, in the use of words. For Bernard, signs are fundamentally communicated through presence of the flesh and not as absence. The (productive and efficient) presence of the signified in the thing, the sign, is what ensures communication between the Word and the soul and indeed, what unites the interior with the exterior, the beautiful and the grotesque. The signification of the body is the process of manifestation.

The body is performative sign and signified. "The words of the body" unite body (*soma*) and sign (*sema*). The voice or sounds precedes the proclamation of beauty: word (sound) and voice (beauty) are distinct. The reason for this is rooted in the Augustinian distinction between voice and word (often used as a paradigm for the incarnation of the Word). The word does not speak because it has no voice. The word is the means by which the voice is transmitted. The word is the vehicle for speech, but words do not speak as such.[86] Hence, words are (signs – *signum*) used to convey beauty (things – *res*) and as such, beauty is prior to words: body is prior to speech. This raises a difficulty. How can signs capture and convey aspects of beauty? In other words, how does the body speak? It seems that the bodily signs, which come from the mouth of the body, must lend words for the soul to speak. And so, the conclusion would be, the soul cannot speak without the body.[87] Bernard briefly considers the position (the soul cannot communicate with the Word without the body) only to nuance it. The communication occurs through the spirit (*Spiritum loqui*) and is therefore spiritual (*spiritualiter*), not bodily. The nuance is *not* a rejection of

---

Quin etiam ratiociniis suadere expedit; quale est, Ab ipso enim salutare meum; et consolari aliquando, juxta illud, Quare tristis es, anima mea, et quare conturbas me? (Psal. XLI, 6.) et interdum velut excitare, et dicere, Lauda, anima mea, Dominum (Psal. CXLV, 1); et nonnunquam diligentius commonere de quibus oportet, ut est, Benedic, anima mea, Domino, et noli oblivisci omnes retributiones ejus (Psal. CII, 2). Nempe cor meum dereliquit me, et necesse habeo ad me ipsum, imo ad me alterum loqui. Atque id interim tanto amplius, quanto minus sum adhuc reversus ad cor, reversus in me, unitus denique mihi ipsi. Nam ne invicem quidem erit jam verbis uti, ubi in unum utique virum perfectum occurremus omnes. Opportune igitur linguae cessabunt; nec medius requiretur interpres, ubi usque adeo medium omne charitate constraverit ille unicus Mediator, ut et nos in unum facti simus in ipsis, qui vere sempiterneque unum sunt, Deo Patre, et ipso Domino Jesu Christo."

86 Bernard of Clairvaux, On the *Song of Songs II*, pp. 237-8. Leclercq (*SC* 452), SCC 45.7, l. 1-20: "Nam verbo loquimur, non verbum loquitur."

87 Bernard of Clairvaux, On the *Song of Songs II*, pp. 237-8. Leclercq (*SC* 452), SCC 45.7, l. 1-20: "Itemque anima non habet unde loquatur, nisi os corporis sibi verba formaverit ad loquendum."

the body. Far from it. Indeed, the introduction of the Spirit grounds the conditions for the communication between the soul and the Word in experience precisely because there is no experience without the Spirit. Furthermore, since the Bernardine experience is fundamentally corporeal and embodied, so too is communication between the soul and the Word. At times, Bernard seems to suggest otherwise.[88] However, the overall point is: the resistance of the weight of the body to the Word is complimented by the force of the body. The Word as the force of the body is therefore sign and signified through the Spirit: the voice of the body becomes Word in the Spirit. Spirit *metamorphoses* the signifying body. The *metamorphosed* body is therefore essential in the communication of the soul and the Word. This is so, in terms of *efficiency* and in *aperity*, which will be fully investigated in the third part of this volume. For now, suffice it to briefly state them and identify them in Bernard's writings first hand. First, *efficiency*: the words of the body are efficient. Bernard writes, "But when the Word addresses such a soul, *desiring to speak to it*, that soul cannot but hear, for '*the word of God is living and active*, sharper than any two-edged sword, piercing to the division of soul and spirit.'"[89] Second, *aperity*. The power of the Word, which is the Spirit, transforms everything, everywhere: "w*hen the soul decides to speak, much less can the Word hide from it*, not merely because *he is present everywhere*, but rather because without his inspiration the soul will lack the *devotion that urges speech*."[90] *Efficiency* and *aperity* are the modes of the *metamorphosed* body. So, based on *efficiency* and *aperity*, how is the body in the background of the communication between the soul and the Word? First, efficiency incorporates all the body. Second, love is not contained in the body indicates the body is overcome. Hence, the body is essential to the communication. From different passages at least two other reasons can be cited. Third, the possibility of such communication depending on the spirit marks the parameters not only of belonging. Fourth, the body and soul are one. Fifth and final, the communication of the beauty and the soul is in a sense a-lingual (*elinguis*), much like that of an infant. Love, which passes through the desire

88 Bernard of Clairvaux, On the *Song of Songs II*, pp. 237-8. Leclercq (*SC* 452), SCC 45.7, l. 1-20: "imaginari quasi corporeas intercurrere."

89 Bernard of Clairvaux, On the *Song of Songs II*, pp. 237-8. Leclercq (*SC* 452), SCC 45.7, l. 21-28: "Ergo hujuscemodi linguam suam cum Verbum movet, volens ad animam loqui, non potest anima non sentire. Vivus est enim sermo Dei et efficax, et penetrabilior omni gladio ancipiti, pertingens usque ad divisionem animae et spiritus (Hebr. IV, 12)."

90 Bernard of Clairvaux, On the *Song of Songs II*, pp. 237-8. Leclercq (*SC* 452), SCC 45.7, l. 21-28: "Et rursum cum suam anima [alias male animam] movet, Verbum latere multo minus poterit; non solum quia ubique est praesens, sed propter hoc magis, quod, nisi ipso stimulante, devotionis lingua minime ad loquendum movetur."

of the flesh, is in fact what gives birth to bodily language, yet a language of the soul is already there. Body, word, experience and desire are intricately weaved in the Bernardine account of the communication between the Word and the soul. Beauty can therefore be communicated by the *efficiency* and the *aperity* of the body. What about the grotesque? Does it too communicate like beauty? This can be laid out by looking at how Bernard makes beauty and love one. Initially, the Word is the power of the body. Now, the power of the body is the beauty of love. Bernard writes, "When the *Word therefore tells the soul, 'You are beautiful,'* and calls it friend, he *infuses into it the power to love, and to know it is loved in return.* And when the soul *addresses* him as beloved and *praises his beauty,* she is *filled with admiration for his goodness* and attributes [...] *she loves and is loved.*"[91] Again, "*The Bridegroom's beauty is his love of the bride,* all the greater in that it existed before hers."[92] Love is prior and so love beautifies and acts. "Realizing then that he was her *lover before he was her beloved,* she cries out with strength and ardor that *she must love him with her whole heart and with words expressing deepest affection. The speech of the Word is an infusion of grace* [...] The more she feels *surpassed in her loving the more she gives in love* [...] Hence, not satisfied to tell him once that he is beautiful, she repeats the word, *to signify by that repetition the pre-eminence of his beauty.*"[93] As power, beauty outpours from the body. The outpouring of beauty is the grotesque. Yet the ugly is also beautiful and as such the ultimate ugliness, the grotesque, becomes one with love. "These are the qualities, and others like them, that the bride contemplated in her beloved when she said, 'B*ehold, how beautiful you are, my Love, how beautiful.*' And not these alone, but beyond them she must have glimpsed something of the beauty of his higher nature, *something that wholly transcends our vision, that eludes our experience.*"[94] The force of the

---

91 Bernard of Clairvaux, On the *Song of Songs II*, pp. 238-9. Leclercq (*SC* 452), SCC 45.8, l. 1-16: "Verbo igitur dicere animae, pulchra es, et appellare amicam, infundere est unde et amet, et se praesumat amari. Ipsi vero Verbum vicissim nominare dilectum, et fateri pulchrum; quod amat et quod amatur."

92 Bernard of Clairvaux, On the *Song of Songs II*, pp. 238-9. Leclercq (*SC* 452), SCC 45.8, l. 1-16: "Siquidem pulchritudo illius dilectio ejus; et ideo major, quia praeveniens."

93 Bernard of Clairvaux, On the *Song of Songs II*, pp. 238-9. Leclercq (*SC* 452), SCC 45.8, l. 1-16: "Medullis proinde cordis et intimarum vocibus affectionum tanto amplius atque ardentius clamitat sibi diligendum, quanto id prius sensit diligens quam dilectum. Itaque locutio Verbi infusio doni, responsio animae cum gratiarum actione admiratio. Et idcirco plus diligit, quod se sentit in diligendo victam: et ideo plus miratur, quod praeventam agnoscit. Unde non contenta est semel dicere pulchrum, nisi repetat et decorum, eminentiam decoris illa repetitione designans."

94 Bernard of Clairvaux, On the *Song of Songs II*, pp. 239-40. Leclercq (*SC* 452), SCC 45.10, l. 1-15: "Haec ergo similiaque puta in dilecto intuentem sponsam advertisse, cum diceret:

body in love outpours and becomes generative. "And therefore, writes Bernard, *repetition is her tribute* to the loveliness of the two natures. Hear then how she dances at the sight and words of her Beloved, *as her love spills over*."[95] In generation beauty is manifested also as the grotesque. "*Non erat ei species neque décor*" (Is 53.2). Beauty is beautiful in giving up beauty. Such is the paradigmatic frame for the communication of the soul and the Word through the mediation of the body. The transformation of desire for the body is prior to the communication: the beauty of the body signifies love and through the efficient love transforms the pre-lingual conditions for communication. Only then is communication possible. The body, through its beauty and ugliness, is the receptacle of words in the Word and through the Spirit. The experience of the body allows communication through the Word, and results in the transformation of love as beauty in efficient action.

Conclusion

How do bodies *extend*? We have been concerned with yet another important moment in the *metamorphosis of love*: the transition of Word to body, specifically, with the relation between *desire and the Word*. This has emerged, in the present chapter, in three moments: *word as force, the weight of the body* and *the body as force*. To recapitulate, the present chapter has attempted to chart how *attraction*, which was previously discussed as *extension*, achieves the *fusion* of bodies. This happens, we have tried to show, because the performative Word gives bodies a gravity which in turn manifests the body as action. The *attraction* of body manifests the force of the Word in the *metamorphosis of love*. The attraction of the body marks yet another series of transformations in the *metamorphosis of love* where desire is manifested as love in the word as force, the weight of the body and the body as force. In the crucified body, the sublime (Edmund) and the grotesque (Bakhtin) are intertwined and manifested as modes of love's desiring-production. The sublime is generation and the grotesque is resistance in the unified dynamic force (*vir*) of love effectuated by the Spirit in the *spreading towards* of *the flesh of the word* within

---

Ecce tu pulcher es, dilecte mi, et decorus. Neque haec sola, sed insuper aliquid procul dubio de naturae decore superioris, quod nostrum omnino praetervolat intuitum, et effugit experimentum."

95 Bernard of Clairvaux, On the *Song of Songs II*, pp. 239-40. Leclercq (*SC* 452), SCC 45.10, l. 1-15: "Ergo iteratio utriusque decorem substantiae designavit. Audi deinde quomodo tripudiat ad aspectum affatumque dilecti, et coram ipso nuptiali carmine quae amoris sunt gratulabunda decantat."

the grotesque body. The grotesque body is, in its manifestation, unbounded yet bounded, ordered yet disordered, resisting confinement yet constantly spreading. Thus, *the grotesque body*, violently fractured yet intimately unified, incomplete and still organic is the metaxoloigcal aperity of bodies without organs (Deluze) and organs without bodies (Žižek) in which destruction like construction are generative resistance, pure ongoing reconfiguration of parts in relation to the *spreading* whole (mer(e)ology). In *the grotesque body* which is the crucified body, *the inverse(d) order of charity*, configures the mode of desiring-production as aperity or as *desire as free will*. The identification of desire with love raises the question of order: how can the disorder of desire frame the order of love? Roughly, this problem constitutes the problem of the next chapter concerning *order*. The problem of order will be analyzed, in the chapter that follows, in three moments: first, *law and order*; second, *love and order*; third, *the (dis)order of desire*.

CHAPTER 6

Order

What *order* ensues from *extension* and *attraction* simultaneously considered? To address this problem, we consider the (re)order or the (dis)order which results from *extension* and *attraction* in the *metamorphosis of love*. Whereas previously love was an outcome of the body, now body is an outcome of love. This reversal constitutes the next moment in the *metamorphosis of love*, wherein body as force is reconfigured into action. The mer(e)ology of *the spread body* as the diffusion of desiring-production returns to *the beginning without beginning* in the guise of *the grotesque body*, where simultaneous wonder before the sublime (attraction) and the grotesque (resistance) are but modes of generation as desiring-production in the expression of love as power (*vir*) beyond reason. A mer(e)ology of *the spread body* within *desire in the word* is situated as the metaxological aperity between onto-metaphysical (Plato and Aristotle), symbolic (Husserl) and formal (Lésiniewski) *mereologies* on the one hand, and *organic merology* (study of fluids and elemental tissues) on the other hand. The *mer(e)ology* of *the spread body*, with *the grotesque body*, achieves the synthesis as metaxological aperity of onto-metaphiscis and logic (mereology) and embodied experience of desiring-production (merology) as *aesthetic mer(e) ology*. The *aesthetic mer(e)ology* of *the spread body* begins therefore with the desiring-production of *the grotesque body* in the (dis)order of charity. The epithet "desire has ordered charity in me,"[1] in the desire as the resistance of the grotesque *in* the crucified body as *the spread body*, roots the order of charity in, and organically grows from, an aesthetic mer(e)ology of the grotesque where "desire impels me, not reason"[2] precisely as desiring-production. The thrust of an organic *aesthetic mer(e)ology* results in *the inverse(d) order of charity*. The *metamorphosis of love* in the (re)order of charity shall be analyzed in this chapter in three moments. First, in *law and order* (6.1), then, secondly, in *love and order* (6.2), and, finally, in *the order of desire* (6.3).

1 Bernard of Clairvaux, On the *Song of Songs III*, Verdeyen (*SC* 452), SSC 50.1, l. 1, cf. Cant. 2.4. "ordinavit in me charitatem."

2 Bernard of Clairvaux, On the *Song of Songs I*, Leclercq (*SC* 441), SCC 9.2: "Desiderio feror, non ratione."

© BRILL FINK, 2023 | DOI:10.30965/9783846767504_008

6.1 Law and Order

The first order in the *metamorphosis of law* is the order of law. In writing "[desire] ordered charity in me,"[3] Bernard succinctly charts the transition, inversion and transformation at the heart of the *metamorphosis of love*, from Word into action through the body. The transformation of desire occurs as a progression of order from affective charity (*caritate in affectu*) to active charity (*caritate in actu*).[4] This progression brings to completion the logic of desire which unfolds from the body as the locus of the *beginning without beginning*, onto the inversion of the order of charity in desire as *aperity* or freedom. The inversion of the order of charity occurs, as is frequently the case for Bernard, gradually or by degrees (*gradus*). Progression by degrees implies movement and continuity across change. Gradual progress results in transformation. The transformation in question is the mode of affection, whereas affection, as an expression of desire, remains a constant throughout the degrees of progress. The Bernardine analysis of the transformation proceeds through a transposition of the order of charity (*caritatis ordine transpositio*) as it passes from affective charity into active charity. The triple affection of interest is the affection of the flesh (*affectione carnalis*), the affection of reason (*affectione rationis*) and finally the affection of wisdom (*affectione apientiae*). What happens to the word passing through the body in the transformation of desire? What is the effect of the order of charity (*ordinavit in me charitatem*) on the efficacy of the body, desire and love? Bernard makes these questions the prime object of the discussion: "[Verses] *are presented from the tray of love*, as sweet as they are delicate, as tasty as they are small. Furthermore, *it is altogether contrary to love to deprive people of love*. So here I am, '*he has set charity in order in me*.'"[5] A plethora of questions arises. What is the order of charity? What does it mean to order charity? The question of the order of charity, which goes to the heart of the problem of the transformation of love arises in terms of the relation among

3 Bernard of Clairvaux, On the *Song of Songs III*, p. 30. Verdeyen (*SC* 452), SSC 50.1, l. 1: "ordinavit in me charitatem."

4 John R. Sommerfeldt, *Bernard of Clairvaux on the Life of the Mind* (Mahwah: Paulist Press, 2004), 40-2, 81.

5 Bernard of Clairvaux, On the *Song of Songs III*, p. 30. Verdeyen (*SC* 452), SCC 50.1, l. 1-11: "Vos forsitan exspectatis tractari sequentia, explicitum putantes versiculum, qui novissime tractabatur. Verum ego aliud molior: habeo enim quod adhuc vobis apponam de fragmentis hesterni convivii, quae mihi collegeram ne perirent. Peribunt autem, si nulli apposuero: nam si voluero ea habere solus, ipse peribo. Nolo proinde vestram illis, quam bene novi, fraudare ingluviem: praesertim cum sint de ferculo charitatis, eo dulcia quo subtilia; eo sapida quo minuta. Alioquin contra charitatem est valde nimis de ipsa charitate fraudare. Itaque hic sum: Ordinavit in me charitatem (Cant. II, 4)."

kinds of charity according to directionality: neighbor, God and self. Is charity in act different from charity in affect? Alternatively, are they rather a continuous progression whereby they fuse to produce something new in a higher level of charity?

The order of charity *does not* require a mutually exclusive choice between *act* and *affect*.[6] Rather, true charity in act remains incomplete without affection because the sentiment of affective charity as such is integrated into active charity through a kind of *liquefaction* of hearts expressed, for instance, in *the gift* of tears. Such *liquefaction* of affective charity is precisely what renders charity effective. The charity in affect is liquefied into charity in act. This is why William of Saint-Thierry often pairs efficient love (*efficiens*) together with affective love (*afficiens*).[7] The difficulty, therefore, lies not in determining whether the expression of charity in affect and charity in act are manifested simultaneously or in tension. For Bernard, they are not the same, they are different, yet *liquefy* into each other. Since the liquefaction of charity in affect is what gives charity in act is efficacy, the question becomes: how does charity in affect liquefy into charity in act to become aperity or free will?

Another way to ask the same question from the vantage point of the *metamorphosis of love*, and by way of transition from desire to free will is as follows. The order of charity is the pathway from corporeal metamorphosis of desire in experience into the power of free will. However, how can desire, inherently beyond reason (*desiderio feror, non ratione*), culminate in any form of order (*ordinavit in me charitatem*)?[8] For now, this is a problem on the possibility of the efficacy of the will. Later, the same problem resurfaces on the possibility of free love. That is, how can free will, under the order of reason and not desire, overcome necessity and therefore come to love at all if the power of the will is fundamentally desire? In other words, is not desire at odds with love (*caritas*), simultaneously threatening love's efficacy and freed? The capital importance of dealing with the (rational) order of love vis-à-vis (irrational) desire cannot be overstated, for what is at stake are the central tenants of love, namely action and choice. A love without act is sterile, it is not love. An act without choice is servile, it remains a prisoner of free will's necessity. Hence, returning to the earlier question, what is the order of desire and how does it emerge, specifically in the transformation of charity in affect and charity in act through the degrees

---

6 Bernard of Clairvaux, On the *Song of Songs III*, pp. 32-3. Verdeyen (*SC* 452), SCC 50.4: "Neque hoc dico, ut sine affectione simus, et corde arido solas moveamus manus ad opera."

7 Bernard of Clairvaux, On the *Song of Songs III*, pp. 31-2. Verdeyen (*SC* 452), SCC 50.2, p. 348, n. 1. Also, Bernard of Clairvaux, On the *Song of Songs III*, Verdeyen (*SC* 452), SCC 50.4.

8 John R. Sommerfeldt, *Bernard of Clairvaux*, 40-50; Mette Birkedal Brunn, *The Cambridge Companion to the Cistercian Order* (Cambridge: Cambridge University Press, 2013).

of affection in the flesh, affection in reason and affection in wisdom? In a revolutionary interpretation of the order of charity, Bernard begins with a double sense of charity: charity in act (or in action) and charity in affect (or in feeling). He writes, "Love exists *in action* and *in feeling*. And with regard to *love in action*, I believe that a law, *an explicit commandment*, has been given to men; yet how can *one's feelings correspond to the commandment*?"[9] The difference between these loves is framed in terms of a framework of consequence. "The former therefore, writes Bernard, is *commanded in view of merit*, the latter is *given as a reward*."[10] Specifically, the consequence is linked with happiness. Some happiness can be achieved already during life by following the commands, though not fully. "We do not deny that the present life, by divine grace, can also experience its *beginning and progress*, but we unreservedly maintain that *its consummation is in the happiness of the life to come. How then should that be ordered which can in no way be fulfilled*?"[11] The two-fold sense of charity, charity in act (*caritas in actu*) and charity in affect (*caritas in affectu*), immediately inscribes the problem of love from the vantage of free will and in so doing echoes closely, in guise of interpretation, the infamous phrase from Augustine's *Confessions* (which triggered the first phase of the so-called Pelagian controversy at the turn of the 4th century on the eve of the fall of the Latin Roman Empire): "give what you command, and command what you will."[12] The Augustinian proposal, taken in isolation, suggests God commands the law only insofar as God gives the strength (grace) for humans to follow (free will) the law. God cannot ask what humans cannot observe freely. Of course, this raises questions concerning how sin can be willed at all in the first place. However, the British monk Pelagius was immediately concerned that the Augustinian formulation (*conf.* 9.20) would blur the boundaries between the grace of merit and the merit of grace. The consequence would be, Pelagius feared, risking foregoing free will by absorbing merit into grace and consequently rendering merit and indeed free will absolutely meaningless illusions of human existence. Bernard's contribution is to have managed to fit a sliver between grace and

9 Bernard of Clairvaux, On the *Song of Songs III*, pp. 31-2. Verdeyen (*SC* 452), SCC 50.2, l. 1-12: "Est caritas in actu, est et in affectu. Et de illa quidem quae operis est, puto datam esse legem hominibus, mandatumque formatum: nam in affectu quis ita habeat, ut mandatur?"

10 Bernard of Clairvaux, On the *Song of Songs III*, pp. 31-2. Verdeyen (*SC* 452), SCC 50.2, l. 1-12: "Ergo illa mandatur ad meritum, ista in praemium datur."

11 Bernard of Clairvaux, On the *Song of Songs III*, pp. 31-2. Verdeyen (*SC* 452), SCC 50.2, l. 1-12: "Cujus initium quidem, profectumque vitam quoque praesentem experiri divina posse gratia non negamus; sed plane consummationem defendimus futurae felicitati. Quomodo ergo jubenda fuit, quae implenda nullo modo erat?"

12 Augustine, *Confessions*, 9.20.

free will precisely in the guise of the (inverse) order of charity. In Bernard's *On the Song of Songs*, the question of grace and free will emerges, above all, as a question of charity. Rather than reducing (perhaps only rhetorically) all love to grace as does Augustine, according to which all love is grace and all grace is love, Bernard multiplies as it were, the senses of charity. This enables Bernard to offer a dialectic question in reply to Augustine's infamous passage in the *Confessions*. Bernard states, "if you prefer to hold that *affective love* has been commanded, I do not dispute it, provided you agree with me that *in this life it can never and will never be able to be fulfilled by any man*."[13] In other words, there is a kind of charity, the charity of affection, which exceeds the law and is therefore beyond the yoke of the law's commandments. How can the law regulate what exceeds the law? This is Bernard's question. The emancipation of affective charity in a sense remains, nevertheless, still close to the law by the second kind of charity, the charity of action, because the charity of action pertains to the law.[14] Interestingly, Bernard draws yet another distinction between the law (*legem*) and the commandment (*mandatum*) of the law. While the charity of action involves both the law and the commandment of the law, which is formulated (*formare*) based on the law, the law/command distinction introduces a descriptive/prescriptive rupture. The charity of action thus emerges within the rupture of what *is* (descriptive or the law) and what *ought* to be (prescriptive or the command). Moreover, to the extent that it emerges thus in the descriptive/prescriptive rupture, the charity of action is not only in a sense (a)moral (beyond the weight of normative limits and boundaries), but more importantly, the charity of action functions, in its (a)moral field, as *the* locus for transformation: from the charity of affect to the charity of action. Hence, Bernard readily accords, inversely, the possibility of conceiving that the charity of affect too, like the charity of action, lies within the umbrella of commands.[15] The inverse relation (charity of affect/command) also inverses the directionality of the rupture. Just as the charity of affect can be (only partially) bound to commands, so too the normative rupture (descriptive/prescriptive)

13 Bernard of Clairvaux, On the *Song of Songs III*, pp. 31-2. Verdeyen (*SC* 452), SCC 50.2, l. 1-12: "Aut si placet tibi magis de affectuali datum fuisse mandatum, non inde contendo, dummodo acquiescas et tu mihi, quod minime in vita ista ab aliquo hominum possit, vel potuerit adimpleri."

14 Bernard of Clairvaux, On the *Song of Songs III*, pp. 31-2. Verdeyen (*SC* 452), SCC 50.2, l. 1-12: "Et de illa quidem quae operis est, puto datam esse legem hominibus, mandatumque formatum."

15 Bernard of Clairvaux, On the *Song of Songs III*, pp. 31-2. Verdeyen (*SC* 452), SCC 50.2, l. 1-12: "Aut si placet tibi magis de affectuali datum fuisse mandatum, non inde contendo, dummodo acquiescas et tu mihi, quod minime in vita ista ab aliquo hominum possit, vel potuerit adimpleri."

is no longer directed from description to prescription but is rather directed now from prescription (*command*) to description (*law*). In fact, because of this inversion alone is it possible for the charity of affection to be bound by the law. In other words, and this gets to the heart of the Bernardine response to the Great Augustine: God *can* and *does* command things beyond human powers to accomplish, yet the momentum, far from constraining the free will, manifests it a fortiori. Bernard writes, "The lawgiver was not unaware that *the burden of the law exceeded the powers of men*, but he judged it *useful for this reason to advise men of their own insufficiency*, that *they might know the proper end toward which they ought to strive according to their powers*."[16] This is because charity transforms the free will in the charity of affect and the charity of action and at the juncture of the descriptive/prescriptive rupture. Such a transformation is anchored on the Bernardine appeal to the Apostle Paul's experience of falling short: "*Accepting that command then, and conscious of our deficiency* [...] we shall know that God has saved us, not by the *righteous works* that we ourselves have done, but *according to his mercy*."[17] Bernard goes on: "Therefore, in commanding impossible things [...] the whole world [is] made subject to God, because nobody will be justified in his sight by *the works of the law*."[18]

That the charity of affect can be partly commanded is considered only in passing because it introduces, only implicitly, the important theme of sin as necessity with relation to the free will and because, as has been noted, it opens the prospect of transformation, from the charity of action to the charity of affect. Bernard continues, "This is what I should say if we were agreed that *affective love was a law commanded*. But that seems *specially to apply to love in action*, because when the Lord said: 'Love your enemies', he *referred right afterwards to actions*, 'Do good to those who hate you.' Scripture also says, 'If your enemy is hungry feed him; if he is thirsty, give him drink.' Here *you have*

16 Bernard of Clairvaux, On the *Song of Songs III*, pp. 31-2. Verdeyen (*SC* 452), SCC 50.2, l. 1-12: "Nec latuit praeceptorem, praecepti pondus hominum excedere vires; sed judicavit utile ex hoc ipso suae illos insufficientiae admoneri, et ut scirent sane, ad quem justitiae finem niti pro viribus oporteret."

17 Bernard of Clairvaux, On the *Song of Songs III*, pp. 31-2. Verdeyen (*SC* 452), SCC 50.2, l. 12-24: "Quis enim sibi arrogare id audeat, quod se Paulus ipse fatetur non comprehendisse? (Philipp. III, 13.) [...] Accipientes quippe mandatum, et sentientes delictum, clamabimus in coelum, et miserebitur nostri Deus: et sciemus in illa die, quia non ex operibus justitiae quae fecimus nos, sed secundum suam misericordiam salvos nos fecit (Tit. III, 5)."

18 Bernard of Clairvaux, On the *Song of Songs III*, pp. 31-2. Verdeyen (*SC* 452), SCC 50.2, l. 12-24: "Ergo mandando impossibilia, non praevaricatores homines fecit, sed humiles, ut omne os obstruatur, et subditus fiat omnis mundus Deo; quia ex operibus legis non justificabitur omnis caro coram illo (Rom. III, 19, 20)."

a question of actions, not of feeling."[19] Why does the charity of action require a commandment, and what is the order of charity? First, Bernard believes that the charity of action is commanded in the injunction (beyond the Greatest Commandment) to love even one's enemies.[20] The love of foe or enemies is formulated mainly in terms of action and not in terms of attitude. What gives efficiency to action, thus, on a first instance, is not the affect (which only comes later). The injunction, uttered by the word (*sermo*) of the Word (*Verbum*), reveals the process: the word then the manifestation of love by following the word. Hence, word proceeds the labor of charity because love is shown by following the commands expressed in words (*Si diligitis me, inquit, sermones meos servate* Joan. XIV, 15). After all, reasons Bernard, what is commanded would not be commanded had it already been accomplished in the charity of the affect. "But listen also to the Lord's command about *love of himself*: 'If you love me *keep my words*.' And here too, by enjoining the observance of the commandments, he *assigns us to action*. It would have been superfluous for him to *warn us to act if love were but a matter of feeling*."[21] Hence, the charity of affect is *not* commanded. It is, as it were, naturally given. The command to love is nature's demand. It would be easy to fall into the trap of equating command and therefore the charity of action with grace on the one hand, and the natural inclination of affection with free will on the other hand. However, such dichotomy would revert to a misrepresentation of the Augustinian debate with the Pelagians absent in Bernard. Bernard's great contribution is to have naturalized the order of love. Like affects, commands and actions too are not only a matter of grace, but are primarily, and fundamentally, a question of nature (*natura*). As with love, so too with desire: Bernard naturalizes desire. The command is to love the enemy emancipated form its revelatory framework and framed in terms of nature or what Bernard, following the Stoic tradition, calls the natural

---

19 Bernard of Clairvaux, On the *Song of Songs III*, p. 32. Verdeyen (*SC* 452), SCC 50.3, l. 1-12: "Atque hoc dixerim, siquidem consenserimus affectualem legem fuisse mandatam. Sed actuali id potius convenire inde vel maxime apparere videtur, quod cum dixisset Dominus: Diligite inimicos vestros, mox de operibus infert: Benefacite his qui oderunt vos (Luc. VI, 27). Item Scriptura: Si esuriet inimicus tuus, ciba illum; si sitit, potum datu (Rom. XII, 20). Et hic de actu habes, non de affectu."

20 Bernard of Clairvaux, On the *Song of Songs III*, p. 32. Verdeyen (SC 452), SCC 50.3, l. 1-12: "Diligite inimicos vestros, mox de operibus infert: Benefacite his qui oderunt vos (Luc. VI, 27) [...] Si esuriet inimicus tuus, ciba illum; si sitit, potum datu (Rom. XII, 20)."

21 Bernard of Clairvaux, On the *Song of Songs III*, p. 32. Verdeyen (*SC* 452), SCC 50.3, l. 1-12: "Sed audi item Dominum etiam de sui dilectione mandantem: Si diligitis me, inquit, sermones meos servate (Joan. XIV, 15). Atque hic quoque ad opera mittimur per injunctam observantiam mandatorum. Supervacue autem de opere monuisset, si in affectione jam fuisset dilectio."

law (or the Golden Rule), the law of reason. The two proposed formulations of the now-called Golden Rule or the law of nature, prescribed by nature and 'codified' in Scripture, not as revelation but as expressions of natural reason, are as follows: "Hence it is necessary that you accept as well that commandment to love your neighbor as yourself, even if it is not expressed as clearly as this."[22] Bernard goes on, "Do you then consider that you do enough to fulfill the command to love of neighbor if you observe perfectly what the *natural law prescribes for every man*: 'What you would not wish done to yourself, avoid doing to another', and also, 'Always treat others as you like them to treat you.'"[23] How about the order of charity? The order of charity is not temporal. The charity of action is not *prior* to the charity of affection. Neither is the order relative. The charity of action is not *greater* than the charity of affection. The order of order, rather, is *modal*. And as such, the apparent tension between reason and desire is resolved. Reason prescribes (law of nature) and desire qualifies. Desire is, it seems, a mode of reason. Summarily, charity of action and charity of affect are natural, they are expressed in the synthesis of reason and desire whereby desire is a mode of reason. The order of law is *an* order of love: the *transformation* of desire and reason into a (re)ordered synthesis essentially manifests a first instance in the mode of love in the *metamorphosis of love*. Law and order yield therefore to *love and order*.

6.2 Love and Order

The second order in Bernard's *metamorphosis of love* is *love and order*. The complementarity between reason (charity of action) and desire (charity of affect) finds perhaps the most explicit expression in the words of the Abbot of Clairvaux: "*I am not saying that we should be without affection*, and that with an arid heart we move only our hands to work. Among the many great and grievous evils [...] I have read this one is reckoned: *to be without affection*."[24] Affection

22 Bernard of Clairvaux, On the *Song of Songs III*, p. 32. Verdeyen (*SC* 452), SCC 50.3, l. 12-20: "Sic te ergo necesse est et illud accipere, quod juberis diligere proximum tuum sicut te ipsum (Matth. XXII, 39), etsi non ita aperte expressum sit."

23 Bernard of Clairvaux, On the *Song of Songs III*, p. 32. Verdeyen (*SC* 452), SCC 50.3, l. 12-20: "An non denique satis tibi esse judices ad implendum istud de proximi dilectione mandatum, si id perfecte observes, in quo omni homini recte de lege naturae praescribitur: Quod tibi non vis fieri, alii ne feceris? (Tob. IV, 16.) Et item illud: Quaecunque vultis ut faciant vobis homines, et vos facite aliis (Matth. VII, 12)."

24 Bernard of Clairvaux, On the *Song of Songs III*, pp. 32-3. Verdeyen (*SC* 452), SCC 50.4, l. 1-4: "Neque hoc dico, ut sine affectione simus, et corde arido solas moveamus manus ad

is what gives the heart a flare of 'freshness' in the implementation of its work's movements. While it is indeed possible to separate affection (*affection*) from work (*opera*), acting thus constitutes a great and serious ill in humanity. This is what, in Bernard's estimation, the Apostle Paul describes in the words: "to be without affection."[25] Hence, affect *adds something* to the aridity (*arido*) of repetitive movement of labour or habit. Or rather, affect modifies habit. What exactly is it? As has been argued, affection (*affectio*) transforms the mode (*modus*) of agency which Bernard charts in the progressive tripartite analysis of affections: affection of the flesh (*affectio caro*), affection of reason (*affectio ratio*) and affection of wisdom (*affectio sapientia*).[26] In each case, the mode of desire expressed in affection is shaped by a different factor, hence the tripartite classification of affection into affection of the flesh, affection of reason and affection of wisdom: "But there is an *affection which the flesh begets*, and *one which reason controls*, and *one which wisdom seasons*. The first [...] *is not subject to the law of God*, nor can be. The second, [is] in *agreement with the law of God* because it is good. [...] the *insubordinate and the agreeable differ from each other*."[27] In all three cases, affection is framed in terms of how it is related to the law. By approximating affection and law Bernard seems, in conformity with earlier remarks, to offer an analysis of affection (charity of affection) vis-à-vis action (charity of action) situated at the intersection of the descriptive/prescriptive overlap: there is no neat duality between affection/action, rather both go together (affection propels action, action draws affection). How then, does affection relate to the law? The first affection is the affection of the flesh. The affection of the flesh is an affection produced (*gignere*) by the flesh (*caro*): "an *affection which the flesh begets*."[28] How exactly the flesh produces affection, is not clear. The expression is close, however, to "the desire of the flesh"

opera. Legi inter alia, quae scribit Apostolus magna et gravia hominum mala, hoc quoque annumeratum, sine affectione scilicet esse (Rom. I, 31)."

25 Jerome, whose Latin Vulgate Bernard probably used, translates the Koine Greek's *storge* as *affectio*. Bernard of Clairvaux, On the *Song of Songs III*, pp. 32-3. Verdeyen (*SC* 452), SCC 50.4, l. 1-4: "sine affectione scilicet esse (Rom 1.31)."

26 Pacificus Delfgaauw, *Saint Bernard, Maître de l'amour divin* (Paris: FAC-éditions, 1994); Vladimir Lossky, "Étude sur la terminologie de saint Bernard," *Bulletin du Cange*, 18 (1942): 82-7.

27 Bernard of Clairvaux, On the *Song of Songs III*, pp. 323. Verdeyen (*SC* 452), SCC 50.4, l. 5-10: "Sed est affectio quam caro gignit; et est quam ratio regit, et est quam condit sapientia. Prima est, quam Apostolus legi Dei dicit non esse subjectam, nec esse posse (Rom. VIII, 7); secunda, quam perhibet e regione consentientem legi Dei, quoniam bona est (Rom. VII, 16); nec dubium distare inter se contentiosam et consentaneam."

28 Bernard of Clairvaux, On the *Song of Songs III*, pp. 32-3. Verdeyen (*SC* 452), SCC 50.4, l. 5-10: "affectio quam caro gignit."

(Gal 5.17)[29] which would suggest an implicit, though quite convincing, contra-position of affection and desire. As such, desire like affection is productive and, to the extent that it is, like desire, affection can also be considered a power. As *desiring-production*, affection of the flesh does not, and this is not surprising, submit (*submittere*) to the law.[30] Again, this is not to say that affection and the law are irreconcilably at odds. For now, the first step, what can be termed the degree of desire, is manifest as production independent of constraints. Hence, it is not subjected to the law. After the affection of the flesh there is the affection of reason. This time, the affection of reason, unlike the affection of the flesh, is not engendered, as would be expected, from reason. There is *no* affection surging from reason. Rather, the affection of reason is an affection which directs/guides (*regit*) reason (*ratio*), "*one which reason controls*."[31] Unlike the affection of the flesh, the affection of reason actively interacts with the law by consenting (*consentire*) to the law: "the second, [is] in *agreement with the law of God* because it is good."[32] Reason *is not* the law and reason *is not* under the law. Reason, in a reflective relation, consents to the law. To say that reason consents is to say that reason con-sents (*con-sentire*), literally "to feel with": reason *feels* with the law through the motor (or indeed power) of affection. Affection as *desiring-production* of the flesh in the affection of the flesh then, though exceeding in a sense the law, nevertheless enters and navigates the dynamic of the affection of reason in the law. Desire is the motor of reason in the interaction of reason and law in con-sent. Thus, the affection of the flesh and the affection of reason are not wholly detached. Quite on the contrary, they function in synchronicity from the first level (*caro*) to the second level (*reason*) while, of course, maintaining a clear distinction.[33] The continuum in the tension of the relation consists in the transformation of the directionality of affection resulting, inversely, in a transformation of the affect's mode itself: from production (affection of the flesh) to regulation (affection of reason). The third affection, the affection of wisdom, accomplishes the highest degree in the progress from the charity of affection to the charity of action. The affection of

29 Jerome's Vulgate, Gal. 5.17: "caro enim concupiscit adversus spiritum spiritus autem adversus carnem haec enim invicem adversantur ut non quaecumque vultis illa faciatis."

30 Bernard of Clairvaux, On the *Song of Songs III*, pp. 32-3. Verdeyen (*SC* 452), SCC 50.4, l. 5-10: "Prima est, quam Apostolus legi Dei dicit non esse subjectam, nec esse posse."

31 Bernard of Clairvaux, On the *Song of Songs III*, pp. 32-3. Verdeyen (*SC* 452), SCC 50.4, l. 5-10: "et est quam ratio regit."

32 Bernard of Clairvaux, On the *Song of Songs III*, pp. 32-3. Verdeyen (*SC* 452), SCC 50.4, l. 5-10: "secunda, quam perhibet e regione consentientem legi Dei, quoniam bona est."

33 Bernard of Clairvaux, On the *Song of Songs III*, pp. 32-3. Verdeyen (*SC* 452), SCC 50.4, l. 5-10: "nec dubium distare inter se contentiosam et consentaneam."

wisdom is only indirectly related to the law. While the affection of the flesh is outside of the limits of the law, yet directs reason to engage with the law, the affection of wisdom synthesizes affection as presented in the first two levels: reason and desire come together in the great transformative synthesis of charity (charity in affect and charity in act): "The third [...] is *far from either of them*, because it *tastes and experiences* that the Lord is sweet; *it banishes the first and rewards the second. The first is pleasant*, of course, but shameful; the second is *emotionless but strong*; the last is *rich and delightful*."[34] The third affection, the affection of wisdom, is characterized in terms of mode: it is the 'taste' and 'savor' of God. Thereafter, the mode of the affect of wisdom transforms the first two; eliminating (*eliminare*) the affection of the flesh and rewarding (*remunerare*) the affection of reason: "*it banishes the first and rewards the second*."[35] The apparent outright rejection of the affection of the flesh by the affection of wisdom is all the more puzzling given that desire, the product of the affection of the flesh, is what propels the very affection of reason which is then rewarded. Why reject desire, yet reap its fruits as desire's reward? "Therefore, by the second, good deeds are done, and *in it love reigns, not that of the feelings* [...] but *that rather which is practical* [...] still *vehemently aflame with the love of love itself*. '*Do not love in word or speech* [...] *but in deed, and in truth*.'"[36] The key to undoing the paradoxical appraisal and rejection of desire in the progression of affection is the phenomenon of "an ardent love of love" (*amore tame amoris*).[37] The expression *love of love* is already found in the writings of the Doctor of Grace.[38] Augustine's *ardent* love of love is a failed locus of inversion because it fails to produce aperity. For Falque, following Chevalier, the precedence of predication according to relation (*secundum relativum*) over predication according to substance (*secundum substantiam*) constitutes an inversion of

34 Bernard of Clairvaux, On the *Song of Songs III*, pp. 32-3. Verdeyen (*SC* 452), SCC 50.4, l. 10-14: "Longe vero tertia ab utraque distat, quae et gustat, et sapit quoniam suavis est Dominus (Psal. XXXIII, 9), primam eliminans, secundam remunerans. Nam prima quidem dulcis, sed turpis; secunda sicca, sed fortis; ultima pinguis, et suavis est."

35 Bernard of Clairvaux, On the *Song of Songs III*, pp. 32-3. Verdeyen (*SC* 452), SCC 50.4, l. 10-14: "primam eliminans, secundam remunerans."

36 Bernard of Clairvaux, On the *Song of Songs III*, pp. 32-3. Verdeyen (*SC* 452), SCC 50.4, l. 14-21: "Igitur per secundam opera fiunt, et in ipsa charitas sedet, non illa affectualis, quae sale sapientiae condita pinguescens magnam menti importat multitudinem dulcedinis Domini; sed quaedam potius actualis, quae etsi nondum dulci illo amore suaviter reficit, amore tamen amoris ipsius vehementer accendit. Non diligamus, ait, verbo, neque lingua, sed opere et veritate (I Joan. III, 18)."

37 Bernard of Clairvaux, On the *Song of Songs III*, pp. 32-3. Verdeyen (*SC* 452), SCC 50.4, l. 19.

38 Bernard of Clairvaux, On the *Song of Songs III*, pp. 32-3. Verdeyen (*SC* 452), SCC 50.4, p. 352, n. 2: *Conf.* 2.1.3 (*CCL* 27.18) and *Conf.* 11.1.6 (*CCL* 27.194).

order leading to the *hypothesis of a new order* ("l'hypothèse d'un autre ordre"), an order apart (*un ordre à part*) not as overcoming substance (Marion) but, rather, as producing a necessary tension in the passage to the order apart (Falque).[39] The Augustinian love of love, attempts to produce such an order in the order of love, but fails to frame in the order of love what he intends in the discussion of relatives and substance.[40] Indeed, for Augustine, love of love is a kind of imprisoned and sterile love at odds with the enjoyment (*frui*) of God because of its failure to use (*uti*) creatures and creation, rather than enjoying (*frui*) them. Hence, for Augustine, love of love is a self-consuming and undesirable love because it is not love at all as it remains ever at odds with the desire of the flesh (concupiscence).[41] Bernard maps out the order apart as the inverse order of love. Implicitly engaging with the Bishop of Hippo, Bernard integrates love of love positively within the logic of desire as it emerges in the progression and transformation of the three affections. The qualitative description of the three affections, far from condemning the affection of the flesh functions to emphasize its unique role in the process of transformation.[42] The shameful, disgraceful or repulsive (*turpis*) mode of the affection of the flesh is neither inherent to the flesh or to the desire/affection of the flesh. Rather, the affection of the flesh is mistrustful and repulsive only when and to the extent that it *is not* effective. After all, work (*opera*) is accomplished by the charity of act and not the charity of affect. The charity of act, however, begins with the second affect, the affect of reason. The affect of the flesh remains at the level of a charity of affection. The charity of act begins only at the charity of act. The great Bernardine synthesis of the affection of the flesh and the affection of reason in the affection of wisdom constitutes a transition from the charity of affection (affection of the flesh) to charity of action (affection of reason). The love of love, bound to charity of affection in the affection of the flesh remains sterile and, to that extent, is indeed, for Augustine as for Bernard, shameful and reprehensible. However, moving beyond Augustine, Bernard safeguards desire as a driving force in the transition of charity of affection to charity of act. The desire of the affection of the flesh *is* the very aperity of *love of love* in efficient, self-transcending action (charity of action). The true reproach of *love of love* is

39 Emmanuel Falque, *Dieu, la chair et l'autre: d'Irénée à Duns Scot* (Paris: Presses Universitaires de France, 2008).

40 Augustine, *On the Trinity*, books 5 and 7.

41 Concupiscence is *not* always synonymous for sinful desire in Augustine, see Timo Nisula, *Augustine and the Functions of Concupiscence* (Leiden: Brill, 2012).

42 Bernard of Clairvaux, On the *Song of Songs III*, pp. 32-3. Verdeyen (*SC* 452), SCC 50.4, l. 10-14: "Nam prima quidem dulcis, sed turpis; secunda sicca, sed fortis; ultima pinguis, et suavis est."

not misdirected concupiscence (Augustine) but rather affection which is not open to its necessary and free flourishing in action (Bernard) which culminates in wholesome love. Love of love thus reveals a dynamic desire emanating from the flesh at the source of love. Thus, desire undergoes a process of manifestation and purification, indeed of metamorphosis, as affective love, from body to word, and from word to action as truth. This is, precisely, the Bernardine sense of *love of love*: an engendering love resulting, contra Augustine, in action and, specifically, in the action of truth or rather in action in truth. Hence, the itinerary of the word advances, from word to action (through the incarnation), and from action to truth (by means of the intentionality of desire): "'*Do not love in word or speech* [...] *but in deed, and in truth.*'"[43] The truth of action is love and the love of action is truth. In the reduction of desire truth is love and love is truth. Hence, there is no absolutely reprehensible affection of charity (source of desire) just as there is no absolutely praise-worthy charity of reason (intentionality of desire) in the affective mode of wisdom (transformation of desire). The fine line separating the three affections, rather, demarks the space in which charity of affection is set apart from the charity of action. Bernard writes: "he takes a middle path between *vitiated and affective love*, while *distinguishing from both the love that is active and salutary*? 'Let us love in deed and in truth', [...] because we are *moved to do good more by the vigorous urging of truth than by the feeling of relished love*. 'He set love in order in me.'"[44] The order of love is therefore achieved, on the one hand, by the transformation of desire in the progress of affections. On the other hand, the order of love is not only transformation, but is, above all, inversion (the *inverse* order of charity), where the charity of action precedes the charity of affection. Within the transformation of desire in the affections (affection of the flesh, affection of reason and affection of wisdom), the inversion of charity yields the order of love as the truth of action (inverse order of charity) rather than as the action of truth (order of charity). What is the content of such an inversion and why is it effectuated thus? Is it necessary and is it irreversible? Can it be otherwise?

---

43 Bernard of Clairvaux, On the *Song of Songs III*, pp. 32-3. Verdeyen (*SC* 452), SCC 50.4, l. 14-21: "Non diligamus, ait, verbo, neque lingua, sed opere et veritate (I Joan. III, 18)."

44 Bernard of Clairvaux, On the *Song of Songs III*, pp. 32-3. Verdeyen (*SC* 452), SCC 50.5, l. 1-9: "Vides quomodo caute medius incedit inter vitiosum atque affectuosum amorem, ab utroque pariter hanc distinguens actualem et salutiferam charitatem? Nec linguae mentientis in hac dilectione recipit fictum, nec rursum afficientis exigit sapientiae gustum. Opere, inquit, diligamus et veritate: quod videlicet moveamur ad bene operandum magis quodam vividae veritatis impulsu, quam sapidae illius charitatis affectu. Ordinavit in me charitatem."

The inverse order of charity is in fact simply an inversion or opposition (*ordine opposito*) of the prescription/description complex. Whereas in fact the charity of affect is the ideal (prescription) and therefore superior (*affectualis superiora*), the charity of action, which is inferior (*actualis inferiora*), remains the measuring rod of the real (description). Bernard wirtes, "Which of these loves do you think He meant? Both of them, but in reverse order. Now the active prefers what is lowly, the affective what is lofty. For example, there is no doubt that in a mind that loves rightly, the love of God is valued more than love of men, and among men themselves the more perfect is esteemed more than the weaker, heaven more than earth, eternity more than the flesh."[45] Hence, the inversion of charity vindicates the order of things as experienced. The flesh takes precedence over the soul, the temporal over the eternal, the earth over the heavens and the imperfect over the perfect. As such, the true order of things begins with the care of the neighbor: "In well-regulated action, on the other hand, the opposite order frequently or even always prevails. For we are more strongly impelled toward and more often occupied with the welfare of our neighbor. We attend our weaker brothers with more exacting care. By human right and necessity, we concentrate more on peace on earth than on the glory of heaven; by worrying about temporal cares we are not permitted to think of eternal things. In attending almost continually to the ills of our body, we lay aside the care of our soul. And finally, in accord with the saying of the Apostle, we invest our weaker members with greater honor, so fulfilling in a sense the word of the Lord, 'the last shall be first, and the first last.' Who will doubt that in prayer a man is speaking with God? But how often, at the call of charity, we are drawn away, torn away, for the sake of those who need to speak to us or be helped! How often does dutiful repose yield dutifully to the uproar of business! How often is a book laid aside in good conscience that we may sweat at manual work! How often for the sake of administering worldly affairs we very rightly omit even the solemn celebration of Masses![46] The second

45 Bernard of Clairvaux, On the *Song of Songs III*, pp. 33-5. Verdeyen (*SC* 452), SCC 50.5, l. 9-14: "Quam putas harum? Utramque, sed ordine opposito. Nam actualis inferiora praefert, affectualis superiora. Etenim in bene affecta mente non dubium, verbi causa, quin dilectioni hominis Dei dilectio praeponatur, et in hominibus ipsis perfectiores infirmioribus, coelum terrae, aeternitas tempori, anima carni."

46 Bernard of Clairvaux, On the *Song of Songs III*, pp. 33-5. Verdeyen (*SC* 452), SCC 50.5, l. 14-34: "Attamen in bene ordinata actione saepe, aut etiam semper, ordo oppositus invenitur. Nam et circa proximi curam et plus urgemur, et pluries occupamur; et infirmioribus fratribus diligentiori sedulitate assistimus; et paci terrae magis quam coeli gloriae jure humanitatis et ipsa necessitate intendimus; et temporalium inquietudine curarum vix aliquid sentire de aeternis permittimur; et languoribus nostri corporis, postposita animae cura, pene continue inservimus; et ipsis denique infirmioribus membris nostris

order in the *metamorphosis of love* transforms the love of the law into action and returns to the order of desire as *love of love*. This is *the order of desire*.

6.3 The Order of Desire

The discussion returns to the question concerning what precisely regulates the order of charity? Though at first there seems to be no order of order – order in the inversion of order – this is far from what Bernard intends. The inversion of the order of love does not imply disorder. Rather, the inversion of the order of charity results in an alternative order of order as transformation. Differently put, how is desire, which is beyond reason, channelled that it may not be destructive, in the inversion through the progression of affection (*affectio*)? The channeling force in the inversion process is necessity: "*A preposterous order, but necessity knows no law. Love in action devises its own order,* in accord with the command of the house holder, beginning with the most recent."[47] The necessity of everyday life trumps all loftier pursuits, even the celebration of the liturgy. Yet again, necessity as such is not a law as such, but rather the force of desire originating in the desire of the flesh and transformed in the levels of affection. Indeed, the defining characteristic of the order of love in the inversion of charity (*ordo praeposterus*) is that necessity has no law (*necessitas non habet legem*): and yet, necessity is a law. Necessity need not mean determinism or absence of free will. Rather, necessity is the self-imposed law of the will upon the will. The will to will (necessity) is the outcome of the inversion and transformation of desire (order of love) as the normalization of love in the Bernardine love of love. The prescriptive love of love (Augustine) becomes a descriptive love of love (Bernard) in the order of charity as inversion through the necessity of desire. The initial closure – morally sin – of the love of love in its prescriptive mode as pure desire gains aperity (free will) or

abundantiorem honorem, juxta sententiam Apostoli, circumdamus (I Cor. XII, 23): per hoc quodam modo facientes verbum Domini, de quo habes: Erunt novissimi primi, et primi novissimi (Matth. XX, 16). Orantem denique hominem cum Deo loqui quis dubitet? Quoties tamen inde charitate jubente abducimur et avellimur, propter eos qui nostra indigent opera vel loquela? quoties pie cedit negotiorum tumultibus pia quies? quoties bona conscientia ponitur codex, ut operi manuum insudetur? quoties pro administrandis terrenis, justissime ipsis supersedemus celebrandis missarum solemniis?"

47 Bernard of Clairvaux, On the *Song of Songs III*, pp. 33-5. Verdeyen (*SC* 452), SCC 50.5, l. 34-38: "Ordo praeposterus: sed necessitas non habet legem. Agit ergo suum actualis charitas ordinem juxta patrisfamilias jussionem, incipiens a novissimis (ibid., 8). Pia certe et justa, quae non sit acceptrix personarum; nec pretia consideret rerum, sed hominum necessitates."

porosity (*metaxu*) precisely through the transformation of desire as necessity in its descriptive mode (inverse order of love). The order of love thus yields not one order, but various orders.[48] The orders of love, be it charity of affect followed by charity of action, or the inverse, are not mutually exclusive or competing loves, but remain complimentary beyond a mere prescriptive/descriptive dichotomy of normativity. Indeed, the orders of love converge, on a first instance, in the unity of desire in the law/necessity synthesis (free will). They also converge in a second instance, no longer as the love of love or the will to will but again in the unity of desire, this time in a double attitude towards truth: the truth of love (*veritas charitas*) and the love of truth (*caritas veritas*).[49] The truth of truth in love is the ultimate vindication of love as aperity, as free will, as prescription rather than description, in the order of love. Desire, not reason, is the pathway to truth in the order of love. Bernard writes, "*But not so affective love, since it always leads the ordering from the first.* It is the wisdom by which *all things are experienced as they are* [...] *The truth of love determines the previous order*, but *this order the love of truth* lays claim to itself."[50] Whereas the primary concern of the charity of action (inverse order of love), the point of departure in the charity of the affect, is the necessity of human beings or their lack thereof (*hominum necessitates*), the intentionality of the charity of affection (order of love) is things as they should be ideally (*prout sunt*). Rather than offering competing senses of in the order(s) of love, their intentionality simultaneously converges partly and diverges partly: the charity of action is horizontal, and the charity of affection is vertical. The encounter of the two occurs in the end process of the transformation of desire beyond free will, this time in truth. Love transforms truth in the inversion of charity. On a first instance (horizontal) the truth of love (*caritatis veritas*) establishes the order of active charity (description).[51] On a second instance (vertical), the love of truth establishes the order of affective charity (prescription): "*true love* is found in this, that *those whose need is greater receive first.* And again, loving truth is evident if we *maintain in our feelings the order it maintains in the reason.*"[52]

---

48 See, Sommerfeldt, *Bernard of Clairvaux*, 81.

49 Verdeyen (*SC* 452), SCC 50.6, p. 357, n. 3; Verdeyen (*SC* 452), SCC 42.6, p. 216, n. 1: on 'truth of love' and 'love of truth'.

50 Bernard of Clairvaux, On the *Song of Songs III*, pp. 35-6. Verdeyen (*SC* 452), SCC 50.6.

51 Eva Rava, "The Loss and Recovery of Truth in Three Treatises of Bernard," *Cistercian Studies Quarterly* 36, no. 1 (2001): 3; Sommerfeldt, Bernard of Clairvaux, 12, 69.

52 Bernard of Clairvaux, On the *Song of Songs III*, pp. 35-6. Verdeyen (*SC* 452), SCC 50.6, l. 1-9: "At non ita affectualis: nam a primis ipsa ducit ordinem. Est enim sapientia, per quam utique quaeque res sapiunt prout sunt: ut, verbi gratia, quae pluris natura habet, pluris quoque ipsa affectio sentiat, minora minus, minima minime. Et illum quidem ordinem charitatis veritas facit; hunc autem veritatis charitas vindicat sibi. Nam et vera in hoc

The point of encounter at the inversion of the order of charity simultaneously produces (desire) the truth of charity in the rule to give in priority according to needs, where love is rendered true. Then the order of charity inverses, i.e. transforms desire, the truth of charity into the charity of truth where affection (of the flesh, of the reason and of wisdom) is true because of reason. The point of encounter, in the aftermath, is the transformation of reason by desire in love: desire produces simultaneously truth and love in the dynamic interplay of truth of *love and love* of truth. As such, the source of desire, the flesh, is at the origin of the order of charity and effectuates the transformation of human experience, in the inversion of the order of love. The transformation of desire, from flesh, through body, then gives the Great Command an alternative light of assimilation. The measure of the love of God as the love without measure is, in the inversion of the order of charity, the transformation of desire.[53] The love of God, with all 'heart, soul and force' (*toto corde, tota anima, tota virtute*) is achieved by overcoming the love of love (active charity). How is the *love of love* surpassed (Bernard) rather than suppressed (Augustine)? The inversion of the order of charity as transformation is the point of repair: "Then *you will experience as well, your own true self, since you perceive that you possess nothing at all for which you love yourself, except insofar as you belong to God. You pour out upon him your whole power of loving.*"[54]

The high point of the order of love as charity of affection coincides with the fourth degree of love in the answer to the divine love as mode without mode (*sine modo*) in its relation, as inversion, to human love, for friend as for foe, in the mode with mode (*cum modo*), in the infamous Bernardine treatise *On the Love of God*.[55] Love is manifested in the progression of the four degrees of love as follows. First, man loves himself for himself. Then man loves God for himself. After, man loves God for God. Finally, man loves himself for God. This final love of self for God exemplifies, the inversion of the charity of affect and the charity of action, and ultimately the order of charity, in the transformation of desire. On the one hand, the transformation of desire in the four degrees of love occurs through the directionality and modes of love based on what motivates love, i.e. 'for whom' (dative) *love* is and not 'whose' (genitive) love *is*: self for self, God for self, God for God and self for God. The love of self

est charitas, ut qui indigent amplius, accipiant prius: et rursus in eo chara apparet veritas, si ordinem tenemus affectu, quem illa ratione."

53 On love 'sine modo' and 'cum modo', see Delfgaauw, *Saint Bernard*, 170-71.

54 Bernard of Clairvaux, On the *Song of Songs III*, pp. 35-6. Verdeyen (*SC* 452), SCC 50.6, l. 9-23: "Deinde sapies etiam ipse tu tibi prout es, cum te senseris nil habere prorsus, unde te ames, nisi in quantum Dei es: quippe qui totum unde amas, in illum effuderis."

55 *DDD* 10.27 (SC 393, pp. 128-129).

for self or the love of love, in charity of the affect, passes through God who transforms not only the directionality (3rd degree) but also the mode (2nd and 4th degree). The passage through God (2nd degree), or the liberation from self-contained love of love, opens beyond itself through experience, the experience of God (*cum ipso experimento amoris tui*) in the body and, specifically, through the desire of the flesh. The experience of God is an experience of love which shatters the illusion of love of love where, in the absence of God, there is only emptiness and nothingness: "you *experience yourself as you are* when *by that experience of love of yourself and of the feeling that you feel toward him, you discover that you are an altogether unworthy object even of your own love*, except for the sake of him without whom you are nothing."[56] However, upon experiencing God, specifically in the desire of the flesh, love and affection simultaneously render depth to the love of love, for self and for God, because of God and not because of self. The condition for the love of God, as the Great Command prescribes, with all heart, soul and power: But you, *if you love the Lord your God* with your whole heart, whole mind, whole strength, *and leaping with ardent feeling beyond* that *love of love with which active love is satisfied* [and] are wholly aflame with that *divine love* to which the former is a step, *then God is indeed experienced* [...] in relation to your *power to enjoy*."[57] This is the experience of God in the love of self (4th degree of love): the order of (affective) charity. In the order of charity, prescriptive love, ideal love, the modeless mode of love (*sine modo*), begins with God and ends with self, in and through experience. The modeless mode of love which earlier emerged as 'power' (*vir*) later is nothing other than aperity which drives human existence towards God by the weight of love, to use the infamous Augustinian expression: "my weight is my love."[58] However, in addition and indeed in hand with the way of grace (the charity of affect), there is also the way of nature (the charity of action). In the inverse order of love, where desire and reason transform the mode of human power (*vir*) in the charity of action, the mode of descriptive love or love with mode (*cum modo*), begins with neighbor and ends with God. How do

56 Bernard of Clairvaux, On the *Song of Songs III*, pp. 35-6. Verdeyen (*SC* 452), SCC 50.6, l. 9-23: "Sapies, inquam, tibi prout es, cum ipso experimento amoris tui, et affectionis quam ad te ipsum habebis, nihil dignum te esse invenies, quod vel a te ipso ametur, nisi propter ipsum, sine quo ipse es nihil."

57 Bernard of Clairvaux, On the *Song of Songs III*, pp. 35-6. Verdeyen (*SC* 452), SCC 50.6, l. 9-23: "Tu ergo si diligas Dominum Deum tuum toto corde, tota anima, tota virtute tua (Matth. XXII, 37); et amorem amoris illum, quo contenta est charitas actualis, affectu ferventiori transiliens, ipso cominus divino amore, ad quem is est gradus, accepto in plenitudine spiritu, totus ignescas: sapit tibi profecto Deus, etsi non digne omnino prout est (quod utique impossibile est omni creaturae), certe prout tuum sapere est."

58 Augustine, *Confessions* 13.10: "pondus meum amor meum."

these two loves, the love of God and the love of neighbor, relate? The progression of degrees of love (*gradus*) need not be a jump or a transcending as the term *transilio*[59] may suggest. Rather, *transilio* may alternatively mean overlap akin to liquefaction: the love of God and the love of neighbour overlap or liquefy in, and indeed because of, the inversion of the order of love.[60] But how? Articulated differently, how are the love of God and the love of neighbor reconciled in the order of charity (*ordinavit in me caritatem*)[61]? The love of neighbor and the love of self are not opposing loves competing with the love of God in the order of love in the City of Man (Augustine): "two loves founded two cities: the city of God and the city of man"(*City of God* 14.28).[62] Quite on the contrary, these various earthly loves, love of self and love of neighbor, and even love of foe, are no longer mixed (Augustine, *mixed Church*) but rather harmonized (Origin) in the order of love. However, in the four degrees of love in *On the Love of God* neither the prescriptive rivalry between the love of God and the love of self (Augustine), nor the mercenary descriptive love of outcomes (Origin) suffices to achieve the *liquefaction* or the inversion of the order of charity because the inversed order of charity is at once prescriptive in the charity of the affect and descriptive in the charity of action (Bernard).

This gets to the ultimate synthesis of desire, and indeed the heart of the problem of love. That is, how to bring together the many loves in the one love: the love of self and the love of neighbor (Mk 12.30), the love of enemies (Matt 5.44) and the love of God (Mk 12.30)? Perhaps Bernard's most succinct elucidation of the puzzle of Christian love is contained in what follows. After expounding the (prescriptive) love of God, Bernard turns to the (descriptive) love of neighbour through the alley of corporeal (embodied) experience: desire and the flesh. "You shall love your neighbor as yourself" (Mk 12.31): the measure (*cum modo*) of love of neighbor is the love of self. The measure of love for self is love *in* God.[63] Hence, the measure is really the condition for the possibility of love: there is no love outside of God. To love *in* God is to be 'effused' or 'poured out'/'spread in' God (*in illum effuderis*): from *effundere*, composed of the particles '*ex*' (preposition) + '*fundō* (verb). The *effusion*, reminiscent of Plotinian theurgy, is inversed in the Bernardine order of charity: humans 'effuse' into

59 Bernard of Clairvaux, On the *Song of Songs III*, pp. 35-6. Verdeyen (*SC* 452), SCC 50.6, l. 12-13.

60 *DDD* 28, l. 25, p. 32.

61 *Cant* 2.4.

62 Augustine, *The City of God*, 14.28 and 15.33 on Cant 2.4.

63 Bernard of Clairvaux, On the *Song of Songs III*, p. 36. Verdeyen (*SC* 452), SCC 50.7, l. 17-20: "Deinde sapies etiam ipse tu tibi prout es, cum te senseris nil habere prorsus, unde te ames, nisi in quantum Dei es: quippe qui totum unde amas, in illum effuderis."

God, not God into humans. Furthermore, the *effusion* is *not* confusion (*confundo*) in which humans are somehow lost or mixed in God (Buddhism). How to understand *effusion*? Either as *liquefaction* in the pouring out of affections into God where they are transformed without confusion or as membership in the spread body, the Church: effusion is the extended and resisting mode of diffusion in the (dis)order of desire. The effect in both perspectives, pouring out and spreading out, is unity in differentiation and differentiation in unity, through transformation *in* God. The transformation of the love of self *in* the love of God is thus a necessary and sufficient prerequisite for the love of neighbor. Who is the neighbor and how does the 'effusion' of self in God triangulate the love of neighbor in the inversion (as liquefaction) of the order of charity? The neighbor is the self (*qui hoc est quod tu*): "As for your neighbor whom *you are obliged to love as yourself, if you are to experience him as he is, you will actually experience him only as you do yourself. He is what you are.*"[64] In fact, the specification of the neighbor as self goes beyond an egotistical love of neighbor for self-analogous to the second degree of love.[65] My neighbor is what I am (*qui hoc est quod tu*) not as self (Augustine), but as a human being (*est enim homo*). Hence, the love of neighbor is based on love of self because by loving self in God, the neighbor becomes lovable in the effusion of the spread body as common humanity transformed *in* God: all love *in* God and *because* of the transformation of desire *through* God, "You who do not love yourself then, *except because you love God*, consequently, *love as yourself all those who similarly love him.*"[66] Hence, if the neighbor can be love as the self is loved is not because the self is loved, but rather because like the self, the neighbor has become, in a common humanity, part of the divine effusion of love in the spread body precisely because of the neighbors love for self. But what about the enemy? Who is the enemy and how is the enemy loved? The enemy, contrary to the neighbor, is *not* part of the spread body: the enemy is the neighbor who, failing to love God, makes it impossible to love as the self is loved because he does not love himself in God, "But you who love God cannot love as yourself a human enemy, for he is nothing in that as he does not love God. *Yet you will love him so that he may*

64 Bernard of Clairvaux, On the *Song of Songs III*, p. 36. Verdeyen (*SC* 452), SCC 50.7, l. 1-9: "Jam vero proximus, quem vere te oportet diligere tanquam te ipsum, ut tibi et ipse sapiat prout est, haud aliud profecto sapiet tibi, quam tu tibi, qui hoc est quod tu: est enim homo."

65 *DDD* 25, l. 18-20 (SC 82).

66 Bernard of Clairvaux, On the *Song of Songs III*, p. 36. Verdeyen (*SC* 452), SCC 50.7, l. 1-9: "Qui itaque te non diligis, nisi quia diligis Deum; consequenter omnes qui similiter diligunt eum, diligis tanquam te ipsum."

love."[67] In other words, the enemy is not part of the spread body where divine effusion transforms human love. Hence, the love for the enemy is not in the same mode or for the same reason as to why the neighbor is loved. The love for enemy renders the enemy capable of love: "*Yet you will love him so that he may love*."[68] The love of neighbor is a shared love (*diligere quia diligit*) whereas the love of enemy is an empowering love (*diligere ut diligat*): "But, *to love in order that he may love, and to love because he loves*, are *not the same thing*."[69] There is an empowering love, therefore, which aims at bringing the enemy to God and though even the enemy deserves love, there is a (rather strange) exception: the enemy who will never come to God, is one who does not deserve even hatred, but only indifference. Love is a potentiality for becoming. The enemy is love that loving may result: "That you may *experience him as he is*, therefore, *you must experience him not for what he is, because he is nothing*, but for *what perhaps he will become*."[70] Love is the cause of love. Outside of such order there is only pure chaos, the disorder of nothingness in the face of sterile love. "But when it becomes clear that he will not return to the love of God, it is essential that you regard him, not as *almost* nothing but *as totally nothing, in that he will be eternally nothing*."[71] Fascinatingly, Bernard gives this as an occasion, the only occasion, where love resorts to hatred: "With this one exception, since *not only is he not to be loved, but even to be looked on with hatred* [...] The *love that is open does not permit the refusal of some feeling*, however small, to any man, *even to one's greatest enemy*."[72] Therefore, the inversion of the order of charity enables the triangulation through God (of self, neighbor and foe) in vertical love

67 Bernard of Clairvaux, On the *Song of Songs III*, p. 36. Verdeyen (*SC* 452), SCC 50.7, l. 1-9: "Porro inimicum hominem, quoniam nihil est, pro eo quod non diligit Deum; non potest quidem diligere tanquam te ipsum, qui Deum diligis; diliges tamen ut diligat."

68 Bernard of Clairvaux, On the *Song of Songs III*, p. 36. Verdeyen (*SC* 452), SCC 50.7, l. 1-9: "non potest quidem diligere tanquam te ipsum, qui Deum diligis; diliges tamen ut diligat."

69 Bernard of Clairvaux, On the *Song of Songs III*, p. 36. Verdeyen (*SC* 452), SCC 50.7, l. 1-9: "Non est autem id ipsum, diligere ut diligat, et diligere quia diligit."

70 Bernard of Clairvaux, On the *Song of Songs III*, p. 36. Verdeyen (*SC* 452), SCC 50.7, l. 9-21: "Proinde ut tibi et ipse sapiat prout est, sapiet tibi, non quidem quod est, qui utique nihil est; sed quod futurus forsitan est."

71 Bernard of Clairvaux, On the *Song of Songs III*, p. 36. Verdeyen (*SC* 452), SCC 50.7, l. 9-21: "Etenim de quo constat quod ad amorem Dei non sit deinceps rediturus, sapiat tibi necesse est, non prope jam nihil, sed nihil ex toto, utpote quod in aeternum nihil est."

72 Bernard of Clairvaux, On the *Song of Songs III*, p. 36. Verdeyen (*SC* 452), SCC 50.7, l. 9-21: "Illo igitur excepto, qui non modo jam non diligendus, insuper et odio habendus est, secundum illud: Nonne qui oderunt te, Domine, oderam, et super inimicos tuos tabescebam? (Psal. CXXXVIII, 21.) De caetero nulli vel inimicissimo homini negari quantulumcunque affectum charitas sane in hac parte ambitiosa permittit. Quis sapiens, et intelliget haec?"

(charity of affect) and in horizontal love (charity of action) to undergo a transformation (effusion) through which love becomes efficient at the juncture of what *is* (description) and what *should be* (prescription). In the final analysis of the ideal wise man, again at the juncture of the inversion of the order of charity, the transformation of desire, from charity of action to-and-fro the charity of affection, renders love interchangeable with affection. "*Da mihi hominem*": a telling description of the wise man ensues. What man does Bernard give us? By way of conclusion, Bernard describes the man who exemplifies the (inverse) order of charity.

The man with the following characteristics embodies the (dis)order of desire. *First*, there is *totality*: absolute love for God, neighbor and even enemy. Bernard writes, "Give me *a man who loves God before all things and with his whole being, self and neighbor in proportion to their love of God*, the enemy as one who *perhaps someday will love*, his physical parents very deeply *because of the natural bond*, but his spiritual guides more generously *because of grace*."[73] However, the love of God *does not* disqualify the natural love of the flesh. *Second*, there is *mode*: "In like manner *let him deal with the other things of God too with an ordered love* [...] *using this world as if not using it*, and *discriminating between the things used and those enjoyed* with an *intimate savoring* in his mind."[74] Rather, with the proper attitude, all turns to the love of God. Experience is thus the measuring rod of *how* (modus) things are used (*uti*) and enjoyed (*frui*).[75] The use and enjoyment of things, qualified by a mode (Bernard), the mode of desire in the 'beginning without beginning', goes beyond a mere dialectic opposition of loves (Augustine). This is possible precisely because the pairs to use/with mode (*uti/cum modo*) and to enjoy/without mode (*frui/sine modo*) reach a transformative synthesis of desire/reason (description/prescription) in the liquefaction of desiring-production as the inverse(d) order of charity as pure resulting in generative aperity or free will. *Third*, there is eternity as *extension*, beyond time and place: "Let him pay but passing attention to things

---

73 Bernard of Clairvaux, On the *Song of Songs III*, pp. 36-8. Verdeyen (*SC* 452), SCC 50.8, l. 1-31: "Da mihi hominem, qui ante omnia quidem ex toto se diligat Deum; se vero et proximum, in quantum diligunt ipsum; inimicum autem, tanquam aliquando forsitan dilecturum; porro parentes carnis suae germanius, propter naturam; spirituales vero eruditores suos profusius, propter gratiam."

74 Bernard of Clairvaux, On the *Song of Songs III*, pp. 36-8. Verdeyen (*SC* 452), SCC 50.8, l. 1-31: "atque in hunc modum ad caetera quaeque Dei ordinato intendat amore, despiciens terram, suspiciens coelum, utens hoc mundo tanquam non utens, et inter utenda et fruenda intimo quodam mentis sapore discernens, ut transitoria transitorie, et ad id duntaxat quod opus, et prout opus est curet, aeterna desiderio amplectatur aeterno."

75 Bernard of Clairvaux, On the *Song of Songs III*, pp. 36-8. Verdeyen (*SC* 452), SCC 50.8, p. 360, n. 1: DDQ 30 (CCL 44 A, 38, 2-16), DDC 1 (CCL 32.8), 30-39 (CCL 32, p. 23-29).

that pass, as existing need demands. Let him embrace eternal things with *an eternal desire*. Give me such a man, I repeat, and I shall boldly proclaim him wise, because *he appreciates things for what they really are*, because he can *truthfully* [...] say, '*He set love in order in me.*'"[76] Fourth, such man is *desired* as inexistent, and in longing order occurs: "But *where* is he, and *when* shall these be? In tears I ask, how long shall we smell and not taste, gazing toward the fatherland and *not taking possession, sighing* for it and saluting from afar? *O Truth, fatherland of exiles, end of their exile!*"[77] Fourthly, and lastly, this exemplary man is identified with the Word in activity of (re)order. Bernard writes, "O Wisdom, *reaching mightily* from *end to end* in *establishing and controlling things*, and *arranging all things sweetly by enriching the affections and setting them in order*!"[78] Specifically, the order is governance: "*Guide our actions as your eternal truth requires*, that each of us may confidently boast in you and say, '*he set love in order in me.*' For you are *the strength of God* and *the Wisdom of God*."[79] The reduction of desire (of love) in the experience of the inverse order of charity emerges no longer *just* as the motor of free will (William of Saint-Thierry),[80] but as pure free will (Bernard): desire *becomes* free will in the inverse order of charity through the aperity of *the beginning without beginning* in the love of love.

---

76 Bernard of Clairvaux, On the *Song of Songs III*, pp. 36-8. Verdeyen (*SC* 452), SCC 50.8, l. 1-31: "talem, inquam, da mihi hominem, et ego audacter illum sapientem pronuntio, cui nimirum quaeque res revera sapiunt prout sunt, et cui in veritate atque securitate competit gloriari, et dicere, quia ordinavit in me charitatem."

77 Bernard of Clairvaux, On the *Song of Songs III*, pp. 36-8. Verdeyen (*SC* 452), SCC 50.8, l. 1-31: "Sed ubi ille, aut quando ista? Quod flens dico, quousque odoramus, et non gustamus, prospicientes patriam, et non apprehendentes, suspirantes, et de longe salutantes? O veritas exsulum patria, exsilii finis? video te, sed intrare non sinor carne retentus, sed nec dignus admitti, peccatis sordens."

78 Bernard of Clairvaux, On the *Song of Songs III*, pp. 36-8. Verdeyen (*SC* 452), SCC 50.8, l. 1-31: "O Sapientia, quae attingis a fine usque ad finem fortiter in instituendis et continendis rebus; et disponis omnia suaviter in beandis et ordinandis affectibus! dirige actus nostros, prout nostra temporalis necessitas poscit; et dispone affectus nostros, prout tua veritas aeterna requirit, ut possit unusquisque nostrum secure in te gloriari et dicere, quia ordinavit in me charitatem."

79 Bernard of Clairvaux, On the *Song of Songs III*, pp. 36-8. Verdeyen (*SC* 452), SCC 50.8, l. 1-31: "Tu es enim Dei virtus et Dei sapientia, Christus sponsus Ecclesiae, Dominus noster, super omnia Deus benedictus in saecula. Amen."

80 William of Saint-Thierry (d. 1148), wrote *On the Nature and Dignity of Love* (*De natura et dignitate amoris*) after 1118: "the principal force that moves the human soul is love".

Conclusion

To conclude, the order or *dis*order of desire as *love of love* constitutes the last moment in the transformation of order of the *metamorphosis of love*. In the *order of charity* in the metaxological aperity of *the grotesque body*, construed as *aesthetic mer(e)ology*, is *desire as free will*. The mode of desiring-production is therefore not only love as the sublime and the grotesque but in the organic generative production of *the spread body*, the desiring-production as pure aperity is free will. Hence, the *desire in the word*, rooted in the organic *desire and the body*, becomes living and efficient desiring-production in *desire as free will*. In the *metamorphosis of love*, therefore, there is neither rationalism, nor sentimentalism, or yet again voluntarism. In the *order of charity* desire is the driving force of the production of bodies because desire orders bodies, as pure organic aperity or free will. In short, *love of love* revolutionizes the order of desire and reason, founded in the body, expressed in the extension, attraction and order of the Word, and finally becomes *aperity* in the *desire as free will*. In the final moments of the *metamorphosis of love*, body arises under the aspect of pure act or aperity. Body as aperity is love, considered from vantage point of free will, in terms of *limits*, then *resistance*, and finally as *aperity*.

PART III

Free Will

CHAPTER 7

Limits

What or where are the *limits* of the body in desiring-production, and is it possible to surpass these? Before plunging into the discussion of *the weight of the word*, some preambles are necessary. The aim of these preambles, succinctly laid out in the section that follows, is to contextualize the discussion on *desire as free will* – the third moment in the *metamorphosis of love* – within the larger philosophical discussion regarding how *desire* and *free will* engage vis-à-vis love. The free will as a mode of desiring-production founded on an *aesthetics mer(e)ology* snatches agency from the framework of description (can) and prescription (ought), no longer as opposites (Hume) but as metaxological dialectic.[1] A debate on free will in the mode of desiring-production flowing from *aesthetic mer(e)ology* is therefore no longer waged in the onto-metaphysical false options which identify free will with the ability to chose (Aristotle),[2] or with rational desire (Aquinas),[3] or irrespective of reason as a capacity within possibility of choice (Hume)[4], or again as pure voluntarism (Scotus) or, at the other extreme, as determination and necessity (Spinoza).[5] Alternatives also

1 David Hume, *An Enquiry Concerning the Principles of Morals* (Oxford: Oxford University Press, 2006), 469: "In every system of morality, which I have hitherto met with, I have always remarked, that the author proceeds for some time in the ordinary ways of reasoning, and establishes the being of a God, or makes observations concerning human affairs; when all of a sudden I am surprised to find, that instead of the usual copulations of propositions, is, and is not, I meet with no proposition that is not connected with an ought, or an ought not. This change is imperceptible; but is however, of the last consequence. For as this ought, or ought not, expresses some new relation or affirmation, it is necessary that it should be observed and explained; and at the same time that a reason should be given; for what seems altogether inconceivable, how this new relation can be a deduction from others, which are entirely different from it."

2 Aristotle, *Nichomachean Ethics*, III.1: "the *originating principle* [*arche*] is outside and nothing is contributed by the person who acts or rather is acted on." Translation by Jonathan Barnes, *The Nicomachean Ethics* (London: Penguin, 2004). The power the *arche* to chose a course of action rather than another (to do A rather than B, where A is not B) is desire (*orexis*), as per John L. Ackrill, "Aristotle on Action," *Mind* 87, no. 4 (1978): 99.

3 Aquinas, *ST* 1-2 q6 a2 ad 1: "voluntas nominat rationalem appetitum." See discussion in T. H. Irwin, "Who Discovered the Will?" *Philosophical Perspectives* 6 (1992), 456-461.

4 David Hume, *An Enquiry*, §8, 23: "a power of acting or not acting, according to the determinations of the will."

5 Baruch Spinoza, *Ethics*, III: "men are conscious of their actions and ignorant of the causes by which they are determined"; *Ethics*, def. 7: "That thing is called free, which exists solely by the necessity of its own nature, and of which the action is determined by itself alone. On

© BRILL FINK, 2023 | DOI:10.30965/9783846767504_009

include flexibility within confines as a combination of absolute freedom and determinism (Hobbes)[6] or the view that free will is more than free action but requires the agent to *cause* the action (Reid).[7] *Desire as free will* is fundamentally *aesthetic mer(e)ological* aperity as production and resistance grounded in *the desire of the body*, passing through the transformation and resistance of the body in *free will and the body* and becoming manifest in the mode of generative love in *free will and love*. As such, the living and efficient word brings full circle the metamorphosis of love to *the beginning without beginning*. The body, it is argued, is *the weight of the word*. Then, the notion of *free will* is introduced as it relates to the body as the *weight of the word* in *free will and the body*. The *limits* of the body emerge in the *weight of the body*. The *limit* of the body, it is argued, is the framework to understand the possibility of *free will*. Finally, the confines of the body are overcome (*how*) at the *limit* of the body where *free will is aperity*. The *free will is aperity* because the *weight of the word* extends the body beyond its confines through the word where, at the limit, the body is production or *aperity*. The central contention of this section on *limits* is that the body is in constant production and therefore, the limits reveal not confines but rather generation: the body is in constant generation. This has an obvious implication, i.e., the body is aperity. In Bernard's *metamorphosis of love*, the question of *limits* arises according to *the weight of the word* (7.1), *free will and the body* (7.2) and *free will as aperity* (7.3).

---

the other hand, that thing is necessary, or rather constrained, which is determined by something external to itself to a fixed and definite method of existence or action." Quotes from Baruch Spinoza, *The Essential Spinoza: Ethics and Related Writings*, trans. Samuel Shirley, ed. Michael L. Morgan (Indianapolis: Hackett Publishing Company, 2006).

6 Thomas Hobbes, *Of Liberty and Necessity*: "Liberty is the absence of all the impediments to action that are not contained in the nature and intrisnical character of the agent. As for example, the water is said to descend freely, or to have liberty to descend by the channel of the river, because there is no impediment that way, but not across becuas the banks are impediments. And though water cannot ascend, yet men never say it wants the *liberty* to ascend, but the *faculty* or *power*, because the impediment is the nature of the water, and intrinsical." Passage from John Bramhall, *Hobbes and Bramhall on Liberty and Necessity* (Cambridge: Cambridge University Press, 1999), 38.

7 Thomas Reid, *Essays on the Power of the Human Mind*: "I consider the determination of the will as an effect. This effect must have a cause which had the power to produce it; and the cause must be either the person himself, whose will it is, or some other being.... If the person was the cause of that determination of his own will, he was free in that action, and it is justly imputed to him, whether it be good or bad. But, if another being was the cause of this determination, either producing it immediately, or by means and instruments under his direction, then the determination is the act and deed of that being, and is solely imputed to him." Derek Brookes, *Thomas Reid: Essays on the Intellectual Power of Man: A Critical Edition* (University Park, Penn State University Press, 2001), IV.i, 265.

7.1 The Weight of the Word

Since *the weight of the body* is the Word, we must now inevitably consider *the weight of the Word*. This is more so the case because the *limit* emerges at the point of origin (*principium*), where the body *extends*, *attracts* and is *ordered* in and by the Word. In other words, the *limit* is the passage, the *metamorphosis*, from body to action in the Word. The central question is, therefore, how does the body *become* Word? Alternatively, in other words, using Bernard's way of framing the question, *what* is the soul's affinity to the Word? Where is the *limit* of the body? The affinity of the soul to the Word passes through the body. Therefore, to ask *what* is the soul's affinity to the Word is to ask, what is the body's affinity to the Word? Furthermore, since the body is production of the Word's force, to inquire into the body's affinity to the Word is, at heart, to pierce through the production of the *metamorphosis of love*. The *limit* is therefore the affinity of the soul to the Word. To probe into affinity is to probe into limits. Indeed, the term affinity in Latin is rendered as *ad* + *finis* which means, literally, towards the limits. At once, there is a sense of dynamism (*ad*) and of confines (*finis*): the movement towards the confines is ongoing. This is at the heart of the Bernardine analysis of the soul's affinity to the Word (*de affinitate animae ad Verbum*). Limits are found in relation. Bernard frames affinity in terms of equality in the love and humility of spouses (*ut more et amore sponsorum*). To be sure, the possibility of equality is predicated on the resemblance of the soul to the Word: although the soul (*anima*) can try to become equal to the Word, equality presupposes some prior resemblance. The resemblance is not merely a substantial configuration but describes rather a relationship (*de affinitate*) akin to the amorous bond of the spouses in the *Song of Songs*. This is the first great insight on limits: limit is not confine but relation (*extension, attraction* and *order*). The modes of relation at the limit are threefold: simplicity, perpetuity or immortality and ultimate freedom. The three modes are progressive and move from one to the next, presupposing the previous one and becoming fulfilled in the next. As such, and paradoxically as it may sound, the limit leads to freedom in relation and of relation. Relation extends the limits. The *metamorphosis of love* is, at the limits, a movement towards aperity of relation. Relation opens rather than collapsing, grows rather than faining, frees rather than confining. Before analyzing the modes of the limit as affinity, it must be noted that Bernard frames the affinity of the Word and the soul in terms of ("theological") aesthetics[8] or modal manifestation: "*No one can be so*

8 Pierluigi Lia, *L'estetica teologica di Bernardo di Chiaravalle. La mistica Cristiana tra oriente e occidente* (Firenze: Sismel, 2007).

blind that he does not see the resemblance between the image and what is made in the image."[9] The use of the term image (*imago*) conjures immediately the question of aesthetics. The aesthetics of *affinity* and resemblance consist in the enfolding (*ad amplexus*) of the Word: "*it will be anxious to make every effort to reform what it sees in its nature to be deformed by sin*, [...] it may rule itself in a way *worthy of its origin*, and faithfully *approach the Word's enfolding*."[10] The unfolding (*ad amplexus*) of affinity is therefore modal aesthetic manifestation. What is a modal aesthetic of manifestation? In other words, why is affinity aesthetic manifestation? The answer, which spans the rest of Bernard's *On the Song of Songs*, is simple: *libero arbitro*, loosely translated, albeit imperfectly, as *free will*. The aesthetic affinity of the Word and the soul is the modal manifestation of the free will (*libero arbitro*). This is significant because the ultimate outcome of *affinity* or *limit* is the manifestation of *free will* in the *metamorphosis of love*. Conversely, the dissimilarity or the soul's aesthetic distance from the Verb is deformation (the grotesque of generative affinity is *resistance*). Love, as (dis) equality of the soul and the Verb, and free will, in the mode of affinity or deformity, are therefore interlaced. Furthermore, the search for affinity through the *aesthetic mer(e)ology* or reformation as reconfiguration of the free will (*libero arbitro*) is achieved through knowledge (*agnoscere*) as an intentionality of conversion to the origin (*origenem*): to know is to touch, to touch is to become and in becoming free will is manifested at the limit.[11] In short, desire as the driving force of affinity/deformity is framed not as onto-metaphysical approximation

9 Bernard of Clairvaux, On the *Song of Songs IV*, pp. 157-8. Zink (*SC* 511), SCC 81.1, l. 1-21: "Quis enim, vel nimis hebes, non videat quam se e vicino respiciant imago et quod ad imaginem est?"

10 Bernard of Clairvaux, On the *Song of Songs IV*, pp. 157-8. Zink (*SC* 511), SCC 81.1, l. 1-21: "Age, jam intendamus declarationi huic, ut quo anima plenius suam agnoscet originem, eo amplius erubescat vitam habere degenerem; imo vero quod peccato vitiatum deprehenderit in natura, studeat reformare industria; ut digne suo genere, Dei quidem munere, sese regens, ad amplexus Verbi fidenter accedat."

11 Michael Casey, *Athirst for God: Spiritual Desire in Bernard of Clairvaux's Sermons on the Song of Songs* (Collegeville: Cistercian Publications, 1988); Paul Moyaert, "Mysticism: The Transformation of a Love Consumed by Desire into a Love without Desire," *Ethical Perspectives*, 7 (2000): 269-278; Pyong-Gwan Pak, "St. Bernard of Clairvaux on the Riddle of Human Desire: The Necessity of a Reversal of Priorities in the Human Life of Desire," *Logos: A Journal of Catholic Thought and Culture* 21, no. 4 (2018): 126-50; Antonio Montanari, "*Desiderium sine anxietate*: *Désir infini et béatitude de l'homme d'après les sermons* 84-86 *super cantica de saint Bernard*," *Collectanea cisterciensia* 70, no. 1 (2008): 4-20; James Zona, ""Set Love in Order in Me": Eros-knowing in Origen and Desiderium-knowing in Saint Bernard," *Cistercian Studies Quarterly* 34, no. 2 (1999): 157.

primarily as "region of unlikeness,"[12] but as the (re)configuration of *bodies* (*aesthetic mer(e)ology*): *bodies* are manifest in the mode of love within *the* whole of *the body*. What then is the soul's *aesthetic* proximity to the Verb? Bernard lays out the three degrees of the soul's proximity (simplicity, perpetuity or immortality and ultimate freedom) to the soul in a gradual ladder of transformation leading to the life of blessedness. Happiness is framed no longer as a moral choice of the free will, but as the progress towards the complete manifestation of the will as *aesthetic* configuration in the affinity of the soul to the Word. There are three *limits*, or progressive modes of affinity: *first*, simplicity; *second*, perpetuity or immortality; and *third*, free will. The rest of this section is concerned with simplicity. The section, which follows, is concerned with perpetuity or immortality. In addition, the last section of this chapter is concerned with free will. All three modes somehow reveal the limits of the body. This chapter aims at elucidating *how* limits manifest within the fabric of finitude. In short, the unfolding of free will through modal degrees of manifestation constitute the *metamorphosis of love* at the limit. *First*, simplicity. Bernard writes, "because of its origin in the divine likeness [the soul] has in itself a *natural simplicity of substance* by which for it *to exist is to live*, even if it does not imply *living in a state of blessedness*; its likeness does not imply equality."[13] To exist is to live (*qua hoc est illi esse quod vivere*). The fundamental capacity of the body is the soul's potency or force: the body is constant becoming. The force of the body is a dynamic power predisposed to performativity modelled after that of the Word. The power of the body is simplicity where *to be* is *to exist*. Within the power of simplicity, a first limit emerges. "*This is a degree, of likeness, but only a degree; it is not synonymous with living in a state of blessedness*, which is the prerogative of the highest virtue."[14] The mode of manifestation of the body is without beatitude or happiness in the absence of the Word. The body is incomplete without the moral texture of blessedness, which is impossible to attain without the Word. The limit of the body is happiness. Blessedness adds quality to life: "If therefore *this quality of life* is the

---

12 Margaret W. Ferguson, "Saint Augustine's Region of Unlikeness: The Crossing of Exile and Language," *The Georgia Review* 29, no. 4 (1975): 842-864; François Chatillon, "Regio dissimilitudinis," in *Mélanges E. Podechard* (Lyon: Facultés Catholiques, 1954): 85-102.

13 Bernard of Clairvaux, On the *Song of Songs IV*, pp. 158-9. Zink (*SC* 511), SCC 81.2, l. 1-21: "Advertat igitur ex hac divinae ingenuitate similitudinis inesse sibi illam suae substantiae naturalem simplicitatem, qua hoc est illi esse quod vivere, etsi non quod bene, quodve beate vivere, ut sit similitudo, non aequalitas."

14 Bernard of Clairvaux, On the *Song of Songs IV*, pp. 158-9. 158-9. Zink (*SC* 511), SCC 81.2, l. 1-21: "Gradus propinquus, gradus tamen. Neque enim unius excellentiae parisve fastigii sunt, hoc habere esse quod vivere, et item habere hoc esse quod beate vivere."

prerogative of the Word, by reason of the perfection of its nature, *life is the prerogative of the soul* because of its *natural affinity* to the Word."[15] The limit emerges in temporality, in the extension from the *first* simplicity to the *present* simplicity. Bernard goes on, "To make this clearer: *it is for God alone that to be is synonymous with being in a state of blessedness, and this is the first and purest simplicity*."[16] The first simplicity (*primum simplex*) alone is pure. Then, the second (*secundam*) simplicity is similar to the first, but lacks quality. "*The second is similar to it*, namely, that *existence is living*, and this is the prerogative of the soul; and even if it is a lower degree, it can be raised not only to living well, *but even to living blessedly*."[17] The quality of the second simplicity is blessedness. This does not mean, however, that blessedness is not possible. The first simplicity can indeed reach a semblance of the second simplicity, which is blessedness. However, the difference remains, "But even for the soul which attains to this (blessedness) *to be is not the same thing as to be blessed*, since it is glorified by *its likeness to the Word* […] *It is a degree of advancement for the soul, from which alone it may rise to the blessed life*."[18] The likeness (*similitudo*) is an additional happiness which however is not equality with blessedness. Yes, to be is to exist, and therefore the body is fundamentally dynamism or force towards affinity (*ad affinitate*) of the Word. However, the degree of likeness in simplicity is never complete such that the soul is never equal to the Word and the body is never fully force. In short, the first *simplicity* is *the weight of the word*. The texture (blessedness) of becoming is the limit of the body. The limit of the body lies in the degrees of becoming, from the soul to the Word. In other words, limits emerge in the process of becoming alike, in the process of resembling more, moving actively towards, but never reaching likeness. There is a third simplicity. In the third degree, the soul rises beyond living as being (first

---

15 Bernard of Clairvaux, On the *Song of Songs IV*, pp. 158-9. Zink (*SC* 511), SCC 81.2, l. 1-21: "Ergo si Verbi est illud propter sublimitatem, hoc animae propter similitudinem, salva quidem eminentia Verbi, palam est affinitas naturarum, palam animae praerogativa."

16 Bernard of Clairvaux, On the *Song of Songs IV*, pp. 158-9. Zink (*SC* 511), SCC 81.2, l. 1-21: "Et ut quod dicitur planius fiat, soli Deo id est esse, quod beatum esse: atque hoc primum et purissimum simplex."

17 Bernard of Clairvaux, On the *Song of Songs IV*, pp. 158-9. Zink (*SC* 511), SCC 81.2, l. 1-21: "Secundum autem simile est huic, id videlicet habere esse quod vivere; atque hoc animae est. Ex hoc, etsi inferiori gradu, ascendi potest, non modo ad bene, sed etiam ad beate vivendum."

18 Bernard of Clairvaux, On the *Song of Songs IV*, pp. 158-9. Zink (*SC* 511), SCC 81.2, l. 1-21: "non quia vel tunc sit hoc esse, quod beatum esse illi qui eo pervenerit; quatenus ita glorietur pro similitudine, ut tamen pro disparitate habeat semper, unde omnia ossa ejus dicant: Domine, quis similis tibi? (Psal. XXXIV, 10). Bonus tamen animae gradus, ex quo, et solo, ad beatam ascenditur vitam."

degree) and good and partially happy living as a quality of being (second degree) to the final step where living well reaches *complete* happiness. In the third degree the soul "is glorified by its likeness to the Word [...] It is a degree of advancement for the soul, from which alone it may rise to the blessed life."[19] The life of the soul has most affinity to the Verb when it (the soul) *is* good because then it is happy. The rising ladder towards the affinity of the Verb as a metamorphosis of aesthetics frames what is good and what is happy (and not the other way around). Simplicity is rooted in the body. The limit of resemblance, we have said it, is rooted in the body. Indeed, the body reaches affinity to the Verb simultaneously with the three degrees of affinity of the soul. Bernard returns to the classification of living bodies into those with sensibility and those without sensibility. Of these, sensible beings are higher than those without sensibility are. The soul is the source of sensibility as it is of life. Indeed, the soul is *not* alive; rather, the soul is the source of life. Life is in the most basic manifestation of movement and self-preservation (*conatus essendi*)[20] manifested in the *mer(e)ological aesthetics* of the body. Configurations of affinity to the Word in degrees result in configurations of bodies with corresponding manifestations of life. Bernard distinguishes two types of living beings: "*those which have consciousness* and *those which do not*. The *sensate rank above the insensate*, and *above them both is life*, by which *one lives and is conscious*."[21] The living beings, therefore, are either sentient (*quae sentiunt*) or insensient (*quae non sentiunt*). A sentient being is one that thinks, feels, experiences, understands, realizes, and sees. None of these is possible, however, without life (*vita*). For this reason, life ranks above "Life and living beings *do not rank equally*; much *less life and lifeless things*. Life is the living soul, but it does not derive its life from any other source than itself; strictly speaking, we describe this as life rather than living."[22] The soul (*anima*) is life. Living (*uita*) and life (*anima*) are

---

19 Bernard of Clairvaux, On the *Song of Songs IV*, pp. 158-9. Zink (*SC* 511), SCC 81.2, l. 1-21: "Gradus propinquus, gradus tamen. Neque enim unius excellentiae parisve fastigii sunt, hoc habere esse quod vivere, et item habere hoc esse quod beate vivere."

20 The definition of *conatus essendi* by Spinoza is (a) striving: "[...] each thing, as far as it lies in itself, strives to persevere in its being," (*Ethics*, part 3, prop. 6); (b) resitence: *conatus essendi* "is opposed to everything which can take its existence away" (*Ethics*, part 3, prop. 6, dem.); finally, (c) essence: "nothing but the actual essence of the thing" (*Ethics*, part 3, prop. 7); with the implication that *conatus essendi* is (d) the power of God. Spinoza, *The Essential*, part 3. The *conatus essendi* is the precursor to the *will to live* (Wille zum Leben) in Schopenhauer and the *will to power* (Wille zur Macht) in Nietzche.

21 Bernard of Clairvaux, On the *Song of Songs IV*, pp. 159-60. Zink (*SC* 511), SCC 81.3, l. 1-8: "Sunt namque viventia, et horum genera duo, quae sentiunt, et quae non sentiunt."

22 Bernard of Clairvaux, On the *Song of Songs IV*, pp. 159-60. Zink (*SC* 511), SCC 81.3, l. 1-8: "Porro insensibilibus sensibilia praeferuntur, atque utrisque vita, qua vivitur et sentitur.

not the same. Life is higher than merely living (as sentient or insensient). Yet, the soul cannot have blessedness on its own. The simplicity of soul in which living is life is the affinity to the Word. The soul stands out from the rest of living beings because, as laid out in the first degree of proximity, being and living is this time framed as life and soul, which are fundamentally the same (*Vita anima est vivens quidem, sed non aliunde quam se ipsa*). Hence, in the human being life, soul and being are the same. This equality constitutes the simplicity on the basis of which the soul has affinity to the Word. Is this simply a configurational or formal similarity to the Verb? In addition, what is its implication for the body? There is no life without the body: the soul's affinity to the Word is inherently attached to the body, as is the incarnate Word, i.e., the affinity becomes complete only in the body where the *sequela Christi* is possible and therefore beatitude. The soul is life and gives life to the body. "Thus it follows that when this is infused into the soul it gives it life, so that the body, through the presence of life, *becomes not life itself but a living thing*."[23] Bernard continues: "From this it is clear that, even for a living body, to *be is not the same as to live*. Much less do those things which are without life attain to this degree. Not even will everything which is described as life, or which is indeed so, be able to reach that point."[24] A characteristic element of the simplicity of the soul vis-à-vis the body is composition. The body is indeed simple when unified, or when the body functions as a single organism. The simplicity of the body, unlike the simplicity of the soul is only temporary, lasting only for as long as composition lasts. When there is composition, there is unity, and for as long as there is unity, there is life. However, existence or being, as such, does not imply life since the composites can disintegrate and life ends but being remains. Bernard explains: "For neither of these does being involve living, since, according to many people, their existence has been in the elements before it was in their limbs. However, according to this view, when they cease to quicken they cease to live, but not to be. They are dissolved and separated, as though they had been not only bound together but also mingled. *For they are not one simple*

Non stabunt pariter in gradu uno vita et vivens; multo minus vita, et quae sunt sine vita. Vita anima est vivens quidem, sed non aliunde quam se ipsa; ac per hoc non tam vivens, quam vita, ut proprie de ea loquamur."

23 Bernard of Clairvaux, On the *Song of Songs IV*, pp. 159-60. Zink (*SC* 511), SCC 81.3, l. 8-26: "Inde est quod infusa corpori vivificat illud, ut sit corpus de vitae praesentia, non vita, sed vivens."

24 Bernard of Clairvaux, On the *Song of Songs IV*, pp. 159-60. Zink (*SC* 511), SCC 81.3, l. 8-26: "Unde liquet, ne vivo quidem corpori id vivere esse, quod esse, cum esse et minime vivere possit. Multo minus quae vitae expertia sunt, ad hunc gradum assurgent. Sed nec omne quod vita dicitur, vel est, continuo valebit pertingere huc."

organism but are compounded of several."[25] The soul as life-giver is what provides simplicity to the composition of elements. Without the body's composition, life, which is the soul, is not living. As such, simplicity is rooted in the body. Yet, without the soul's life, the composite of the body returns to nothing: "*Therefore it is not reduced to nothing but dissolved into its component parts, and each returns to its first principle*; for example, air returns to air, fire to fire, and so forth. For such a quality of life *to be is by no means the same as to live*; it is even when it does not live."[26] Without composition, the body is not living; without a body, the soul is only life, not living. Simplicity is unity of composition, which in turn brings together life (soul) and living (body). How does the simplicity in composition of the soul and body approximate the soul to the Word? The soul infuses life in the body and as such, the soul's simplicity, which approximates it to the Verb, is not present in the body, be it human or otherwise. However, it is rooted in the body. The aim of the distinction is certainly to avoid approaching the body to the Verb (as is the case in the Patristic tradition) on the one hand and, on the other hand, to show the superiority of the soul over all creation. However, this need not come at the detriment of the body. Simplicity emerges at the limit of the body, which is disintegration of composition, or affinity to the body. The limits of the body are found in the simplicity of life which is the condition for living, but they can also be delineated from the other side, in the multiplicity of fragmentation where elements in parts (*in parte*) still exist, but without life (*quae est et quando non vivit*). The limits are found where the body disintegrates. Then alone is the body either one, simple like the Word, and therefore with affinity to the Word, or many when the body is not living but only existing in elements at the origin (*origenem*). The limit emerges not in simplicity as such, but at the point where the limit is constituted or collapsed, where both body and soul are necessary: at the opposite end of the simplicity of the living body is the multiplicity of the non-living body at the origin. Both origin and simplicity have affinity to the Word.

---

25 Bernard of Clairvaux, On the *Song of Songs IV*, pp. 159-60. Zink (*SC* 511), SCC 81.3, l. 8-26: "At neutri tamen idem esse quod vivere est: cum, ut quidem multorum opinio est, ante in elementis, quam vel illa in membris, vel ista in ramis exstiterint, At secundum hoc cum desinunt vivificare, simul vivere cessant, sed non et esse. Solvuntur pariter et dissolvuntur, tanquam non alligatae tantum, sed et colligatae. Neque enim unum simplex est quaeque harum; sed ex pluribus constans."

26 Bernard of Clairvaux, On the *Song of Songs IV*, pp. 159-60. Zink (*SC* 511), SCC 81.3, l. 8-26: "Et propterea non redigitur in nihilum, sed dissilit in partes, ut et ad suum quodque recurrat principium; verbi causa, aer ad aerem, ignis ad ignem, et reliqua in hunc modum. Nequaquam igitur tali vitae idem esse et vivere est, quae est et quando non vivit."

What is the non-living body and what is its affinity to the Word? A series of bodies were previously introduced, but not this one. The non-living body (*non vivus*) is different and it is crucial in the mediation and transformation of desire as well as the experience of God. Through the vivification of the soul alone (desire?) does the human being *fully* experience the simplicity of affinity to the verb (life, soul, being) through the body. The bottom line is, the simplicity of the soul does not prejudice the complexity of the body. On the contrary, the contrast seems to reinforce the importance of the body in conjunction with the soul. Whereas the soul vivifies, the body, even in its non-living state, returns to a *principium* where the *origenem* is regenerative limit in affinity: "Therefore it is not reduced to nothing but dissolved into its component parts, and each returns to its first principle."[27] The body thus displays a double movement of return to the elements (Aristotelianism) which the bodies endure in conversion (Neoplatonism).[28] The body, then, in a sense even irrespective of the soul naturally returns to the beginning (*principium*). There is no resemblance on this about simplicity, but there is definitely a sense of affinity in that by means of complexity (cf. the various members of the body), the body has a natural tendency towards its origin: the elemental, the body. The limit is conversion and therefore the same affinity to the Word in exit (*exitus*) from the beginning (*originem*) or in the return (*reditus*) to the beginning (*principium*). This much is clear thus far: there is no affinity of the soul to the Word without the Body. On the contrary, the body manifests the truth of limits in affinity. Indeed, the Bernardine quibble on the affinity to the Word is not with the body (*corpus*), but with the flesh (*caro*). The flesh (*caro*), and not the body, is under the specter of sin. What is that specter? Death. Natural death or decomposition of complexity in the absence of the soul is natural for Bernard and different from the death of sin, which is spiritual, and stands in contrast to natural death.[29] He explains: "For *the death of sinners is very evil.* Thus the soul which lives according to the flesh is dead though it lives, for it would have been better for it never to have lived than to live in such a way. And it will never rise from *that living death except through the Word of life*, or rather through *the Word which is life, both living and life-giving*."[30] In this marvelous turn of phrase, the Word is the

27 Zink (*SC* 511), SCC 81.3, p. 303, n. 1: *Et propterea non redigitur in nihilum, sed dissilit in partes, ut et ad suum quodque recurrat principium.*" The idea that all returns to the beginning is a recurring Bernardine theme (cf. SBO V, p. 13-14); SCC 7.2, pp. 156-8, SCC 13.1, SCC 83.4.

28 Brague, *Saint Bernard*, 183. Zink (*SC* 511), SCC 81.3, p. 302, n. 1.

29 John M. Rist, *Augustine Deformed: Love, Sin and Freedom in the Western Moral Tradition* (New York: Cambridge University Press, 2014).

30 Bernard of Clairvaux, On the *Song of Songs IV*, pp. 160-1. Zink (*SC* 511), SCC 81.4, l. 24-30: "Mors potius est: et ideo gravior, quia peccati, non naturae Denique mors peccatorum

life to the flesh after the death of the body much as the soul was the life of the body during life. A new kind of life is possible: a life where, living according to the flesh, the body is dead while still alive. The life of the soul according to the flesh is a life of death: "Thus the soul which lives according to the flesh is dead though it lives, for it would have been better for it never to have lived than to live in such a way."[31] The condemnation of the soul is, on the reverse of the coin, a vindication of the body. The bottom line is that the simplicity of the soul does not come to the detriment of the body. Rather, the body offers a second and indeed complimentary point of affinity to the soul's natural affinity to the Word based on the body. Whereas the soul offers simplicity, the body offers complexity in a single movement of conversion and return to the origin. Furthermore, this underscores the efficient aspect of the Word. The life of the soul is truly a life through the Word. In the first degree towards the affinity of the Word therefore lies the simplicity and complexity of the soul and the body respectively, from being as living (first step), to living well (second step) and finally reaching happiness (third step). To summarize this first section of our chapter on limits, the first limit of the body is simplicity according to which the soul finds affinity to the Word. Central to this Bernardine contention is the retrieval and celebration of the goodness of the body and of the body's integration with the soul. The body contributes to the first affinity. The distance from the Word is not the body, but the flesh. Therefore, the true lack of simplicity is the body which though living is also in a spiritual sense dead. The soul that lives according to the body, not the flesh, lives in simplicity of the Word. In addition, this is the first limit: life is *the weight of the Word* on the body. Just as life depends on *the weight of the Word* on the body, so too does *free will* depend on it in the second simplicity: immortality.

7.2 Free Will and the Body

What is the limit of immortality in the *affinity* of the soul to the Word? In addition to simplicity, the soul (*anima*) resembles (*similitudo*) the Word in immortality. Immortality and simplicity are intertwined since only what is composite is mortal; what is not composite, simple, or one or inherently

pessima (Psal. XXXIII, 22). Ita ergo quae secundum carnem vivit anima, vivens mortua est; quippe cui bonum erat omnino non vivere, quam sic vivere. A qua nimirum vitali quadam morte minime unquam resurget, nisi per verbum vitae, imo per Verbum vitam, viventem utique et vivificantem."

31 Bernard of Clairvaux, On the *Song of Songs IV*, pp. 160-1. Zink (*SC* 511), SCC 81.4, l. 24-30: "Ita ergo quae secundum carnem vivit anima, vivens mortua est."

immortal. Immortality, like simplicity too, is similar to the Word, but not equal to the Word. Bernard explains, "now the soul is immortal, and in this it is also similar, but not equal to, the Word. For the immortality of the Godhead is so far above it [...] 'He who alone possesses immortality.'"[32] In what sense is the Word immortal and in what sense is the soul immortal and like, but not equal, to the Word? Furthermore, how does the body mediate the immortality of the soul, when resembling the Word? First, immortality is unchanging – this presumes simplicity. Immortality (*immortalitas*) is immutability (*immutabilitas*). What is not composite, cannot change and is therefore immortal. Therefore, the immortality of God surpasses all other immortality because God is by nature (*natura*)[33] immortality; that is to say, immutable. Bernard writes, "For the immortality of the Godhead is so far above it that the Apostle says of God, 'He who alone possesses immortality.' This was said of him, I think, because only God is by nature unchangeable – he said 'I am God, and I do not change.'"[34] To be God, is to be unchanging. The Word too is unchanging, because the Word is *with* God, the Word *is* God.

Whereas immortality is without end because immortality is unchanging, what changes is mortal. Since change is in a sense an aspect, and indeed *the* defining aspect of mortality, true (divine) immortality is immutable and, additionally, unending (*nec finem*). Bernard thus explores the verso and perhaps even reverses the Plotinian epithet "time is a shadow of eternity"[35] into "change is an imitation of death."[36] Bernard writes, "For true and integral immortality does not admit change any more than it does ending, because all change is in some way an imitation of death."[37] Why is change an imitation of death? Because change *is* transformation or metamorphosis. What changes transitions from a being into another such that what is transformed ceases to be

32 Bernard of Clairvaux, On the *Song of Songs IV*, pp. 161-2. Zink (*SC* 511), SCC 81.5, l. 1-11: "Alias autem immortalis est anima, et in hoc nihilominus Verbo similis quidem, sed non aequalis. Nam in tantum superexcellit immortalitas Deitatis, ut Apostolus dicat de Deo: Qui solus habet immortalitatem (I Tim. VI, 16)."

33 Silveira da Costa and Ricardo Luiz, "El concepto de naturaleza en la metafísica teológica de San Bernardo de Claraval (1090-1153)," *Medio Aevo*, no. 1 (2012): 131-44.

34 Bernard of Clairvaux, On the *Song of Songs IV*, pp. 161-2. Zink (*SC* 511), SCC 81.5, l. 1-11: "Nam in tantum superexcellit immortalitas Deitatis, ut Apostolus dicat de Deo: Qui solus habet immortalitatem, I Tim. VI, 16. Quod ego reor pro eo dictum, quod solus sit natura incommutabilis Deus, qui ait: Ego Dominus, et non mutor, Malach. III, 6."

35 Gordon H. Clark, "The Theory of Time in Plotinus," *The Philosophical Review* 53, no. 4 (1944): 337-358.

36 Bernard of Clairvaux, On the *Song of Songs IV*, pp. 161-162. Zink (*SC* 511), SCC 81.5, l. 1-11: "omnis mutatio quaedam mortis imitatio sit."

37 Bernard of Clairvaux, On the *Song of Songs IV*, pp. 161-2. Zink (*SC* 511), SCC 81.5.

one thing and becomes another. Therefore, death is a condition for life at the limits of the body: "This was said of him, I think, because only God is by nature unchangeable – he said *'I am God, and I do not change.'* For true and integral immortality does not admit change any more than it does ending, because *all change is in some way an imitation of death*. Everything which changed, *in passing from one state to another*, necessarily dies to what it is, so *that it may begin to be what it is not*."[38] The focus is not on the end itself, but on the limit infinitely approaching, but never actually reaching an end. The limit is change. Change is the condition for mortality. Moreover, even what changes, and what is by definition composite, may nevertheless resemble the Word: existence alone implies change. Change is a limit. Without the body, the limit of change is incomprehensible and indeed impossible, as Bernard goes on to show.

The immortality of the Word includes a beginning without end. This is the key. Transformation includes simultaneously the end as much as the beginning in the process of the *enfolding* of the Word. The beginning is embedded in the end (*incipio*). However, how does the transformation (*transire*) of being within the tension of the beginning or 'what is' (*quod est*) and the end or 'what is not' (*quod non est*), manifest the affinity of immortality (*immortalitas*)? *Where* in the beginning of the end is transformation and imitation of immortality located? In other words, how is the soul (*anima*) (un)like unto the Word (*verbum*) concerning immortality? So far, we have shown, immortality is a limit of the body implying no end and, more importantly, ongoing change. Immortality is the limit of the body changing *towards the end* (affinity) of the Word. The reverse of the coin of immortality in the body is what it reveals, outside of the body, as a limit: what is unchanging and without. Specifically, what is *similar* to the Word's immortality? The soul "seems to resemble the Word in two respects: *simplicity of essence and perpetuity of life*."[39]

---

38 Bernard of Clairvaux, On the *Song of Songs IV*, pp. 161-2. Zink (*SC* 511), SCC 81.5, l. 1-11: "Alias autem immortalis est anima, et in hoc nihilominus Verbo similis quidem, sed non aequalis. Nam in tantum superexcellit immortalitas Deitatis, ut Apostolus dicat de Deo: Qui solus habet immortalitatem (I Tim. VI, 16). Quod ego reor pro eo dictum, quod solus sit natura incommutabilis Deus, qui ait: Ego Dominus, et non mutor (Malach. III, 6). Vera namque et integra immortalitas tam non recipit mutationem, quam nec finem, quod omnis mutatio quaedam mortis imitatio sit. Omne etenim quod mutatur, dum de uno ad aliud transit esse, quodam modo necesse est moriatur quod est, ut esse incipiat quod non est."

39 Bernard of Clairvaux, On the *Song of Songs IV*, pp. 161-2. Zink (*SC* 511), SCC 81.5, l. 11-26: "Non mediocris tamen animae dignitas praesenti disputatione comperta est, quae gemina quadam vicinitate naturae Verbo appropiare videtur, simplicitate essentiae, et perpetuitate vitae."

Possibly the first aspect for immortality in what is human is the soul. However, this is not the case for Bernard. This is partly because of the union of body and soul. Indeed, though there is an immortal element to the soul, Bernard notes: "*it is plain that* [*the soul*] *changes in its affections* and it so recognizes that its likeness to God in its immortality *is incomplete* [...] *absolute and complete* immortality is [...] *in God alone*, in whom is *no change*."[40] The limit of immortality reveals the *likeness*, imperfect as it may be, to the Word, in whom perfection alone is unchanging, but also the soul's *likeness* to the body in that the soul's *affections*, like the body's element, change.

If there are as many deaths as are there are changes, where is immortality? In Bernard's formulation: "*But if every change necessarily involves death, where is immortality*?"[41] In other words, if change is inherent to human mortality, what aspect human existence is immortal? Of course, the obvious, first answer, is the immortal soul (*immortalis anima est*). As previously discussed, the soul is immortal because there is no distinction between its life (*vita*) and its existence, "[b]ut the soul is immortal, and since it has life in itself, and there is no way in which it can fall away from itself, so there is no way in which it can fall away from life."[42] The suggestion seems to place immortality in the soul and mutability in the body. However, this is *not* what Bernard does nor what he intends. The soul is immortal, not because it does not change, but only to the extent that, contrary to mutation, its life is *not* a shadow of death: the soul is its life and therefore the soul is never in the process of becoming. Hence, though motion *is* change for Bernard, motion is *not* also the same as death. The separation of motion and death allows reconciling the immortality of the soul (as *not* the shadow of death) on the one hand, and the possibility of the soul undergoing change (though *not* change of being). For indeed, the soul undergoes changes in affection, "But *the soul is immortal*, and since *it has life in itself*, and there is *no way* in which it can *fall away from itself*, so there is *no way* in which it can *fall away from life*."[43] These changes emphasize the one part of immortality, which distances the soul from the Word.

---

40 Bernard of Clairvaux, On the *Song of Songs IV*, pp. 161-2. Zink (*SC* 511), SCC 81.5, l. 11-26: "Verum cum constet suis affectibus mutari eam; agnoscat ita se Deo in immortalitate similem, ut sciat sibi deesse non modicam immortalitatis partem, soli cedens absolutam perfectamque immortalitatem, apud quem non est transmutatio, nec vicissitudinis obumbratio."

41 Bernard of Clairvaux, On the *Song of Songs IV*, pp. 161-2. Zink (*SC* 511), SCC 81.5, l. 11-26: "Quod si tot mortes quot mutationes, ubi immortalitas?"

42 Bernard of Clairvaux, On the *Song of Songs IV*, pp. 161-2. Zink (*SC* 511), SCC 81.5, l. 11-26: "quoniam cum ipsa sibi vita sit; sicut non est quo cadat a se, sic non est quo cadat a vita."

43 Bernard of Clairvaux, On the *Song of Songs IV*, pp. 161-2. Zink (*SC* 511), SCC 81.5, l. 11-26: "Attamen immortalis anima est; quoniam cum ipsa sibi vita sit; sicut non est quo cadat a se, sic non est quo cadat a vita."

To close this section on the second affinity of the soul to the Word, which is immortality, it may be asked, where is the body in the approximation of the soul to the Word? Far from being a repudiation of the body, the consolidation of change in the soul within immortality emerges as the Bernardine integration of location, intensity and duration. Change and motion, and by extension transformation or metamorphosis can, and indeed *do happen*, within the confines of immortality. The affects signify the body. So, the change of affects (*affectibus mutari*) in the immortal soul signify that which is not immortal in the soul, or that which passes. It is not so much that affects are *not* part of immortality. Change in affect is interesting to Bernard in the analysis of the soul in that they do not imply a change of being while providing a window into the movements of the soul, which are the very reflection of the soul's life. These transformations are *psycho-somatic* (to use an anachronistic term): they happen *in* the soul but cannot happen without interacting with the body because the soul affects the body and the body affects the soul. In short, immortality as perpetuity of life (*perpetuitate vitae*), like the simplicity of essence, in the identification of soul-life, reveals the (a)proximity of the soul to the Word *in* and *through* change as motion. Change as motion, as a derivative of desire, is the beginning of the end in the ongoing process of becoming and brings to the surface, though only superficially, of the body as inherent necessity characteristic of human immortality, i.e. of human existence vis-à-vis the eternity of the Word. The complete vindication of the body in motion concludes in the necessity of freedom as aperity. For this reason, freedom is appended to simplicity and immortality in-between the soul and the Word. Freedom is also at the limit of affinity where *free will is aperity*.

7.3 Free Will as Aperity

The final approximation of the soul to the Word is freedom or what can be literally translated as freedom of the will (*arbitrii libertas*), which is henceforth *free will*.[44] Of the three approximations, freedom of the will is what makes human beings most like the Word. The ladder of affinity brings the limits closer to the Word. At the limit, free will is aperity. This section explores *free will as aperity*, specifically vis-à-vis the body. Bernard devoted a whole oeuvre to the free will, entitled *De libero arbitrio*. The views are not always consistent across

44 Colleen McCluskey, "Bernard of Clairvaux on the Nature of Human Agency," *Revista Portuguesa de Filosofia* 64 (2008): 297-317, particularly 298: "In the later part of the 13th century, Walter of Bruges, writing in 1269, mentions Bernard by name in connection with the view that the will cannot be coerced by the intellect's judgement."

works. This section focuses on the commentaries of *On the Song of Songs*. In *On the Song of Songs, free will* is a quality, rather than a faculty, and a mode, rather than quantity, which gives *texture* to the pure aperity of limits in the affinity towards the Word. Free will extends as *aperity* as the body's limit tends towards the Word's power. The mode of the free will is therefore power (*forte*),[45] a power that increases the power of the soul's proximity to the Word. Bernard writes, "But one point has occurred to me which I cannot neglect, and which in no way detracts from the soul's greatness and its similarity to the Word, but *enhances* them."[46] The power (*forte*) of the free will in the approximation to the Verb is thus an instantiation of the power (*vir*) of the Verb as love. Hence, the soul's affinity of the Word to the body is extension of limits manifested in *aperity*. Free will thus is *the* limit of the body: ever producing, ever open, ever growing. As *limits* extend in aperity, only *resistance*, and *resistance* alone, is the counter-blow to *extension* which reveals the other side of the limit in *attraction*. These points are developed in the last two chapters of this section, namely *resistance* and *aperity*. The rest of this section is concerned with showing that the Word is the root of the free will in terms of *efficiency*. For this, the soul depends on the body and resembles mostly the Word. Free will is like the Word in origin and production. The free will is rooted in God through its proximity to the Word and like the Word, the free will is efficient manifestation of the divine in human beings. Bernard writes: "I cannot neglect [something] which in no way detracts from *the soul's greatness and its similarity to the Word*, but enhances them [...] free choice, *something clearly divine which shines forth in the soul like a jewel set in gold*."[47] As a mode of desiring-production the free will derives opposites during (*inter*) – which is preferable to between (*inter*) – as resistance in generation. Some capacities follow from the free will: "From it the

45 Emmanuel Falque, "Saint Bernard de Clairvaux : le pouvoir de la liberté," in *Dieu et la cité, le statut contemporain du théologico-politique*, ed. P. Capelle (Paris: Cerf, 2008), 49-61; Nico Den Bok, "Human and Divine Freedom in the Theology of Bernard of Clairvaux: a Systematic Analysis," *Bijdragen* 54, no. 3 (1993): 271-295; Vincent Brümmer, "Calvin, Bernard and the Freedom of the Will," *Religious Studies* 30, no. 4 (1994): 437-55; Dalia Marija Stanciene, "The Concept of Free Will in the Treatise by Bernard of Clairvaux Concerning Grace and Free Will," *Logos-Vilnus* 56 (2008): 39-49; Michel Corbin, *La grâce et la liberté chez saint Bernard de Clairvaux* (Paris: Cerf, 2002).

46 Bernard of Clairvaux, On the *Song of Songs IV*, pp. 162-3. Zink (*SC* 511), SCC 81.6, l. 1-21: "Sed enim adhuc unum occurrit, quod minime praeteribo: nec enim minus insignem similemve minus Verbo animam facit, et forte etiam plus."

47 Bernard of Clairvaux, On the *Song of Songs IV*, pp. 162-3. Zink (*SC* 511), SCC 81.6, l. 1-21: "Arbitrii libertas haec est, plane divinum quiddam praefulgens in anima, tanquam gemma in auro."

soul derives its *power of judgment*, and its *option of choosing* between *good and evil*, between *life and death*, in fact between light and darkness, and *any other concepts which are perceived by the soul as opposites*."[48] The recognition of opposites *as* opposites is only posterior to their production by the free will. The desiring-production of the free will produces good (production) and evil (resistance). Hence, the manifestation of free will is production, then recognition. Recognition of opposites within production is choice. The free will "is the eye of the soul which as censor and arbiter exercises discrimination and discernment between these things, and arbiter in discerning and free in choosing. It is *called free choice* because it is *exercised in these matters* in accordance with the *freedom of the will*."[49] The question of merit enters at the end process of freedom (production) and will (recognition) as a further process of generation in the circle of desiring-production. The *incipio* of the Word is the root of the creative power of the free will: in free will, like in the Word, origin and production (e)merge. Will is flow. Will emerges where origin and production merge. The will's quality for free choice is the condition for the possibility of the mode of willing freely, therefore, in the face of options. To will freely is to actualize options. The will is free (*liberum*) because it has arbitration or choice (*arbitrium*) concerning the actualization or desiring-production of the will (*voluntatis*). The will is free only within the dialectic of production where the arbitration of opposites is instantiated. Within the ongoing flow of desiring-production, desiring-production *is* the force (*fortis*) of the will and only becomes free by the ongoing production of *resistance* within generation and the subsequent recognition of this generation as opposites. The metaxological mode of desire is free will in *aesthetic mer(e)ology*. The limit of freedom reveals merit. What is the merit of flow? Does not flow inevitably lead to a synthesis of opposites where free will acts or to resistance where free will is omniscient? Merit gives texture to flow. The (de)merit or responsibility for generation is always after-the-fact, following generation and the *recognition* of emerging opposites within generation. Through the choice of the free will "a man can *acquire merit*; everything you do, whether good or ill, *which you had the choice*

48 Bernard of Clairvaux, On the *Song of Songs IV*, pp. 162-3. Zink (*SC* 511), SCC 81.6, l. 1-21: "Ex hac nempe inest illi inter bonum quidem et malum, nec non inter vitam et mortem, sed et nihilominus inter lucem et tenebras."

49 Bernard of Clairvaux, On the *Song of Songs IV*, pp. 162-3. Zink (*SC* 511), SCC 81.6, l. 1-21: "Nihilominus inter ipsa censorius quidam arbiter (is animae oculus) dijudicat et discernit, sicut arbiter in discernendo, ita in eligendo liber. Unde et liberum nominatur arbitrium, quod liceat versari in his pro arbitrio voluntatis."

of doing or not doing, is duly imputed to you for *merit or censure*."[50] The will (*voluntatis*), within the force of desiring-production, is manifest in a free (*liberum*) mode upon encountering and engaging with resistance (evil) within generation (good). The free will's engagement (*conatus*) with desiring-production, upon recognition of opposites, can be active (generation) or passive (resistance). Merit is the impetus of the will towards the manifestation of desiring-production (*conatus*), either of generation (*conatus recendendi*) or of resistance (*conatus a centro*), within the metaxological aperity of opposites. The *aesthetic mer(e)ological* configuration is diffused (*diffuso*) in the manifestation of the absolute beauty. As beauty (good) extends and ugliness (evil) contracts, so too goodness diffuses and evil infuses, for the efficient Word is active and efficient within the *body* precisely *as* the mode of generation in the will as it approximates the Word. The Word's efficiency gives texture to flow through the will: this is merit. The limit of freedom shows merit and demerit go in hand. Bernard writes, "And as a man is *rightly praised for refraining from doing wrong* when he *might* have done wrong, so also someone who *could have refrained from doing wrong* but *did* wrong, like someone who *could have done right but did not do so*, is *not free* from censure."[51] (De)merit is a mode of desiring-production in generation (good) and resistance (evil) as either necessary possibility (*conatus*) within possible necessity (free will) or as possible necessity (free will) within necessary possibility (*conatus*). There is merit when the choice or arbitration of free will as possible necessity determines the resistance-to-resistance (*conatus a centro*) within necessary possibility (*conatus*) to yield generation to the periphery (*conatus recendendi*) as manifestation of beauty. On the contrary, when there is no resistance-to-resistance by the arbitration or choice of the free will within possible necessity, then demerit follows. Inversely, within the choice or arbitration of free will as necessary possibility this time, generation *in* generation of desiring-production reconfigures *mer(e)ological* diffusion to yield modal manifestation of the will or merit. Again, inversely, the resistance in generation in necessary possibility of possible necessity, results in the desiring-production redirected towards the center (*conatus a centro*) or the ugly. The merit of the free will is the reconfiguration of the free will in

50 Bernard of Clairvaux, On the *Song of Songs IV*, pp. 162-3. Zink (*SC* 511), SCC 81.6, l. 1-21: "Unde et liberum nominatur arbitrium, quod liceat versari in his pro arbitrio voluntatis. Inde homo ad promerendum potis. Omne etenim quod feceris bonum malumve, quod quidem non facere liberum fuit, merito ad meritum reputatur."

51 Bernard of Clairvaux, On the *Song of Songs IV*, pp. 162-3. Zink (*SC* 511), SCC 81.6, l. 1-21: "Et, ut merito laudatur, non is tantum qui potuit facere mala, et non fecit, sed et qui potuit non facere bona, et fecit; ita malo non caret merito tam is qui potuit non facere mala, et fecit, quam is qui potuit facere bona, et non fecit."

desiring-production by the manifestation of beauty or ugliness. Merit, necessary possibility of possible necessity or in possible necessity of necessary possibility as generation or resistance, is possible alone with free will in *production, recognition* and *reconfiguration*. Naturally, without free will the modality of the free will, which is merit, is not possible: "*when there is no freedom, there is no merit or blame*."[52] Merits are therefore the office of human beings in contrast to animals who are "devoid of reason gain no merit, for they lack *deliberation* just as they lack *freedom*."[53] Yet the signification of the gesture remains powerful communication regardless of merit in animals, which humans also must reclaim.[54] The limits of free will in merit (*production, recognition* and *reconfiguration*) are rooted in the body, specifically in the human body. The animal body emphasizes the limits characteristic to the human body, which allow for merit and demerit. There is no merit in animals because they lack judgement. Animals, Bernard writes, "are *prompted by the senses, led by impulse, dominated by appetite*. They have *no judgment to rule their actions*, nor any *faculty for exercising judgment*, which is *reason*. It follows that they can incur *no judgment* since they exercise none."[55] What drives animals is pure impulse of the appetites due to lack of reason. "How can they reasonably be expected to exercise a faculty of reason which they have not received?"[56] Free will depends on reason. Yet, animal bodies move. What is the source of animal movement if not free will? Animals will, but not freely. The will of non-free animals is pure production void of possibilities, it is pure desiring-production as manifestation. Production void of possibilities implies that there is no active recognition or reactive reconfiguration. Desire and impulse are therefore not at odds with reason. However, they integrate only within desiring-production of free generation. The animal will is subject to nature. Nature moves animals. The human will is not subject to nature. Bernard writes, "It is only man who has not thus

52 Bernard of Clairvaux, On the *Song of Songs IV*, pp. 162-3. Zink (*SC* 511), SCC 81.6, l. 21-29: "Ubi autem non est libertas, nec meritum."

53 Bernard of Clairvaux, On the *Song of Songs IV*, pp. 162-3. Zink (*SC* 511), SCC 81.6, l. 21-29: "Propterea quae sunt carentia ratione animalia, nihil merentur; quia sicut deliberatione, ita et libertate carent."

54 Umberto Eco and Costantino Marmo, eds. *On the Medieval Theory of Signs*. Amsterdam: John Benjamins Publishing, 1989.

55 Bernard of Clairvaux, On the *Song of Songs IV*, pp. 162-3. Zink (*SC* 511), SCC 81.6, l. 21-29: "Sensu aguntur, feruntur impetu, rapiuntur appetitu. Neque enim judicium habent, quo se dijudicent sive regant, sed ne instrumentum quidem judicii, id est rationem."

56 Bernard of Clairvaux, On the *Song of Songs IV*, pp. 162-3. Zink (*SC* 511), SCC 81.6, l. 21-29: "Inde est quod non judicantur, quia non judicant. Quanam quippe ratione ab his exigatur ratio, quam non acceperunt?"

been dominated by nature, therefore he alone among living creatures is free."[57] Man may be dominated, not by nature, but by sin; man sins willfully, therefore man can be dominated by his will. Bernard goes on, "Yet *when sin intervenes*, even man is *dominated*, but *by his will*, not by *nature*, and he is *not thereby deprived of the liberty* which is his birthright. *What is done willingly is done freely*."[58] Yet, even when dominated by sin, the faculty of liberty is not lost. This is Bernard's attempt to *naturalize* an aspect of sin (*peccatum*). Sin is self-imposed by the will as limit, sin is willed limit, not by an external passive factor, but by an internal active will. The free will, in willing sin (resistance), manifests its limit whereby, much like animals dominated by nature, the body's function arises at the limit. In short, as with the other *affinities*, simplicity and immortality, the body is not a body of death in free will, the third affinity.

The *weight of the body* on the soul is not sin, but *the power of love*. Bernard notes, "It is by sin that *the corruptible body oppresses the soul*, but it is *the result of love, not of force*. For although the soul *fell of itself*, it *cannot rise of itself*, because the *will lies weak and powerless* through the *vitiated and depraved love of a corrupt body*, yet is at the same time *capable of a love of justice*."[59] Love as power is what explains not only why the body is a weight to the soul, but also why the body remains capable of free will and justice. At the limit, the body emerges as a power where *free will is aperity*. The bondage of sin has an effect on the body, which is compulsion: "in some strange and twisted way *the will deteriorates* and *brings about a state of compulsion* where *bondage cannot excuse the will*, because *the action was voluntary*, nor can the will, being fettered, *free itself from bondage*."[60] The compulsion of the will interferes with the freedom of the will and so, compulsion is deterioration. What is absolutely "strange and twisted" is that the deterioration and compulsion is voluntary:

57 Bernard of Clairvaux, On the *Song of Songs IV*, pp. 163-4. Zink (*SC* 511), SCC 81.7, l. 1-5: "Hanc vim a natura solus homo non patitur, et ideo solus inter animantia liber."

58 Bernard of Clairvaux, On the *Song of Songs IV*, pp. 163-4. Zink (*SC* 511), SCC 81.7, l. 1-5: "Et tamen interveniente peccato patitur quamdam vim et ipse, sed a voluntate, non a natura, ut ne sic quidem ingenita libertate privetur. Quod enim voluntarium, et liberum." The passage echoes the *voluntarist* formulations by Scotus.

59 Bernard of Clairvaux, On the *Song of Songs IV*, pp. 163-4. Zink (*SC* 511), SCC 81.7, l. 5-31: "Et quidem peccato factum est ut corpus quod corrumpitur, aggravet animam; sed amore, non mole. Nam quod surgere anima per se jam non potest quae per se cadere potuit, voluntas in causa est, quae corrupti corporis vitiato ac vitioso amore languescens et jacens, amorem pariter justitiae non admittit."

60 Bernard of Clairvaux, On the *Song of Songs IV*, pp. 163-4. Zink (*SC* 511), SCC 81.7, l. 5-31: "Ita nescio quo pravo et miro modo ipsa sibi voluntas, peccato quidem in deterius mutata, necessitatem facit: ut nec necessitas, cum voluntaria sit, excusare valeat voluntatem; nec voluntas cum sit illecta, excludere necessitatem."

"For this *bondage is in some sense voluntary*. It is an agreeable bondage which *flatters while it overcomes*, and *overcomes by flattery*, so that when the will has *betrayed itself* by consenting to sin, it cannot of itself throw off the yoke, nor reasonably excuse itself."[61] In other words, the free will, in its ultimate power of aperity at the limit, is capable of willing away its ability to will: the will has the power not to will! "For it is the will which, although free, by consenting to sin became slave to sin; and it is the will which puts itself in subjection to sin by its willing servitude."[62] At the limit of the will, the body reveals *necessity*. The affinity of the soul to the Word in the free will is necessity. The idea of necessity will be the subject of the following chapter entitled *resistance*. The rest of this section aims to set up the discussion for the following chapter by showing how necessity is the limit of the free will, which manifests *free will as aperity*. What follows proceeds by first numbering the characteristics proper to necessity, which are aperity, passivity, resistance, and transformation. These dimensions of necessity illustrate how the body is involved in the *affinity* to the Word. Necessity, as the will's limit, is the free will's mode of manifestation. Necessity reveals aperity. The will's capacity to will not willing freely reveals its limit in ultimate aperity: the will's capacity more manifested as free insofar as it can unwill its capacity to will freely. As such, the limit is not negative. The will imposes upon itself necessity by a mysterious, depraved, and vicious (*parvo et miro modo*) mode. This voluntary imposition of necessity is a change of the will by sin (*peccato quidem in deterius mutata*). However, and here is a capital caveat, the change of the will is *not* altogether negative or reprehensible precisely because it is *not* altogether voluntary. Hence, there is an ambivalent attitude towards the will's auto imposition of necessity (as limit) in amiable violence, in caressing while oppressing and in oppressing while caressing. In fact, the term for violence pre-eminently prejudges the nature of the constraint of necessity upon the will. Here, the term *vis* need not be translated as violence but translates, better, as power. Hence, there is on the one hand the violence (*vim*) of sin which imposes necessity on the free will by the free will, but there is also, on the other hand, the power (*vis*) of necessity, consequence of free will, beyond the grasp of sin. The rehabilitation of a part of necessity as power thus requires determining in what this power, which is not obvious at first, consists.

---

61 Bernard of Clairvaux, On the *Song of Songs IV*, pp. 163-4. Zink (*SC* 511), SCC 81.7, l. 5-31: "Est enim necessitas haec quodammodo voluntaria. Est favorabilis vis quaedam, premendo blandiens, et blandiendo premens: unde sese rea voluntas, ubi semel peccato consenserit, nec excutere jam per se, nec excusare tamen ullatenus de ratione queat."

62 Bernard of Clairvaux, On the *Song of Songs IV*, pp. 163-4. Zink (*SC* 511), SCC 81.7, l. 5-31: "Voluntas enim est, quae se, cum esset libera, servam fecit peccati, peccato assentiendo: voluntas nihilominus est, quae se sub peccato tenet, voluntarie serviendo."

The movement of the free will is double: application of necessity (*vis*) and continuation in necessity (*voluntarie serviendo*), in view of which the mutation of the free will after power and violence can be traced. The movement in question is the first one: how is violence separated from power in it and how is limitation of freedom a power? Where is the desire and the body? Necessity is passive. Necessity is a consequence of free will which is experienced passively as something undergone or suffered (*necessitate quam patior*) yet it is caused actively by the free will. Necessity in its double movement therefore holds captive the free will in that it is suffered and suffers the free will. Paradoxically, because of free will, necessity transforms free will and is at odds with it. Necessity makes the individual an alien to itself in terms of experience and in terms of body. The alienation of embodies experience is a consequence, in fact, of the necessity of the will. Bernard fleshes out the necessity upon the free will in what follows. In the closing words of the current sermon, there is a powerful description of the alienation of embodied necessity, which is key for the analysis because the experience of alienated embodiment is the origin and starting point of the treatment of free will and necessity. The reflection on the necessity of the will and the will to necessitate therefore is rooted in experience (*experior*), personal and social, and constitutes to that extent, a *hermeneutics of the body*, which is this time reversed, from the body, through freedom, to the Word. Necessity transforms or mutates the free will (*libero arbitro*). A dialogue with the listener expresses this fittingly, which is a rarity in the work of Bernard.[63] Necessity is resistance. Free will is the metaxological synthesis of necessity and possibility achieved through the reconfiguration of the free will in the merit of resistance or generation. The necessity imposed on possibility as demerit is simply a resistance to the aperity of desiring-production in *resistance to resistance* or in generation. The necessity of impossibility as demerit (sin) is a limit of aperity by the very possibility of aperity. The condition for the possibility of aperity as a mode of desiring-production is the necessary possibility for the limitation of the aperity in the necessary impossibility of the free will imposed by the free will. Hence, while the free will is never lost, it may be limited. Necessity transforms the will. Transformation of the will in the choice or arbitration of free will within self-imposed necessity of desiring-production yields also a transformation of the body. The description of the experience of necessity as bondage is framed in terms of a struggle from within, which is later transformed in the body through the body of the Word. What is the experience of the bondage? "'But,' you say, 'you will not make me deny the bondage which *I suffer*, which *I experience in myself and against which I struggle*

63 Zink (*SC* 511), SCC 81, p. 312, n. 1. Also, SCC 9.1-2 (*SC* 414, pp. 194-200).

continually.' '*Where* do you experience this bondage?' I ask. 'Is it *not in the will?*'"[64] The bondage of necessity is not in the will; otherwise, the will would diminish. Yet, "*Your will is not diminished because it is in bondage. Your will is strong to do what you cannot refuse to do, even if you struggle. Now where there is will there is freedom.*' But I speak of *natural freedom*, not spiritual, by which [...] *Christ has set us free*. [...] '*Where the spirit is, there is freedom.*'"[65] The experience of bondage or necessity is passive suffering (*patior*) which arises from within as resistance. "'But,' you say, 'you will not make me deny the bondage which *I suffer*, which I experience in myself and against which I struggle continually'."[66] The resistance in desiring-production is suffering merely as resistance that reveals opposites. This resistance is not the resistance *of* generation (the grotesque) but rather the resistance *within* generation that makes the *flow* of desiring-production possible in the first place. Intensity, duration and extension condition resistance *within* generation. The experience of bondage is therefore an interior tension inherent to desiring-production. Therefore, the locus of the experience of necessity as bondage is not in the will: "'Where do you experience this bondage?' I ask. 'Is it not in the will? Your will is not diminished because it is in bondage. Now where there is will there is freedom."[67] The will as power (*vis*) is free in uninterrupted desiring-production. The necessity of the free will, as condition for the possibility of desiring-production as power (*vir*) however is natural. Yet insofar as the will freely fails to resist resistance or resists generation, has an imposed necessity. The necessity of the free will in the necessary possibility or possible necessity of production and resistance is natural in the manifestation of the will as power (*vir*) within desiring production. The will's mode of manifestation is necessity. The constitutivity to the

64 Bernard of Clairvaux, On the *Song of Songs IV*, pp. 165-6. Zink (*SC* 511), SCC 81.9, l. 1-10: "Sed non me, inquis, decredere facies necessitatem quam patior, quam in memetipso experior, contra quam et assidue luctor. Ubinam, quaeso, hanc necessitatem sentis? Nonne in voluntate?"

65 Bernard of Clairvaux, On the *Song of Songs IV*, pp. 165-6. Zink (*SC* 511), SCC 81.9, l. 1-10: "Non ergo parum firmiter vis, quod et necessario vis. Multum vis quod nolle nequeas, nec multum obluctans. Porro ubi voluntas, et libertas. Quod tamen dico de naturali, non de spirituali, qua libertate, ut dicit Apostolus, Christus nos liberavit (Galat. IV, 31). Nam de illa idem ipse dicit: Ubi spiritus Domini, ibi libertas (II Cor. III, 17)."

66 Bernard of Clairvaux, On the *Song of Songs IV*, pp. 165-6. Zink (*SC* 511), SCC 81.9, l. 1-10: "Sed non me, inquis, decredere facies necessitatem quam patior, quam in memetipso experior, contra quam et assidue luctor."

67 Bernard of Clairvaux, On the *Song of Songs IV*, pp. 165-6. Zink (*SC* 511), SCC 81.9, l. 1-10: "Ubinam, quaeso, hanc necessitatem sentis? Nonne in voluntate? Non ergo parum firmiter vis, quod et necessario vis. Multum vis quod nolle nequeas, nec multum obluctans. Porro ubi voluntas, et libertas."

manifestation of the will is necessity as willed necessity or self-imposed restriction. The limit of the will is revealed in simultaneity of opposites, not contradiction: "the soul [...] is both held as a slave in this *voluntary and yet irresistible bondage*, and it *is free*."[68] The opposites are freedom and bondage. Bernard goes on to explain: the will "is *enslaved and free at the same time*; enslaved through bondage, free because of its will, and, which is *even stranger and more unfortunate*, guilty in proportion to its freedom, *and enslaved in proportion to its guilt, and therefore enslaved in proportion to its freedom*."[69] The simultaneous necessity and freedom of the free will is at the heart of desiring-production as pure aperity in the metaxological synthesis of opposites (necessity and possibility). The origin or beginning (*incipio*) of the manifestation of the will as free is the possibility of imposing restrictions upon the will in proportion to the will's freedom. To the extent that the will can manifest itself within the bounds of restriction as resistance against generation, the will manifests itself as truly free within the very parameters of the configuration of the *aesthetic mer(e) ological* mode of the body.

To summarize, necessity is the limit of the free will. We have said it: necessity, as the will's limit, is the free will's mode of manifestation. The central characteristics of necessity, which are aperity, passivity, resistance and transformation, express the modality of the free will at the limit. It is now time to bring to a conclusion our discussion on the *affinity* of the soul to the Word. We start by quoting from a later work by Bernard, *On Grace* where the treatment of free will (*libero arbitrio*) is laid out consistently with what is covered in *On the Song of Songs*. Bernard writes, "Let that be enough about freedom. In the book I have written on grace and free choice you may find other observations about the image and the likeness, but *I do not think they contradict the things I have been saying* [...] *I leave it to your judgment which is preferable*."[70] He goes on, "I have particularly mentioned three qualities: *simplicity,*

68 Bernard of Clairvaux, On the *Song of Songs IV*, pp. 165-6. Zink (*SC* 511), SCC 81.9, l. 1-10: "Ita anima miro quodam et malo modo sub hac voluntaria quadam ac male libera necessitate, et ancilla tenetur, et libera."

69 Bernard of Clairvaux, On the *Song of Songs IV*, pp. 165-6. Zink (*SC* 511), SCC 81.9, l. 1-10: "ancilla, propter necessitatem; libera, propter voluntatem: et quod magis mirum, magisque miserum est, eo rea quo libera, eoque ancilla quo rea, ac per hoc eo ancilla quo libera."

70 Bernard of Clairvaux, On the *Song of Songs IV*, pp. 165-6. Zink (*SC* 511), SCC 81.9, l. 1-10: "Miser ego homo, quis me liberabit a calumnia hujus pudendae servitutis? Miser, sed liber. Liber, quia homo; miser, quia servus. Liber, quia similis Deo; miser, quia contrarius Deo. O custos hominum, quare posuisti me contrarium tibi? Posuisti enim, cum non prohibuisti. Alioquin ipse me posui, et factus sum mihimetipsi gravis (Job VII, 20). Justissime quidem, ut hostis tuus hostis sit et meus; et qui tibi repugnat, repugnet et mihi. Ego vero

immortality, and freedom. And I think it must be clear to you *that through its inborn likeness* [...] the soul has a *great affinity with the Word.*"[71] The three qualities, which approximate the soul to the Word, are simplicity, immortality and freedom. These three approximations have been treated in this chapter as *affinities* (*affinitas*) – towards the end – or limits. The limits revealed in each of the affinities are weight, body and aperity. These, in turn, build on one another as they move in degrees towards the necessity of the free will which is limit and resistance. Furthermore, the Bernardine position makes clear there is no denigration of the body. On the contrary, the approximation of the soul also reveals the intimate relation of the body to the soul in simplicity and immortality, and ultimately the transformation of the will, which has as its point of departure embodied experience.

Conclusion

Limits, then, reveal the body's possibilities. Consequently, the chapter has explored the *limits* of the body in desiring-production and the possibility of overcoming *limits*. In response, the body was presented as *the weight of the word*. Then, *free will* was introduced, as it relates to the body as the *weight of the word* in *free will and the body* and, in direct response, it was stated that the *limits* of the body emerge in the *weight of the body*. The *limit* of the body thus provide the framework to understand the possibility of *free will*. Finally, the confines of the body arise at the *limit* of the body where *free will is aperity*. The *free will is aperity* because the *weight of the word* extends the body beyond its confines through the word where, at the limit, the body is production or *aperity*. The central contention sustained throughout this chapter was that the body is in constant production and therefore, the limits reveal not confines but rather generation: the body unfolds in constant generation. The important implication, according to this reasoning, is that *the body is aperity*. This aperity, before its manifestation as *aperity* proper, first arises as *limit* and *resistance* and, thereafter, as *apeirty* in necessity. Accordingly, the next chapter explores *resistance*.

---

qui tibi, ego qui mihimet contrarius factus sum, atque in membris meis invenio quod contradicat, et menti meae, et legi tuae; quis me liberabit de manibus meis?"

71 Bernard of Clairvaux, On the *Song of Songs IV*, pp. 168-9. Zink (*SC* 511), SCC 81.11, l. 1-14: "tria quaedam impraesentiarum praecipua commendata tenetis; simplicitatem, immortalitatem, libertatem."

CHAPTER 8

Resistance

For Bernard, limits are not reducible to confines, as they reveal the ongoing dynamic generation of the body. In generation, the body overcomes limits only by enduring *resistance*. For this reason, an exploration of *resistance* is the next moment of interest in the *metamorphosis of love*. *Where* and *how* do bodies *resist*? *Resistance* arises at the *limit* where the tension between possibility and necessity unravels the constitution of aperity, which is for Bernard the unfolding of free will. Accordingly, the present chapter aims to understand *how resistance* arises at the *limit*, or better, from the *limit*, and at articulating *why* free will arises therein. A reflection on *resistance* is a reflection on free will. Free will arises from resistance in three moments: necessity, possibility and production. The first moment is *the necessity of the free will* (8.1), wherein Bernard grounds free will in the simplicity of the soul construed as the image of God. As such, for Bernard, free will is the image of God's simplicity in the soul. Paradoxically, the limit of free will is the *resistance* of the will or, alternatively, necessity, for the free will, in willing necessity against itself as a limit, constitutes *resistance*. This *resistance*, whereby the free will wills most freely, is transformative. The second moment, *possibility and free will* (8.2), focuses on the paradoxical dynamic whereby the free will *wills* necessity, rather than mere possibility, against itself, giving way to duplicity. In duplicity, the will operates in necessity and in possibility. The third moment of *resistance* is *free will as desiring-production* (8.3). In it, necessity, which is *resistance*, is a *sine qua non* for the possibility of willing at all, because the free will *wills* fully, ultimately as aperity or action, only when will *wills* against itself in resistance. Then alone is the free will fully free or generative in desiring production. The itinerary of resistance originates in necessity of the limits, therefore, and culminates in the *aperity* of the free will's efficiency where free will is *aperity*. *Resistance* is the condition for *aperity*, which Bernard understands as pure will or action.

8.1 The Necessity of the Free Will

The first aspect of *resistance* is *the necessity of the free will*. For Bernard, *resistance* arise at the *limits*. What are these *limits*? In common parlance, limits delineate the confines of a space, a place or a capacity. The limits arise, for Bernard, *towards the end* (*ad + finem*), construed not in terms of confinement,

 | DOI:10.30965/9783846767504_010

delineation and constrain, but in terms of *affinity* or a kind of attraction. The attraction in question is, for Bernard, the *affinity* of the soul to the Word, which is the soul's simplicity. The simplicity of the soul is more than the mere absence of composition. Simplicity is perfect unity in action. Simplicity is therefore the integrity of the soul, expressed most perfectly as free will, from whence arises the possibility of multiplicity and faction, and based on which a reflection on the nature of human action begins. *Affinity* is simplicity as free will. The will is free, because it is simple, and when it is simple, and the will is simple only insofar as it can (possibility) *will* against its constitutive simplicity, whereas the *will* resists the divine image even at the expense of simplicity (necessity) in refusing freedom. Accordingly, the limit is found precisely where the will *wills* against itself. The will that wills against itself resists possibility and, in willingly resisting the possible, imposes necessity upon itself, that is, the will thus recognizes limits as constitutive of freedom. Therein, the free will undergoes pressure, which scatters its power from the harmony of simplicity into the chaos of multiplicity. Since limits are constitutive of freedom, necessity arises as resistance, hence the paradox, not contradiction, on *the necessity of free will.* Because necessity is *resistance,* the will, as will, may *will* against itself. In the paradox of the free will's necessity, *resistance* arises at the point where the will manifests itself in its greatest form, which is in its capacity for negation. The *necessity of the free will* was historically identified with sin, either as an inherent ontological state of the soul (Augustine) which can be alleviated by grace but which is never truly healed, or as a weight on free will, but nothing really which a well-disposed will cannot overcome (Pelagius) and as something only which grace improves and transforms. The first approach underscores the will's utter dependence on grace even for the possibility of willing to will well, while the second (especially later with Julian of Aeclenum), emphasizes the ability of the free will to will what is good irrespective of grace. These alternative approaches to the nature of free will overlook the nature of *necessity*, resulting in a bifurcation of realities at play in human agency: grace and nature. It is within the heritage of this century-old debate that Bernard attempts to articulate *resistance* as the *necessity of the free will.* Bernard's position is as follows: necessity is not coterminous with sin and necessity is constitutive of human existence. Therefore, *resistance* does not hinder free will. Rather, and conversely, *resistance* reveals will as will in its necessity. Bernard presents his vision of the *necessity of free will* from the vantage point of *affinity* thereby showing how the *limits*, which emerge in *affinity*, give way to *resistance*. Thus, the *affinity* of the soul to the Word, in simplicity, is *first* experienced in *resistance* as constitutive of the soul's affinity to the Word, then, *second*, the possibility for the soul's *duplicity* explains multiplicity, or the possibility of *limits*, and third, the unfolding of the Word in the *necessity of the free will* is a transformative act of desiring-production.

Turning first to *resistance* and *the necessity of the free will*, according to Bernard, *resistance is constitutive* of the soul's affinity to the Word, so that, as stated above, *necessity* is *resistance*. Yet again, not all necessity is the product of sin. This raises the question: how does sin affects the will or, alternatively, what is natural, and thus not sinful, about the necessity of the will? Failure to distinguish the sinful and the natural in necessity results in a failure to understand the process of transformation of the body and soul in the *affinity* to the Word. Simplicity is the basis for the *affinity* of the soul to the Word. Moreover, simplicity, for Bernard, implies free will, which is, in turn, the basis of the soul's immortality. To determine whether *resistance* is natural or sinful, we must ask whether the *affinity* is inherent to the soul and to the Word. In other words, do human beings enjoy a natural *affinity* to the Word and if so, how is this *affinity* affected by sin (necessity) or is the *affinity* altogether lost and is it at best purified by grace or at worst restored by grace? In other words, does grace effect a metamorphosis or, rather, does grace subvert human nature thereby not metamorphosing but rather replacing human nature? The answer to these questions depends on the notion of *resistance* at the *limit* in *affinity*. When discussing *affinity* at the limit, the relationship between the soul and the Word depends on similarity, the measure for which is resemblance. Now, conversely, in *resistance, affinity* depends on inequality or *dissemblance*, which presupposes, naturally, some foundational equality. In light of this, the question arises, then, on the nature of the *dissemblance* of the free will. The soul approaches the Word in a three-fold likeness. As in semblance, in dissemblance the affinity to the Word is not *lost* but simply deformed, which implies *metamorphosis* in the interplay of semblance and dissemblance, rather than mere subversion, and therefore complete loss and replacement. To express the dynamism of semblance and dissemblance, Bernard uses the word *impression*. The *affinity* of the Word is impressed as the soul's simplicity. Accordingly, Bernard frames the question, "Now there is one point made which I fear may cause offence unless it is explained. If I am not mistaken, there are some standing here who will be somewhat irritated by what I have to say. Do you remember that when I attributed to the soul a *threefold likeness to the Word*, I said it would be more accurate to say it was *impressed into the soul*?"[1] The threefold (*Trina*) likeness of the soul to the Word is impressed (*insigna*) on the soul.

1 Bernard of Clairvaux, On the *Song of Songs IV*, pp. 171-3. Zink (*SC* 511), SCC 82.2, l. 1-25: "Est itaque in his quae dicta sunt aliquid, quod, ut vereor ego, offendiculum dare queat, si non complanetur. Et, ni fallor, sunt de hic stantibus, quibus scrupulum movit quod dicere volo.

However, Bernard hastens to articulate the problematic. He writes, "Now this may seem to conflict with some passages in the Scriptures, as, for example, that one in the Psalms: 'Although a man is held in honor, he has no understanding; he is compared to foolish beasts and has become like them;' and again: 'They changed their glory into the likeness of a calf who eats hay', and what has been said plainly by the Person of God: 'You thought, wicked man, that I was like you.' *There are many other passages which seem to state that God's likeness in man was utterly destroyed by sin.*"[2] While some passages suggest the likeness of God in human beings is signed (*insigna*), which means it cannot be lost, other passages state that human beings become like beasts, thereby suggesting, this time, that the likeness to God may be lost, effaced or destroyed (*deleo*). The question is then, whether *affinity* is natural (*insigna*) or whether it is a labour of grace after its destruction (*delo*) or, perhaps, something of each? Bernard wirtes, "What shall we say to that? Are we to deny that *these attributes exist in God at all, and say that we must look for others in which to find this likeness? Or can we say that they do exist in the soul, but not necessarily, and therefore they are not inseparable from it?* Far from it. *They do exist both in God and in the soul, and do so always.* And we need have no regrets for anything we have said; it is all supported by unquestionable and absolute truth."[3] The strategy to address the question begins with how Bernard frames the question. Remarkably, the first step is not to deny the possibility of the existence of free will or attributes of simplicity in human beings, but to emphasize the need for a foundation of these attributes outside of human beings. This assumes, for Bernard, that the constitution of the soul includes necessarily free will such that if free will is destroyed, the soul is destroyed as well. This is why the first question is not whether the soul is free in fact, but that if freedom is not found in God as its

---

Trina illa Verbi similitudo, quam animae assignavimus, imo qua insignitam advertimus, recolitisne quod etiam inseparabiliter inesse illi visa fuerit nobis?"

2 Bernard of Clairvaux, On the *Song of Songs IV*, pp. 171-3. Zink (*SC* 511), SCC 82.2, l. 1-25: 'Id quidem videatur aliquibus Scripturarum testimoniis obviare, ut verbi gratia, est illud in psalmis: Homo, cum in honore esset, non intellexit; comparatus est jumentis insipientibus, et similis factus est illis (Psal. XLVIII, 13, 21); et item illud: Mutaverunt gloriam suam in similitudinem vituli comedentis fenum (Psal. CV, 20), sed et quod aperte dictum est in persona Dei: Existimasti inique, quod ero tui similis (Psal. XLIX, 21): et pleraque alia, quae similitudinem Dei in homine post peccatum deletam concorditer asseverare videntur."

3 Bernard of Clairvaux, On the *Song of Songs IV*, pp. 171-3. Zink (*SC* 511), SCC 82.2, l. 1-25: "Quid ergo dicemus ad haec? Tria illa in Deo minime esse, et sic alia quaerenda, in quibus similitudinem assignemus? aut esse quidem in Deo, sed non in anima, et ne sic quidem in his similitudinem inveniri? aut esse et in anima, sed posse etiam non inesse, ac per hoc non inseparabilia esse? Absit! Et in Deo, et in anima sunt, et semper insunt; nec est quod nos aliquid horum dixisse poeniteat, ita totum subnixum est indubitata et absolutissima veritate."

source, then it must be found elsewhere. Human beings cannot be human beings without God in terms of grace, but simply in terms of their inherent constitution, which most fundamentally includes free will. The alternative option, and this is the second step in the Bernardine reflection, is to grant that the free will is not necessarily part of the human soul. In this case, the free will can be separated from the soul and so it is not part of the constitution of a human being. This would amount to saying that the free will is given by God by means of grace. In other words, according to the second interpretation, free will is grace. Therefore, the first option includes free will in the human constitution while the second option does not. In both cases, free will comes from God. This leads to the Bernardine conclusion, which offers a *middle way*. Since free will exists in God *always*, according to Bernard, God's *free will* is therefore the source of free will in human beings. Thus, free will in a sense exists also in the soul, *always*, which means free will is necessary, and therefore inseparable from the soul. Free will, for Bernard, is the human imprinted likeness of the triune simplicity of God in the soul, and it is constitutive of human beings. As such, it cannot be destroyed, for to destroy free will would amount to destroying what it means to be human. In addition, in this way free will is naturalized: whatever its weaknesses, will is not such only or primarily because of sin, but because of finitude. Whereas in God free will exists always, is therefore eternal, and without fault, in human beings, because of *limits*, free will is manifested as *necessary resistance. Resistance* is free will as necessity of human constitution.

Thus, for Bernard, free will is resistance in the limit, irreducible to sin. Resistance at the limit is modal manifestation. Modal manifestation can express vestiges of divine free will which are necessary for human constitution but which always remain imperfect and which always fall short of divine free will, the source of human free will. For Bernard, free will is manifested as a sign such that free will in necessity signifies. The free will is impressed (*in+signare*) in a three-fold likeness of the soul to the Word: "Do you remember that when I attributed to the soul a *threefold likeness to the Word,* I said it would be more accurate to say it was *impressed into the soul*?"[4] Bernard, like Augustine, identifies the image of God in humanity with a triune vestige, the image of the Trinity (*vestigia trinitatis*) or the traces of God left behind as an imprint of the divine origin of humanity. There are, however, some important aspects of departures. The vestige of the trinity as the image of God (*imago dei*) in Augustine reflects the Trinity in the soul's triangulation of mind-love-knowledge or alternatively

4 Bernard of Clairvaux, On the *Song of Songs IV*, pp. 171-3. Zink (*SC* 511), SCC 82.2, l. 1-25: "Trina illa Verbi similitudo, quam animae assignavimus, imo qua insignitam advertimus, recolitisne quod etiam inseparabiliter inesse illi visa fuerit nobis?"

mind-will-word.[5] However, as mere images in the Plotinian scheme of emanation, the images of the Trinity always fall short as signs of the Trinitarian image and signify without efficiency or performativity, much like the smoke of a fire signifies a fire without being the fire itself.[6] In other words, the image of God in Augustine is not efficient. The Bernardine sign in the *On the Song of Songs* goes beyond Augustine and indeed tradition by postulating the three-fold likeness of the soul, ultimately expressed in the freedom of the will, as efficient signification.[7] The model is the incarnation of the Word as the basis for the efficient soul-Word approximation: "For the Word of God is living and efficient" (Heb 4.1). The free will as sign of God's Trinity is therefore not simply a vague reminder of God in creation but rather the very governance and presence of God in the constant manifestation of the Word embracing *all* bodies: "I will pour my spirit on all flesh" (Joel 2.28). Free will and body are therefore intimately interweaved in Bernard's conception of the necessity of the free will. Not only is the free will therefore the way God governs the world through a deeply intimate and organic presence within the world through the Word (possibility of action) and Spirit (possibility of experience) in the manifestation of generation (beauty), it is also the way human beings are granted the possibility of becoming organs of that body. The body emerges as action, then, because the divine likeness is imprinted on the soul as embodied efficiency in the Word. In this sense, the free will is manifested as efficiency – the free will is manifested as pure aperity. However, if the free will is pure aperity as the efficient mode of divine agency in the world, what and how does the *necessity of the free will* signify? In other words, if free will necessarily signifies, then is signification not meaningless or, at least, irrelevant and needless? Bernard approaches this question by drawing a distinction between free will and necessity. For Bernard, the free will, the vestige of the Trinity, is *impressed* (*insignare*) on the soul, whereas necessity is not. Bernard is aware that the necessity of free will distances the soul from the Word: "Now this may seem to conflict with some passages in the Scriptures, as, for example, that one in the Psalms: 'Although a man is held in honor, he has no understanding; he is compared to foolish beasts and has become like them;' and again: 'They changed their glory into the likeness of a calf who eats hay', and what has been said plainly by the Person of God:

5 Augusitne, *On the Trinity*, 9.4.
6 Augustine, *On Christian Doctrine*, 2.3.
7 Susannah Ticciati, *A New Apophaticism: Augustine and the Redemption of Signs* (Leiden: Brill, 2013).

'You thought, wicked man, that I was like you.'"[8] It may even be suggested that there is the suggestion that necessity (sin) destroys (*deleo*) affinity altogether, which would amount to the loss of the freedom of the will: "There are many other passages which seem to state that God's likeness in man was utterly destroyed by sin."[9] At stake is the freedom of the will in the face of necessity. How does the freedom of the will and the will's imposed necessity coexist as opposites? Bernard writes, "What shall we say to that? Are we to deny that *these attributes exist in God at all, and say that we must look for others in which to find this likeness? Or can we say that they do exist in the soul, but not necessarily, and therefore they are not inseparable from it?*"[10] If lost, then free will is not the basis for the affinity of the soul to the Word, or else it is in the soul, but only as a contingency so that even if lost, the soul remains the soul and it remains somehow, on the basis of a different affinity, like unto the Word. Bernard answers, "Far from it. *They do exist both in God and in the soul, and do so always.*"[11] In spite of the dissemblance, the affinity of the Word in efficient action as desiring-production is not lost precisely because the production does not end but continues diffusion as a mode of the free will. The freedom of the will is not lost or destroyed by necessity. What then is necessity of the free will? The idea that free will is somehow governed by necessity is overwhelming, for how could free will remain free under the schedule of sin? Augustine struggled with the question of the effects of sin on the image of God in human beings. While Augustine's views are difficult to summarize, he postulated original sin as a way to understand why the free will inherently tends towards what Bernard later calls necessity or the imposition of limits. Bernard follows (the 'later')

8 Bernard of Clairvaux, On the *Song of Songs IV*, pp. 171-3. Zink (*SC* 511), SCC 82.2, l. 1-25: "Id quidem videatur aliquibus Scripturarum testimoniis obviare, ut verbi gratia, est illud in psalmis: Homo, cum in honore esset, non intellexit; comparatus est jumentis insipientibus, et similis factus est illis (Psal. XLVIII, 13, 21); et item illud: Mutaverunt gloriam suam in similitudinem vituli comedentis fenum (Psal. CV, 20)."

9 Bernard of Clairvaux, On the *Song of Songs IV*, pp. 171-3. Zink (*SC* 511), SCC 82.2, l. 1-25: "et pleraque alia, quae similitudinem Dei in homine post peccatum deletam concorditer asseverare videntur."

10 Bernard of Clairvaux, On the *Song of Songs IV*, pp. 171-3. Zink (*SC* 511), SCC 82.2, l. 1-25: "Quid ergo dicemus ad haec? Tria illa in Deo minime esse, et sic alia quaerenda, in quibus similitudinem assignemus? aut esse quidem in Deo, sed non in anima, et ne sic quidem in his similitudinem inveniri? aut esse et in anima, sed posse etiam non inesse, ac per hoc non inseparabilia esse? Absit! Et in Deo, et in anima sunt, et semper insunt; nec est quod nos aliquid horum dixisse poeniteat, ita totum subnixum est indubitata et absolutissima veritate."

11 Bernard of Clairvaux, On the *Song of Songs IV*, pp. 171-3. Zink (*SC* 511), SCC 82.2, l. 1-25: "Et in Deo, et in anima sunt, et semper insunt."

Augustine in the view that the free will, and therefore the image of God, is never destroyed but only deformed. Augustine explains the stain of original sin on free will in terms of Plotinian ontology of similitude. The image of God may resemble Christ in various degrees. Hence, the free will is deformed or reformed by grace. Bernard agrees in substance with Augustine. However, by identifying free will with the image of God, the Abbot of Clairvaux frames necessity in terms of manifestation and concealment. The necessity of the free will is the concealment of the freedom of the will rather than its destruction: "Now when Holy Scripture speaks of the unlikeness that has come about, *it says not that the likeness has been destroyed, but concealed by something else which has been laid over it.*"[12] The exact term used to signify the effect of necessity on the freedom of the will is not *to cover* in the Latin but the compound verb *superducta* (sufix *super* + verb *ductare*). The prefix can imply space (besides/over/on top), time (duration) and degree (beyond). The verb ductare, therefore, means to lead – later, the free will returns to the Word in *reduction*. To frame the necessity of the free will in terms of the verb *superductare* is much richer and conveys a dynamism which the translation *to cover* hardly captures. The necessity of the free will alters the modality of the expression of the will *as* free in terms of the movement of desiring-production. The manifestation of the desiring-production changes in terms of intensity, duration and extension in the metaxological aperity of generation and resistance: relative direction of diffusion (to the center or to the exterior), duration of the extension, and its limits as extension. The necessity of the free will transforms in a sense the free will and conditions its manifestation thereby limiting its modality while always maintaining desiring-production. Moreover, the constraints of modal expression, necessity, constitute the limits of free will. The constraints of necessity on the freedom of the will is simply a restriction on the modal quality of the expression of aperity by the freedom of the will. The transformation of the free will as a super-cover (*superducta*) or *necessitating-production* is deeply rooted in the *body*. The process of transformation is not only spiritual, but also corporeal. To explain this, Bernard employs language of the incarnation (*forma*): "The soul *has not in fact put off its original form* but has put on one foreign to it. *The latter is an addition; the former has not been lost.* This addition *can hide the original form, but it cannot blot it out.* The gold laments that it has grown dim, but it is still gold; its pure color is faded, but the base of the color is not altered. The *simplicity of the soul remains unshaken in its fundamental being,* but it is not seen because it is

12 Bernard of Clairvaux, On the *Song of Songs IV*, pp. 171-3. Zink (*SC* 511), SCC 82.2, l. 1-25: "Sed quod Scriptura loquitur de dissimilitudine facta, non quia similitudo ista deleta sit loquitur, sed quia alia superducta."

covered."[13] The metaphor of gold on the one hand is revealing of the question of intensity, signified by the shining gold, changed through necessity. Furthermore, the metaphor frames, as has been the discussion of the free will as image in the affinity of the soul to the Word, in terms of beauty because gold is generally associated with beauty or as an adornment of aesthetic coveting. These are reinforced by the powerful employment of the term *forma*, which is not only aesthetic but also deeply rooted in bodily beauty as an alternative to image, or *imago* which Bernard brings together. The *forma* refers to the incarnation, which the Word assumes. The desire of the Word for the *body* in the incarnation introduces a further element of desire-transformation in the willed necessity of the free will. The necessity of the free will is no longer another aspect obstructing the aperity of the free will, but becomes a condition for the possibility of desiring-production. Summarily, Bernard emphasizes the simplicity of the soul. He preserves the freedom of the will at all cause. "The *simplicity of the soul remains unshaken in its fundamental being*, but it is not seen because it is covered by the disguise *of human deception, pretence, and hypocrisy*."[14] In spite of sin, the soul's simplicity is preserved inherently, albeit in disguise, and covered because of sin. The process of the manifestation of free will within the bounds of limits constitutes necessity. In short, while necessity does overlap with sin, it is not only, nor primarily, sin. The necessity of the free will as a *stance* emerges in the limit where necessity is not free will but constitutive modal manifestation.

8.2 Possibility and Free Will

So, *resistence* is necessity, and necessity is, accordingly, constitutive of the soul's affinity to the Word through manifestation. As such, the simplicity of the soul's affinity to the Word is preserved. However, the free will is fundamentally experienced as divided in duplicity. The second moment in *resistance* is therefore focused no longer on the necessity of the free will, but on its possibility, specifically the possibility of duplicity and multiplicity. While the simplicity of the Word is preserved, the duplicity of the free will is inevitable in the necessity

13 Bernard of Clairvaux, On the *Song of Songs IV*, pp. 171-3. Zink (*SC* 511), SCC 82.2, l. 25-37: "Non plane anima nativam se exuit formam, sed superinduit peregrinam. Illa addita, non ista perdita est. Obscuratum aurum plangit, sed aurum tamen; mutatum colorem optimum, sed non fundamentum coloris evulsum."

14 Bernard of Clairvaux, On the *Song of Songs IV*, pp. 171-3. Zink (*SC* 511), SCC 82.2, l. 25-37: "Obscuratum aurum plangit, sed aurum tamen; mutatum colorem optimum, sed non fundamentum coloris evulsum. Manet in fundamento prorsus inconcussa simplicitas, sed minime apparet duplicitate operta humanae dolositatis, simulationis, hypocrisis."

of resistance. The most puzzling aspect of this is that simplicity and duplicity co-exist in the free will. In other words, how can the free will impose necessity on itself (simplicity) and yet maintain the possibility of duplicity? The central contention of this chapter is that the possibility of duplicity is a condition for generation in the resistance of necessity. Differently put, the resistance of the free will, which is constitutive of what it means to be human, is conditioned on the possibility of duplicity. This is because there is no necessity without possibility. The free will *wills* only insofar as it can possibly *will* otherwise. That is, insofar as the free will is duplicitous. What, then, is duplicity? Duplicity arises in experience as originary and unifying, engendering chaos while accounting for the possibility of imposing necessity on the body.

First, duplicity arises in experience. The necessity of the free will imposed by the free will is duplicitous, not simple. In fact, if generation and resistance is possible at all, it is because the mode of the will is *experienced* fundamentally as duplicity. The duplicity of human experience and the tensions that ensue therein and which are then manifested in the natural and foundation affinity of the soul to the Word, must not be overlooked or confused because duplicity, like resistance, is constitutive of human beings. Failure to appreciate it constitutes a failure to understand the human free will under a threefold scheme of necessity, possibility, and ultimately under the transformation of desire.

Second, duplicity is manifested as oringinary and unifying. Duplicity as *committere*, in addition to the proposed translation as *incongruous*, implying resistance and tension, also has the double meaning to unite or to begin. Bernard writes, "How *incongruous is the mixture of simplicity and duplicity*! How unworthy is so base an *addition* to so pure a foundation!"[15] There is, paradoxically and simultaneously, unity, tension and resistance in the beginning. Hence, in the duplicity of the necessity and possibility of the freedom of the will, there is an image of unity: the image of God, which is the image of the free will.

Third, duplicity engenders chaos akin to the disintegration of death. The effects of duplicity engender death: "*For although it is not deprived of life, yet the gift of life cannot preserve it in the body*."[16] The duplicity of necessity raises therefore confusion (*confussion*) or disorder: "*Yet the original simplicity persists in every soul along with the duplicity, and the co-existence of these increases the confusion*. Its immortality continues also, but in an obscure and debased form,

15 Bernard of Clairvaux, On the *Song of Songs IV*, pp. 173-4. Zink (*SC* 511), SCC 82.3, l. 1-35: "Quam incongrue simplicitati duplicitas admiscetur! quam indigne tali fundamento talis structura committitur!"

16 Bernard of Clairvaux, On the *Song of Songs IV*, pp. 173-4. Zink (*SC* 511), SCC 82.3, l. 1-35: "Nam, etsi non privatur vita, vitae tamen beneficium suo corpori jam non sufficit vindicare."

with the dark clouds of physical death of the body overshadowing it."[17] The suggestion is that duplicity is not only a spiritual force, but also a physical one which undertakes decomposition first of the soul's simplicity and progressively of the body as well.

Fourth, duplicity weighs on the body. Necessity, as previously noted, weighs on the body when manifested as the source of the law, which regulates the members after the free will imposes necessity on itself. Now just as the spirit of God comes down upon all flesh, so too the law of rebellion holds *all* members of the body captive insofar as what the will imposes in necessity now surpasses the reach of the will in the new law directing the members under necessity. Bernard continues: "Now this necessity, incurred voluntarily, and the rebellious law which has descended upon the members [...] weighs upon that freedom, and binds the creature which is free by nature, subjecting it to slavery by its own will. Then it covers it with ignominy, so that it will serve the law of sin in its flesh, though unwillingly."[18] Duplicity includes the possibility of imposing necessity on the body.

Fifth, duplicity veils freedom. The metaphor of gold as the shining object, which the law of necessity blurs, has a complimentary metaphor in the cloak covering freedom. The law of necessity has its utmost expression at the threshold where the body and freedom intertwine. That is, at the moment where freedom loses grip even over the body. Hence, in spite of the deep consequences that necessity has even on the regulation of the body which are most visible *in* the body, freedom remains intact. Bernard writes, "Duplicity of heart does not wipe out essential simplicity; nor does death – whether the voluntary death due to sin or the necessary death of the body – destroy the immortality of nature; again, the compulsion of voluntary servitude does not extinguish free will."[19] Duplicity veils freedom, and with this veil, produces a counterfeit of freedom, which gives the appearance either of a false freedom or of

---

17 Bernard of Clairvaux, On the *Song of Songs IV*, pp. 173-4. Zink (*SC* 511), SCC 82.3, l. 1-35: "Sed perseverat nihilominus in omni anima cum originali duplicitate generalis simplicitas, ut de collatione confusio augeatur: perseverat aeque immortalitas, sed fusca et tetra, irruente tenebrosa corporeae mortis caligine."

18 Bernard of Clairvaux, On the *Song of Songs IV*, pp. 175-7. Zink (*SC* 511), SCC 82.5, l. 1-22: "Sed et voluntaria illa necessitas, et contraria lex inflicta membris, de qua proximo sermone disserui, eidem incubat libertati, et liberam natura creaturam per propriam ipsius voluntatem, dum allicit, subjicit servituti, implens faciem ejus ignominia, ita ut vel carne serviat legi peccati, et non volens."

19 Bernard of Clairvaux, On the *Song of Songs IV*, pp. 175-7. Zink (*SC* 511), SCC 82.5, l. 1-22: "Neque enim essentiae simplicitati praescribit duplicitas cordis; non naturae immortalitati mors, aut voluntaria peccati, aut necessaria corporis; non arbitrii libertati necessitas voluntariae servitutis."

a destroyed freedom. Thus, the image of free will, with its counterfeit being a semblance of necessity, is also, contrariwise, an impression of the real will, which duplicity discloses.

Sixth, freedom is manifested by degrees because of duplicity. Bernard matches the degrees of bodies to the degrees whereby freedom is unveiled from duplicity's counterfeit veil: "for as the soul retains its *freedom by virtue of the will*, yet it conducts itself as a slave; and this imposes compulsion on it."[20] On a side note, the body and the will are then inscribed within the degrees of love. Conversely, the affinity to freedom, within the self-imposed *law* of the members issued by necessity, also results in degrees of dissimilarity or unlikeness. Freedom framed in terms of necessity as the law of the body is therefore a *necessity in becoming*: the freedom of the will in the face of necessity stands between voluntarism and determinism and beyond compatibilism as manifestation of will or *mer(e)ological aesthetics* – the process whereby the parts in multiplicity progressively and by degrees manifest the unity of the whole in agency of free willing.

Seventh, duplicity as the cloak covering but not destroying freedom is the basis for Bernard's paradigm of knowledge (epistemology) and morality (ethics) rooted not in vision, but in the body. Interestingly, Bernard offers a glimpse of a paradigm (*mer(e)ological aesthetics*) as the basis of epistemology in a revolutionary paradigm of knowledge grounded not in vision but in the body.[21] He writes, "Is *deceit not like the folds of a cloak*, asks Bernard, being not inborn but put on and, so to speak, with the needle of sin stitched on to simplicity, as death is to immortality, and compulsion to freedom?"[22] The cloak metaphor binds necessity not only with the servitude of the members, but this time also with deceit, as *diplois* (a cloak or layer), which implies at once the imposition of necessity as well as its delusion, fraud or deceit. The fraud of necessity on the body is not only one of escaping the freedom of the will but, in the process of becoming *as* freedom, necessity also colors or modifies the body's capacity to know. In the process of desiring-production, necessity is thus expressed as not only resistance to generation. In the recognition and the resisting of resistance *as* resistance by the freedom of the will, the free will is impaired, thus resulting in the failure to resist resistance. The manifestation of desiring

20 Bernard of Clairvaux, On the *Song of Songs IV*, pp. 175-7. Zink (*SC* 511), SCC 82.5, l. 1-22: "Et bene sicut diploide, ubi veste veluti duplicata, manente libertate propter voluntatem, servilis nihilominus conversatio necessitatem probat."

21 Emmanuel Falque, *Ca n'a rien à voir: Lire Freud en philosophe* (Paris: Cerf, 2018), 54.

22 Bernard of Clairvaux, On the *Song of Songs IV*, pp. 175-7. Zink (*SC* 511), SCC 82.5, l. 1-22: "Annon diplois, ubi non innata, sed affixa, et quadam quasi acu peccati assuta est simplicitati fraus, immortalitati mors, necessitas libertati?"

production is therefore also affected in the unfolding of desiring-production as *mer(e)ological aesthetics*. As such, necessity is the basis of the law, which affects knowledge and action: the production of generation as *the beautiful* (good) and the failure to resist resistance as the grotesque (evil) within the diffusion of the body. The efficient word, diffused on all flesh by the spirit, does not lose its efficacy but is rather resisted by the body at the juncture where necessity modifies the will and therefore, in return, modifies the body as well.

For Bernard, in *possibility and free will*, the possibility of necessity emerges within the duplicity of the free will. This section has laid out the elements of duplicity. These are as follows: first, duplicity arises in experience; second, duplicity is originary and unifying; third, duplicity engenders chaos; fourth, duplicity accounts for the possibility of imposing necessity on the body; fifth, duplicity veils or counterfeits freedom; sixth, duplicity is manifested in degrees; seventh, and finally, duplicity unravels a paradigm for knowledge and ethics (herewith called *mer(e)ological aesthetics*). In the possibility (duplicity) of necessity (resistance), the will's freedom is manifested in degrees. The freedom, which the possibility of necessity manifests in degrees, is modal manifestation of desiring-production.

8.3 Free Will as Desiring-Production

Thus far, in exploring *resistance*, it has been argued that the *limit* is the locus of *resistance*; first, *resistance* is constitutive of the soul's affinity to the Word where *resistance* is necessity; *second*, from the vantage point of the possibility for the soul's *duplicity* which explains multiplicity as the possibility of necessity. Thus, *resistance* is necessity and resistance as duplicity is the basis for the possibility of free will. Within the limit, resistance manifests the free will as modal aperity or desiring-production, which is the point of discussion at hand. It will be argued that desiring-production is manifested in the resistance at the limit as transformation or metamorphosis, or the *metamorphosis of love*. Transformation as desiring-production is construed in terms of *affinity*, namely the affinity of the soul to the Word. Affinity, in the manifestation of the free will as desiring production, is progressive *disclosure* of love as knowledge. Disclosure of the free will as desiring-production is knowledge and love, which is also the corrective to duplicity whereby the soul becomes enstranged. Later, it is argued that disclosure of the free will as desiring production is fundamentally (re)configuration, first, and then *aperity*. (Re)configuration, as aesthetic manifestation and epistemological knowledge, emerges in disclosure from duplicity in the depths of human nature.

First, reconfiguration from the estrangement of *body*. The tension of duplicity produces a radical transformation of the *body*. In duplicity of the soul, whereby the soul is unlike God and the soul becomes a stranger even unto itself, the tension between free will and necessity engenders a radical transformation. What does it mean to say, in the face of necessity willed by the free will on itself, "that the soul is unlike God and consequently unlike itself as well"?[23] Bestiality is the soul's unlikeness to God. Passing through bestiality, the free will actualizes its becoming as reconfiguration of the matrix of finitude. The bestiality as manifestation of necessity is nature or *natura*. The body's alienation therefore is a passage in the process of transformation or reconfiguration of modal manifestation. The bestiality of humanity as different from itself must not be understood as a failure to reach an ideal (Augustine), but rather as a passage of transformation, of metamorphosis, through the incarnate Word in the veil or *cloak* of *the assumed man* (*assumptus homo*) – this time assumed as the bestiality of man *alien* or *different* to the animality of man: man is alien to itself by becoming alien to God in the incarnation. Necessity is not only a restriction on the free will, as modal aperity; it is a necessary transformation, experienced as tension, in the process of the generation of the free will as desiring-production. Necessity is rooted in the organic of man, in the "cracks of the body" – or what Falque calls the "failles de la chair"[24] – where the *flesh* of bodies is grafted, the *grafted flesh*, and interlaced in suffering of the grotesque as a condition for the possibility of the diffusion of the *whole body*. Necessity is radically (as roots) grafted on to the organic whole as the source of modal aperity in the animal-beast tensions of the free will and necessity. The free will as becoming *must* necessarily pass through the bestiality of the grotesque. Free will is hence a grafting of necessity on the body.

Second, reconfiguration of *vision*. The radical transformation of the body also reconfigures *vision*. The transformation of the body inevitably alters the free will passing through the body and *becomes* vision as love. The proximity to the Word as vision reaches its accomplishment in the vision of God (*Dei visio*) which is tangible in charity (*ego autem dico in caritate*). This is the last step of the transformation of desire in the free will's necessity within the duplicity of experience. In the vision of God, the ultimate proximity to the Word is love itself. Touch in the "cracks of the flesh" – the *failles de la chair* – are tissue which unite the body to *whole* in the transformations of necessity from touch to vision. These are all synthesized in a metaxological aperity of the free will

23 Bernard of Clairvaux, On the *Song of Songs IV*, pp. 175-7. Zink (*SC* 511), SCC 82.5, l. 1-22: "Inde anima dissimilis Deo, inde dissimilis est et sibi."

24 Emmanuel Falque, "Ceci Est Mon Corps," *Études*, no. 4 (2012): 483-93.

as ultimate efficiency of the Word in love. Love, anchored in the touch of the *failles de la chair, is* efficiency of desiring-production accomplished in vision.

Third, reconfiguration of limit as *resistance*. The two Bernardine reconfigurations in duplicity, first of the body and then of the vision, offer an alternative understanding of the problem of distance in the *affinity* of the soul to the Word at the *limit* where *resistence* emerges – the third reconfiguration. The growing affinity or likeness as transformation of the free will by necessity is not a question of distance (Augustine), metaphysical or ontological, but rather a question of *modal efficiency* – which will be discussed as *aperity*. The third reconfiguration marks, therefore, a passage from vision (eye) to love (touch). An epistemology flowing from and *based* on touch of the body is fulfilled in the dynamic expression of the body as vision of God: "It is assuredly a thing most marvelous and astonishing, *that likeness which accompanies the vision of God, and is itself the vision*. I can only describe it as *subsisting in charity. This vision is charity*, and the likeness is charity."[25] The final transformation of the body through desire is vision as love. The ultimate expression of the body in the affinity of the soul to the Word is the pure efficiency of love. There is no distinction between the love reached in affinity and the love of the vision, for the single continuum is the process of a free will in becoming, passing through necessity, which is manifested in the expression of the efficiency of the word in the modes of love. Body in the becoming of free will *is* love.

Three reconfigurations, therefore, lead to desiring production in resistance – first the body, then vision and lastly vision becoming body as love. For Bernard, love as desiring-production, or manifestation, is the vision of God in a process of reconfiguration, from vision to love or from duplicity to unity in which the soul, through the Word, is no longer estranged, but wholesome and unified. The corrective to duplicity in resistance is the reciprocity of love. The elements of reconfiguration, from vision to love are as follows: memory, capacity, unity and reciprocity, partiality, perfection and aperity. These constitute the modal disclosure of free will as desiring-production. *First*, memory. Bernard asks, "Who would not be amazed at the charity of God in recalling someone who has spurned him?"[26] The memory of rejection incites a sense of wonder at God's goodness. Revisiting memory begins the process of reconfiguration. *Second*,

25 Bernard of Clairvaux, On the *Song of Songs IV*, pp. 175-7. Zink (*SC* 511), SCC 82.8: "Admiranda prorsus et stupenda illa similitudo, quam Dei visio comitatur, imo quae Dei visio est; ego autem dico in caritate. Caritas illa visio, illa similitudo est. Admiranda prorsus et stupenda illa similitudo, quam Dei visio comitatur, imo quae Dei visio est; ego autem dico in caritate. Caritas illa visio, illa similitudo est."

26 Bernard of Clairvaux, On the *Song of Songs IV*, p. 179. Zink (*SC* 511), SCC 82.8, l. 1-20: "Quis non stupeat caritatem Dei spreti et revocantis?"

capacity. Bernard notes, "the unrighteous man [...] appropriating to himself the likeness of God, but who by choosing unrighteousness becomes incapable of *loving either himself or God*."[27] Unrighteousness has for its effect the incapacity to love and creates a distance not only from God but also from oneself. The loss of capacity due to iniquity leads to duplicity. *Third*, unity and reciprocity. The corrective to duplicity, which is caused by iniquity, is goodness. Goodness produces unity. Bernard writes, "You know the words, 'He who loves iniquity hates his own soul.' When the iniquity [...] is taken away, there will be a oneness of spirit, *a reciprocal vision, and reciprocal love*."[28] The outcome of unity is reciprocity. In reciprocity, vision begins to manifest affinity to love. *Fourth*, partiality. Bernard continues, "When what is perfect comes, what is *partial* will be done away with."[29] Reciprocity only begins the process of unity, but the unity from duplicity is fragile and in reconfiguration remains only partial. *Fifth*, perfection. The reciprocity of love becomes perfect in vision. Bernard continues, "*love between them will be chaste and consummated, full recognition, open vision, strong unity, indivisible fellowship and perfect likeness*."[30] The *affinity* of the Word and the soul becomes perfect only when there is full conformity between vision and love, i.e. when vision is manifested as love. *Sixth*, aperity. In perfection, there is aperity. The soul overcomes duplicity when in reciprocity it loves and is loved, not as it wishes it were, but as it really is. Bernard concludes, "the soul will *know as it is known and love as it is loved*, [...] *knowing and known, loving and loved*, Jesus Christ."[31] The elements of reconfiguration chart the *metamorphosis* of desire into desiring-production, wherein *free will* is *desiring-production*. *Desiring-production* consists in the *disclosure* of the will within the framework of affinity at the limit where resistance emerges, from

27 Bernard of Clairvaux, On the *Song of Songs IV*, p. 179. Zink (*SC* 511), SCC 82.8, l. 1-20: "Merito iniquus arguitur ille, qui supra inductus est, Dei similitudinem usurpans sibi, cum diligendo iniquitatem, neque possit se diligere, neque Deum."

28 Bernard of Clairvaux, On the *Song of Songs IV*, p. 179. Zink (*SC* 511), SCC 82.8, l. 1-20: "sic enim habes: Qui diligit iniquitatem, odit animam suam (Psal. X, 6). Facta igitur de medio iniquitate, quae eam quae ex parte est dissimilitudinem facit, erit unio spiritus, erit mutua visio, mutuaque dilectio."

29 Bernard of Clairvaux, On the *Song of Songs IV*, p. 179. Zink (*SC* 511), SCC 82.8, l. 1-20: "Siquidem veniente quod perfectum est, evacuabitur quod ex parte est."

30 Bernard of Clairvaux, On the *Song of Songs IV*, p. 179. Zink (*SC* 511), SCC 82.8, l. 1-20: "eritque ad alterutrum casta et consummata dilectio, agnitio plena, visio manifesta, conjunctio firma, societas individua, similitudo perfecta. Tunc cognoscet anima, sicut cognita est (I Cor. XIII, 10, 12)."

31 Bernard of Clairvaux, On the *Song of Songs IV*, p. 179. Zink (*SC* 511), SCC 82.8, l. 1-20: "Tunc cognoscet anima, sicut cognita est (I Cor. XIII, 10, 12); tunc amabit, sicut amata est; et gaudebit sponsus super sponsam, cognoscens et cognitus, diligens et dilectus, Jesus Christus Dominus noster, qui est super omnia Deus benedictus in saecula. Amen."

vision to touch. Disclosure of free will as desiring-production happens as a reconfiguration of the body, followed then by a reconfiguration of vision, and finally by a disclosure, in a third reconfiguration, of vision as touch. Free will is disclosed as desiring-production in the resistance of duplicity in memory, capacity, unity and reciprocity, partiality, perfection and aperity.

Conclusion

Overall, this chapter on *resistance* has addressed the question: *where* and *how* do bodies *resist*? It has been argued that resistance arises at the limit. Resistance gives way to disclosure wherein the free will emerges as aperity. This was discussed in three sections. For Bernard, it was shown that resistance is constitutive of human existence, that duplicity allows for possibility of necessity, and that in the tension of necessity and possibility, the *necessity of the free will* reconfigures the free will to produce (metaxological) aperity. The last chapter of this volume analyzes *aperity* and, as such, brings to a close the *metamorphosis of love,* which has been charted throughout our analysis in general, with special attention to the pathway from limit to resistance and, finally, into aperity.

CHAPTER 9

Aperity

The body *extends* beyond the confines of the body in production through the Word and *resistance* arises at the limits where the free will emerges as *aperity*. Exploring free will as aperity is the subject matter of this closing chapter, which addresses the question of the body's *aperity* as act in the midst *resistance* at the *limits*, where free will is *aperity* tout court and where the body manifests itself as pure action. To be sure, in the final moment of the *metamorphosis of love*, in its purest and fully incarnate expression, desire is indistinguishable from love, wherein the willed aperity of the free will – and in this consists the full sense of the soul's affinity *to* the Word, *in* the soul's desire for the Word, *through* the Word's efficiency – is love or aperity. With this final moment of love's metamorphosing dynamism, which is the mechanism of incarnation, aperity's endless possibilities for becoming return to the *beginning without beginning*. The free will is the body's aperity in love, according to three moments: first, in *free will as power* (9. 1); secondly, in *the power of love* (9. 2); and, finally, in the *love of love as free will* (9.3).

9.1 Free Will as Power

As *aperity*, the free will is power, and its locus is return (*reditus*) in conversion. Moreover, conversion is based on *affinity*, where the *limits* of the body emerge as *limits*, in *resistance* and in *extension*. The limit *resistence-extension* is *free will as aperity* of the body. The counterside of the limit as constitutive aperity is resistance. In light of *resistance*, free will emerges in *desiring-production* (8.3). Now, from the vantage point of *limits* and *resistance, free will* is pure *aperity* and simply *power*. Free will emerges as power in a three-fold dynamism, which includes *conversion, conformation* and *efficacy*. This is, in short, the basis for Bernard's view of free will as a power. For Bernard, conversion is the initial impetus grounding aperity (*limits*); conformation is the transformative experience at the limit (*resistance*); and the outcome of the dynamism of conversion and conformation is efficacy (*aperity*). The efficiency of the free will, in limits and resistance, is power. Therefore, dynamics of power are conversion, conformation and efficacy.

First, conversion. Bernard grounds *aperity* in incarnate conversion. The soul is inclined towards the Word in *affinity* because the Word is the origin of

 | DOI:10.30965/9783846767504_011

the soul. *Affinity* is therefore a return to the source-beginning. Alternatively, return is conversion as *affinity*. Bernard writes, "*showing the affinity between the Word and the soul.* What was the value of all that labor? [...] we have seen how *every* soul [...] standing thus under *condemnation* and *without hope*, has the *power to turn and find it* [and] *also dare to aspire to the nuptials of the Word*, [...] to bear the *sweet yoke of love*."[1] The weight of love marks the return of the soul to the Word. At work in the dynamism of conversion is the *exitus-reditus* model. Importantly, the body is at the centre. Christianity reimagined the *exitus-reditus* model: exit like return are only possible via the mediation of the Word in the incarnation; hence the importance of the body. The affinity of the verb is deeply embedded in the Augustinian Trinitarian Christianisation of the Plotinian triadic scheme of procession and return. Much of Bernard's originality risks being overlooked at the expense of reducing the triadic formulation to a Trinitarian imposition on the old Plotinian scheme following Augustine. Already Augustine departs from Plotinus in important respects, especially on the fundamental role of the incarnation of the Word in the movement of return (*reditus*), which 'the philosophers' failed to appreciate because of pride. For Augustine, the God of 'the philosophers' is never a mediator in the flesh between God and humanity. While Bernard certainly agrees fundamentally with Augustine, important departures are also evident. Augustine frames conversion, the procession-return itinerary, mostly around an often-ambivalent dynamic of *cooperation* between the freedom of the will in the post-fall state and divine grace. Hence, Augustine does not shy away from making seemingly contradicting statements at times optimistic of the human capacity to overcome sin while cooperating with the grace of God ("God who made you without you will not save you with out you"[2]). At times, Augustine stresses the helpless state of the human condition in the absence of divine intervention, as when commenting on *To Simplicianum* just prior to death ("I have tried hard to maintain the free choice of the will, but the grace of God prevailed").[3] These result in an equally ambiguous assessment of how grace

1 Bernard of Clairvaux, On the *Song of Songs IV*, pp. 180-1. Zink (*SC* 511), SCC 83.1, l. 1-25: "licet, inquam, sic damnatam, et sic desperatam, docuimus tamen hanc in sese posse advertere, non modo unde respirare in spem veniae, in spem misericordiae queat; sed etiam unde audeat aspirare ad nuptias Verbi, cum Deo inire foedus societatis non trepidet, suave amoris jugum cum Rege ducere angelorum non vereatur."

2 Augustine, *Sermons*, trans. John E. *Sermons on the New Testament* (New York: New City Press, 1992), *Sermon* 169.13: "Qui ergo fecit te sine te, non te iustificat sine te."

3 Augustine, *Retractations*, in *Augustine: Earlier Writings*, ed. J. H. S. Burleigh (Philadelphia: Westminster Press, 1953), 370: "In cuius questionis solutione laboratum est quidem pro libero arbitrio uoluntatis humanae, sed uincit dei gratia" (CCL 57, pp. 89-90).

and free will interact. In short, the role of grace and free will overlap in the process of return.[4] This overlap is particularly evident in the Augustinian treatment of the restoration of the divine image. Augustine even at times outright states that the image of God is destroyed by sin, only to later back down and opt for distortion rather than destruction. The weight of sin is such that grace in the process of reformation is indispensable within the onto-metaphysical Plotinian framework of image inherited by Bernard from Augustine. In one sentence: the Augustinian free will is helpless in the absence of the mystery of God's dispensation of grace. In stark and unprecedented contrast to Augustine, the abbot of Clairvaux *naturalizes* free will and articulates the limits of the body, and their implications on the free will's powers, in terms other than sin. This is not to say that sin does not weigh on the free will. Rather, the limit of the free will (necessity and resistance) is *not* all accounted by sin alone but mostly by the limits of corporeality. The empowerment of the freedom of the will, even in the face of sin as necessity, is possible by reframing the exile-return movement within the *metamorphosis of love*. In the *metamorphosis of love*, the power (*vir*) of the will as desiring-production is affected by necessity in the modality of generation and in the capacity to resist resistance. Thus, the free will as the divine image in human beings is central within desiring-production: the image of God as free will allows the free will to overcome self-imposed necessity. In fact, there is not only overcoming of necessity, but even aspiration to the love of God: "but *also dare to aspire to the nuptials of the Word*, not fearing to enter into alliance with God or to bear the *sweet yoke of love* with the King of angels."[5] The love of God as the capacity of human free will (not of grace as in Augustine) constitutes a return to the *origin*. After all, "[w]hy should [the soul] not venture with confidence into the presence of him by whose image it sees itself honored, and in whose likeness it knows itself made glorious?"[6] The soul is empowered and able to return to the likeness of the image precisely because the return is *a* beginning at the origin. The soul's "very *origin* gives it ground

4 Else Marie Wiberg Pedersen, "This Is Not About Sex? A Discussion of the Understanding of Love and Grace in Bernard of Clairvaux's and Martin Luther's Theologies," *Dialog* 50, no. 1 (2011): 15-25; Dalia Marija Stanciene, "The Concept of Free Will in the Treatise by Bernard of Clairvaux Concerning Grace and Free Will," *Logos-Vilnus* 56 (2008): 39-49.

5 Bernard of Clairvaux, On the *Song of Songs IV*, pp. 180-1. Zink (*SC* 511), SCC 83.1, l. 1-25: "sed etiam unde audeat aspirare ad nuptias Verbi, cum Deo inire foedus societatis non trepidet, suave amoris jugum cum Rege ducere angelorum non vereatur."

6 Bernard of Clairvaux, On the *Song of Songs IV*, pp. 180-1. Zink (*SC* 511), SCC 83.1, l. 1-25: "Quid enim non tute audeat apud eum, cujus se insignem cernit imagine, illustrem similitudine novit?"

for confidence."[7] Furthermore, the *return* is in a sense inevitable, produced by the gravitational attraction of *the weight of love*. The axiomatic law *like returns to like* governing physical elements therefore applies also to the organic soul. In short, the movement of the free will as conversion is but a natural return of the body to its divine likeness, which is the Word. Inscribed in the possibility of exit (*exitus*) is the necessity of return through the free will (*reditus*). Conversion is the free will's first expression.

Secondly, conformation. The first important aspect of *conformation* is its aesthetic dimension. The description of the kind of actions which return the image to its origin are wholly alien to the Augustinian framework of "the region of unlikeness" (*regio dissimilitudinis*) where evil as privation distances from God and good as action and where, through the use of reason, the soul approaches God. Bernard shies away from making moral predicaments but rather describes the return to God in terms of aesthetics where the return to the *origin* is the beauty of action: "All [the soul] it has to do is to take care to preserve its natural purity by innocence of life, or rather *to study to beautify and adorn with the brightness of its actions and dispositions the glorious beauty which is its birthright*."[8] The beauty of action fully approximates and completes the pure manifestation of the modality of the free will in spite of necessity as desiring-production in the *mer(e)ological* reconstitution of *the spread body*. The *weight of love* thus manifests the *free will as power* in *mer(e)ological* dissipation in the mode of beauty at the origin. The final moment in the transformation from desire to love in *free will as love* occurs in the *conformation* of the beauty of actions to the efficiency of the Word, or as the efficiency of the Word, precisely as love, where free will is power: "For the Word of God is living and efficient." What is the conformation (*comformatio*) of the free will to the Word in the beauty of action as love beyond reason (Augustine) and moral prescription? The inherent movement towards beauty is in the origin and expressed in the habit (*morum*) and affect (*affectus*): "*to study to beautify and adorn with the brightness of its actions and dispositions the glorious beauty which is its birthright*."[9] There is a natural aesthetics of desire where beauty propels affects,

7 Bernard of Clairvaux, On the *Song of Songs IV*, pp. 180-1. Zink (*SC* 511), SCC 83.1, l. 1-25: "quid, inquam, vereatur de majestate, cui de origine fiducia datur?"

8 Bernard of Clairvaux, On the *Song of Songs IV*, pp. 180-1. Zink (*SC* 511), SCC 83.1, l. 1-25: "quid, inquam, vereatur, de maiestate, cui de origine fiducia datur? Tantum est ut curet naturae ingenuitatem vitae honestate servare, imo caelestes decus, quod sibi originaliter inest, dignis quibusdam studeat morum affectuumque venustare et decorare coloribus."

9 Bernard of Clairvaux, On the *Song of* Songs *IV*, pp. 180-1. Zink (*SC* 511), SCC 83.1, l. 1-25: "imo caeleste decus, quod sibi originaliter inest, dignis quibusdam studeat morum affectuumque venustare et decorare coloribus."

from the origin, back to the Word as the origin of *the beginning without beginning*. The conformation of the free will to the verb happens through the impetus of a natural gift (the freedom of the will) which embraces all of human nature: "There is a great *natural gift* within us, and if it is not allowed full play *the rest of our nature will go to ruin* [...] eaten away by the rust of decay."[10] The conformity happens, furthermore, through the *affinity* of the soul and Word to approach as a double force of preservation, or continuity, and return, or resistance (akin to the *conatus essendi* of Spinoza).[11] Bernard continues, "This is why God, its Creator, desires the divine glory and nobility to be always preserved in the soul, so *that it may have within itself that by which it may always be admonished by the Word, either to stay with him or to return to him if it has strayed.*"[12] The tri*part*ite movement of conformation can be charted as the channelling of the force of the will 'out *of* the Word' (*ex Verbo*), 'staying *with* the Word' (*stare cum Verbo*) and 'returning *to* the Word' (*redire*). The constant unfolding of divine beauty in the process of conformation through the Word ensures a paradigm effusion as *mer(e)olgoical* transformation in *the spread body*. The Ambrosian paradigm of conformation, later exhibit in Augustine, which follows formation, deformation and reformation through conformation is supplanted by a process of divine manifestation in the Verb ('*out of* the Word', '*staying with* the Word', '*returning to* the Word'): the *compressed word*, the *assumed man* and finally the *spread body*. Since there is no deformation strictly speaking in the necessity of the will, but only modal metaxological aperity, the conformation is not simply a return to an original form, but a joining in the efficiency of the Word's ongoing process of manifestation in *the spread body* precisely as desiring-production in the force (*vir*) of the will in an ongoing aesthetic unfolding of becoming. The complete conformation of the soul and the Word is ultimately achieved not simply as reformation but also as transformation. The free will, at the heart of approximation to the Word, achieves *mer(e)ological aesthetic* aperity in *fusion* (not *confusion*) with the Word. Conformation to the Word is essentially (*trans*) *fusion*. The fusion is the modal manifestation of the free will, which stands in sharp contrast to the necessity of free will as love.

Finally, efficacy. Love is the efficiency of the Word in the epithet "For the love of God is living and efficient" (Heb 4.1). The efficiency of love as a modal

10 Bernard of Clairvaux, On the *Song of* Songs *IV*, pp. 181-2. Zink (*SC* 511), SCC 83.2, l. 1-21.

11 Baruch Spinoza, *The Essential Spinoza: Ethics and Related Writings*, trans. Samuel Shirley, ed. Michael L. Morgan, Hacket Publishing Company, 2006.

12 Bernard of Clairvaux, On the *Song of* Songs *IV*, pp. 181-2. Zink (*SC* 511), SCC 83.2, l. 1-21: "Et utique ad hoc auctor ipse Deus divinae insigne generositatis perpetuo voluit in anima conservari, ut semper haec in sese ex Verbo habeat, quo admoneatur semper, aut stare cum Verbo, aut redire, si mota fuerit."

aperity of free will is conditioned on the Word. Hence, the movement of the soul (*motus*) is measured in terms of affective and defective (*affectibus-defectibus*) *displacement*: "It does not stray by changing its place or by walking, but it strays [...] *in its affections, or rather its defections* and it degenerates and becomes *unlike itself* when it becomes *unlike him*."[13] The reformation and conformation of the soul to the Verb is a kind of positive expression of the necessity of freedom directed towards the Verb. The soul's "unlikeness *is not the destruction* of its nature but a *defect*, for natural goodness is increased as much by comparison with itself as it is spoiled by communication with evil."[14] By restricting its movement, and directed/impulse by beauty, the soul moves towards the Verb. Ultimately, the conformation of affectivity to God, the mapping out of the vestiges of the divine manifestation (*insignum*) is love, this time as charity in conformation through mimesis. Bernard exhorts the listeners to "'*be imitators of God* [...] and walk in love, *as Christ also has loved you*."[15] Imitation as production is grounded in love and produces love. Love is the power of the will. The product of transformation, achieved by the aesthetic gravitation of love, through desire and movement of affects, is a specific kind of divine love, charity (*charitate*). The same charity is, in practice, manifested as dilection (*dilectione*). The empowerment of love, in the movement of the affects, is the affect of Christ returned. To love is to be loved. All movement is a reaction not simply as resistance, nor again as resistance of resistance, but most fundamentally as generation of the free will, as power passing through desire, to love (*dilectio*) in the conformation of the Word. Bernard writes, "*So the soul returns and is converted to the Word to be reformed by him and conformed to him. In what way? In charity* -- for he says, '*Be imitators of God* [...] and walk in love, *as Christ also has loved you*.'"[16] Imitation offers aperity as *a* beginning in the Word, *the beginning without beginning*. Indeed, the Word is the origin to which the organic soul returns as all elements do to the beginning in and through the power of love as *desiring-production* in *mer(e)ological* aperity. The

13 Bernard of Clairvaux, On the *Song of Songs IV*, pp. 181-2. Zink (*SC* 511), SCC 83.2, l. 1-21: "Non mota quasi locis migrans, aut pedibus gradiens, sed mota (sicut substantiae utique spirituali moveri est cum suis affectibus, imo defectibus) a se quodam modo in pejus vadit, cum se sibi vitae et morum pravitate dissimilem facit, reddit degenerem."

14 Bernard of Clairvaux, On the *Song of* Songs *IV*, pp. 181-2. Zink (*SC* 511), SCC 83.2, l. 1-21.

15 Bernard of Clairvaux, On the *Song of Songs IV*, pp. 181-2. Zink (*SC* 511), SCC 83.2, l. 1-21: 'In quo? In charitate. Ait enim: Estote imitatores Dei."

16 Bernard of Clairvaux, On the *Song of Songs IV*, pp. 181-2. Zink (*SC* 511), SCC 83.2, l. 1-21: "Jam vero animae reditus, conversio ejus ad Verbum, reformandae per ipsum, conformandae ipsi. In quo? In charitate. Ait enim: Estote imitatores Dei, sicut filii charissimi; et ambulate in dilectione, sicut et Christus dilexit vos (Ephes. V, 1, 2)."

dynamic of the organic soul's affinity *towards* the Verb/Word through *the free will as power* reveals *the power of love.*

9.2 The Power of Love

In conversion, or the affinity of the soul to the Word, free will is considered as love's power, or the power of love. *Affinity* has magnitude or *power* and directionality, which is love, so that while magnitude is the impetus of conversion, conformation depends equally as much on direction. Tracing the magnitude and direction of love, in affinity, reveals thus the power of love. The power of love, which directs the soul to the Word, is fundamentally *return*, the true power of love. Therefore, while free will is power, the power of the free will is love. This is so because love brings back the will's power to the beginning-origin, which is the pattern revealing the blueprint of *the power of love* or love's reduction. The reduction of *the power of love* is, following the Latin (*re* + *ducere*), to restore, to return, to lead back. Reduction of the power of love is is comformation. Return is conformation which is governed by the maxim: *like returns unto like, like becomes unto like.* The power of love is the result of the *fusion* (*conformitas*) or *conformity* of the free will to the efficacy of the Word. Bernard writes, "Such conformity *weds the soul to the Word, for one who is like the Word by nature shows himself like him too in the exercise of his will, loving as she is loved.* When she loves perfectly, the soul is wedded to the Word."[17] The wedding feast of the Word culminates in the marriage of the soul to the Word where reciprocal love, first directed from the Word and only then returned to the soul, constitutes the consumption of the marriage. The fusion without confusion is the instantiation of the free will as pure efficiency. What ensues is a reduction of the power of love. Power (*potestas*) is construed as a fundamental mode of action whereby modal transformation is manifested within a spectrum of rates. Power is *intensity* as resistance (necessity) and as free will (generation). In the reduction of *power* the power of love *is* power or pure intensity. Comformation is later explored in terms of aperity.

Now, the reduction of *the power of love* in conformation manifests degrees of intensity advancing towards modal aperity in *joy, fusion, equality, self-sufficiency, all-encompassing, reciprocal* and *self-surpassing. First, the joy of love.*

---

17 Bernard of Clairvaux, On the *Song of Songs IV*, pp. 182-3. Zink (*SC* 511), SCC 83.3, l. 1-23: "Talis conformitas maritat animam Verbo, cum cui videlicet similis est per naturam, similem nihilominus ipsi se exhibet per voluntatem, diligens sicut dilecta est. Ergo, si perfecte diligit, nupsit."

The soul approaches the image of God, the Word, and becomes similar to it in the exercise of the will. As the will conforms to the Word, there is joy. Love is loved, and the love of love is en-joyable. Bernard writes, "What is lovelier than this conformity? What is more *desirable than charity*, by whose operation, O soul, not content with a human master, you *approach* the Word with confidence *cling to him with constancy, speak to him as to a familiar friend*, and *refer to him in every matter* with an intellectual grasp proportionate to the boldness of your desire?"[18] The joy of conformation is love in the desire of charity, confidence and constancy, familiarity and counsel. Joy of love, therefroe, accompanies conformation. Second, the *fusion* as *diffusion* and *transfusion* of wills into a single spirit (production). In acting, the will becomes like unto the Word and as such, a kind of *fusion* results. Bernard writes, "Truly this is a spiritual contract, a holy marriage. It is more than a *contract*, it is an *embrace*: an embrace where *identity of will* makes of *two one spirit*."[19] The identification of the members of the body now become one by partaking in a single spirit. The marriage of wills results in one single flesh. Third, the identification produces equality. Bernard continues, "There need be no fear *that inequality of persons should impair the conformity of will*, because *love* is no respecter of persons. *It is from loving, not revering, that love receives its name*."[20] Inherent to the conformity of difference in fusion is equality. Love renders the lovers equal. Fourth, the power of love is self-sufficient because it is all-encompassing and governs all other affections. *"Love is sufficient for itself; when love is present it absorbs and conquers* [in se omnes traducit] *all other affections*."[21] The use of *conquer* to render *tradure* is misleading. Love does not subject the affections (*affectus*) but moves, displays, leads through, transforms – in one word, love *metamorphoses* the affections

---

18 Bernard of Clairvaux, On the *Song of Songs IV*, pp. 182-3. Zink (*SC* 511), SCC 83.3, l. 1-23: "Quid hac conformitate jucundius? quid optabilius charitate, qua fit ut humano magisterio non contenta, per temet, o anima, fiducialiter accedas ad Verbum, Verbo constanter inhaereas, Verbum familiariter percuncteris, consultesque de omni re, quantum intellectu capax, tantum audax desiderio?"

19 Bernard of Clairvaux, On the *Song of Songs IV*, pp. 182-3. Zink (*SC* 511), SCC 83.3, l. 1-23: "Vere spiritualis, sanctique connubii contractus est iste. Parum dixi, contractus: complexus est. Complexus plane, ubi idem velle, et nolle idem, unum facit spiritum de duobus."

20 Bernard of Clairvaux, On the *Song of Songs IV*, pp. 182-3. Zink (*SC* 511), SCC 83.3, l. 1-23: "Nec verendum ne disparitas personarum claudicare in aliquo faciat convenientiam [alias, conniventiam] voluntatum, quia amor reverentiam nescit. Ab amando quippe amor, non ab honorando denominatur."

21 Bernard of Clairvaux, On the *Song of Songs IV*, pp. 182-3. Zink (*SC* 511), SCC 83.3, l. 1-23: "Honoret sane qui horret, qui stupet, qui metuit, qui miratur: vacant haec omnia penes amantem. Amor sibi abundat, amor ubi venerit, caeteros in se omnes traducit et captivat affectus. Propterea quae amat, amat, et aliud novit nihil."

into a single self-sufficient state of unity. The unity is the condition for conformation and fusion of the wills. Fifth, love functions in conformation as the criterion for knowledge. Bernard states, "[*t*]*herefore it loves what it loves, and it knows nothing else*."[22] The conformity of wills opens the possibility of knowing the object or subject of love. What is loved is also known. Furthermore, love demarks the limits of knowledge: love knows nothing other than what it loves. Knowledge, in other words, is not possible without love. As such, love is the rule of knowledge. Sixth, love is reciprocal and, in reciprocity, there is generation. In reciprocity, there is *love of love* as to *love and be loved* (*amari et amare*).[23] Bernard writes, "He who is justly honored, held in awe, and admired, prefers to be loved [...] What other bond or compulsion do you look for between those who are betrothed, *except to love and be loved*?"[24] The reciprocity of love is essential to the possibility of love altogether. Seventh, and final, the bond of love is the locus of oversaturation. The object of desire is charity for nothing is as desirable as charity itself. The mode of erotic love is overdetermined power, which not only overcomes all affects, but also is the overcoming of love itself. The efficiency of the Word expressed in the will is a bond, which is beyond all other bonds. Bernard explains: "This bond is stronger even than nature's firm bond between parents and children. [...] it is *stronger not only than other affections, but even than itself*."[25] The bond is stronger than itself! The bond (*nexus*) is not simply construed as an *emotional community* where belonging and a sense of group identity is forged by a common emotional experience. The bond which love forges between the soul and the Word is not identification only, either, but mainly identity, as is specially suggested when compared to a biological parental bond. Summarily, the reduction of love is a return in the echelons of *joy, fusion, equality, self-sufficiency, all-encompassing, reciprocal*

22 Bernard of Clairvaux, On the *Song of Songs IV*, pp. 182-3. Zink (*SC* 511), SCC 83.3, l. 1-23: "Honoret sane qui horret, qui stupet, qui metuit, qui miratur: vacant haec omnia penes amantem. Amor sibi abundat, amor ubi venerit, caeteros in se omnes traducit et captivat affectus. Propterea quae amat, amat, et aliud novit nihil."

23 Thomas Aquinas, *Suma Theologiae*, I-IIae, 27.1: "amare quam amari."

24 Bernard of Clairvaux, On the *Song of Songs IV*, pp. 182-3. Zink (*SC* 511), SCC 83.3, l. 1-23: "Ipse qui honori merito, merito stupori et miraculo est: amari tamen plus amat. Sponsus et sponsa sunt. Quam quaeris aliam inter sponsos necessitudinem vel connexionem, praeter amari, et amare?"

25 Bernard of Clairvaux, On the *Song of Songs IV*, pp. 182-3. Zink (*SC* 511), SCC 83.3, l. 24-28: "Hic nexus vincit etiam quod natura arctius vinxit, vinculum parentum ad filios. Denique, propter hoc, ait, relinquet homo patrem suum et matrem suam, et adhaerebit sponsae (Matth. XIX, 5). Vides iste affectus quam sit in sponsis, non caeteris tantum affectibus, sed etiam se ipso potentior."

and *self-surpassing*. The reduction culminates in the happiness of the free will. Happiness is the conformation of the soul to the Word.

From conformation results love in degrees. Bernard notes, "*Love is a great reality; but there are degrees to it*."[26] Only in God is *caritas* also *amor* because freedom and act are one for God. There is a lag, however, between freedom and act in human beings. The aperity of freedom constitutes, in conformation, the metamorphosis or transformation from freedom to act by way of degrees. Transformation is conformation, yet conformation does not mean confusion but rather implies difference. Difference is facilitated by the *affinity* (*ad* + *finem*) or limits of degrees. Degrees (*gradus*) are modes of *intensity* in the power of love rather than progressions. Again, degrees are dynamic manifestations in continuity, rather than unrelated and broken developments. The power of love as intensity is manifested in degrees or quantities. Humans, inevitably, experience the great reality of love by degrees. First, *interested* love. To illustrate interested love, Bernard sets forth the example of the love between a father and a child. Paternal-filial love is rooted in the biology, i.e., the nature, of human existence. What characterizes fundamentally love based on natural relations is interest. Of interested love, he writes, "Children love their father, but they are thinking of their inheritance [...] I suspect the love which seems to be founded on some hope of gain. It is weak, for if the hope is removed it may be extinguished, or at least diminished."[27] Interest in natural relations is the very expression of nature. Love has a specific natural inclination of desire which is only aimed at lovers at first. Bernard notes, "a man is bidden to honor his father and his mother; nothing is said about love [...] because most children are inclined to honor their parents rather than love them."[28] Bernard does not intend on criticizing the interest element of love. Love is given from the outset within the framework of human composition itself. The first challenge is not the possession of love, but submitting love to the servitude of reward. Again, that love be rewarded is not a problem for Bernard. The problem arises when the reward of love is other than love itself. Then, the following degree is *wholesome* love. While interested love is the root of all other loves, it is not yet fully love.

26 Bernard of Clairvaux, On the *Song of Songs IV*, pp. 184-5. Zink (*SC* 511), SCC 83.5, l. 1-25: "Magna res amor; sed sunt in eo gradus."

27 Bernard of Clairvaux, On the *Song of Songs IV*, pp. 184-5. Zink (*SC* 511), SCC 83.5, l. 1-25: "Sponsa in summo stat. Amant enim et filii, sed de haereditate cogitant: quam dum verentur quoquo modo amittere, ipsum a quo exspectatur haereditas, plus reverentur, minus amant."

28 Bernard of Clairvaux, On the *Song of Songs IV*, pp. 184-5. Zink (*SC* 511), SCC 83.5, l. 1-25: "Suspectus est mihi amor cui aliud quid adipiscendi spes suffragari videtur. Infirmus est, qui forte spe subtracta, aut exstinguitur, aut minuitur."

"It is not pure, as it desires some return. Pure love has no self-interest. Pure love does not gain strength through expectation, nor is it weakened by distrust."[29] Love becomes *wholesome*; love is the fullness of existence. The being and existence was the same only when there is love. "Love is the *being and the hope of a bride*. She is full of it [...] He asks nothing else, and she has nothing else to give."[30] Love becomes wholesome when it seeks nothing but itself as merit and reward. Furthermore, wholesome love is most unlike natural love or interested love when it becomes exclusive: "this love is the property only of the couple. No-one else can share it, not even a son."[31] The model, therefore, for the development of love, from *interested* love to *wholesome* love is no longer a *given* love (as is the case in the father-child relation) but a *chosen* love (as is the case in the couple relation). This is not because natural love is inferior. On the contrary, the love of the couple is also natural. It is rather because giving makes the choice of love for its own sake difficult, not impossible, but quite difficult. The love of a couple, however, is chosen as its own reward when it is first developed and as long as it is maintained. In the couple, love is no longer natural interest, but culminates in the love of love. Then, the wage of love is love. Love is love's currency and can only be repaid with love, "the Bridegroom who is love -- *asks only the exchange of love* and trust. Let the Beloved love in return. How can the bride -- and the bride of Love -- do other than love? *How can Love not be loved*?"[32] Furthermore, Bernard writes, in the love of love, love seeks no reward beyond itself but is content with the *love of love* as desiring-production or the efficiency of the Word: *"Love is sufficient for itself; it gives pleasure to itself, and for its own sake. It is its own merit and own reward. Love needs no cause beyond*

---

29 Bernard of Clairvaux, On the *Song of Songs IV*, pp. 184-5. Zink (*SC* 511), SCC 83.5, l. 1-25: "Impurus est, qui et aliud cupit. Purus amor mercenarius non est. Purus amor de spe vires non sumit, nec tamen diffidentiae damna sentit."

30 Bernard of Clairvaux, On the *Song of Songs IV*, pp. 184-5. Zink (*SC* 511), SCC 83.5, l. 1-25: "Sponsae hic est, quia hoc sponsa est quaecunque est. Sponsae res et spes unus est amor. Hoc sponsa abundat, hoc contentus et sponsus. Nec is aliud quaerit, nec illa aliud habet."

31 Bernard of Clairvaux, On the *Song of Songs IV*, pp. 184-5. Zink (*SC* 511), SCC 83.5, l. 1-25: "Hinc ille sponsus, et sponsa illa est. Is sponsis proprius est, quem alter nemo attingat, nec filius quidem."

32 Bernard of Clairvaux, On the *Song of Songs IV*, pp. 184-5. Zink (*SC* 511), SCC 83.5, l. 1-25: "Denique ad filios clamat: Ubi est honor meus? et non. Ubi est amor meus, dicit; servans sponsae praerogativam. Sed et jubetur homo honorare patrem suum et matrem suam (Deut. V, 16), et de amore tacetur: non quia non amandi sint parentes a filiis, sed quia multi filiorum honorare parentes magis quam amare affecti sunt. Esto quod honor regis judicium diligat: sed sponsi amor, imo sponsus Amor solam amoris vicem requirit et fidem. Liceat pro inde redamare dilectam. Quidni amet sponsa, et sponsa Amoris? Quidni ametur Amor?"

itself, nor does it demand fruits; it is its own purpose."[33] In short, interested love becomes wholesome love when it is *exclusive*.

Wholesome love is *generative*. Bernard explains, "*I love because I love; I love that I may love. Love is a great reality, and if it returns to its beginning and goes back to its origin, seeking its source again, it will always draw afresh from it, and thereby flow freely. Love is the only one of the motions of the soul, of its senses and affections*, in which the creature can respond to its Creator, even if not as an equal."[34] The dynamic of love, like the conformation of the soul to the Word, is one of *exit* – and later of *return*. Conformation in the freedom of the will, in spite of necessity, is achieved, truly *as* love.

Summarily, *the power of love* exhibits directionality of love in return as conformation. This happens, first, in the *reduction* (*re-ducere*) of love, through the echelons of *joy, fusion, equality, self-sufficiency, all-encompassing, reciprocal* and *self-surpassing*; and then in the manifestation of love through these echelons as *interested love*, *wholesome love* and *generative love*. Love is generative in the excercize of free will.

9.3 Love of Love as Free Will

The generative function of love is efficacy. Efficacy is the final moment in the manifestation of *aperity*; efficacy of the free will is *aperity* itself and the outcome of conversion and conformation. Effiacy resolves in *aperity* as love's end, which is not only love oriented towards an object, or subject, but the *love of love* itself. For Bernard, the greatness of love, resulting from degrees of transformation, is purified fully when desiring nothing except itself. Then, love, as love of love, is self-sufficient. Love of love expands in the efficiency of the Word. Love of love is self-sufficient because it is efficient. Bernard presents *love of love* in the closing sermons of *On Song of Songs*, while emphasizing its basis in the Word, particulalry in actualizing love as free will. From the *affinity* to the Word in the *limits*, and passing through *resistance*, the soul (and body) attains *aperity* in conformation and return to the Word by the power of love. The Word,

33 Bernard of Clairvaux, On the *Song of Songs IV*, pp. 183-4. Zink (*SC* 511), SCC 83.4, l. 1-37: "Is per se sufficit, is per se placet, et propter se. Ipse meritum, ipse praemium est sibi. Amor praeter se non requirit causam, non fructum. Fructus ejus, usus ejus."

34 Bernard of Clairvaux, On the *Song of Songs IV*, pp. 183-4. Zink (*SC* 511), SCC 83.4, l. 1-37: "Amo, quia amo; amo, ut amem. Magna res amor, si tamen ad suum recurrat principium, si suae origini redditus, si refusus suo fonti semper ex eo sumat, unde jugiter fluat. Solus est amor ex omnibus animae motibus, sensibus atque affectibus, in quo potest creatura, etsi non ex aequo, respondere auctori, vel de simili mutuam rependere vicem."

through its asymetrical relationship to the soul, and conversely, through the soul's *affinity* to the Word, renders the soul efficacious in action. In the asymetry of soul-*affinity*-Word, *love of love* is free will. In *affinity*, the limit of the soul, and therefore its extension, lies *aperity*. Thus, the *limit* constitutes action and, as action, the *limit* manifests *aperity*, from whence arises the question of the structure of the *limit* in asymetric love, which is the structure of *love of love*, and of free will tout court. Bernard explores two underlying aspects of *efficacy*'s manifestation according to the said structure: the renunciation to the gift of the Word's love and, thereon, the *metamorphosizing* rebirth in the Word.

First, renunciation to the gift of the Word's love. The love of the Word is asymmetric to human love because the Word loves more than it can be loved. The asymmetry is without prejudice, for humans love only when loved more than they can be loved and according to human limits of love. Bernard writes on this point: "Rightly, then, does [the soul] *renounce all other affections and devote herself to love alone,* for it is in *returning love that she has the power to respond to love.*"[35] The condition for loving, that love may love, is complete commitment, the basis for which is renunciation. Renuanciation prepares the response to an otherwise unattainable assymetric love. Bernard elegantly illustrates the asymmetry of love, "Although she may *pour out her whole self in love,* what is that compared to the inexhaustible fountain of his love? *The stream of love does not flow equally from her who loves and from him who is love, the soul and the Word.*"[36] Asymmetry is not detrimental to love because, while the soul loves, the Word is love; therefore, to love in this asymetry of soul-Word, is to *will* the Word as love, and thus to *love* love truly. Bernard then wonders how the loving soul is able to respond with love to the ineffable Word-love. Bernard writes, "*Will the desire of* [the soul's] *heart, her burning love, her affirmation of confidence, fail in their purpose because she has not the strength to keep pace with a giant, or rival honey in sweetness, the lamb in gentleness, or the lily in whiteness*?"[37] Nothwisthanding the asymetric love in quesiton, the soul

---

35 Bernard of Clairvaux, On the *Song of Songs IV*, pp. 185-7. Zink (*SC* 511), SCC 83.6, l. 1-37: "Merito cunctis renuntians affectionibus aliis, soli et tota incumbit amori, quae ipsi respondere amori habet in redhibendo amore."

36 Bernard of Clairvaux, On the *Song of Songs IV*, pp. 185-7. Zink (*SC* 511), SCC 83.6, l. 1-37: "Nam et cum se totam effuderit in amorem, quantum est hoc ad illius fontis perenne profluvium? Non plane pari ubertate fluunt amans et Amor, anima et Verbum, sponsa et sponsus, Creator et creatura, non magis quam sitiens et fons."

37 Bernard of Clairvaux, On the *Song of Songs IV*, pp. 185-7. Zink (*SC* 511), SCC 83.6, l. 1-37: "Quid ergo? peribit propter hoc, et ex toto evacuabitur nupturae votum, desiderium suspirantis, amantis ardor, praesumentis fiducia, quia non valet ex aequo currere cum gigante, dulcedine cum melle contendere; lenitate cum agno, candore cum lilio, claritate cum sole, charitate cum eo qui charitas est?"

is able to love wholly and paradoxically by giving all and thus lacking nothing. Bernard continues, "Although *the creature loves less*, being a lesser being, yet if *it loves with its whole heart nothing is lacking, for it has given all* [...] a soul cannot love like this and not be beloved [...] the exchange of love."[38] Wholesome love, even in asymetric love, ensures fullness, so to give is to receive, and to renounce to all for the sake of love is to receive the exchange of love, which is reciprocity. Asymetric love ensures reciprocity in wholesome reunciation. The limit of the soul's insufficiency thus reveals in renunciation the fullness of the gift of the Word-love. Word-love, moreover, is active in the gift of love.

Renunciation for the gift of love leads into transformation, or rebirth, in the Word, who is Word-love, because the soul does not love, but is loved first and because love in fullness reveals the soul's *aperity* or free will. Bernard notes, "No-one can doubt that the soul *is first loved*, and *loved more intensely*, by the Word; for it is *anticipated* and *surpassed* in its love."[39] The assymetry of the Word-love's action in the soul is here qualified by time (precedence and anticipation) and modality (intensity and surpassing), whereby in renunciation the soul achieves aperity in conformation to God, who as pure love *is* pure act. Upon willing no more to will, the soul is united with God in the union of which the efficacy of aperity is manifested, for "'He who is united to God is one spirit with him.'"[40] To be one with love, is to partake, as one, in love, wherein union marks the full return (*redditus*) to the origin-beginning (1.1), for just as *all* engenders from the Word, so too, in love, all returns to the beginning of the Word, in the love-Word. Bernard thus notes that "by God's help [the soul] may rule itself in a way worthy of its origin, and faithfully approach

38 Bernard of Clairvaux, On the *Song of Songs IV*, pp. 185-7. Zink (*SC* 511), SCC 83.6, l. 1-37: "Non. Nam, etsi minus diligit creatura, quoniam minor est; tamen si ex tota se diligit, nihil deest ubi totum est. Propterea, ut dixi, sic amore, nupsisse est: quoniam non potest sic diligere, et parum dilecta esse, ut in consensu duorum integrum stet perfectumque connubium."

39 Bernard of Clairvaux, On the *Song of Songs IV*, pp. 185-7. Zink (*SC* 511), SCC 83.6, l. 1-37: "Nisi quis dubitet, animam a Verbo et prius amari, et plus. Prorsus et praevenitur amando, et vincitur. Felix, quae meruit praeveniri in tantae benedictione dulcedinis! Felix, cui tantae suavitatis complexum experiri donatum est!"

40 Bernard of Clairvaux, On the *Song of Songs IV*, pp. 185-7. Zink (*SC* 511), SCC 83.6, l. 1-37: "Quod non est aliud, quam amor sanctus et castus, amor suavis ei dulcis; amor tantae serenitatis, quantae et sinceritatis; amor mutuus, intimus, validusque, qui non in carne una, sed uno plane in spiritu duos jungat, duos faciat jam non duos, sed unum, Paulo ita dicente: Qui adhaeret Deo, unus spiritus est (I Cor. VI, 17)."

the Word's enfolding."[41] The transformative return to the Word in God's comformation is the pattern for self-rule and, therefore, for *aperity*, which is the metamorphosizing metamorphosis of free will. Moreover, in *aperity*, the love-Word is incarnate life: "*When you see a soul leaving everything and clinging to the Word with all her will and desire, living for the Word, ruling her life by the Word, conceiving by the Word what it will bring forth by him, so that she can say, 'For me to live is Christ, and to die is gain', you know that the soul is the spouse and bride of the Word.*"[42] Aperity of free will is the life of Christ, so to live is Christ, writes Bernard citing Paul. The Word's enfolding and incarnate efficacy is the free will. The labor of freedom, then, as the outcome of aperity, is the conception and, eventually, also the incarnation of Christ in one's life *as* life itself, following Paul: "My little children, with whom I travail in birth again, until Christ shall be formed in you."[43]

Love of love is *free will* within the aperity possible only through the realization of human *limits*. To love is to love as beloved, first in renunciation, then in the transformation of conformation. With *love of love*, thus, the *metamorphosis love* culminates in free will or in the efficacy of the Word. The return (*redditus*) of love in the Word-love or incarnate life is *aperity*.

Conclusion

The body's *aperity* in the midst of *resistance* at the *limits* is free will in three moments, according to, firstly, *free will as power*, to *the power of love*, secondly, and finally, in the disclosure of *aperity* as the *love of love* or *free will*. *Aperity* as free will is the final moment in the manifestation of the *metamorphosis of love*, where the soul's return to God, through conversion, conformation and efficacy in the Word-love, is a return to *beginning without beginning* in experience. Free will is, therefore, the actualized expression of the body in the efficacy of the Word, and the creative force, first metaphysical, then moral, of *metamorphosis*.

---

41 Bernard of Clairvaux, On the *Song of Songs IV*, pp. 157-8. Zink (*SC* 511), SCC 81.1: "Dei quidem munere, sese regens, ad amplexus Verbi fidenter accedat."

42 Bernard of Clairvaux, On the *Song of Songs IV*, pp. 208-9. Zink (*SC* 511), SCC 85.12: "Ergo quam videris animam relictis omnibus Verbo votis omnibus adhaerere, Verbo vivere, Verbo se regere, de Verbo concipere quod pariat Verbo; quae possit dicere: Mihi vivere Christus est, et mori lucrum (Philipp. I, 21): puta conjugem, Verboque maritatam."

43 Bernard of Clairvaux, On the *Song of Songs IV*, pp. 208-9. Zink (*SC* 511), SCC 85.12: "Filioli mei, quos iterum parturio, donec formetur Christus in vobis (Galat. IV, 19)."

Consequently, the full expression of body, in its incarnate Word-love constitution, is free will in the possibility of *aperity*'s creative becoming. The instantiation of the Word's efficacy in the body follows conversion, conformation and lastly, in efficacy, *aperity* manifests free will. The return to the origin-beginning is a return to *experience* by way of *limits*, where the *metamorphosis of love* originates in the desire *of* (genitive) the body and to which it returns in the desire *of* the body (constitutive), thus marking the pathway of generative exit and aperitive return. Aperity is pure act of body through Word.

Conclusion

Précis for a Triune Ontological Reduction

If the hypothesis on the *metamorphosis of love* is right, then a seamless line of interpretation – wherein *eros* and *agape* harmonize into a creative *becoming* of will in act, albeit with notable variances – unifies Christian commitments to the *problem of love* across the centuries (from Ignatius of Antioch's *Letter to the Romans*, to *On the Song of Songs* by Bernard of Clairvaux). Irrespective of establishing any consequential reflections on reception history, which may exist or not, therefore, the hypothesis of the *metamorphosis of love* accentuates the importance of a long-eclipsed model, now, hopefully, retrieved as a starting point for further reflection, beyond mere *univocity* (inclusive or exclusive), *equivocity* and *analogy* (of being). In (contemporary) French phenomenology (of religion), the model of Bernard's *metamorphosis of love* – past Falque's scholastic *metamorphosis of finitude*, and wholly opposed to Marion's Dionysian model of *univocity* – in its *experiential* monastic embedding and metaphorical, or poetic expression, masterfully anchors the abstract model of *analogy* within the fabric of the body's finitude which desire constitutes. The method of phenomenological analysis of the *metamorphosis of love*, and the ensuing hermeneutic and *systematized* mechanics thereof, thus beckon revisiting medieval texts anew in the medieval philosophy of religion and in monastic theology. In closing, and by way of précis, a synthesis firstly revisits the structure or *mechanics* of the *metamorphosis of love*, in view of hermeneutic considerations, and, secondly, identifies and clarifies key findings in view, and this time mainly speculatively, of the Trinitarian lens of Bernard's *ontological reduction* which precedes the hermeneutics and phenomenology of the *metamorphosis of love*.

Beyond the formal mechanics of the *metamorphosis of love* herein carefully articulated, an additional phenomenological meditation may elsewhere seeks to give flesh to the bones of what may seem to have been in this volume a mainly formal and therefore seemingly inadequate rendering of the *book of experience*. Inevitably, however, experience arises *as* the *metamorphosis of love* for Bernard in *On the Song of Songs* at the tightly knit juncture of phenomenology and hermeneutics. Hence, navigating *experience* presupposes *fleshing out* the bones of its structure as a preamble to recognizing authentic experience. Therefore, if the task of unveiling the structure of the *metamorphosis of love*, while worthy *in se* is initially, though seemingly and mistakenly, a barrier to accessing experience, it is only because articulating the *mechanics* of

 | DOI:10.30965/9783846767504_012

love (hermeneutics) is an indispensable phase, often ignored, to then describe love's *metamorphosis* (phenomenology). *To experience* paradoxically demands, for Bernard, reading a world inhabited *in* experience and *as* experience – seeking, that is, the *experience of experience* – wherefore the complicated task *to speak* about a phenomenon (*metamorphosis*), which precedes and supersedes all forms of speech in the *infancy* of life, while learning *how* to speak thus (*mechanics*). Recognizing that something, perhaps unknown, is lost in daring to unveil and undergo *metamorphosis* from *the between* (*metaxu*), where time and eternity intersect, the hope of gain in discovering all things anew (Rev 21.5) requires untangling the finely interlaced hermeneutics-phenomenology which is for Bernard's *On the Song of Songs* mechanics-metamorphosis. From whence a meditative elaboration of *mechanics* may further attain an appreciation of the *metamorphosis of love* and its central movements.

The *mechanics* of love reveal love as inherently tripratite, or Triune. The *metamorphosis of love* is therefore tripartite – considered *in* body, *through* word and *as* free will – and desire is love's unifying force. Within the tripartite superstructure of the mechanics of the *metamorphosis of love*, an inner dynamism reveals yet another interior mirror tripartite infrastructure. In a first moment, the body emerges in *experience, desire* and the *body*. The field of *experience* (1.) is recognized, first, in the modality of its infinite limits upon inhabiting it as a saturated source of the divine, the mirror of humanity, which Bernard calls the *beginning without beginning*.[1] Beyond reason, though not in spite thereof, therefore, *desire*, is the driving force of *experience*.[2] The existential stance to encounter the saturated phenomenon of *experience* is one presupposing belief, whereby *I believe, that I may experience*.[3] Belief, basis of experience, prepares the senses to recognize reality and the body to navigate experience. As the driving force of experience, *desire* (2.) arises from the body, affects the body, and finally, constitutes bodies. Experience reveals the *body* (3.), then, through desire. Moreover, the body while source of desire, is also transformed by desire and, in the process, which is the manifestation of the *metamorphosis of love*, body is formed; body is desire's *production* accordingly. Word transcends corporeality. Then, in a second moment, the word unfolds in *extension, attraction* and *order*. Through *extension* (4.) of desire, the efficacy of

1 Bernard of Clairvaux, On the *Song of Songs I*, pp. 3-4. Leclercq (*SC* 441), SCC 1.5, l. 19: "*principium sine principio.*"

2 Bernard of Clairvaux, On the *Song of Songs I*, pp. 54-55. Leclercq (*SC* 441), SCC 9.2, l. 7: "*Desidero feror, non ratione.*"

3 Kilian McDonnell, "Spirit and Experience in Bernard of Clairvaux," *Theological Studies* 58, no. 1 (1997): 4.

the word, in the Word (incarnate), surpasses the physical constraints of body, from whence word in body is desire's act. By a complimentary and reverse movement, in the Word's performative act, desire's force is at once extension and *attraction* (5.). Within the complimentary aesthetic reconfiguration of desire's extension and attraction, the body is revealed as the Word's force which orients and orders (6.) the weight of the body according to the weight of love. There arises the will. The closing moment unveils will in *limits, resistance* and *aperity*. Whereas will is manifest in the act of the Word's body, the dynamics of extension and attraction only reveal the freedom of the will at the limit (7.). The limit *is* limit because of its constuitive *resistance* (8.), in the absence of which a limitless will is unfree and only bound to necessity. Conversely, only because of experiencing the limit as resistance does the free will emerge in *aperity* (9.). The *metamorphosis of love,* through a doubly tripartite structure, charts desire's transfiguration into aperity, through body, word and free will.

Prior to articulating the foundations for a *triadic ontological reduction,* select clarificatory notes are in order on aspects of Bernard's *metamorphosis of love.* Firstly, a point on meta-questions and method. For Bernard, the use of *metaphor* maintains a link between hermeneutics and phenomenology, not through symbolic or allegorical representation only, but mainly by recognizing the performative thrust of speech, which grounds a framework of analysis between performativity of language (sermon) and creative performativity (creative language of God), and which entrenches the one in the other. Through the sermon (indicative language), Bernard exhorts concrete action for the life of the listener, whose relationship to the *sermo* is governed by, and analyzable according to *locutionary* categories: elocutionary (*loucoutoire*), illocutionary (*illocoutouire*) and perlocutionary (*perlocutoire*).

Second, a note on the model of *metamorphosis.* The *metamorphosis of love* in Bernard's *Song of Songs* is not the same as the *metamorphosis* of which Falque writes in *The Wedding Feast of the Lamb,* where Falque proposes, by means of *incorporation,* a radical transformation of *eros* in the *agape* of the Eucharist, thereby implying ontological discontinuity in *The Metamorphosis of Finitude* and its passage from death to resurrection. Whereas Nygren defends exclusionary *equivocity,* Falque adopts, albeit implicitly, a constructive or integrative *equivocity,* which is unlike Bernard's *metamorphosis of love.* The *metamorphosis of love,* situated in the *metamorphosis of finitude,* nevertheless exceeds finitude by postulating a creative and productive synthesis of *equivocity* and *analogy,* where *analogy* is located within the tissue of the body's finitude. Therefore, for Bernard, there is no experience without belief, and there is no love without the body – such is *the* defining trait of the *metamorphosis of love.*

Third, given its centrality, a clarifying note on the body is due. The body central vehicle for experience and the locus of human-divine love in *metamorphosis* in *On the Song of Songs*, is multifaceted, and refers fundamentally to the body of God, which, unlike Tertullian's material or spiritual body, is for Bernard *act*, the body of Christ – the real body of incarnation, the mystical body of the Church, the body of the resurrection, and the body of the Eucharist – *and* the human body. Desire and its transformations in the *metamorphosis of love* weave these bodies into a continuum in the fabric of finitude, or so it seems, from the vantage point of human experience. To speak about the body, furthermore, is not to exclude the soul, for again, desire is what unites body and soul in *On the Song of Songs*, particularly in the aperity of free will at the *limits*, where body is spirit in act, but also in that the body grounds the dynamism of desire and therefore, the movements of the soul. Complimentary explorations on the role and status on the spiritual sense in Bernard's interpretation and on the liturgical context and the role of gestures therein, may shed light on the place of body, and its relation to the soul, in *On the Song of Songs.*

Fourth, some remarks on desire. Desire and its transformation is the driving force of the *metamorphosis of love*. Therefore, in order to chart the *metamorphosis of love*, and given the tight – even inseparable – hermeneutic connection between experience and the articulation thereof, consequently, on a first instance, and necessarily, the *mechanics* of the *metamorphosis of love* must be elucidated by tracking the vestiges of desire in Bernard's *On the Song of Songs*. Experience is a book, for Bernard, and just as reading is impossible without first learning the mechanics of language, *metamorphosis* is impossible without first learning the mechanics of desire, from whence arises the methodological, and ultimately ontological question of how desire, construed as *lack*, is observable, if at all. In the *metamorphosis of love* desire, passing from body and through word in the Word, is not lack, but, as has been argued, desire is for Bernard a *creative dynamism*, which is the power of free will in *aperity*, the locus of active saturation. In other words, desire is not lack; desire is creative production and the fulfillment of human love *as* action. For this reason, the expression *desiring-production*, first used by Deluze and Guattari – and *only* the expression, with a different meaning –, has been adopted to emphasize the creative dimension of longing, which the Greek notion of *eros* and its equivalent in Latin *amor* convey in Plato and Plotinus, and which the early Christian writers like Origen adopt or, in the case of Gregory of Nyssa reformulate – also in commenting the *Song of Songs* – with expressions like *epectasis* (ἐπέκτασις), meaning the soul's *active* progression towards God.

Fifth, a note on reason. Bernard's enigmatic and paradigmatic statement "desire impels me, not reason"[4] is *not* a rejection of reason. Rather, Bernard aims to emphasize the primacy of desire over reason in the navigation of experience through belief. He therefore exclaims, "I believe, that I may experience."[5] To avoid the rationalization of the experiencing 'I', and therefore, the objectification of *experience* tout court against the later Cartesian *cogito ergo sum*, Bernard's approach may well be, *I desire, therefore I am.* Desire is the point of departure for Bernard, and for the monastic theologians of the 12th century, who orient the exercise of reason in experience and, in the process, unveil the divine vestiges of reason's constitution *as* Triune, after God. From whence the structure of reason, really the structure of the soul, implies a unified physiological, psychological and ontological integrity – beyond subject-object, body-soul, reason-desire dichotomies – in the Trinitarian order saturated with God's *vestiges* of experience and irreducible to the demands of reason alone.

By way of *envoi*, and affording speculative leeway for further reflection and for creative development, the final remarks present a *précis* for a (triply triadic) *ontological reduction* of the *metamorphosis of love*, wherein *aperity* – it is necessary to repeat – is the *active* or *actualizing* locus of saturation. Consider then, that if, as John writes, "God is love" (Jn 4.8) and, as Augustine reformulates, "love is God", and, furthermore, if truly God is triune, and, if finitude bears a divine vestige, the image of God (*imago dei*), then it follows that the *metamorphosis of love* bears a Triadic *dynamism*. Hence, the *metamorphosis of love* is an experiential and relationally performative *analogia amoris*, which effects the foundational *ontological reduction* of reality and reveals it as Triadic, and not as monadic in the excess proper of the erotic phenomenon (Marion). The *Love* who *is* God in the *metamorphosis of love* bears, in the structure of experience, a triply triadic structure, as not only the hermeneutic key to navigate experience but possibly, also, and this time by way of speculation, as the *very* ontological composition of the fabric of finitude governing *all* phenomenological revelation. In this sense, it is to be presupposed that the vestige of love's Trinity are formative of experience (*book of experience*), thus making it possible to recognize experience thus (hermeneutics) and, thereafter, allowing

4 Bernard of Clairvaux, On the *Song of Songs I*, pp. 54-55. Leclercq (*SC* 441), SCC 9.2, l. 7: "*Desiderio feror, non ratione.*"

5 Jean Leclerq, *The Love of Learning and the Desire for God: A Study of Monastic Culture* (New York: Fordham University Press, 1962), 7, 263; Kilian McDonnell, "Spirit and Experience in Bernard of Clairvaux," *Theological Studies* 58, no. 1 (1997): 4. Also, Lode Van Hecke, *Le désir dans l'expérience religieuse: l'homme réunifié – relecture de Saint Bernard* (Paris: Cerf, 1990).

to describe it accordingly (phenomenology). Experience *as* experience bears the vestige of God's Trinity. In the *book of experience*, the love of God is manifest as Trinity – not by analogy *only* (although by analogy also), not by equivocity *only* (although also sometimes thus) – and, while never disclosing the divine economy as strictly monadic, in *metamorphosis* love is excess *always* in the *immanent-economy* of divine relation. From whence the *metamorphosis of love* is the creative and unsaturated givenness of God's Trinitarian immanence, life and presence, even in the triad of time's past-present-future orientation, always, everywhere. God as love is only experienced in God's unifying yet Trinitarian *immanent-economy*, which the *metamorphosis of love* enacts. The *metamorphosis of love* achieves, therefore, an *ontological reduction* of love whereby the vestiges of love are unveiled *as* Trinitarian. The *metamorphosis of love* therefore escapes the conceptual and abstract *analogy* of onto-theology, the mere *univocity* of a (practically) monadic God without being, and the exclutionary *equivocacy* of metaphysical dualism. The *metamorphosis of love* is the experience of God as Triune – it cannot be otherwise, for Bernard – and, accordingly, as the unravelling of reality's divine vestiges in a Trinitarian *ontological reduction*. The final hypothesis of a Triadic *ontological reduction* is, beyond speculative debates, a concrete and daring invitation to consider the practice of theology and philosophy, and the ensuing demands arising from love's transfigurations, in terms of bearing the responsibility of ordinary *commitments* as the sole rule to discern authentic reflection and authentic life in *relations*.

Bibliography

Primary sources

French-Latin Editions

Callerot, Françoise. *L'amour de Dieu, La grâce et le libre arbitre. Sources Chrétiennes 393.* Paris: Cerf, 1993.

Leclercq, Jean. *Sermons sur le Cantique. 1 : Sermons 1-15. Sources Chrétiennes* 414. Paris: Cerf, 2006.

Leclercq, Jean. *Sermons sur le Cantique. 2 : Sermons 16-32. Sources Chrétiennes* 431. Paris: Cerf, 1998.

Verdeyen, Paul. *Sermons sur le Cantique. 3 : Sermons 33-50. Sources Chrétiennes* 452. Paris: Cerf, 2000.

Verdeyen, Paul. *Sermons sur le Cantique. 4 : Sermons 51-68. Sources Chrétiennes* 472. Paris: Cerf, 2003.

Zink, Michel. *Sermons sur le Cantique. 5 : Sermons 69-86. Sources Chrétiennes* 511. Paris: Cerf, 2007.

English Editions

Bernard of Clairvaux, *On the Song of Songs I* (Sermons 1-20). Translated by Kilian Walsh. Kalamazoo: Cistercian Publications, 1971.

Bernard of Clairvaux, *On the Song of Songs II* (Sermons 21-46). Translated by Kilian Walsh. Kalamazoo: Cistercian Publications, 1976.

Bernard of Clairvaux, *On the Song of Songs III* (Sermons 47-66). Translated by Kilian Walsh and Irene M. Edmonds. Kalamazoo: Cistercian Publications, 1979.

Bernard of Clairvaux, *On the Song of Songs IV* (Sermons 67-86). Translated by Kilian Walsh and Irene M. Edmonds. Kalamazoo: Cistercian Publications, 1980.

Latin Critical Editions

Bernardus Claraevallensis. *Sermons sur le Cantique. Sources Chrétiennes* 414-431. Edited and translated by Jean Leclercq, Henri Rochais, Charles Hugh Talbt, Paul Verdeyen and Raffaele Fassetta. Paris: Cerf, 1996.

Other primary sources

Aquinas, Thomas. *On Love and Charity: Readings from the* Commentary on the Sentences *of Peter Lombard.* Translated by Peter A. Kwasniewski, Thomas Bolin and Joseph Bolin. Washington: The Catholic University of America Press, 2008.

Augustinus, Aurelius. *Confessions, Opera Omnia, editio Latina, Patrologia Latina* 32. URL: http://www.augustinus.it/latino/confessioni/index2.htm.

Augustinus, Aurelius. *Sermons (148-183) on the New Testament*. Translated by John E. Rotelle. New York: New City Press, 1992.

Augustinus, Aurelius. *Responses to Miscellaneous Questions*. Translated by Raymond F. Canning. New York: New City Press, 2007.

Augustinus, Aurelius. *Late Have I Loved Thee: Selected Writings of Saint Augustine on Love*. Translated by John F. Thornton and Susan B. Varenne. New York: Vintage Spiritual Classics, 2006.

Augustinus, Aurelius. *The City of God*. In *The Works of Saint Augustine*. Translated by William Babcock. New York: New City Press, 2012.

Francis de Sales. *On the Love of God*. Translated by Henry Benedict Mackey. London: Burns & Oates, 1884. URL: https://ccel.org/ccel/desales/love/love.i.html.

Hume, David. *An Enquiry Concerning the Principles of Morals*. Oxford: Oxford University Press, 2006.

Hume, David. *A Treatise of Human Nature*. Chelmsford: Courier Corporation, 2003.

Ignatius of Antioch. *Epistle to the Romans*. In *Ante-Nicene Fathers, Vol. 1*. Edited and translated by Alexander Roberts, James Donaldson, and Cleveland Coxe. Buffalo: Christian Literature Publishing Co., 1885.

Lombard, Peter. *Book of Sentences, The Mystery of the Trinity*. Translated by Giulio Silano. Toronto: Pontifical Institute of Medieval Studies, 2007.

Origenes, *Ante-Nicene Fathers, Vol. 4*. Edited and translated by Alexander Roberts, James Donaldson and Cleveland Coxe. Buffalo: Christian Literature Publishing Co., 1885. Revised and edited for *New Advent* by Kevin Knight, URL: http://www.newadvent.org/fathers/0416.htm, accessed throughout June 2022.

Origenes. *The Song of Songs: Commentary and Homilies*. Translated by R. P. Lawson. London: Longmans, 1957.

Pascal, Blaise. *Pensées*. Edited by Jacques Chevalier. Flammarion: Paris 1949.

Pseudo-Dionysius. *The Divine Names*. In *The Complete Works: Dionysius Areopagita*. Translated by Colm Luibheid. New York: Paulist, 1987.

Secondary Sources

Ackrill, John L. "Aristotle on Action." *Mind* 87, no. 4 (1978): 595-601.

Alvis, Jason. *Marion and Derrida on the Gift and Desire: Debating the Generosity of Things*. Cham: Springer, 2016.

Ashworth, Jennifer, and Domenic D'Ettore. "Medieval Theories of Analogy." In *The Stanford Encyclopedia of Philosophy*. Edited by Edward N. Zalta (Winter 2021 Edition).

Assunto, Rosario. "Sulle idee estetiche di Bernardo di Chiaravalle." *Rivista di Estetica* 4 (1959): 240-68.

Astell, Ann W. "Telling Tales of Love: Julia Kristeva and Bernard of Clairvaux." *Christianity and Literature* 50, no. 1 (2000): 125-48.

Astell, Ann W. *The* Song of Songs *in the Middle Ages*. London: Cornell University Press, 1990.

Austin, John L. *How to do Things with Words*. Oxford: Oxford University Press, 1975.

Bäck, Allan. *Aristotle's Theory of Predication*. Leiden: Brill, 2000.

Bala, Ilona. "La phénoménologie de l'amour de Jean-Luc Marion : l'expérience de la passivité en tant que dépassement de l'égologie." *Studia Litteraria Universitatis Iagellonicae Cracoviensis* 10, no. 4 (2015): 299-315.

Baladier, Charles. *Érôs au Moyen Âge : amour, désir et délectation morose*. Paris: Cerf, 1999.

Belloso, José María Rovira. "Palabra y Sacramento como signos de la Iglesia." *Diálogo ecuménico* 18, no. 61 (1983): 417-34.

Benke, Christoph. *Unterscheidung der Geister bei Bernhard von Clairvaux*. Würzburg: Echter, 1991.

Black, Fiona C. *The Artifice of Love: Grotesque Bodies in the* Song of Songs. London: Clark, 2009.

Blanc, Cécile. "L'attitude d'Origène à l'égard du corps et de la chair." *StPatr* 17 (1982): 843-58.

Jacques Blanpain, *S'ouvrir au désir : En lisant le* Cantique des cantiques *avec Bernard de Clairvaux*. Scourmont: Veilleux, 2003.

Bodard, C. "La Bible, expression d'une expérience religieuse chez S. Bernard." *Analecta Sacri Ordinis Cisterciensis* 9, no. 3-4 (1953): 24-45.

Boersma, Hans, and Matthew Levering. *The Oxford Handbook of Sacramental Theology*. Oxford: Oxford University Press, 2015.

Bok, Nico Den. "Human and Divine Freedom in the Theology of Bernard of Clairvaux: a Systematic Analysis." *Bijdragen* 54, no. 3 (1993): 271-95.

Boquet, Damien. *L'ordre de l'affect au Moyen Âge: autour de l'anthropologie affective d'Aelred de Rievaulx*. Caen: CRAHM, 2005.

Boquet, Damien, and Piroska Nagy. "Medieval Sciences of Emotions during the Eleventh to Thirteenth Centuries: An Intellectual History." *Osiris* 31, no. 1 (2016): 21-45.

Boquet, Damien, and Piroska Nagy, *Medieval Sensibilities: A History of Emotions in the Middle Ages*. Translated by Robert Shaw. New York: John Wiley & Sons, 2018.

Boquet, Damien, and Piroska Nagy. "Une Histoire Des émotions Incarnées." *Médiévales* 61, no. 2 (2012): 5-24.

Bosch, A. "Christologie Bernardine." *Cîteaux* 9 (1958): 5-17.

Bosch, A. "Dieu devenu connaissable dans le Christ d'après saint Bernard." *Collectanea Ordinis Cisterciensum Reformatorum* 22 (1960): 11-20.

Bosch, A. "Dieu rendu accessible dans le Christ d'après saint Bernard." *Collectanea Ordinis Cisterciensum Reformatorum* 21 (1959): 185-205.

Bosch, A. "Le Christ, Dieu devenu imitable d'après S. Bernard." *Collectanea ordinis Cisterciensium Reformatorum* 22 (1959): 341-55.

Bosch, A. "Le Christ, Dieu devenu imitable d'après S. Bernard." *Collectanea ordinis Cisterciensium Reformatorum* 22 (1961): 42-57.

Bosch, A. "Le mystère de l'Incarnation chez saint Bernard." *Cîteaux* 10 (1959): 85-92; 165-77; 245-67.

Bosch, A. "Présupposés à la christologie Bernardine." *Cîteaux* 9, (1958): 85-105.

Brady, Bernard V. *Christian Love*. Washington: Georgetown University Press, 2003.

Bramhall, John. *Hobbes and Bramhall on Liberty and Necessity*. Cambridge: Cambridge University Press, 1999.

Brookes, Derek. *Thomas Reid: Essays on the Intellectual Power of Man: A Critical Edition*. University Park: Penn State University Press, 2001.

Bruun, Mette Birkedal. *Parables: Bernard of Clairvaux's Mapping of Spiritual Topography*. Leiden: Brill, 2007.

Bruun, Mette Birkedal. *The Cambridge Companion to the Cistercian Order. Cambridge Companions to Religion*. Cambridge: Cambridge University Press, 2013.

Bruun, Mette B. "Wandering Eyes, Muttering, and Frowns: Bernard of Clairvaux and the Communicative Implications of Gesture." In *Understanding Monastic Practices of Oral Communication*. Turnhout: Brepols, 2011.

Brümmer, Vincent. "Calvin, Bernard and the Freedom of the Will." *Religious Studies* 30, no. 4 (1994): 437-55.

Bynum, Caroline W. "Did the Twelfth Century Discover the Individual?" *The Journal of Ecclesiastical History* 31, no. 1 (1980): 1-17.

Cange, Charles du. *Glossarium mediae et infimae latinitatis*. Niort: L. Favre, 1883-1887.

Carruthers, Mary. *The Experience of Beauty in the Middle Ages*. Oxford: Oxford University Press, 2013.

Casey, Michael. *Athirst for God: Spiritual Desire in Bernard of Clairvaux's* Sermons on the Song of Songs. Collegeville: Cistercian Publications, 1988.

Chatillon, François. "Regio dissimilitudinis." In *Mélanges E. Podechard* (Lyon: Facultés Catholiques, 1954), 85-102.

Chrétien, Jean-Louis. *Symbolique du corps: la tradition chrétienne du* Cantique des Cantiques. Paris: Presses Universitaires de France, 2005.

Clark, Gordon H. "The Theory of Time in Plotinus." *The Philosophical Review* 53, no. 4 (1944): 337-358.

Cohen, Alix, and Stern, Robert. *Thinking about the Emotions: A Philosophical History*. Oxford: Oxford University Press, 2017.

Congar, Yves. "L'ecclésiologie de St. Bernard." *Analecta Sacri Ordinis Cisterciensi* (1953): 1-56.

Constant, Eric Alan. *Concepts of Prophecy in the Middle Ages: Inspired Exegesis, Visions from God, and the Interaction of Theories and Practice*. East Lansing: Michigan State University, 2016.

Corbin, Michel. *La grâce et la liberté chez saint Bernard de Clairvaux*. Paris: Cerf, 2002.

Costa, da Silveira, and Ricardo Luiz. "El concepto de naturaleza en la metafísica teológica de san Bernardo de Claraval (1090-1153)." *Medio Aevo*, no. 1 (2012): 131-44.

Czachesz, István. *The Grotesque Body in Early Christian Discourse: Hell, Scatology, and Metamorphosis*. Abingdon: Routledge, 2014.

Darrell Jackson, B. "The Theory of Signs in St. Augustine's *De doctrina christiana*." *Revue d'Etudes Augustiniennes et Patristiques* 15, no. 1-2 (1969): 9-49.

Davidson, Scott and Marc Antoine Vallée. *Hermeneutics and Phenomenology in Paul Ricoeur: Between Text and Phenomenon*. Cham: Springer, 2016.

Debbasch, Hubert. *L'homme de désir, icône de Dieu*. Paris: Beauchesne, 2001.

Déchanet, Jean-Marie. "Le mystère du salut. La christologie de saint Bernard." In *Saint Bernard théologien*, Actes du Congrès de Dijon (15-19 sept. 1953), ASOC, 9, fasc. 3-4 (1953): 78-91.

Déchanet, Jean-Marie. *William of Saint-Thierry: The Man and His Work*. Translated by R. Strachan. Kalamazoo: Cistercian Publications, 1972.

Deleuze, Gilles and Félix Guattari. *Anti-Oedipus*. London : A & C Black, 2004.

Delfgaauw, Pacificus. "La nature et les degrés de l'amour selon saint Bernard." In *Saint Bernard theologien: Actes du congres de Dijon* (Dijon, 1953), 15-19.

Delfgaauw, Pacificus. *Saint Bernard, Maître de l'amour divin*. Paris : FAC-éditions, 1994.

Diepen, H. M. "L'*assumptus Homo* patristique." *Revue thomiste*, 63 (1963): 225-245.

Dodaro, Robert. *Christ and the Just Society in the Thought of Augustine*. Cambridge: Cambridge University Press, 2004.

Eco, Umberto, and Costantino Marmo, editors. *On the Medieval Theory of Signs*. Amsterdam: John Benjamins Publishing, 1989.

Elliot, Mark W. *The* Song of Songs *and Christology in the Early Church*. Tübingen: Mohr Siebeck, 2000.

Evans, G. R. *The Church in the Early Middle Ages*. London: IB Tauris, 2007.

Falque, Emmanuel. "Après la métaphysique ? Le 'poids de la vie' selon saint Augustin." In *Après la métaphysique : saint Augustin ?* Edited by Alain de Libera. Vrin : Paris, 2013.

Falque, Emmanuel. *Ca n'a rien à voir: lire Freud en philosophe*. Paris: Cerf, 2018.

Falque, Emmanuel. "Ceci est mon corps." *Études*, no. 4 (2012): 483-93.

Falque, Emmanuel. "Christ doesn't saves us by his Words first of all, but by his body." Interview with Arthur Rossman. 7 June 2018. *Church Life Journal*, University of Notre Dame.

Falque, Emmanuel. *Dieu, la chair et l'autre: d'Irénée à Duns Scot*. Paris: Presses Universitaires de France, 2008.

Falque, Emmanuel. "Expérience et empathie chez Bernard de Clairvaux." *Revue des sciences philosophiques et théologiques* 89, no. 4 (2005): 655-96.

Falque, Emmanuel. *Le combat amoureux: disputes phénoménologiques et théologiques*. Paris: Hermann, 2014.

Falque, Emmanuel. *Le livre de l'expérience: d'Anselme de Cantorbéry à Bernard de Clairvaux*. Paris: Cerf, 2017.

Falque, Emmanuel. *Les noces de l'agneau: essai philosophique sur le corps et l'eucharistie*. Paris: Cerf, 2011.

Falque, Emmanuel. "Saint Bernard de Clairvaux : le pouvoir de la liberté." In *Dieu et la cité, le statut contemporain du théologico-politique*. Edited by P. Capelle. Paris: Cerf, 2008.

Falque, Emmanuel. "Saint Bernard et le champ de l'expérience." In *Expérience philosophique et experience mystique*. Edited by P. Capelle. Paris: Cerf, 2005.

Falque, Emmanuel. "The Hidden Source of Hermeneutics: The Art of Reading in Hugh of St. Victor." *Journal of French and Francophone Philosophy* 25, no. 1 (2017): 121-31.

Falque, Emmanuel. *The Metamorphosis of Finitude: An Essay on Birth and Resurrection*. Translated by George Hughes. New York: Fordham University Press, 2012.

Falque, Emmanuel. *The Wedding Feast of the Lamb: Eros, the Body, and the Eucharist*. Translated by George Hughes. New York: Fordham University Press, 2017.

Falque, Emmanuel. "Y at-il une chair sans corps?" In *Phénoménologie et Christianisme chez Michel Henry*. Paris: Cerf, 2004.

Ferguson, Margaret W. "Saint Augustine's Region of Unlikeness: The Crossing of Exile and Language." *The Georgia Review* 29, no. 4 (1975): 842-864.

Fitzgerald, Brian. *Inspiration and Authority in the Middle Ages: Prophets and Their Critics from Scholasticism to Humanism*. Oxford: Oxford University Press, 2017.

Gaffiot, Félix. *Dictionnaire Illustré Latin-Français*. Paris: Hachette, 1934.

Gastaldelli, F. "Ricerca ed esperienza di Dio secondo san Bernardo." *Rivista cistercense* 8 (1991): 133-54.

Gilson, Etienne. *La théologie mystique de saint Bernard*. Paris: Vrin, 1986.

Harris, Jennifer. "The Fate of Place in the Twelfth Century: Creation, Restoration and Body in the Writings of Bernard of Clairvaux." *Viator* 39, no. 2 (2008): 119-41.

Hecke, Lode Van. *Le désir dans l'expérience religieuse: l'homme réunifié – relecture de Saint Bernard*. Paris: Cerf, 1990.

Hood, Pamela Michelle. *Aristotle on the Category of Relation*. Lanham: University Press of America, 2004.

Howe, Elizabeth. "The Mystical Kiss, and the *Canticle of Canticles*. Three Interpretations." *American Benedictine Review*, 33 (1982): 302-11.

Hufgard, M. Kilian. *Bernard of Clairvaux on Being and Beauty: Bernard's Aestheticism Re-examined*. Lewiston: Mellen Press, 2000.

Irwin, T. H. "Who Discovered the Will?" *Philosophical Perspectives* 6 (1992): 453-73.

Kearney, Richard. "What Is Carnal Hermeneutics?" *New Literary History: A Journal of Theory and Interpretation* 46, no. 1 (2015): 99-124.

Kereszty, R. "Relationship between Anthropology and Christology. St. Bernard, a Teacher for our Age." *Analecta Cisterciensia*, 46 (1990): 271-300.

Kienzle, B. "*Verbum Dei et Verba Bernardi*: The Function of Language in Bernard's Second Sermon for Peter and Paul." *Cîteaux commentarii cistercienses* 42, no. 1-4 (1991): 149-159.

Kilby, Karen. "Susannah Ticciati, A New Apophaticism: Augustine and the Redemption of Signs." *Augustinian Studies* 47, no. 2 (2016): 258-61.

Kirchner, Renato. "A Intimidade Da Experiência Religiosa: Uma Aproximação Fenomenológica Da Mística De Bernardo De Claraval." *Revista Pistis Praxis* 8, no. 738 (2016): 307.

Knight, Hilary. "Saint Bernard of Clairvaux on Experience." *Medieval Mystical Theology* 24, no. 1 (2015): 59-79.

Knuuttila, Simo. *Emotions in Ancient and Medieval Philosophy*. Oxford: Clarendon, 2004.

Lane, Anthony N. S. *Bernard of Clairvaux, Theologian of the Cross*. Collegeville: Liturgical Press, 2013.

Le Goff, J. *Les gestes symboliques dans la vie sociale. Les gestes de la vassalité*. In *Simboli et simbologia nell'Alto Medioevo* (3-9 aprile 1999). Spoleto: CISAM, 1976.

Le Goff, Jacques, and Nicolas Truong. *Une histoire du corps au Moyen Âge*. Paris: Liana Levi, 2003.

Leclercq, Jean. *The Love of Learning and the Desire for God: A Study of Monastic Culture*. New York: Fordham University Press, 1962.

Leclercq, Jean. "Voir le monde par les affects: Bernard de Clairvaux et la voie monastique." *Revue des sciences philosophiques et theologiques* 95, no. 2 (2011): 323-41.

Lewis, Charlton T. *A Latin Dictionary*. Oxford: Claredon Press, 1879.

Lia, Pierluigi. *L'estetica teologica di Bernardo di Chiaravalle. La mistica Cristiana tra oriente e occidente*. Firenze: Sismel, 2007.

Lia, Pierluigi. *Un'estetica del verbum in Bernardo di Chiaravalle*. Milano: Facoltà teologica dell'Italia settentrionale, 2011.

Lindberg, Carter. *Love: A Brief History Through Western Christianity*. Oxford: Blackwell Publishing, 2008.

Liston-Kraft, Philip. "Bernard's Belching Bride: The *Affectus* that Words Cannot Express." *Medieval Mystical Theology* 26, no. 1 (2017): 54-72.

Lloyd, Geoffrey. *Polarity and Analogy: Two Types of Argumentation in Early Greek Thought*. Cambridge: Cambridge University Press, 1966.

Lossky, Vladimir. "Étude sur la terminologie de saint Bernard." *Bulletin du Cange*, 18 (1942): 82-7.

Marion, Jean-Luc. “Substantia. Note sur l’usage de Substantia par st. Augustin et sur son appartenance à l’histoire de la métaphysique.” In *Mots médiévaux offerts à Ruedi Imbach*: 691-701.

Marion, Jean-Luc. *The Erotic Phenomenon*. Translated by Stephen E. Lewis. Chicago: Chicago University Press, 2006.

Markus, R. Austin. *St. Augustine on Signs*. Assen: Vangorcum, 1957.

McCluskey, Colleen. “Bernard of Clairvaux on the Nature of Human Agency.” *Revista Portuguesa De Filosofia* 64, no. 1 (2008): 297-317.

McDonnell, Kilian. “Spirit and Experience in Bernard of Clairvaux.” *Theological Studies* 58, no. 1 (1997): 3-18.

McGrath, Sean, and Andrzej Wierciński. *A Companion to Heidegger’s Phenomenology of Religious Life*. Amsterdam: Rodopi, 2010.

Montanari, Antonio. “*Desiderium sine anxietate*: Désir infini et béatitude de l’homme d’après les sermons 84-86 super cantica de saint Bernard.” *Collectanea cisterciensia* 70, no. 1 (2008): 4-20.

Monti, James. *A Sense of the Sacred: Roman Catholic Worship in the Middle Ages*. San Francisco: Ignatius Press, 2012.

Montserrat, Dominic. *Changing Bodies, Changing Meanings: Studies on the Human Body in Antiquity*. London: Routledge, 1998.

Morrow, Derek J. “The Love ‘Without Being’ That Opens (To) Distance Part One: Exploring the Giveneness of the Erotic Phenomenon With J-L. Marion.” *Heythrop Journal* 46, no. 3 (2005): 281-98.

Moyaert, Paul. “Mysticism: The Transformation of a Love Consumed by Desire into a Love without Desire.” *Ethical Perspectives* 7, no. 4 (2000): 269-278.

Musto, Ronald G. “The Kiss of Peace: Ritual, Self, and Society in the High and Late Medieval West.” *Speculum* 80, no. 2 (2005): 652-54.

Nagy, Piroska. *Le don des larmes au Moyen-Âge*. Paris : Albin Michel, 2000.

Nayak, Ajit. “Heraclitus (540-480 BC).” In *The Oxford Handbook of Process Philosophy and Organization Studies*. Edited by Jenny Helin, Tor Hernes, Daniel Hjorth and Robin Holt. Oxford: Oxford University Press, 2014.

Nisula, Timo. *Augustine and the Functions of Concupiscence*. Leiden: Brill, 2012.

Nygren, Anders. *Agape and Eros*. Translated by P. S. Watson. London: Westminister Press, 1953.

O’Brien, Denis. “*pondus meum amor meus*: Saint Augustine and Jamblique.” *Revue de l’histoire des religions* (1981): 423-8.

Pacchi, Arrigo. “Hobbes and the Passions.” *Topoi* 6, no. 2 (1987): 111-9.

Pedersen, Else Marie Wiberg. “This Is Not About Sex? A Discussion of the Understanding of Love and Grace in Bernard of Clairvaux’s and Martin Luther’s Theologies.” *Dialog* 50, no. 1 (2011): 15-25.

Pak, Pyong-Gwan. "St. Bernard of Clairvaux on the Riddle of Human Desire: The Necessity of a Reversal of Priorities in the Human Life of Desire." *Logos: A Journal of Catholic Thought and Culture* 21, no. 4 (2018): 126-50.

Palmer, John. "Zeno of Elea." In *The Stanford Encyclopedia of Philosophy*. Edited by Edward N. Zalta. (Spring 2017 Edition).

Petkov, Kiril. *The Kiss of Peace: Ritual, Self, and Society in the High and Late Medieval West*. Leiden: Brill, 2003.

Prieur, J-M. *La croix chez les Pères (du IIe au début du IVe siècle)*. Strasbourg: Cahiers de Biblia Patristica, 2006.

Rava, Eva. "The Loss and Recovery of Truth in Three Treatises of Bernard." *Cistercian Studies Quarterly* 36, no. 1 (2001): 3.

Reddy, William M. *The Navigation of Feeling: A Framework for the History of Emotions*. Cambridge: Cambridge University Press, 2001.

Reeves, Marjorie. *The Influence of Prophecy in the Later Middle Ages: a Study in Joachimism*. Oxford: Oxford University Press, 1969.

Ricœur, Paul. *The Rule of Metaphor: The Creation of Meaning in Language*. London: Routledge, 2004.

Rist, John M. *Augustine: Ancient thought Baptized*. New York: Cambridge University Press, 1994.

Rius-Camps, Josep. *El dinamismo trinitario en la divinización de los seres racionales según Orígenes*. Rome: *Pont. Institutum orientalium studiorum*, 1970.

Rosenwein, Barbara H. *Generations of Feeling: A History of Emotions, 600-1700*. Cambridge: Cambridge University Press, 2016.

Rosenwein, Barbara H. "Thinking Historically about Medieval Emotions." *History Compass* 8, no. 8 (2010): 828-42.

Rosenwein, Barbara H. and Riccardo Cristiani. *What Is the History of Emotions?* Cambridge: Polity Press, 2018.

Rosenwein, Barbara H. "Worrying about Emotions in History." *The American Historical Review* 107, no. 3 (2002): 821-45.

Rudy, Gordon. *Mystical Language of Sensation in the Later Middle Ages*. New York: Routledge, 2002.

Santos, Bento Silva. "Hodie Legimus in Libro Experientiae. Heidegger's Appropriation of Bernard of Claraval's Formula." *Trans-Form-Acao* 39, no. 3 (2016): 101-20.

Schuster, Marja. "Hermeneutics as Embodied Existence." *International Journal of Qualitative Methods* 12, no. 1 (2013): 195-206.

Sommerfeldt, John R. *Bernard of Clairvaux on the Life of the Mind*. Mahwah: Paulist Press, 2004.

Sonnet, J-P. "Le Cantique, entre érotique et mystique: sanctuaire de la parole échangée." *Nouvelle Revue Théologique* 119, no. 4 (1997): 481-502.

Soskice, Janet. "Being and Love: Schleiermacher, Aquinas and Augustine." *Modern Theology* 34, no. 3 (2018): 480-91.

Stanciene, Dalia Marija. "The Concept of Free Will in the Treatise by Bernard of Clairvaux Concerning Grace and Free Will." *Logos-Vilnus* 56 (2008): 39-49.

Ticciati, Susannah. *A New Apophaticism: Augustine and the Redemption of Signs.* Leiden: Brill, 2013.

Torstein T. Tollefsen, *Eros and agape – a critique of Anders Nygren.* In *Love – ancient perspectives.* Edited by K. Grødum, H. F. Hägg, J. Kaufman and T. T. Tollefsen. Oslo: Cappelen Damm Akademisk, 2021.

Triomphe, Micheline. "La rationalité de la passion chez Hobbes." *Revue de la Société d'études anglo-américaines des XVIIe et XVIIIe siècles* 7, no. 1 (1978): 49-60.

Van Hecke, Lode. *Le désir dans l'expérience religieuse: l'homme réunifié – relecture de saint Bernard.* Paris: Cerf, 1990.

Viladesau, Richard. *Theological Aesthetics: God in Imagination, Beauty, and Art.* New York: Oxford University Press, 1999.

Williams, Rowan. "Language, Reality and Desire in Augustine's *De Doctrina.*" *Literature and Theology* 3, no. 2 (1989): 138-150.

William of Saint-Thierry, Arnold of Bonneval, and Geoffrey of Auxerre. *The First Life of Bernard of Clairvaux.* Translated and edited by Hilary Costello. Kalamazoo: Cistersian Publications, 2015.

Wojtyła, Karol. *Love and Responsibility.* Dedham: Pauline Books & Media, 2003.

Zizek, Slavoj. *Organs without Bodies: Deleuze and Consequences.* London: Routledge, 2016.

Zona, James. ""Set Love in Order in Me": Eros-knowing in Origen and Desiderium-knowing in Saint Bernard." *Cistercian Studies Quarterly* 34, no. 2 (1999): 157.

Index of Terms